The Correspondence of
WOLFGANG CAPITO

VOLUME 1: 1507–1523

Edited and translated by
ERIKA RUMMEL
with the assistance of Milton Kooistra

Wolfgang Capito (1478–1541) was one of the most important figures of the Reformation, a prominent Catholic churchman who converted to Protestantism. Following appointments as a professor of theology in Basel and advisor to the Archbishop of Mainz, he moved to Strasbourg, where he worked for two decades as a leader in the Reformation movement.

This volume – the first of three – is a fully annotated translation of Capito's existing correspondence, covering the years 1507–1523. The letters reveal his ongoing dialogue with leading humanists and reformers, such as Erasmus and Luther (with whom Capito had a contentious relationship), and reflect the cultural and political milieu of the time. While offering significant insights into the progress of the Reformation, the volume elucidates Capito's thoughts on such matters as the promotion of concord between reformers, the Eucharistic controversy, tolerance towards Anabaptists, and the relationship between secular and church governments.

ERIKA RUMMEL is a professor emerita in the Department of History at Wilfrid Laurier University and an adjunct professor at Emmanuel College, University of Toronto.

MILTON KOOISTRA is a PhD candidate in the Centre for Medieval Studies at the University of Toronto.

THE CORRESPONDENCE OF WOLFGANG CAPITO

VOLUME 1
1507–1523

Edited and translated by Erika Rummel
with the assistance of Milton Kooistra

University of Toronto Press

Toronto / Buffalo / London

Reprinted in paperback 2020

ISBN 978-0-8020-9017-1 (cloth)
ISBN 978-1-4875-2588-0 (paper)

Library and Archives Canada Cataloguing in Publication

Title: The correspondence of Wolfgang Capito / edited and translated by
Erika Rummel ; with the assistance of Milton Kooistra.

Other titles: Correspondence

Names: Capito, Wolfgang, 1478–1541, author. | Rummel, Erika, 1942– editor,
translator. | Kooistra, Milton, editor, translator.

Description: Reprint. Originally published 2005. | Includes bibliographical
references and index. | Contents: v. 1. 1507–1523

Identifiers: Canadiana 20200166832 | ISBN 9781487525880 (v. 1 ; softcover)

Subjects: LCSH: Capito, Wolfgang, 1478–1541 – Correspondence. | LCSH:
Theologians – Europe – Correspondence. | LCGFT: Personal correspondence.

Classification: LCC BR350.C2 A4 2020 | DDC 284/.2092–dc23

University of Toronto Press acknowledges the financial assistance to its publishing
program of the Canada Council for the Arts and the Ontario Arts Council, an agency
of the Government of Ontario.

Contents

Preface

This edition was conceived a decade ago, when I discovered, in the course of my research, how difficult it was to access Capito's writings. The neglect of these sources is surprising in view of Capito's historical significance. He was an active and well-respected member of the humanist circle in Basel, where he taught theology. On his appointment as cathedral preacher in Mainz, Capito became a close advisor to the archbishop, Albert of Brandenburg, chancellor of the German Empire. Capito was sympathetic to the Reformation, but disapproved of Luther's radical tactics. Luther in turn despised Capito's diplomatic approach. Playing his cards close to his chest, Capito formally remained obedient to the Catholic Church until he secured a position as preacher in Strasbourg. Over the next two decades he collaborated with Martin Bucer in directing the reformation of that city.

A prolific writer, Capito authored or contributed to more than forty books and pamphlets. He wrote and received a large number of letters, of which more than seven hundred are extant. His correspondence reflects the cultural and political milieu of the time. It provides significant insights into the progress of the Reformation and the ongoing negotiations for religious peace. In spite of Capito's stature as reformer, however, neither his works nor his correspondence are available in modern editions. Among his works, an important Latin commentary on Romans remains in manuscript; and of his correspondence, about a third is either still in manuscript or printed in publications that appeared before 1900. In many cases, these publications offer only the text, providing no translation and supplying no historical or biographical background information. The exception are letters addressed to famous contemporaries such as Erasmus, Luther, Bucer, and others whose correspondence is available in critical, annotated editions and includes Capito's letters.

The present work attempts to build a bridge to the sources for modern readers. It provides an annotated translation of a selection of letters to and from Capito. The selection is based on two criteria: the history and the accessibility of the text in question. All letters previously unidentified or unpublished are included, as are those that were published before 1900 or in periodicals and books of limited circulation. Letters that do not fall into those categories are listed and summarized in the appropriate chronological slot to preserve the context. My first task accordingly was to locate and collect the source material and to transcribe the manuscript letters. Although the source texts are not included in the present book, they have been posted on a website, www.wolfgang-capito.com, which may be consulted by specialists wishing to read the letters in the original Latin or German.

My search for texts built on the work of three scholars who have made significant contributions to our knowledge of Capito's life and thought. Beate Stierle (*Capito als Humanist* [Gütersloh, 1974]) examined the early life of the reformer and his career up to 1520 and provided a detailed analysis of the manuscript containing Capito's commentary on Romans. James Kittelson (*W. Capito: From Humanist to Reformer* [Leiden, 1975]) wrote an intellectual biography of the humanist turned reformer. Olivier Millet (*La Correspondance de W.F. Capiton* [Strasbourg, 1982]) put together a ground-breaking list of Capito's correspondence, which also contains summaries in French.

The correspondence of Capito will appear in three volumes, covering the periods 1507–23, 1524–31, and 1531–41, respectively. By the end of 1523 Capito had clearly turned away from the Catholic Church. The year constitutes a caesura in his life, which is also reflected in his correspondence. Fifteen thirty-one was another crucial year for Capito: Zwingli died in the battle of Kappel, and Capito was well positioned to fill the vacuum and become a leading voice in the Swiss Reformation. In the same year, he also lost his wife to the plague and married Wibrandis Rosenblatt, the widow of the Basel reformer Johannes Oecolampadius. These events provide a natural dividing line between volumes 2 and 3.

Almost two hundred letters survive from the period covered in volume 1, the majority written in Latin, a few in German, and one (Ep. 66 by Christoph Hegendorf) in Greek. Ninety-three of the letters are translated here in full; the remainder, which have been published in modern editions, are summarized. Many of the letters were first transcribed under the direction of J. Baum at the end of the nineteenth century. The result of this group effort, deposited in the library of the University of Strasbourg, remains in manuscript. Only an index to the collection, entitled *Thesaurus Baumianus: Verzeichnis der Briefe und Aktenstücke,* has been published (by J. Ficker [Strasbourg, 1905]). For modern readers, however, the nineteenth-century script is as difficult (and in some cases, more difficult) to decipher than the sixteenth-

century original. For that reason, the texts transcribed in the *Thesaurus* have
been redone on the basis of the original manuscripts, and translations of the
texts have been included in this volume.

The headnote to each letter provides a brief biography of the writer and/
or addressee, notes the location of the manuscript, and supplies publication
data if there is a printed text. The footnotes supply biographical data for the
persons mentioned in the letter, clarify issues raised, and identify quotations
from classical, biblical, patristic, and scholastic sources. In a very few in-
stances, a letter exists in more than one version. In that case, significant variants are discussed in the footnotes.

The numbering of the letters follows that of Millet's finding list. Additional letters that have come to light in the course of my research and others
that have been redated are inserted in the appropriate places and marked by
an 'a,' 'b,' or 'c' after the number. Accordingly, the list now contains the following items apostrophized by a letter:

- 1a: a poem addressed to Johann Eck on his departure from the University
  of Freiburg in 1510 and published in Eck's *Quattuor orationes* (Augsburg,
  1513).
- 3a: a poem addressed to Eck published in his *Disputatio Viennae habita*
  (Augsburg, 1517).
- 11a: a letter prefacing the second part of Capito's Hebrew grammar.
  Millet's Ep. 11 is the preface to the first part (1518).
- 15a: a letter prefacing Andreas Karlstadt's *Contra D. Ioannem Eckium ...
  propositiones* (Basel, 1518) and ascribed to Capito (not listed by Millet).
- 15b and c: a pair of letters from and to the jurist Udalricus Zasius (1518),
  not listed by Millet.
- 19a: a letter prefacing Capito's Latin translation of Luther's *De decem prae-
  ceptis* (originally published in German), not listed by Millet. It is included
  in a collection of Luther's writings published by Froben in 1518. Millet's
  Ep. 19 is Capito's preface to that edition.
- 31a: a letter listed as 7a in Millet. It appeared as the preface to the second
  edition of Josse Clichtove's *Elucidatorium* (Basel, 1519) and contains significant variants on the preface in the first edition (Ep. 7, 1517).
- 32a: the second of two letters prefacing a translation of Chrysostom.
  Millet's Ep. 32 is the first letter (1519).
- 36a: a letter fragment listed by Millet in his appendix.
- 45a: a letter from Cochlaeus to Capito (1520), not listed by Millet.
- 46a: a prefatory letter introducing Hermann Buschius's *Hypanticon* (1520),
  not listed by Millet.

– 60a: a letter from Albert of Brandenburg to Leo X drafted by Capito, not listed by Millet.

In addition, Millet's Epp. 107, 114, 155, and 178 have been redated. Ep. 56 from Hutten (1520), which Millet lists but was unable to locate, has been traced to the holdings of the Pierpont Morgan Library in New York. It was published in 1949.

I gratefully acknowledge the financial assistance of the Social Sciences and Humanities Research Council of Canada as well as the material assistance of Emmanuel College (University of Toronto), which provided me with office space and the amenities that go with it for the duration of the project. My research would not have been possible without the assistance I received at the libraries and archives whose collections I used, notably the Centre for Reformation and Renaissance Studies at the University of Toronto (Professor William Bowen), the Archive municipale in Strasbourg (Drs Schwieger and F.J. Fuchs), the Universitätsbibliothek in Basel (Dr Martin Steinmann), the Universitätsbibliothek in Würzburg (Dr Hans-Günther Schmidt) and the Staatsarchiv in Würzburg (Dr Werner Wagenhöfer), the Herzog-August Bibliothek in Wolfenbüttel (Dr Gillian Bepler), the Vatican library and the Archivo Secreto (Dr Christine Maria Grafinger, Father William Sheehan), the Staatsarchiv in Vienna (Leopold Auer), and the Zentralbibliothek in Zürich (Dr Christoph Eggenberger).

Special thanks go to a number of colleagues who have contributed directly to this edition by transcribing or translating individual letters: Chris Nighman at Wilfrid Laurier University (Epp. 55 and 60), Gisela Argyle at York University (the lengthy Ep. 177), Tim Hegedus at Wilfrid Laurier University (Ep. 66), Gavin Hammel at the University of Toronto (Appendices), and Jason Sager at Wilfrid Laurier, who did some of the summaries. Much credit goes to Milton Kooistra, whose substantial and sustained contribution over the past three years I have acknowledged on the title page of this edition. I also want to express my gratitude to Reinhard Bodenmann, who read part of this manuscript, and from whose comments I have greatly benefited.

Many other friends and colleagues have supplied information or offered valuable suggestions and comments: Mark Crane, Elizabeth Brown, Anthony Lane, Greta Kroeker, Jill Kraye, Heinrich Dilly, Franz Küchle, Thomas Brady, Elaine Fantham, Charles Fantazzi, James Estes, D.F.S. Thomson, James Farge, Rolf Decot, Lawrin Armstrong, James Hirstein, Matthieu Arnold, Christoph Römer, Ron Schoeffel, Rainer Heinrich, Virginia Brown, and James Hankins. Merely listing their names is an inadequate return for their scholarly services. I owe a great debt to them for taking a kind interest in my research and volunteering their time and effort to answer my queries.

They checked barely legible manuscripts, supplied biographical data, and mediated access to manuscripts and the acquisition of microfilms. To put it briefly, they acted as exemplary citizens of the Res Publica Literaria, carrying on a tradition honoured already four hundred years ago, by the men whose letters are published in this edition.

ERIKA RUMMEL

Abbreviations and Short Titles

Allen	*Opus epistolarum Des. Erasmi Roterodami*, ed. P.S. Allen, H.M. Allen, and H.W. Garrod (Oxford, 1906–58)
Amerbachkorrespondenz	*Die Amerbachkorrespondenz*, ed. A. Hartmann and B.R. Jenny (Basel, 1942–)
AMS	Archives municipales de Strasbourg
ARG	*Archiv für Reformationsgeschichte/ Archive for Reformation History*
ASD	*Opera Omnia Desiderii Erasmi Roterodami* (Amsterdam, 1969–)
AST	Archives du Chapitre Saint-Thomas (in AMS)
Ballenstedt	J.A. Ballenstedt, *Andreae Althameri vita* (Wolfenbüttel, 1740)
Barge, *Karlstadt*	H. Barge, *Andreas Bodenstein von Karlstadt* (Leipzig, 1905)
BDS	Martin Bucer, *Deutsche Schriften: im Auftrage der Heidelberger Akademie der Wissenschaften* (Gütersloh, 1960–)
Briefe Mutians	*Der Briefwechsel des Conradus Mutianus*, ed. Karl Gillert (Halle, 1890)
Briefe Oekolampads	*Briefe und Akten zum Leben Oekolampads*, ed. E. Staehelin, Quellen und Forschungen zur Reformationsgeschichte (Leipzig, 1927–34; repr. 1971)
Briefwechsel des Beatus Rhenanus	*Briefwechsel des Beatus Rhenanus*, ed. A. Horawitz and K. Hartfelder (Leipzig, 1886; repr. 1966)
Bullinger, *Briefwechsel*	*Heinrich Bullinger Werke. Briefwechsel*, ed. J. Staedtke et al. (Zurich, 1973–)
Corr Bucer	*Correspondance de Martin Bucer*, ed. J. Rott et al. (Leiden, 1979–)
CR	*Corpus Reformatorum*

CWE	*Collected Works of Erasmus* (Toronto, 1974–)
ERSY	*Erasmus of Rotterdam Society Yearbook*
Gerdesius	D. Gerdesius, *Introductio in Historiam Evangelii XVI seculo passim per Europam renovati* (Groningen, 1744–6)
Herminjard	*Correspondance des Réformateurs dans les pays de langue française*, ed. A.-L. Herminjard (Geneva and Paris, 1866–97; repr. 1965–6)
Herrmann	F. Herrmann, *Die evangelische Bewegung zu Mainz im Reformationszeitalter* (Mainz, 1907)
Holborn	*Desiderius Erasmus Roterodamus. Ausgewählte Werke*, ed. H. and A. Holborn (Munich, 1933)
Hutteni opera	*Ulrichi Hutteni equitis Germani opera*, ed. E. Böcking (Leipzig, 1859–61; repr. 1963)
Kalkoff, *Capito*	P. Kalkoff, *W. Capito im Dienste Erzbischof Albrechts von Mainz. Quellen und Forschungen zu den entscheidenden Jahren der Reformation (1519–23)* (Berlin, 1907)
Kalkoff, *Depeschen*	P. Kalkoff, *Die Depeschen des Nuntius Aleander* (Halle, 1886)
Kalkoff, *Festschrift*	P. Kalkoff, *Festschrift zur Jahrhundertfeier der Universität Breslau* (Breslau, 1911)
Kawerau	*Der Briefwechsel des Justus Jonas*, ed. G. Kawerau (Halle, 1884–5; repr. 1964)
Ki.Ar.	Kirchenarchiv
Kittelson	J. Kittelson, *Wolfgang Capito: From Humanist to Reformer* (Leiden, 1975)
Kolde	*Analecta Lutherana, Briefe und Aktenstücke zur Geschichte Luthers*, ed. Th. Kolde (Gotha, 1883)
Kolde, *Beiträge*	Th. Kolde, 'Beiträge zur Reformationsgeschichte,' in *Kirchengeschichtliche Studien, H. Reuter zum 70. Geburtstag gewidmet* (Lepizig, 1888), 197–201
Krafft	*Briefe und Dokumente aus der Zeit der Reformation*, ed. K. and W. Krafft (Elberfeld, 1875)
LB	*Desiderii Erasmi Roterodami opera omnia*, ed. J. Leclerc (Leiden, 1703–6; repr. 1961–2)
Melanchthons Briefwechsel	*Melanchthons Briefwechsel: Kritische und kommentierte Gesamtausgabe*, ed. H. Scheible (Stuttgart-Bad Cannstatt, 1977–)

Migne, PG	*Patrologiae cursus completus, Series graeca*, ed. J.-P. Migne (Paris, 1857–66)
Millet	O. Millet, *Correspondance de Wolfgang Capiton (1478–1541)* (Strasbourg, 1982)
NAKG	*Nederlands Archief voor Kerkgeschiedenis*
Pflug, *Corr*	Julius Pflug, *Correspondance*, ed. J.V. Pollet (Leiden, 1969–)
QGT	*Quellen zur Geschichte der Täufer in Elsass*, ed. M. Krebs and H.G. Rott (Gütersloh, 1959–60)
RTA	*Reichstagsakten*
Schiess	*Briefwechsel der Brüder Ambrosius und Thomas Blaurer*, ed. T. Schiess (Freiburg, 1908–12)
Scultetus	A. Scultetus, *Annalium Evangelii passim per Europam ... renovati, Decas prima et secunda* (Heidelberg, 1618–20)
Seitz	O. Seitz, *Der authentische Text der Leipziger Disputation* (Berlin, 1903)
Stierle	B. Stierle, *Capito als Humanist* (Gütersloh, 1974)
TB	Thesaurus Baumianus (manuscript in the Bibliothèque Nationale et Universitaire, Strasbourg)
Vadianische Briefsammlung	*Vadianische Briefsammlung*. Mitteilungen zur Vaterländischen Geschichte 24–5, 27–30, ed. E. Arbenz and H. Wartmann (St Gallen, 1890–1913)
WA	*D. Martin Luthers Werke: Kritische Gesamtausgabe* (Weimar, 1906–61)
Wackernagel	R. Wackernagel, *Geschichte der Stadt Basel* (Basel, 1924)
WBr	*D. Martin Luthers Werke. Briefwechsel* (Weimar, 1930–)
Wimpfelingi Opera	*Iacobi Wimpfelingi Opera selecta*, ed. O. Herding et al. (Munich, 1965)
ZKG	*Zeitschrift für Kirchengeschichte*
Zwingli, *Briefwechsel*	*Zwinglis Briefwechsel*, ed. E. Egli et al. (Leipzig, 1911–35)
Zwingli, *Opera*	*Zwinglis Werke / Ulrici Zwinglii Opera*, ed. M. Schuler and J. Schulthess (Zurich, 1828–42)
Zwingli, *Werke*	*Huldreich Zwinglis Sämtliche Werke*, ed. E. Egli et al. (Berlin-Leipzig-Zurich, 1905–)

Introduction

Wolfgang Fabritius Capito (Köpfel) was a native of Haguenau near Strasbourg in Alsace. His father was a smith, as the middle name 'Fabritius' indicates, and a member of the respected guild of Constoflers. His date of birth, usually given as 1478, is unconfirmed. There is no information about his early schooling, but we know that he matriculated at the University of Ingolstadt in 1501. That would suggest a birth date in the 1480s, since most young men began university studies in their teens.[1] In 1504 Capito is listed in the records of the University of Heidelberg, but he moved to the University of Freiburg the following February. There he matriculated as BA and earned his MA in 1506, when Johann Eck was dean. In 1511 he himself served as dean of the faculty of arts. He lectured at the university and pursued studies in theology under Johannes Caesarius and Georg Northofer. He also attended the lectures of the jurist Udalricus Zasius, with whom he remained in touch after he left the university (Epp. 15b, 15c). He received his licence in theology in 1512 and his doctorate in 1515.[2] From a letter to Hutten in 1519 (Ep. 34) we gather that Capito planned to take a doctorate in law as well, but there is no evidence that he executed this plan.

The first letter of the present volume dates from 1507, when Capito was a student at the University of Freiburg and doing occasional work for the Haguenau printer Heinrich Gran. There is an unfortunate gap of nine years between Ep. 1 and Ep. 2, the first letter from Capito to Erasmus. It is for this reason that I included two poems (1a and 3a). Addressed to Johann Eck, they may be regarded as letter-poems and attest to the good relations that existed between the two men before the religious debate found them in opposite camps. Indeed in those early days, Capito was willing to suffer on Eck's behalf. When the latter left Freiburg in a huff, his enemies and sup-

* * * * *

1 On Capito's birthdate see Stierle, 11, n.1.
2 On his university studies, see ibid. 22–7.

porters engaged in a poster war. Capito's contributions to the polemic landed him before a senate committee and led to a brief incarceration. The two poems included in this edition offer rare glimpses of the early, cordial relationship between Capito and Eck. Indirect evidence also comes from Johannes Cellarius's eyewitness report of the Leipzig Disputation, which is favourable to Eck and dedicated to Capito (Ep. 31). Among fellow students at Freiburg, with whom Capito remained in touch, were Matthew Zell and Urbanus Rhegius who, like Capito, embraced the Reformation, and Johann Fabri, later bishop of Vienna, who was a staunch defender of the Catholic faith and became Capito's foe. In later years Capito deprecated his studies at Freiburg and expressed regret at having wasted his time on medieval authors, 'the snares of the sophists and the nauseating writings of Scotus' (Epp. 30, 32). His generation had 'languished under indolent, or rather, ignorant teachers,' he wrote, but a golden age was dawning, and students now had an opportunity to study superior authors and learn from classical and patristic sources (Epp. 11, 25).

In 1512 Capito left the university of Freiburg to take up an appointment as preacher in Bruchsal, a new foundation in the see of Philip von Rosenheim, bishop of Speyer. He found the post uncongenial, however. He chafed at the time spent in chapter meetings, in dealing with 'the superstitions' of old women, and in answering legal questions, a field in which he did not feel entirely competent (Ep. 30). In 1515, finally, he was able to improve his position. Christoph von Utenheim, bishop of Basel, appointed him cathedral preacher in that city. He remained in Basel until 1520.

The Basel years are fairly well documented in Capito's correspondence. From 1517 on we have a steady flow of letters, many of them prefaces to his own works or to those of friends and fellow scholars. The most significant of these are the anonymous prefaces to the works of Karlstadt (Ep. 15a) and Luther (Epp. 19, 19a), published by Froben in 1518. By that time Capito was in correspondence with Luther and clearly moved by the reformer's ideas, although either unable or unwilling to see their schismatic thrust. On balance, it was Erasmus rather than Luther who shaped Capito's thought during the Basel years. He made Erasmus's acquaintance during the latter's stay in Basel in 1515/16, when he was preparing his New Testament edition for publication. In the letters written during the Basel years, Capito projects a typically Erasmian attitude towards biblical scholarship and the nascent movement of the Reformation: enthusiasm for language studies, a disdain for scholastic authors, a preference for patristic authors over medieval exegetes, and a desire to remain on the sidelines of the religious debate. He used the slogans of the New Learning (Epp. 4, 7, 8, 19) and promoted the ideals of Christian humanism epitomized by Erasmus. Indeed, Capito's programmatic letter concerning the formation of a theologian from child-hood on (Ep. 8) is reminiscent of Erasmus's *Methodus* and echoes the curric-ular proposals made there. In 1520 Capito became involved in a polemic between Erasmus and Edward Lee, an Englishman at the University of Louvain. Lee found fault with Erasmus's edition of the New Testament (Basel, 1516), contending that the changes he made to the Vulgate version were unnecessary and indeed doctrinally suspect. When Erasmus pub-lished an apologia, Capito added a preface defending biblical humanism (Ep. 54).

The Basel letters show Capito as an active member of the scholarly circle at Froben's press. He maintained epistolary contact with the Amerbach brothers, Beatus Rhenanus, Johannes Oecolampadius, and Conradus Pelli-canus. Their correspondence evinces a fervent longing for the restoration of classical learning and of a genuine theology based on biblical and patristic sources. Although Capito sharply criticized church abuses (Ep. 7), there is no indication that he intended to challenge Catholic doctrine at the time. He was, however, in touch with men whose teaching would soon be declared heterodox by the Catholic Church. Luther, Oecolampadius, Karl-stadt, and Pellicanus have already been mentioned. In addition, Capito corresponded with Melanchthon, Zwingli, and Bucer, his future colleague in Strasbourg.

In 1520 Capito received an invitation from Albert of Brandenburg, arch-bishop of Mainz, to join his court and assume the post of cathedral preacher. The invitation came about through the recommendations of two friends, Ulrich von Hutten and the physician Heinrich Stromer, who were at that time in the archbishop's service (Ep. 32). In May Capito left Basel for Mainz, accompanied by his student Hartmann von Hallwyl and his secretary Jakob Truchsess. He was soon involved in the business of the court. His principal task, it appears, was to look after the archbishop's correspondence with Rome. After being appointed to Albert's council, Capito's former student Caspar Hedio took over his duties as preacher and succeeded him in that post in January 1521 (Ep. 102 note 2).

For the next two years Capito attempted to steer the archbishop towards a rapprochement with Luther or, failing that, a policy of toleration. Much has been made of Capito's influence on the archbishop. He is credited with per-suading Albert to act with moderation and, in particular, to delay the publi-cation of the Edict of Worms and decline the title of apostolic legate, which would have obliged him to enforce the Edict (Ep. 104). No doubt, however, Albert's Hohenzollern relatives, in particular his brother Joachim of Brandenburg, were more influential than Capito in directing Albert's policy.[3] He closely collaborated with them in efforts to extract favours from Rome and had no need to take lessons in diplomacy from Capito. Albert was alert to the political and material benefits of playing the waiting game and using the Luther affair as a bargaining chip with Rome. His correspondence with the Holy See (some of it drafted by Capito, but no doubt under the archbishop's direction) makes it clear that he expected a reward for his loyalty to the church (see, e.g., Ep. 93). His restraint may therefore be interpreted as a strategic move and a bid for Rome's largesse more than a reflection of his religious leanings or of Capito's personal influence. One must remember, moreover, that Capito himself was engaged in bargaining with Rome at the time. He acknowledged his duplicity in a letter to an unknown recipient, admitting that he ' studiously concealed' his inclinations.[4] In a bid to obtain a benefice in Strasbourg, he assured the papal legate Girolamo Aleandro of his support for the Catholic Church (see, e.g., Ep. 97). In letters to Luther, by contrast, Capito claimed to have served the cause of the Reformation in Mainz and to have convinced the archbishop of the need for a personal reform. He portrayed Albert as a man earnestly engaged in biblical studies and striving to fulfil his episcopal mandate. He therefore implored Luther to bear with the bishop and make allowances for the prelate, to refrain from publishing any criticism of Albert, to temper his radicalism and adopt a more diplomatic stance. Luther disagreed with Capito on every count. He perceived Albert as worldly, unwilling to abandon the lucrative trade in indulgences, and lacking the will to reform. In January 1522 he wrote a candid letter rejecting Capito's policy of accommodation, condemning his backroom tactics, and stopping short only of calling him a hypocrite (Ep. 131). In response, Capito travelled to Wittenberg in person and, according to Caspar Hedio, effected a complete reconciliation (Ep. 135 note 1). Some scholars date Capito's conversion to the meeting with Luther in March 1522. It may well have left a deep impression on Capito's mind, but there was no appreciable change in his actions until the beginning of 1523, when Luther's letter condemning his Nicodemism appeared in print. The unauthorized publication effectively 'outed' Capito.

Throughout his years at the court of Mainz, Capito was involved in litigation over the provostship at St Thomas in Strasbourg. Aleandro secured the

* * * * *

3 The impression that Capito had considerable influence is based on the testimony of Capito's friend and disciple Hedio and on Capito's own testimony, which must be taken with a grain of salt.

4 *Sedulo dissimulo* (Ep. 36a).

position for him, but the claim was contested by two notorious benefice hunters. One was bought out at an early stage, but the other, Jacob Abel, a protonotary at the papal court in Rome, doggedly pursued his claim. Capito did not abandon litigation, until the publication of Luther's embarrassing letter ruined any chance of seeing the lawsuit settled in his favour. The quest for the provostship is first mentioned in Capito's correspondence in Ep. 50 of July 1520. For the remainder of the year, Capito's legal representatives battled Abel's claim (see Appendix). In 1521 the matter was settled in Capito's favour on the intercession of Aleandro, who described the benefice in a confidential letter as a bribe to keep Capito in the Catholic camp.[5] Before he could take possession, however, Pope Leo X died, and Abel renewed his suit under the incoming pope, Adrian VI. In February 1522 Aleandro informed Capito of Adrian's favourable decision, again stating that he expected quid pro quo. 'If you imitate Luther and yourself strive for revolution,' he warned Capito, '... you can expect to turn the pontiff and indeed the whole Catholic Church against you' (Ep. 149). The publication of Luther's letter in 1523 revealed that Capito had been a secret supporter of the reformer all along. Not surprisingly, Abel made a third attempt to unseat his competitor, and the pope reversed his judgment (Ep. 161), furnishing Abel with executorial letters. Capito, however, forestalled the consequences by travelling to Strasbourg in March 1523 and taking possession of the provostship in person. The move was successful. The canons were now divided over the religious question. Some openly supported the reformers, the remaining conservative party was not strong enough to oust Capito. In June 1523 he officially left the service of the archbishop, and in July he took out citizenship in Strasbourg. In November Capito notified his legal representatives in Rome of his intention to drop the lawsuit against Abel (Ep. 175). Abel continued to press his claim, taking his case to the city of Strasbourg in 1534, but the city had by then embraced the Reformation, and the councillors declined to enforce papal mandates (Ep. 50, headnote).

Capito's letters from the summer of 1523 contain mixed messages about his confessional status. He tailored his words to the creed of the recipient, depicting himself alternatively as a maligned Catholic (Epp. 161 and 164 to Erasmus) or a supporter of the Reformation (Ep. 163 to Urbanus Rhegius). As late as November 1523 he assured the bishop of Strasbourg of his obedience and subordination (Ep. 174, headnote). The quest for financial security

* * * * *

5 In February 1521, Aleandro recommended that Capito be given a prebend because he was 'learned and eloquent and just as capable of being of service as of doing harm' (Kalkoff, *Depeschen*, 41).

was no doubt the underlying motive. When his diplomatic game threatened to unravel in 1522, he competed against his friend and former student, Caspar Hedio, for the position of cathedral preacher in Strasbourg and bitterly resented Hedio's appointment. Mutual friends were surprised at his angry response, but eventually effected a reconciliation between the two men (Epp. 145 note 4, 169, 170, 173). In March 1524 the congregation of Young St Peter's in Strasbourg invited Capito to become their preacher. His call accorded with the Reformation principle, which ignored the Catholic hierarchy and placed the appointment in the hands of the congregation. It was at this point, finally, that Capito openly abandoned the Catholic Church. On 1 August 1524 he married Agnes Roettel, the daughter of a Strasbourg city councillor.

Capito's commitment to the Reformation brought about a gradual shift in his attitude towards humanistic learning. The prefatory letters to his early works are full of humanistic catchphrases. He calls on the Muses, praises the authors of classical antiquity, and castigated the 'barbarous' style of medieval theologians.[6] Such phrases are all but absent from the letters written after his conversion. In their place we find the slogans of the Reformation, reflecting his new commitment.[7] This is not to say that Capito turned his back on humanism. He continued to subscribe to the humanistic slogan 'Ad fontes' and to engage in the quintessential humanistic activities of translating and commenting on texts, but he imposed on these pursuits a different rationale. He insisted on the importance of philological and historical training for theologians, but distinguished between human skills that allowed an exegete to understand the text and divine inspiration that allowed him to fully grasp its meaning. His commentary on Habakkuk (1526) contains the most comprehensive statement on the relationship between acquired knowledge and inspired understanding. The exegete, he says, needs 'an exact knowledge of the history of the period and a reasonable command of languages, especially Hebrew,' but in addition he must beware of 'confusing the prophetic faith with human conceits.'[8]

No one will deny the importance of philological skill, but

* * * * *

6 See the footnotes for Capito's prominent use of classical proverbs, his tirades against the 'barbarians,' the deprecating term used by humanists to denote medieval authors (e.g., Epp. 6, 8, 11, 32a), and the references to the Muses and the Graces indicating his literary interests (e.g., Epp. 3a, 32, 37).
7 Compare Capito's usage in Epp. 146, 163 with the catchphrases listed by H. Diekmannshenke, 'Der Schlagwortgebrauch in Karlstadts frühen Schriften' in S. Looß and M. Matthias, eds., *Themata Leucoreana* (Wittenberg, 1998), 283–302.
8 *In Habakuk prophetam ... enarrationes* (Strasbourg, 1526), A4 r–v.

how can you expound an author correctly and clearly, if you do not even understand his words? I hear you say: 'By using a faithful translator.' But no translator, however learned and however felicitous in his translation, can reflect every facet of an idiom in a foreign language. Yet the weight of the whole sentence often rests on a detail, such as a trope, a phrase, a little word, or the emphasis contained in one specific word ... I am speaking here only of the understanding and precise explanation grammarians promise and offer in their treatment of secular authors, which you will never achieve without a knowledge of languages, even if you are equipped with the best translation. For, as I said, a good part of a sentence is understood in the light of the usage of the native speaker and the idiom of the language.[9]

Yet the exegete must remember that it is the Spirit who perfects our understanding of scripture and beware of intellectual arrogance. God's counsel is hidden in the allegorical language of the prophets. 'We will discover it only by the grace promised to us in Christ, by faith in God, and by hope in his mercy and forgiveness.' Without faith, exegetes can explain scripture no better than 'Eustathius explained Homer, Servius Virgil, and Donatus Terence.' They cannot offer a full explanation without the aid of God, for 'the heavenly kingdom is to be found, not in language, but in the power of God.'[10]

Consulted on the subject of a preacher's qualifications, Capito warned of putting too great a value on university training. An academic degree was merely a professional designation and did not serve as proof of learning. An understanding of the Bible could not be obtained through study alone. It was granted to the elect through divine inspiration.[11] In the preface to his commentary on Hosea (1527), Capito emphasized that the title 'doctor' belonged to Christ alone, for 'the church of Christ is completely taught by God.' He saw his commentary as a repository, 'not of [his] own knowledge, but of the knowledge of God.'[12] The preface is full of warnings against the arrogance of worldly learning. Capito uses the language of the *spirituali*, which may have particular appeal for the addressee of the preface, Marguerite of Navarre, herself an advocate of evangelism. Capito praises Marguerite

* * * * *

9 Ibid., A5v–6r.
10 Ibid., 6v–7r.
11 AMS Varia ecclesiastica 18: 329–43v, esp. 330v, using a historical argument: 'If the doctorate were merely deceit and vainglory, Christians would not praise but condemn it' (quoted Kittelson, 216, n.20.).
12 *In Hoseam prophetam ... commentarius* (Strasbourg, 1527) 2v, 3v.

for having transcended popish superstition through contemplation. 'To make all empty confidence vanish, we must look at the internal light.' The true knowledge of God is found by 'looking within oneself.' We do not all have the same degree of knowledge and understanding, 'the supply of which is regulated by the spirit.'[13] Intellectual humility and distrust in human wisdom must not lead us to disdain education, however. 'We all need to be educated,' Capito wrote in a letter to the mayor of Basel. 'What harm is there in my having learned in school the things that God gave to others through spiritual understanding?'[14]

Erasmus once complained that there were no truly learned men among the reformers,[15] a surprising statement, given the active role reformers played everywhere in establishing schools and making education widely available. What Erasmus meant was that the reformers had no interest in literature per se or in literary accomplishments and used language studies merely to further confessional goals. Indeed, Protestant school orders often included provisions for language studies, but clearly for the purpose of allowing students to study the scriptural text in the original.

Capito exemplifies this purpose. He writes entirely in the spirit of a reformer when he advises a cautious approach to secular authors. He praises Cicero for his stylistic perfection and encourages students to read Livy and other historians to 'exercise their minds' but urges them never to lose sight of the fact that the benefits derived from the study of secular authors are limited. 'Only faith and love offer certainty and are beneficial.' History books, he writes, cannot 'improve us inwardly or offer instruction to the common people. Therefore all teaching, exhortation, criticism, and correction must take its origin in the spirit of Christ and the divine scripture.'[16]

In the years leading up to 1529, when the city officially embraced the reformed creed, Capito found himself in continued negotiation with the secular authorities. Strasbourg was an imperial city, and the senate was sharply divided over confessional policy. Some councillors openly supported the Reformation, while others did not wish to antagonize or defy the Catholic emperor or the local ecclesiastical ruler, Bishop Wilhelm von Hohnstein. The first test came in the fall of 1523 over the question of celibacy. Anton Firn, a priest under the jurisdiction of Capito, then provost of St Thomas,

* * * * *

13 Ibid., 5r, 5v, 7v.
14 TB 12:63 (Millet, Ep. 279).
15 ASD 9-1, 344, 396; Allen Ep. 2615: 427–9.
16 *Kinderbericht und fragstück van glauben* (Strasbourg, 1529) 40r, *Berner Synodus: Ordnung wie sich pfarrer und prediger zu Statt und Land Ber in leer und leben halten sollen* (Basel, 1532; repr. Basel, 1830), 111.

and other members of the clergy married and appealed to the city council for support against the sanctions of the bishop and the chapter.[17] The appeal, *Supplication des pfarrhers unnd der pfarrkinder zu sant Thoman*, was drafted, but not signed, by Capito, who promoted Firn's cause discreetly. Capito's refusal to enforce the bishop's decree against married priests and the qualified support of the city council allowed Firn and others who flouted the rule of celibacy to retain their positions. When Conrad Treger, the Augustinian provincial, attacked Capito's position on celibacy in 1524, he replied with the *Verwarnung der diener des worts*. He did so under the cover of anonymity, but went public as the polemic continued and signed his second response, *Antwurt ... auff Bruder Conradts Augustinerordens Provincials vermanung*, published in September 1524. Indeed, he openly identified himself as a Lutheran and praised the reformer as the foremost exegete of his time: 'I would like to say that no writer in our time ... has treated scripture more skilfully than Luther.'[18]

In the *Antwurt*, Capito furthermore defended the reformers against the accusation of inciting unrest and insubordination. 'Does dissension follow from the Gospel?' Capito asked. 'Yes, it does. But that is the fault of the princes of the world, who have thus far defended their hope for peace with arms, and whom God kills with the sword of his mouth.'[19] The perception that the reformers condoned insubordination was reinforced by the radical preaching of Karlstadt, who visited Strasbourg in October of 1524, and by the peasant revolts, which marred the spring of 1525. In an effort to dissociate the reformation movement from the goals of the rebels, Capito composed the *Warhafftige verantwortung uff eins gerichten vergicht* (1525), in which he condemned the riots but, unlike Luther, stopped short of recommending violent retribution.

In the following years, Capito and his colleagues focused their efforts on securing the endorsement of the city council for the abolition of the mass and the removal of images from the churches. The council gave its support only reluctantly. In December 1523 the senate decreed that preachers must preach the Bible, but declined to act on the petition of the pastors for a more general reform. With the help of Nicolaus Kniebs, a member of the council and an ardent supporter of the Reformation, the pastors finally succeeded on 1 July 1525, in obtaining a decree mandating the celebration of the Lord's Supper alongside the mass. A second petition in August 1525 resulted in the

* * * * *

17 See *Appellatio sacerdotum/Appellatio der eelichen Priester* (Ep. 189); Ep. 177.
18 *Antwurt ... auff Bruder Conradts ... vermanung* (Strasbourg, 1524), O iiii recto.
19 Ibid., Cii recto.

senate ordering the removal of statuary and images from the churches. In a third petition in May 1526, the pastors again urged the abolition of the mass, calling it a 'hateful thing and the height of blasphemy against God.'[20] Finally, Bucer's and Capito's preaching prompted a citizens' petition in March 1528, requesting that the mass be abolished. The council continued to resist, fearing the political consequences of such an action. Their fears were reinforced by the imperial vice-chancellor, Balthasar Merklin, who visited Strasbourg in June 1528, reminding the council of its obligations to the emperor. In response, Capito and Hedio wrote and addressed to the vice-chancellor a defense of the religious changes they had advocated and in part executed in Strasbourg.[21] In February of 1529, the council finally embraced the Reformation and abolished the mass.

The reformation of Strasbourg went forward against the backdrop of the Sacramentarian Controversy, which caused a rift between Lutherans and Zwinglians. Luther affirmed the real presence of Christ in the bread and wine consecrated at the Lord's Supper. Capito inclined towards Zwingli's interpretation of the Eucharist as symbolic and 'a daily remembrance of Christ's one sacrifice on the cross,'[22] but his pronouncements on the subject lack consistency. In the controversy with Treger, he stated that the Eucharist was 'a recollection of Christ's death on the cross. We refresh our memory and clearly affirm it by accepting the Lord's bread and wine.' He added: 'We know, however, that we become blessed through the body and blood alone.'[23] Commenting on the feud between Karlstadt and Luther in 1524, he chose his words carefully: 'We should nourish our faith with the Lord's bread and wine, through the remembrance of his body and blood alone, and let everything else go.'[24] A letter from the Strasbourg pastors to Luther in November 1524, to which Capito subscribed, rejected the formula 'the body is in the bread and the blood is in the wine, for scripture does not contain phrases of this kind.' The pastors did not, however, reject consubstantiation out of hand. They merely questioned the importance of focusing on that concept. 'The bread and the cup are external things, and however much the bread may be the body of Christ and the cup his blood, it nevertheless con-

* * * * *

20 BDS 2:483–96, with Bucer's marginalia.
21 *Kurtze Summ aller Lere und Predig* (Strasbourg, 1528).
22 *An den ... Bischoffen ... Entschuldigung* (Strasbourg, 1523), DD iii recto.
23 *Antwurt* (cf. above, note 18), Hi verso.
24 *Spaltung* (= Millet, Ep. 224, of 1524) B iiii recto: 'Unsern glauben sollen wir mit des herren brot und wein, durch die gedechtnuss seins leibs und bluts allein speissen, und das übrig farn lassen.' Cf. also ibid.: 'Weits zu forschen is über-flüssig' (to search further is superfluous).

tributes nothing to our salvation, seeing that the flesh is of no benefit at all. To remember the Lord's death is the only thing here [in the Eucharist] that brings salvation; it is for that purpose that we must eat the bread and drink the cup. For the Christian must reflect more on the purpose of eating and drinking than on the nature of what he eats and drinks [in the Eucharist].'[25]

In October 1525, the Strasbourg pastors sent Georg Cassel to Wittenberg to discuss the Sacramentarian question and seek agreement on the matter. Capito sent along a letter, in which he affirmed once again that the bread was 'the external symbol by which we confess ourselves to be members of the external body of Christ.' At the same time he appealed for concord and warned of the danger of 'minutely examining' details that were not essential to salvation.[26] Luther's reply to the Strasbourg mission was belligerent. He insisted that Zwingli erred when he assigned a symbolic meaning to the biblical phrase 'This is my body.' Luther's uncompromising stand forced the Strasbourg pastors to take sides. Between 1526 and 1528 Bucer and Capito threw their support behind Zwingli's interpretation. Capito, in his catechism of 1527, agreed with Luther that the bread and wine was 'truly Christ,' but denied that 'he goes either under or with the bread. For Christ attends to the spiritual matter with physical signs.' In his commentary on Hosea (1527) Capito repeated that the Eucharist was 'a sign' but buried his view under complex language: 'The Eucharist is assuredly a sign both of our internal anointing and of our being members of the one body, the one lump of bread, the one spirit, and heirs of one and the same father.'[27]

In 1528 Bucer resumed efforts to reach an agreement with the Wittenberg theologians, suggesting in his *Vergleichung* (1528) that he might have misunderstood Luther. Both Bucer and Capito were under the impression at that time that agreement was a matter of language and depended only on finding the right formula. Luther's intransigence at the Marburg Colloquy (September 1529) shocked them. Poor health kept Capito from attending the meeting in person, but Bucer witnessed Luther's aggressive rejection of Zwingli's interpretation. No agreement was reached between the parties on the nature of the Eucharist.

In the catechism of 1529, Capito abandoned diplomacy and unequivocally

* * * * *

25 WBr. 3:383.

26 *Dr. Johannes Bugenhagens Briefwechsel*, ed. O. Vogt (Stettin, 1889–99; repr. 1966) 32, 35–7 (Millet, Ep. 248). In January 1526 he had written to Oecolampadius that the Lord's supper was 'an external thing ... and therefore not necessary for salvation' (*Briefe Oekolompads* 1:454 = Millet, Ep. 273).

27 *Kinderbericht* (1527, see above, note 16), C1r (quoted in Kittelson, 150); commentary on Hosea, 155v.

supported Zwingli's position. The dialogue between instructor and catechumen ran as follows:

> YOUTH: He has given his body and blood for the disciples to eat and to drink spiritually, that is, for faith ...
>
> INSTRUCTOR: Therefore, you do not believe that he transformed his body and blood in the Lord's Supper in a fleshly way or has hidden them under the bread and wine?
>
> YOUTH: I do not believe it.[28]

The Diet of Augsburg (1530) afforded another opportunity for a peaceful settlement of the religious strife. Capito and Bucer, who had been dispatched to advise the Strasbourg delegates on religious questions, set to work on outlining their position. It constituted a significant rapprochement to the Lutheran position. In a statement written in Capito's hand we read: 'We teach that in the sacrament and in the Supper taken by the believers, there is the true body and blood of our Saviour Christ, through whom all the believers are being nourished for their eternal life.'[29] The Confessio Tetrapolitana, which grew out of these deliberations and was subscribed by Strasbourg, Lindau, Constance, and Memmingen, omitted the phrase that seemed to limit the sacramental benefit to believers. It stated: 'In the sacrament, Christ gives his true body truly to eat and his blood truly to drink, for the nourishment of their souls and eternal life, that you may remain in him and he in you.'[30] Capito then went to Switzerland to make the formula palatable to the Zwinglians, while Bucer negotiated with the Wittenberg theologians. Capito did not achieve his goal. Zwingli's response, he wrote in a report to the Strasbourg city council, was 'too sharply expressed and much too heated' to allow further progress in the negotiations.[31]

Nor could a rapprochement be achieved after Zwingli's death in 1531. The formula employed at the Bern Synod of January 1532, in which Capito played a prominent role, was uncompromising. It read: 'The body of Christ Jesus and his precious blood are therefore in the Supper, but the physical body is not contained in the bread nor the physical blood in the wine, as the old error maintained.' In a letter to Jacob Meyer, the mayor of Basel, Capito

* * * * *

28 *Kinderbericht* (1529, see above, note 16), 20v–21r (quoted in Kittelson, 152).
29 *Ratschlag B* of March 1530 (BDS, 3:348).
30 BDS 3:125.
31 Quoted Kittelson, 158; cf. Millet, Ep. 428.

himself reverted to a formula closer in spirit to Zwingli than to Luther. He asserted that Christ's body was given as 'food for the soul' and that believers 'ate the bread with the mouth, the body of Christ, however, with faith in a renewed soul.'[32]

In 1532 the emperor extended a peace offering to those who subscribed to the Augsburg formula. After some negotiations, Strasbourg became a signatory, and Bucer embarked on a series of pamphlets to prepare the way for concord with the Wittenberg theologians, beginning with the *Entschuldigung der diener* (1532). In 1534 he recapitulated the development of his thought in a letter to Johann Hess. His interpretation of Luther's words had been mistaken, he said. He had not realized that Luther was postulating a 'sacramental union' (*sacramentalis unio*) between the bread and the body of Christ. This being the case, 'what disagreement is there between us?'[33] We see a similar effort to accommodate Luther's position in Capito's writings. In 1535 he stated that the body and bread were not mixed together physically but acknowledged that there was a 'sacramental union' (*sacramentalis conjunctio*).[34] In his correspondence he expressed optimism that 'the commotion in the churches would soon be settled.'[35] The following year Luther and the Strasbourg theologians agreed that 'the bread was Christ's body through a sacramental union, that is, Christ is present in the bread and his body truly given ... and this does not depend on the worthiness of the minister or the communicant ... even the unworthy receive it.'[36] Capito and Bucer signed the Wittenberg Concord with only a mental reservation. The Concord stated that both worthy and unworthy communicants received the body and blood of Christ in the Eucharist; the Strasbourgers maintained that those who lacked faith (as distinct from 'unworthy' sinners) could not benefit from the sacrament. In his explanation of the Concord before the Strasbourg city council, Bucer therefore noted that 'those who have no faith at all ... receive only the bread and wine.'[37]

In the *Hexemeron*, a commentary on the first chapters of Genesis published

* * * * *

32 *Berner Synodus* (see above, note 16), 60; undated letter to Meyer (after 1 July 1535), TB 5:178v (= Millet, Ep. 559): 'Also gibt der Herr zwen ding, das brot zum lib, und befiehlet sie beyden zu essen, aber synen lib zum spis der selen.'
33 Letter of Oct. 1534 to Johann Hess, BDS 6-1:48–9.
34 According to a letter from Myconius to Bullinger, 4 Feb. 1535 (Bullinger, *Briefwechsel* 5, Ep. 521). 'Capito,' he wrote, 'asked us for nothing more than a verbal agreement ... and we obliged him.'
35 Sept. 1535, Capito to Brenz (Millet, Ep. 575).
36 BDS 6-1:122–4; signed by Bucer, Capito, and their colleagues 28 May 1536.
37 BDS 6-1:152–3.

in 1537, Capito toed the Lutheran line. The Eucharist, he wrote, contained the 'true body and blood of Christ ... for in that mystical supper the host himself is present and he refreshes those who share his supper with heavenly food.' Yet we find traces of the Strasbourg position in his emphasis on the sacrament being 'vested in faith, which contemplates the whole Christ, who is truly God and truly man, and most certainly present, according to his words, "I shall be with you until the end of the world."' He adds, moreover, that 'faith indeed does not seek to know more than what is appropriate to our knowledge' – an echo of his earlier warning not to examine minutely the meaning of the words in the Last Supper.[38]

Bucer's and Capito's efforts to bring the Swiss theologians into the fold were fruitless. Capito attempted to win over Bullinger with a reconstructed account of the negotiations at the Diet of Augsburg. In a letter of 28 March 1536 he claimed that 'Zwingli saw the [Confessio Tetrapolitana] before we presented it to the emperor. He approved it, saying only that it seemed rather emasculated ... It also pleased Oecolampadius to whom it was likewise presented for reading, ... nor did he see anything in it that was at odds with his belief or that of his churches.' Taking his interpretation of the events a step further, Capito claimed that there was a general perception among the imperial councillors that 'that our confession was not at odds with that of the Lutherans.' Luther's teachings concerning the sacrament were 'not different, although they were less explicit' (*non diversum, sed minus explicatum tamen*). Since the Lutherans had not fared well at the Diet of Augsburg, he said, the Strasbourg representatives decided to keep a low profile. Diplomacy was necessary, for they were dealing with 'crass princes and nobles.' It was imperative, moreover, to achieve a consensus among the reformers. Eck had already noted gleefully that 'there were as many churches as there were men,' or at any rate, that there were three distinct groups: Lutherans, Zwinglians, 'and we in the middle' (*nos medios*). To reinforce his plea for concord, Capito cited the late Zwingli's admonitions to the same effect. It remained to be hoped that 'this fatal disagreement would come to an end, that we may become one in the Lord.'[39] Capito's attempts to level the differences between the Lutheran and the Swiss churches had no effect. Until 1538 he held out hopes that verbal finessing would bring about an agreement. He was unable to understand why Luther and Bullinger refused to compromise and, in a letter to Joachim Vadian, expressed sur-

* * * * *

38 *Hexemeron dei opus* (Strasbourg, 1539) 190r–191v. See above, note 27 and text.
39 TB 9:54–6 (=Millet, Ep. 600).

prise at the ultimate failure of the negotiations between the parties.[40] Tracing the development of Capito's thought on the Sacramentarian Controversy, it is clear that he favoured Zwingli's interpretation but made concessions to Luther's stand for the sake of achieving consensus among the parties. The shifts in Capito's thought parallel Bucer's and no doubt reflect the dialogue between the two Strasbourg reformers. Neither of them was successful in his efforts to make their rapprochement to the Lutherans palatable to the Swiss theologians.

Capito furthermore failed to win partisans for his views on the Anabaptist question. He joined fellow reformers in condemning the Anabaptists' refusal to take the oath or bear arms, and he never endorsed their position on infant baptism,[41] but he showed a much greater willingness than his colleagues to find excuses for the Anabaptists. In Capito's eyes they were merely overzealous. In his commentary on Hosea (1527), he pleaded their cause: 'There are good men among them, whom the fear of God, which is a virtue, has driven to this error. They have ceased to look to the true glory of God, superstitiously involve themselves in minutiae, and go beyond the limits, but they are wretched rather than evil.'[42] He even admitted to a certain admiration for the Anabaptists, who confessed Christ in the face of persecution. He firmly believed therefore that 'they sin without malice, if they sin at all.'[43] He added, however, that the willingness of Anabaptists to become martyrs for their cause was inappropriate and *praeter vocationem certam*, beyond what they were called to do. The alternative he proposed to Anabaptists and other dissenters amounted to Nicodemism. There was no need to act rashly, he said, or to choose voluntary martyrdom. 'There is a middle way. Let us all embrace it. It consists in this: Let us first consider that we truly bear the symbol of death and resurrection, that is, baptism. Secondly, do we not participate in the Eucharist with our brethren? For that is the image of consummate charity: eating of one bread we are all one bread. Finally, in the matter of fear and love of God and the desire for his kingdom,

* * * * *

40 *Vadianische Briefsammlung*, 5:504–5 (26 Aug. 1538): 'The people in Zurich are in an uproar over Luther's letter, which we think has been written in a most friendly spirit.' Luther does not disapprove of the Basel confession; he merely notes that it is somewhat obscure (ea aliud occultum celet, quod ex natura sermonis non intelligatur).

41 He wrote an enthusiastic preface (Ep. 335) to Martin Cellarius's *De operibus dei* (1527), who noted that 'infant baptism should not be forbidden' (66v). Capito furthermore assured Zwingli: 'There is the strictest agreement among us concerning the baptism of infants' (Ep. 338).

42 Hosea (see above, note 12), 177v.

43 Ibid.: 'sine malicia peccant, si peccant.'

we must consider over and over again, whether God has given us a suitable opportunity and whether he supplies us with the ability and the spirit to realize our desire. For one without the other is deficient and useless.'[44]

Capito's solution to the problem of dissent consisted of reducing orthodoxy to the lowest common denominator: the rites of baptism and communion. They were the chief marks of belonging to the Christian community. Pronouncements on other matters of faith should be made only under favourable conditions and by those who had a special vocation. Preachers must closely examine themselves and the circumstances before acting rashly and causing discord.

The views expressed covertly in the commentary on Hosea appeared more plainly in a document circulating under Capito's name in 1540. A young Frisian, Joannes a Bekesteyn,[45] visited Capito to ascertain that the document, which openly advocated Nicodemism, actually represented the views of the Strasbourg reformer. Capito met with him and told him that it was a pastor's vocation or first duty to stand by his congregation. An evangelical pastor in Catholic territory should therefore 'not rashly leave it, but remain instead in the parish to which he was called, patient and tolerant of the corruptions.' Indeed, he must tolerate even the mass. Similarly, it was the duty, or vocation, of the head of a household to look after his family. He must therefore avoid any action that might imperil his family and affect their welfare. Bekesteyn was disappointed and repelled by Capito's view that a man 'should connive with the degenerate church because he would be unable to look after his family, living in distant exile.' Although Capito emphasized that his advice was meant for the weaker brethren, Bekesteyn regarded him as a 'pseudo-scholar' and a 'dissimulating' hypocrite.[46]

Capito maintained that heroism was not required of Christians, except in matters concerning salvation. Accordingly, he wrote to Bullinger: 'The truth must be proclaimed with a constant mind. Once we have received it by Christ's favour, we shall maintain it to our last breath. But what truth? For not just any truth must be attested by one's life and blood, only the truth necessary for salvation. Otherwise, one would have to face death in defence of the

* * * * *

44 Ibid. 178r.
45 It is unclear what document Bekesteyn had seen, but what he describes resembles the *Consilium theologicum* (1540) of Bucer, which may have been composed with input from Capito.
46 The quotations come from a letter of Bekesteyn to Felix Rex, librarian at Königsberg, which describes the interview in detail. The text is printed in A. Hegler, *Beiträge zur Geschichte der Mystik in der Reformationszeit* (Berlin, 1906), 31–41.

true teachings of the philosophers, because all truth comes from God.'[47] Conversely, the authorities should avoid driving dissenters to martyrdom and take action only against those who openly challenged central articles of faith.

Applying this view to the Anabaptists, Capito wrote: 'It is too deep for me to judge their inner faith.' He was content to judge them by their actions: 'They must not publicly traduce the Word; they must not gather in secret assemblies; and they must not refuse to take the public oath. Rather, they must submit to the commands of the magistracy, according to the common custom.'[48] One must distinguish between Anabaptists who held their, albeit mistaken, beliefs in peace and those who were rebellious and resisted the authorities. The latter, Capito agreed, needed to be punished.[49]

The Strasbourg magistrates passed a number of decrees against the Anabaptists between 1527 and 1535. As a result Anabaptists preaching in Strasbourg were subjected to interrogation, incarceration, and expulsion. Capito participated in a number of examinations, of Hans Denck, for example, who arrived in the city in 1526, of Gall Vischer in 1528, and of Jacob Kautz and Wilhelm Reublein in 1529. On the request of the magistrates, he lodged Kautz, providing a form of house arrest; in other cases he sheltered Anabaptists without official sanction.[50] Although he dutifully supported the disciplinary actions of the council, he complained that they were oppressive: 'A new ecclesiastical tyranny creeps along these underground passages while the old [Catholic] tyranny still continues. I admit that we act in this inept fashion for the higher glory of God, but our efforts are marred by overconfidence in our own powers ... We must protect the public peace, but not by suppressing prophets, lest the Spirit be extinguished and the gifts of God slandered, which were provided for the common good.'[51]

Capito preferred conversion to punishment and persuasion to coercion. He repeatedly pleaded for mercy on behalf of dissenters. He asked Zwingli to be lenient to Balthasar Hubmaier, and the mayor of Horb to take pity on the Anabaptists imprisoned in his city.[52] What was the use, he asked, of forcing

* * * * *

47 To Bullinger in Nov. 1535 (Bullinger, *Briefwechsel* 5, Ep. 671 = Millet, Ep. 579).
48 QGT 7:332, letter to Musculus, April 1531 (= Millet, Ep. 438).
49 QGT 7:184 (Sept. 1528, Capito to Blaurer, Schiess 1:167; Millet, Ep. 367).
50 Cf. QGT 7:66, containing the testimony of the tailor Jörg Ziegler, who lodged Anabaptists 'on the request of Capito' in 1526.
51 Preface to Hosea (see above, note 12), 7–8. The pagination is faulty and confusing. It begins [1], 3 [=2], 3, 4, [5, 6, 7, 8]; then starts over again: 1, 2, 3. The quotation is in the first quire.
52 27 Dec. 1525 to Zwingli (Zwingli, *Briefwechsel*, Ep. 428 = Millet, Ep. 267); letter to Mayor of Horb and a letter of consolation to the prisoners of Horb, 31 May 1527, QGT 7:80–91 (= Millet, Epp. 330–1).

dissenters to conform. 'They confess their error out of fear, yet cling to their former belief in their heart. For belief is in the heart.'[53] Capito's tolerant attitude aroused suspicion, as he regretfully reported to Zwingli in 1525.[54] He also irritated colleagues by his readiness to offer hospitality to dissenters like Caspar Schwenckfeld, Ludwig Hetzer, Martin Cellarius, Guillaume Farel, and perhaps even Michael Servetus. Of Schwenckfeld, he wrote in 1529 that he was 'a truly noble man. He wholly breathes Christ.' At a disputation with Schwenckfeld in 1533, he said that 'he was not against him' and would willingly listen to what he had to say. As late as 1534, he praised Schwenckfeld's moral integrity, although he had to admit that his teaching was problematic.[55]

Capito himself eventually came to realize that he had underestimated the danger dissenters posed to the public peace. In 1526 he described the Anabaptists as merely a nuisance: 'They cause some disturbance, but it will shortly be resolved, I think.' A year later, he acknowledged that it amounted to a 'great conspiracy against the lawful authorities and the ministers of the Word,' but he still believed that 'there are among them some innocent men.'[56] Strasbourg soon acquired a reputation for lax enforcement of laws against dissenters. No doubt many observers saw Capito as one of the men responsible for creating the tolerant climate. His lenient attitude towards dissenters led Oecolampadius to comment: 'Our Capito leaves something to be desired in my opinion. For the Anabaptists glory a great deal in his support, whenever he deals with them in his rather benevolent manner, although I have no doubt that he is not in agreement with them.' He asked Zwingli to warn Capito against supporting them and compromising his reputation.[57] In November 1533 Myconius pointedly observed: 'Everything is full of Anabaptists. There has never been seen a greater number of doctrinaire preachers. All are being tolerated. The pastors keep silent. The city council is either ignorant or negligent.'[58] During an examination at the Stras-

* * * * *

53 QGT, 7:86.
54 20 Nov. 1525 to Zwingli (Zwingli, *Briefwechsel*, Ep. 409 = Millet, Ep. 266).
55 18 May 1529 to Zwingli (Zwingli, *Briefwechsel*, Ep. 842 = Millet, Ep. 391) TB 7:109 (5v); QGT 7-2:79.
56 26 Sept. 1526 and 9 July 1527 to Zwingli (Zwingli, *Briefwechsel*, Epp. 531, 634 = Millet, Epp. 304, 334); 7 Nov. 1527 to Zwingli (Zwingli, *Briefwechsel*, Ep. 666 = Millet, Ep. 344).
57 QGT 7:173, 3 July 1528, Oecolampadius to Zwingli (Zwingli, *Briefwechsel*, Ep. 733).
58 QGT 8:209, 23 Nov. 1533, Myconius to Capito (= Millet, Ep. 524). For a summary of the situation in Strasbourg in the context of the reformers' thought on law and order see J. Estes, *Peace, Order and the Glory of God* (Leiden: Brill, forthcoming).

bourg Synod in 1533 Capito was obliged to acknowledge his former impru-
dence and his 'special weakness for foreign guests.'[59] Bucer took this as a
sign that Capito had seen the error of his ways and was now 'wholly ours.'
He blamed the city council for being too lenient on the dissenters, and noted
that the atmosphere had changed: 'Necessity will now force a different kind
of action, for the sects are becoming too strong.[60]

Capito's inclination had always been to submit to authority, although he
repeatedly found himself caught between jurisdictions. In negotiating his
way between them, he usually voiced disagreement in an apologetic rather
than a confrontational style and used covert or carefully qualified language rather than unequivocal and absolute terms. Capito's handling of
the question whether the clergy should take out citizenship, affords an
example both of his willingness to collaborate with the authorities and of
his tendency to obfuscate when caught in a conflict of interest. He took out
citizenship on his arrival in Strasbourg in 1523, an act that many interpreted as a challenge to the Catholic ecclesiastical authorities. The clerical
foundations traditionally paid *Schirmgeld* to the city for the protection of
their legal interests. In April of 1523 the city declined to accept the payment of St Thomas. In discussions with Capito, the chapter's provost, the
magistrates indicated that the clergy might take out citizenship individually and thus enjoy legal protection. Clergymen would be exempted from
serving as delegates on political missions and could pay for being released
from watch duty, but would be required to swear an oath of loyalty. An
increasing number of priests bought citizenship before it became mandatory in November of 1524.

When Capito took the oath in July 1523, he portrayed the move as a voluntary sharing in the burden of a community. Downplaying the implications of his actions in an apologia addressed to the bishop, he insisted that
he remained the bishop's obedient subject. A year later, in December 1524,
he published a pamphlet, *Das die Pfafheit schuldig sey Burgerlichen Eyd
zuthun*, in which he took a more radical position, declaring it unfair for
'clerical freedom to exist at the expense of the community.' Since the clergy
shared the privileges of the citizens, he said, they must also share their
expenses. When the council demanded that the collegiate churches contribute to the common chest and to poor relief, however, Capito signed an

* * * * *

59 The censure read: 'Capito hat ein sonder anmutung zu fremden gästen und
   prüssen (= heretics?]' (QGT 8:52).
60 QGT 8:270, Bucer to Blaurer, Jan. 1534, Schiess 1:466); ibid. 209 (Bucer to
   Myconius, Nov. 1533).

appeal, asking the bishop to protect their prerogatives.[61] In the spring of 1524 the city council made a more direct inroad into clerical privileges by appointing preachers to parish churches. A few months later they formalized their right to make such appointments and voted to support the preachers financially.

Capito, who had become preacher of Young St Peter's, was one of the beneficiaries of this provision. His position as provost of St Thomas, however, put him at odds with the city authorities. His efforts to navigate between the two positions left him liable to the accusation of duplicity. This difficulty was resolved when he resigned the provostship in 1525,[62] but another difficulty arose in its stead. As an evangelical preacher, Capito found himself in conflict with imperial authority. This was, however, a problem he shared with the city council. The beginning of 1525 saw an exodus of canons from Strasbourg, some of whom took along property belonging to their foundations. Nicolaus Wurmser, assuming the leadership of the conservative canons of St Thomas, fled to Offenburg, taking away the great seal and other legal documents crucial to the administration of St Thomas. In February 1525 he appealed to the imperial court, then sitting at Esslingen, on behalf of the Strasbourg foundations. He complained of the innovations to religious ceremonies that had gone forward under Capito's provostship, contrary to the mandate of the Diet of Nürnberg, which had declared a moratorium on changes. Capito in turn charged Wurmser with theft. He defended the reformation of the church in Strasbourg in a pamphlet, *Von drey Strassburger Pfaffen* (1525), insisting that he had preached the gospel truth and had instituted such worship as was in agreement with the gospel. The conflict dragged on into the 1530s when the city agreed to compensate the Catholic canons who had fled Strasbourg.

The year 1526 saw Capito involved in another conflict with the imperial authorities. After the Baden Disputation (May–June 1526) he provided a transcript of the proceedings to his relative, the printer Wolfgang Köpfel. Köpfel published the text without authorization. The city of Basel prosecuted the printer and Capito in the imperial court. His difficulties were compounded when the Catholic apologist Johannes Fabri published a letter in which Capito allegedly spoke of secret meetings and subversion. Capito extricated himself from the affair by showing that Fabri had misrepresented

* * * * *

61 TB 2:49–50v.
62 In 1525 he ceded the post to Lorenz Schenckbecher in exchange for the latter's position as cantor; in 1537 the provostship reverted to Capito.

the meaning of his words. He did not explain his involvement in the unlawful publication of the Baden proceedings.[63]

Fifteen thirty-one was a bleak year in the annals of the Swiss Reformation and in Capito's personal life: Zwingli was slain in the battle of Kappel; Oecolampadius passed away in Basel; and Capito's wife died of the plague. On the advice of Bucer, Capito married Oecolampadius's widow, Wibrandis Rosenblatt, in the spring of 1532. In 1533, when the Strasbourg city council granted the pastors permission to hold a synod to define doctrine, Capito delivered the opening sermon, but his contributions to the proceedings were sparse. He was eclipsed by Bucer, who by that time had emerged as the principal theologian of Strasbourg. Thus Capito never fulfilled the promise he showed in the early years of the Reformation, when he was regarded as the leading voice in the city. His authority was undermined by his involvement with dissenters and the embarrassing Baden episode. Later, ill health, personal misfortune, and financial problems beset him and sapped his strength.

Although Bucer took over the helm in Strasbourg during the thirties, Capito's counsel continued to be valued and was sought repeatedly by other communities. He attended the Synod of Bern in 1532 and played a skilful role in establishing peace in the fractured community.[64] In 1534 Jakob Truchsess, his former student and now a councillor to the Duke of Würtemberg, asked for advice on means of furthering the Reformation. On Capito's recommendation, Ambrosius Blaurer was invited to draw up a church order and reform the university of Tübingen.[65] In 1535 Capito helped restore order to the Frankfurt church,[66] and in 1537 he counselled Duke Ruprecht of the Palatinate-Zweibrücken concerning his rights and obligations in directing the reformation of his realm.

* * * * *

63 In his letter to Zwingli (Zwingli, *Briefwechsel*, Ep. 494) he had used a Greek term, *to tes zeteseos syggramma*, for 'proceedings of the meeting' and noted that it was important to publish the outcome of the disputation (*catastrophe disputationis*). As Capito explained in his exculpation, *Warhaftige Handlung ...*, Fabri mistranslated the two phrases, rendering *zetesis* into German as *geselschaft* 'to create the suspicion that there was a secret society' and *catastrophe* as *verkere*, i.e., overturning, falsifying (quoted in Zwingli, *Briefwechsel*, 624–5, nn.8–9).

64 He brought about a reconciliation between the city council and the outspoken preachers Franz Kolb and Kaspar Megander. Reporting on Capito's diplomatic success, Berchthold Haller wrote that 'he achieved everything he wanted' (letter to Bucer, 16 Jan. 1532, quoted in Kittelson, 191).

65 Cf. his letter to Truchsess of 21 May 1534, TB 7:109, 4 (= Millet, Ep. 533).

66 TB 8:74–86 (= Millet, Ep. 550). Capito recommended that the council retain Dionysius Melander, whose preaching had caused a great deal of unrest, but require him to give no more trouble ('on Ergernis,' TB 8:75v).

In each case, Capito commented on the relationship between church and state and the respective duties and responsibilities of church leaders and secular authorities. In his report to the city council of Frankfurt, *An einen Ehrbarn Rath ... Ermahnung,* he explained that God set up two governments, one secular and one spiritual. 'The secular government is concerned with the physical person, with possessions, and all external things, and in the case of a pious nation, also with the external government of the church. The spiritual government is concerned only with the conscience and governs it with the Word, the Sacrament, brotherly punishment, and the like. The secular government is vested in your Honourable Council, the spiritual in the church [as a whole], and not merely in the servants of the church, and even less in the secular authorities. Therefore, what Matthew says in chapter 18[:17], "tell the church" [about excommunication in case of disobedience to the church], should and must also apply.'[67] Since the church government (*seniores* or elders) included not only pastors, but also members of the city council and other respectable laymen, there was an overlap between secular and spiritual government in matters concerning church discipline.

Capito's most extensive, and because of its late date of publication, definitive statement on the subject is found in his response to Duke Ruprecht's queries. The published version, entitled *Responsio de missa, matrimonio et iure magistratus in religionem* (1537) contained a prefatory letter to King Henry VIII of England, in which Capito emphasized the active role the secular authorities are expected to play in promoting piety and the reformation of the church. Responding to the old accusation that the reformers incited unrest, he noted that the Catholic Church usurped powers that rightly belong to the secular authorities, while the reformers wished to restore the correct balance. It was only when legitimate reformers were suppressed that radicals, such as Anabaptists or peasant rebels, took the field and caused trouble, 'for which our enemies now blame us.' Where the people were taught by legitimate reformers, law and order was upheld and respected. 'For all administration is easier if the people are rightly instructed in the teaching of God and Christ.' Reformers did not endorse rebellion. On the contrary, they taught that it was incumbent on the people to obey their rulers, whether or not they fulfilled their duty. Capito believed that it was 'right for the people to obey, according to God's decree, and impious to refuse obedience, and most wicked to keep secret counsel, incite a rebellion, and resist violently.'[68] The ruler, in turn, must always consider that his

* * * * *

67 TB 8:78v.
68 *Responsio de missa, matrimonio, et iure magistratus in religionem* (Strasbourg, 1537), prefatory letter to Henry VIII (= Millet, Ep. 639), iiii recto-verso, v verso, vi recto, viii recto.

power comes from God and take care not to violate God's Word or go against God's church. He must be virtuous, God-fearing, and gentle, rather than 'officious and overbearing, as are the princes of Germany.' Far from fomenting unrest, the reformers 'cherish peace among the people,' Capito says, 'but under the right conditions, that is, without injury to God.' These conditions include: 'First, that the word of the Lord and the freedom of faith is not obstructed by any human inventions; secondly that the sacraments be taught as instituted by Christ, that is, as instruments of grace through which faith is strengthened; thirdly, that church laws and church discipline honour the Word, preserve impeccable moral principles, be based on tradition, or reform the tradition when it has been corrupted.'[69]

Here, as in his advice to the Frankfurt city council, Capito explains the respective functions of the secular and ecclesiastical governments. The secular government is concerned with external matters, which includes public morality and the proper observance of rites. 'It is the special duty of pious princes to support religion and moral integrity among their people'; it is the duty of ecclesiastical rulers 'to teach the gospel, to remit sins publicly and privately, to make [doctrinal] pronouncements, to administer the sacraments, to excommunicate those who are guilty of public crimes, and to absolve them again, when they repent.' Of course 'clerics are men, and as such subjects of the king and the secular authorities ... and piety is not obviated by their subjection and obedience.' Their crimes, like those of any other citizen, are liable to punishment by the state. In so far as they are the messengers of God's Word, however, they are not subject to secular authorities, 'for in that role they acknowledge no superior and yield to no one. For they hold their office by the gift of God and for the purpose of correcting the interior man, a duty they cannot relinquish to any man; rather they must observe the injunction "In the things of God we must obey God rather than men."'[70]

Discussing the respective roles of secular and ecclesiastical governments in enforcing orthodoxy and, more generally, public morality, Capito returns to the subject of Nicodemism. He wants enforcement to be restricted to public behaviour and demands conformity of action rather than thought. It is the joint duty of secular and ecclesiastical leaders to promote the glory of God by 'making certain that the words of the preacher are honoured among the people and treated with the dignity they deserve, that good morals prevail among the people entrusted to their care and that they live in accor-

* * * * *

69 Ibid., 92r, 92v–93r, 94r–v.
70 Ibid., 191v, 193r, 194r.

dance with religion.'[71] It is necessary to take action against manifest sinners because they corrupt the people by their example. 'Their punishment will likewise serve as an example and purify the religion of the people.'[72] Sins committed in private do not fall under the jurisdiction of the authorities, Capito says. 'Hypocrisy, hiding in the heart, will find an avenger in God.' The authorities cannot look into the heart and therefore must not attempt to regulate conscience or administer punishment for sinful thoughts. No good can come from judging a man's thoughts. 'You cannot successfully bring accusations against a hypocrite or, conversely, free him from suspicion. You run the risk of giving a good man a bad name, or an evil man a good reputation. You may put a burden on innocent people or even treat guilty people with greater suspicion and prejudice than they deserve. There is less risk in inclining to leniency.' A magistrate should act only on certain evidence (*documentis certis*) and 'leave thoughts and the conceits of the heart, which are hidden, to the secret judgment of God, according to the popular saying "Thoughts are free and exempt from taxation." They go unpunished among men, as long as they remain unknown.'[73]

Capito's advocacy of Nicodemism accords with his own practice in 1523, when he concealed his conversion and published pamphlets containing Reformation thought anonymously. His view that dissenters ought to be discreet in advertising their position and his corresponding plea to the authorities to show a measure of tolerance toward dissenters stemmed in part from the conviction that public concord must be preserved at all costs and was an essential mark of the true church; but his tendency to nuance his doctrinal pronouncements and oppose the rigid enforcement of orthodoxy was no doubt also informed by epistemological considerations.

The impotence of the human intellect is a theme that runs through all of Capito's writings. Knowledge of the Truth, he said, was given by God to the elect. Capito himself never laid claim to divine inspiration, never talked of a religious experience, never adopted the decisive language that springs from a sense of divine mission. Instead he frequently talked about the inability of the human mind to penetrate the mysteries of faith. There were two ways to acquire a knowledge of God, he explained in the *Hexemeron*: one God-given; the other natural. Natural or 'speculative' knowledge 'is handed down in the books of the philosophers, or can be acquired by reading Scripture, that

* * * * *

71 Ibid., 89v–90r.
72 Ibid., 74v. Cf. also 89r: only manifest sinners are to be punished, who 'by their evil example harm the church ... we tolerate absurd men and those who are secretly vicious.'
73 Ibid., 80v, 81v, 82r.

is, through the agency of the human intellect and without the illumination of the Spirit.' This kind of knowledge allows a person to contemplate God, but provides no moral or spiritual guidance. God-given or revealed knowledge, however, 'is acquired through divine oracles, if the teaching of the Spirit accommodates our ears to them, for without his teaching they surpass our natural grasp.'[74] Those who have only natural knowledge may be terrified of God and despair. They see God's creation and are filled with 'fear and awe, flee from God and hate him. Knowledge that has been divinely revealed, however, experiences God in what he has wrought in heaven and earth and, through faith in Christ his son, sees him as a beloved father, approaches him with prayers, worships him spiritually, and loves him intensely.' Revealed knowledge, which cannot be sought with the mind but is received as a special gift from God, 'gently strengthens the soul, dispels the clouds of doubt, and gives peace to those illumined by faith.'[75]

Because Capito believed that revealed knowledge produced peace and consensus, he saw religious strife as a sign that the protagonists lacked inspiration.[76] In his attempts to achieve concord, the mark of the divinely guided church, he was therefore inclined to gloss over disagreements, reducing them to semantics. 'But if it were to happen that we disagreed,' he told Zwingli, 'we must dissent humbly and charitably. For we should not allow the bond in which we are united through the Spirit to be broken by a difference of opinion.'[77]

Capito's lack of decisiveness – whether based on an irenic ecclesiology or rooted in epistemological considerations – was unpopular with his contemporaries. Bucer identified two flaws in his colleague's approach to doctrine: Capito was inclined to subject traditions to a critical examination, and he tended to conceal his views if they were likely to cause a polemic. Bucer spoke of these habits of mind as afflictions and expressed the hope that his friend would overcome them in time. Capito, he said, 'has rather complex thoughts on many subjects. The Lord has allowed him to fall prey to this evil: he does not readily accept received opinion or teaching handed down by others. That quality is the mother or sister of heresy. At the same time

* * * * *

74 *Hexemeron* (see above, note 38), 100v–101r.

75 Ibid., 119v–120r.

76 Cf. Bucer's *Apologia circa Christi caenam* (1526): 'Nothing can less benefit the servant of God than favouring sectarianism and indulging in disputes which dispel the truth, sow envy and malice, and occasion the total shipwreck of the whole of the authentic Christianity' (trans. D.F. Wright in *Commonplaces of Martin Bucer* [Appleford, 1921], 33).

77 Zwingli, *Briefwechsel*, Ep. 634, 18 Aug. 1527 (Ep. 338).

God has given him such love and zeal for preserving the unity of our church, that he does not teach his views openly, although he sometimes conceals them poorly. But it seems this sickness of his is now abating.'[78]

It was Capito's misfortune to live in an age that did not care for nuanced or qualified opinions and was averse to latitudinarianism. An exchange between Luther and Capito in 1522 is symptomatic of the tensions between moderate and proactive reformers. Capito had advocated diplomacy and suggested that it was best to act with pious cunning, *vafre, sed pie*. Luther rejected that approach out of hand. It was a denial of Christ, he said. He did not wish to see the gospel advanced through compromise and smooth talk. The doctrinal truth must be argued candidly and defended vigorously. The Holy Spirit, he said, 'was no flatterer.'[79] The developments of the 1530s made it clear that Capito's approach ran counter to the spirit of the time. It was Luther who captured the *zeitgeist*, promoting confessionalization, favouring clear doctrinal definitions, and expecting 'Stoic' assertions from the believer.[80]

* * * * *

78 Bucer to Blaurer, 29 Dec. 1531 (Schiess 1:305).
79 WBr. 2:417 (= Millet, Ep. 121); WBr. 2:431 (= Millet, Ep. 131).
80 Luther, *De servo arbitrio* (WA 18, 603): 'Beware of Christian Sceptics and Academics. Let us be pertinacious asserters, more so than the Stoics themselves.'

THE CORRESPONDENCE OF WOLFGANG CAPITO

VOLUME 1: 1507–1523

Letter 1: 25 April 1507, Haguenau, Capito to the Reader

> This recommendation to the reader appears at the end of Conrad Summer-
> hart's *Commentaria in Summam Physice Alberti Magni* (Haguenau: Gran, 1507)
> fol. 5z verso. Summerhart (or Summenhart, 1465–1502) studied at Paris (MA
> 1478) and Tübingen (ThD 1489), where he also taught. He was interested in
> practical aspects of theology, writing against simony and usury. The present
> work was published from lecture notes edited by Johannes Caesarius, who
> matriculated at Tübingen in 1486 and from 1507 taught at Freiburg. The book
> has, in addition to Capito's preface, a preface by Jacob Wimpheling and com-
> mendatory poems by Wimpheling and Capito himself. The text of the letter
> is printed in J. Baum, *Capito und Butzer, Straßburgs Reformatoren* (Strasbourg,
> 1920) 37.

Here you have, most friendly reader, the theologian Conrad Summerhart's
learned commentaries on Albert.[1] They have been edited as fully as they
could be edited on the basis of a corrupt copy and have been printed with
amazing skill by the careful printer Heinrich Gran of Haguenau.[2] They have
the savour of great craftsmanship and high culture, so that what has so far
appeared rather obscurely in other books now is readily apparent and at
your disposal and can be understood without a guide (though requiring frequent practice). Buy it quickly, read it attentively, for from these pages you
will learn the whole of natural philosophy. Farewell from Haguenau in
haste, on the 25th of April, in the year 1507.

HEXASTICHON BY THE SAME AUTHOR

Best reader, here is the true foundation of wisdom, such as a not too distant
age has contributed. The commentary is better, I believe, than the twisted
prose [of the text] which involves fair thoughts in complexities. From this
book you can learn the difficult nature of things by yourself. Pray, read it
assiduously.

* * * * *

1 Albert the Great (d. 1280), Doctor of the Church and teacher of Thomas
  Aquinas, made the works of Aristotle accessible to Latin readers through paraphrases and commentaries.
2 Heinrich Gran (1489–1527) began publishing in Haguenau in 1489. He concen-
  trated on theological works and study aids (grammars, dictionaries). His output amounted to some three hundred publications.

Letter 1a: [1510, Freiburg], Capito to Johann Eck

At the end of Eck's *Orationes quattuor* (Augsburg: Johann Otmar, 1513), there is
a poem by Capito addressed to the author. The text is printed in Th. Wiede-
mann, *Dr. Johann Eck, Professor der Theologie an der Universität von Ingolstadt*
(Regensburg, 1865), 30. Entitled *In Eckii discessum a Friburgo Saphicum endecasyl-
labum adonicum*, the poem attests to Capito's friendly relations with Eck at this
early stage in his career. For modern readers, who know Eck primarily as a
Catholic theologian, it is interesting to see him praised here for his literary
accomplishments. For another poem to Eck, see below Ep. 3a.

Johann Maier von Eck (1486–1543) studied at Heidelberg and Tübingen (BA
1499, MA 1502), then moved to Cologne and Freiburg (ThD 1510). Capito
obtained his MA there when Eck was dean. When anonymous verses were
posted at the university ridiculing Eck, Capito took his side. Eck left Freiburg
in 1510 for Ingolstadt, where he taught theology until his death. He became
the principal Catholic apologist and was the bearer of the papal bull *Exsurge
Domine* excommunicating Luther and his followers. He was a well-versed
theologian and ready debater, and equally admired by Catholics and reviled
by Protestants.

Eck is about to leave our region. We wish him health and many years like
Nestor;[1] may Juno[2] bring him back and preserve him for his faithful friends.
A learned man with a strong genius, Eck is skilled in secular and sacred literature alike, but especially in the tunes of Minerva.[3] Eck often took the time
to absorb smooth orators and prophetic poets, indeed to drink in the dew of
noble learning. He exceeds all in knowledge. Let those who hear us singing
with Sapphian lyre[4] praises worthy of Eck's shining intellect respond in
verse and sing in turn with me. May all the Muses and the three beautiful
sisters, the Graces, may winged Mercury,[5] the divine craftsman, and may
the chaste Pallas[6] accompany Eck. Ah, dear Eck, you desert the friends who

* * * * *

1 Proverbial for longevity, cf. *Adagia* 1.6.66.
2 Juno, chief Roman goddess, in her capacity as guardian and protective mother.
3 Minerva, Roman goddess of wisdom and skills, identified with the Greek goddess Athena.
4 Sappho, seventh-century BC Greek lyric poet.
5 Mercury, the gods' messenger (hence 'winged'), Roman god identified with
the Greek god Hermes, inventor of the flute and leader of the Muses and
Graces.
6 I.e., Athena, cf. above, note 3.

have been taught in the languages, you leave the lectern orphaned of languages, you force all the faithful brethren to shed tears of grief. Who will lecture to us, now that you are leaving? With whom shall we share an eager laugh? Who will with strong argument overcome proud newcomers? Eck is about to leave our region. We wish him well. May he, like a wrestler, artfully subdue sparkling minds.

Letter 2: 2 September 1516, [Basel], Capito to Desiderius Erasmus

Printed in Allen 2:333–8, #459 and CWE 4, Ep. 459

[*Summary*]: Capito professes his friendship for Erasmus. During Erasmus's absence from Basel Capito has begun to teach St Paul's Epistle to the Romans and is directing his students to adopt the Erasmian style and spirit. Referring to Erasmus's work on a second edition of the New Testament [first edition published in 1516], Capito suggests that he hire two assistants to compare the Greek and Latin texts with the relevant notes in order to silence critics accusing Erasmus of inconsistency. Capito also advises Erasmus to tone down his attacks on the superstitious observance of rites and other doctrinal matters to avoid arousing animosity towards his work. Capito fears that the 'wounds inflicted by Erasmus's eloquent pen' will lead to his condemnation. Finally, he asks Erasmus to direct him in the method of scriptural exegesis. His friendly reply will confirm their friendship.

Letter 3: November 1516, Basel, Capito to the Reader

This is the preface to Capito's *Institutiuncula in Hebraeam linguam*, which was printed at the end of Conradus Pellicanus's *Hebraicum Psalterium* (Basel: Froben, 1516) fols. aa2v–bb8v. On Pellicanus (1478–1556), see below, Ep. 89, headnote.

Behold, dear reader, the psalter, a handbook most useful, in my opinion at any rate, and of the foremost benefit which, taken in hand, will supply a handy resource and ready provisions for use in making your way through the world of scripture. This is what I call resources and generous supplies and abundant wealth: to know the language of the holy scriptures, with which, as with ready coin, we acquire any benefit and any pleasure whatsoever to nourish the spirit fatigued by the magnitude of the task. Once the light of the divine word has shone upon a man, it leaves even in the laziest fellow a wonderful zeal and an incredibly powerful impetus to study and to come as close as possible to capturing its sweet savour. But the knowledge of only one language blinds the eyes to this pleasant light, for in that case we cannot see it and are blinder than any mole.[1] Therefore learn how something is expressed and you will immediately understand the attractive purity of speech densely packed with sententious sayings, the best arrangement of matters and their tight mutual connection. If, however, you disdain to learn this (as many have done), that majestic speech will seem to you in your ignorance uncultured and harsh and quite inane and frivolous, *stale nonsense*.[2] And you will never change your mind; indeed you will not even feel doubts, for one values a thing according to one's perception. Therefore I want you to acquire a knowledge of the sacred language from this little book of psalms, for it is the only key that will open the doors to its mysteries; and if you turn its pages with zealous hand, so to speak, you will understand it better in its own language. Then, without a doubt, the truth will come to you, flowing plentifully as from a very clear spring. Hence you will receive into your open heart the first gushing waters, a source of splendid erudition, unsoiled and undisturbed by the tracks of wild animals. These are the attractions that lead to the scriptures, these the sweet gains that will keep you intent on your labours. These are the quite incomparable riches whose supply will allow you to leave the poorhouse of commentaries and, no longer homebound, range through the open sea of scripture, living a life of splendour on the resources provided by your industry, as becomes a free man. Such advantages are conferred by this little book of psalms when *read with careful attention to the writing*, to use Fabius's words.[3] I also cite Adrianus Titanus,[4] who has such great experience in sacred writings, who drew on the language of David to shed much light on both the Old and the New Testament in the work which he entitled *Introduction to the Aims of the Holy Scriptures*.

Nor is there any reason to despair because you are still inexperienced in the sacred language, for the task is certainly easy and you have at hand the means to overcome all difficulty if there is any: *great labour*, as the poet says,[5] and persistent effort. Just try, and the outcome will surpass all your expecta-

* * * * *

1 Lit. 'blinder than a slaked skin,' a proverbial expression: Erasmus *Adagia* 1.3.56.
2 Lucian *Dialogues of the Dead* 16.405.
3 Quintilian Faber on reading good authors: 'legendus est, sed diligenter ac paene ad scribendi sollicitudinem.' *Institutiones oratoriae* 10.1.20.
4 Adrianus's biographical data are unknown. The work cited here is printed in Migne, PG 98:1271ff.
5 Virgil *Georgics* 1.146.

tions. In two days you will acquire the facility to read, after six months you will understand the meaning when you collate the text word for word with the Latin. You can do it without any help from a teacher. Why hesitate to make even the ultimate effort, if you could soon enjoy an intimate taste of scripture? Make the effort, and I freely promise my help if you make a faithful attempt, for I have put together a book of instruction[6] in Hebrew during the past holidays[7] to support you in your studies. I wrote it for the personal use of the noble young man Hartmann von Hallwyl,[8] in the expectation of spurring his talented mind to run the course with this friendly invitation and speeding him on the way. However, on the advice of Beatus Rhenanus,[9] who seems born for good literature and for the promotion of your studies, I have given the manuscript to Froben[10] for publication. It is of course more than unpolished, still blustering bellows, as they say,[11] for it benefited only from a few days and those interrupted by business.

I have rashly cast the die, to benefit you. Therefore, if you pass adverse judgment on me, I ask that you do so without arrogance. Remember: whatever the nature of the work, however paltry, it comes from a loyal heart wishing to advance your case, dear reader. I regard it as well done if it makes you a keener student of sacred scripture. I am convinced that zealous piety by itself provides a sure trailhead that can lead to the highest peaks of erudition. Continuous reading of holy writ leads you to a better understanding of it, as St Vulgarius asserts.[12] Therefore read and reread our firstborn, although born prematurely, if there is no better book available and you want to look after your interests. The type of theology will please you, and you will admit that I have not sung to you in vain and, as the proverb says,

* * * * *

6 It was published under the title *Hebraicarum Institutionum libri duo* (Basel: Froben, 1518). See below, Ep. 11, headnote.

7 I.e., in August.

8 See below Ep. 11, headnote.

9 The famous Alsatian humanist (1485–1587) studied in Paris. He worked with the printers Matthias Schürer in Strasbourg and Johann Froben in Basel, where he lived from 1511 to 1527. To avoid the Reformation debate in that city he returned to his native Sélestat, where he continued his scholarly work and wrote his magnum opus, *Rerum Germanicarum libri tres* (1531).

10 Johann Froben (1460–1527), influential printer in Basel.

11 Erasmus *Adagia* 4.9.37, explains 'in folle offere' as offering something that is unclear (see also his use at Allen Ep. 311: 23–4). Juvenal *Satires* 7.111 uses 'spirant ... folles' of blustering lawyers.

12 The name is a corruption for 'Bulgarius,' i.e., the Bulgarian archbishop of Akrida, Theophylactus (d. 1107). Cf. Migne, PG 123:980B.

played the flute like Agathon.[13] It seems to me that I have performed a worth-while task if I give you here, too, a summary of the contents:

There are twenty-two letters in Hebrew ...[14]

If you desire more help in learning the sacred language, you can obtain it from our booklet entitled on the frontispiece *Institutio in Hebraicam liter-aturam.*[15] There I have laid out a path for those who want to progress in their knowledge; here, however, I must take care not to add too much and seem oblivious to what is appropriate in a pocketbook, which must be short and easy to carry – for the booklet of psalms by itself now extends over many gatherings. Take this in good part, to be trained more fully at another time by means of the *Institutio.* Farewell, dear reader, and think kindly of me. Basel, in the month of November, 1516.

Letter 3a: Before 27 January 1517, [Basel], Capito to Johann Eck

> This poem appears at the end of Eck's *Disputatio ... Viennae Pannoniae habita* (Augsburg: Miller, 1517; cf. cc6, 74). Eck sent a copy of the book to Erasmus.

By the counsel of the gods above, Minerva[1] was wedded to you. With you she has brought forth such scholars, and those unscholarly men she brought forth jointly with her former weak husband, she has through your genera-tive powers born again. We are fortunate to be reborn in a golden age. Indeed, I regret rubbing the bald spot.[2]

Letter 4: 26 February 1517, Antwerp, Desiderius Erasmus to Capito

> Printed in Allen 2:487–92, #541 and CWE 4, Ep. 541

[*Summary*]: Erasmus replies to Capito's letter [Ep. 2] expressing his delight in what he sees as the beginning of a new golden age. He expresses the hope

* * * * *

13 Proverbial expression meaning 'bland rather than useful speech.' Cf. Erasmus *Adagia* 2.4.63.
14 A brief explanation of the Hebrew alphabet and its pronunciation follows on fols. bb1r–bb7v.
15 See below, Ep. 11, headnote.

1 Minerva, the goddess of wisdom.
2 I.e., labouring in vain over medieval commentaries; a variant on the proverb 'calvum vellis' (you are tweaking a bald man), Erasmus *Adagia* 2.8.37.

that the new learning will lead to a general peace among Christian rulers. And it is in this atmosphere that scholarship in the humanities will flourish. Even among the theologians some, who were previously opposed to the humanities, have now begun to use Greek, Latin, and Hebrew to interpret holy writ properly. At the same time, Erasmus also expresses concern that studying antiquity will revive paganism and that the study of Hebrew will reintroduce religious legalism, which will obscure the pure and simple teaching of Christ more than scholasticism did. He praises Capito extravagantly as a man with an 'uncommon knowledge of the three languages' and proclaims him as his intellectual heir, to whom he will 'hand on the torch.'

Letter 5: 24 March 1517, [Basel], Capito to Desiderius Erasmus

Printed in Allen 2:519–21, #561 and CWE 4, Ep. 561

[*Summary*]: Capito informs Erasmus of an unnamed critic who has pointed out errors in the Hebrew words appearing in Erasmus's annotations. Capito himself is preparing an introduction to Hebrew in three books. He continues to praise Erasmus's learning and intellect. His works are still winning him new friends, including the Basel canon Johann Rudolf von Hallwyl, whom Erasmus regards as an opponent of humanist learning. On the contrary, says Capito, Hallwyl encourages his cousin Hartmann to pursue humanistic studies.

Letter 6: 15 July 1517, Basel, Capito to Desiderius Erasmus

Printed in Allen 3:9–10, #600 and CWE 5, Ep. 600

[*Summary*]: Capito reports that he is defending Erasmus against his critics. He regrets that his earlier association with scholastic theologians has prevented him from fully breaking free of 'the ancient taint of ingrained barbarism.' He encourages his students to do better and learn 'their Erasmus' so that they may master his style. In response to Erasmus's inquiry he reports that the critic mentioned in his earlier letter (Ep. 5) has been silenced. He informs Erasmus of his intention to publish his *Hebraicarum institutionum libri duo* in time for the next Frankfurt book fair because Froben's presses are now occupied with Chrysostom's works. He will resume his regular studies and devote his remaining energy to Hebrew and Chaldean. Capito concludes by expressing his desire to live up to Erasmus's expectations.

Letter 7: 11 August 1517, Basel, Capito to Christoph von Utenheim

This prefatory letter appears on the verso of the title-page of the *Elucidatorium ecclesiasticum* of Josse Clichtove (Basel: Froben, 1517). Clichtove (d. 1543) received a doctorate of theology from the University of Paris in 1506. He was, for some years, attracted to the reforming circles of Jacques Lefèvre d'Etaples and published a number of commentaries on Lefèvre's expositions of Aristotle as well as on the works of church fathers. He increasingly devoted his energies to the reform of the clergy. After a controversy with the theologians of Paris in 1520/1, however, he became cautious and conservative. He broke with Lefèvre and joined the Paris theologians in their battle against Erasmus and Luther. The addressee, Christoph von Utenheim (d. 1527), bishop of Basel from 1502 on, was responsible for Capito's appointment as cathedral preacher. Utenheim, who had studied at Erfurt (MA 1466) and Basel (doctorate in canon law 1474), was a patron of humanistic learning and sympathetic to church reform, but after 1522 distanced himself from the reformers and forbade his clergy to attend the lectures and sermons of Oecolampadius, whom he himself had brought to Basel. Tired of continued wrangles over power with the city of Basel, he resigned his office in 1527 and died before a successor could be elected.

Wolfgang Fabritius Capito to the Reverend Father in Christ and Lord, Lord Christoph von Utenheim, Bishop of Basel, his lord to whom he owes obedience: Greetings.

In the two years during which I have served as preacher[1] in the most beautiful cathedral of Basel whose bishop you are, reverend and most deserving Father, I have much and often inquired into the source from which this great host of universal evils has invaded the clergy. At first it occurred to me that it stems from the carelessness of those who sit at the helm of the church and wink at any impious action whatsoever, thus encouraging licence and the habit of sinning. These evils would easily be uprooted, if only the leaders themselves made the smallest effort and pretended at any rate to fight them (since they have no real will), if at least they took the task seriously and were unfavourably disposed towards the impudence of the multitude and did not receive those inveterate rascals into their household and company. On the other hand, they may perhaps be excused for being unwilling to undertake the reformation of morals, a goal they are

* * * * *

1 Capito was appointed cathedral preacher in 1515.

not sure they can achieve even if they tried with all their might. Indeed, the evils have gathered strength over time; they have grown roots that are too deep to be dug up and uprooted, even if the prelates put their spade to them and corrected them with zealous care. Yet it seems to me that one must make an effort nevertheless and consistently stay the course, correcting errors as much as possible. For those who undertake to straighten every-thing out will never be totally disappointed in their hopes. Indeed they will achieve much more than if they make no effort, and lie helplessly on their backs crippled by vain despair. For people usually do their duty, if not from the heart, at least from fear of being fined: *they flee the rope covered with ruddle*.[2] To such an extent does a stern example guarantee good morals.

However that may be, I do not deny that one may find in this age some men who are truly bishops, among whom I count Your Honour, who greatly respect piety and religion, who are moved by the injury done to Christ, who, with the gravity proper to priests, prosecute the vices of the insane multi-tude. In pursuing my accusation, I may seem to show a lack of appreciation for their complete integrity. I therefore will mention another reason for this evil: lack of knowledge and the supine ignorance of sacred rites, which we who are called priests perform daily, carrying with the sons of Cath[3] the secret burden of the mysteries on our shoulders. Without understanding and without any involvement we go through the prayers of the hour in a loud voice and have no clear understanding of the reason for the mass, no clear understanding of the rite of singing hymns in church. And nothing is worse than acting by rote.[4] As a result, we are not mindful of our duty and fall headlong into sins, behaving more shamefully than a pimp (excuse the expression). Josse Clichtove, the celebrated Paris theologian, wanting to eliminate this great evil, has explained the responsibility of the church in four books which he has entitled, according to the contents, *Elucidation of the Church*. He has explained it in simple as well as appropriate terms, occasion-ally even defining the meaning of the terms. He has, moreover, adorned the work with the most delightful flowers plucked throughout from the garden of scripture, shown the meaning of the passages and indicated the biblical

* * * * *

2 I.e., the rope applied to loiterers in the agora in ancient Athens, who did not do their duty as citizens; cf. Aristophanes *Acharnians* 22.
3 Cf. Num. 4:15. The sons of Cath (or Kohath) were one of the three main divi-sions of the tribe of Levi and responsible for the tabernacle service.
4 The phrasing is reminiscent of Cicero *Rep.* 1.17, 'nunquam se plus agere quam nihil cum agat.'

book from which they are taken. And in doing so, he clearly lacks neither eloquence nor learning.

I dedicate these books to you, reverend father, and considering their suitability and usefulness, I declare that this small gift is a worthy gift for a bishop. For the well-known Hebrew proverb says [Heb.] *tov aruchat yaraq*,[5] that is, when offered in time, a simple meal of fresh herbs makes a sweet and sumptuous meal. And there is nothing more timely than these commentaries, nothing more beneficial both for our understanding and the purity of our feelings. And once we understand the sacred words repeated so often, the 'stomach' of our memory will take them in and digest them. We will absorb them into our nature and imitate their virtue.

It will be your task, then, most vigilant prelate, to accept in your kindness the excellent commentaries I present to you and to commend them to the priests entrusted to your care for their improvement, that they may understand the mysteries properly. Through your care, you will open the gates to piety, which after a long exile will return to the church, and you will see her, like Antaeus, [6] with the whole world at her feet. No one, by God, who reads these commentaries can fail to experience Christ's religion more fully in himself, not to speak of the knowledge he obtains from them. There is no one for whom they will not be salutary and inspirational. There is no one in whom they will not inspire good hopes for good results, unless he is a man quite deserted by God, like the Pharaoh, whose heart was turned to stone.[7] Or he may resemble Gryllus,[8] whom Circe bewitched and turned into a pig, and whom Ulysses, according to Plutarch, could not persuade in any way to want to return to his human nature. I dare not yet hope for a total turnaround in our time. For shame! There are even now men stuck in the evil ways, who stubbornly wish to end their days among shameful love affairs, sordid simony, and every pomp and circumstance. We shall be free of their blood only if we press on and rebuke them loudly *in season and out of season.*[9] Thus we shall have done our duty, and will confront with a staunch heart the avenger of evil when he passes the last judgment, knowing that we have

* * * * *

5 Prov. 15:17.
6 Mythological giant who challenged and killed all comers until he himself was killed by Hercules.
7 Exod. 7:13.
8 The sorceress Circe turned men into animals. Gryllus, one of her victims who refuses to resume human nature, is a speaker in Plutarch's dialogue entitled 'Beasts are Rational' (*Moralia* 986–92).
9 2 Tim. 4:2.

acted our part well. Farewell in Jesus Christ, reverend prelate, and may he long protect you from harm for the sake of restoring piety and good morals. Basel, 11 August 1517.

Letter 7a: [Before August 1519], Basel, Capito to Christoph von Utenheim.

This letter now appears as Ep. 31a.

Letter 8: 28 August 1517, Basel, Capito to Johann Rudolf von Hallwyl

This letter is printed with Conrad Summerhart's *Philosophia naturalis ... absolutissima, dilucide breviterque explicans, quicquid alii verbis ieiunis involverunt, qua, amice lector, si tibi ingenium venae mediocris et si tradentem habueris, et ipse noveris discere, paucis mensibus universam assequeris* (no publisher, no year of publication). On Summerhart, see above Ep. 1, headnote. The *Philosophia naturalis* is a reprint of the 1507 edition by Gran, for which Capito wrote a letter to the Reader and a poem (Ep. 1 above). The reprint differs from the first edition in the title and in the peripheral matter included. Capito's letter to the Reader and his poem have been omitted. A prefatory letter by Jacob Wimpheling, which preceded the text of 1507, has been moved to the end of the volume in the 1517 edition. In its place, at the head of the text (fols. AIv–IIr), we find Capito's *Epistola de formando a pueris theologo* (A letter on grooming a theologian from childhood on = Ep. 8).

The addressee is Johann Rudolf von Hallwyl (d. 1527), from 1504 provost of the Basel cathedral chapter, a position he exchanged in 1510 for that of treasurer (*custos*). He was nominated for the post of coadjutor to the bishop of Basel, but died before he could assume that duty. He was interested in classical learning, taking up the study of Greek in his old age, and he promoted the studies of his younger relative, Hartmann von Hallwyl (see below, Ep. 11, headnote).

Wolfgang Fabritius of Haguenau to Johann Rudolf von Hallwyl, canon and treasurer of [the church of the] Holy Virgin in Basel, greetings.

Johann Rudolf, most honourable and illustrious on account of your learned nobility: In former times peripatetic philosophy, that is, dialectic or some details of metaphysics and physics, comprised just a small part of the entire training ground of theology. These subjects, pursued excessively by acute minds with too much leisure, have now grown into an almost infinite mass, so that they can no longer be comprehended even by those who live for them exclusively and have chosen to study only them and are very keen learners. Spending their whole life on them in daily exercise and unwilling to do anything else, they have introduced a great deal of awkwardness and fastidious prolixity, to the greatest detriment of Christendom. For in the meantime the writings of the ancient authors are falling by the wayside; the gospel and the Pauline epistles, the monuments of our nascent faith are neglected; morality perishes, as does knowledge of religion and all holy rites, and in their place that pagan Aristotle alone remains, and he is more complex and thorny now through the unfortunate diligence of his follow-ers.[1] And finally legal usage[2] has been admitted to explain human affairs, which is in itself a very large field, but more appropriate and more closely related to the heart of theology. For if there is an ambiguity that worries the people, we [the theologians] must provide a clear definition, we must indicate the way to salvation as from the tripod,[3] a way that is not only free of doubt but also safe and easily accessible, and we must recall what has gone astray in obscure and remote byways and reduce and compress it into a compendious form, so to speak. For a long time now we have claimed teaching authority, for a long time we have claimed to be *leaders of the blind, lights for those who are in darkness, and instructors of the foolish.*[4] Yet the apostle of the gentiles seemingly attaches blame to this perception of oneself, even in a Jew. Indeed, human nature is better elucidated and brought out in the open by the life-giving precepts of Christ which are like the pin of a sun-dial or indeed a Lydian stone, as they say,[5] than by human sanctions, which ought to be corrected by that standard. For the law, explained in the gospels, *makes straight the crooked places, makes low the hills and exalts the valleys,*[6] and links everything most closely by the chains of mutual love. Our minute distinctions, by contrast, are not only without effect but leave behind poison to be sucked by those spiders. They teach the skill of covering up a crime to those who are keen on such things or are afflicted by some other sickness and draw on our inventions to foster their desires and their avarice, giving dishonest acts the appearance of respectability, borrowing their arguments from the workshop of the theologians. As a result no monetary gain is ever

* * * * *

1 I.e., the medieval translations, summaries, and commentaries on Aristotle are more complex than the original Aristotelian text.
2 I.e., canon law.
3 I.e., like the Pythia at Delphi, who made her oracular pronouncements seated on a tripod.
4 Rom. 2:19–20.
5 I.e., a catalyst. See Erasmus *Adagia* 1.5.87.
6 A combination of Isa. 40:4 and 42:16.

regarded as shameful ... [7] There is no chance, then, that scruples of this kind can keep evil from flowing through the cracks, but it can be easily dried out and cauterized with the fire of Christian love, which rises with great intensity from the path of scripture, once you remove the barrier of commentaries. That is how matters stand now, in my opinion.

Just as antiquity tells us that it *is ruinous to cultivate a field too well,*[8] nothing seems to me less expedient than to be too delicate in judging the profound and innumerable errors of this corrupt world. Indeed, clever people often arm themselves with dark schemes by taking advantage of the so-called dictates of their conscience, to act all the more freely, whereas the tacit judgment of nature which is a stranger to such arguments resists strenuously but is covered with a fog. I do not deny that one must support the timid and explain the tenets of our faith to those who ask for it. Nevertheless I believe that the apostle gives more salutary instructions in that respect, and we would perhaps be more careful with human interpretations, if we did not believe that the decrees of men are more powerful than the spirit speaking through Paul.

Thus, I wish, if possible, to recover our territory and concede to that pagan philosophy, which has recently invaded our patrimony, only a part of our city, the remotest corner in fact, for we cannot do completely without it. It appears, I say, that apostolic dignity and the aid of the old authors no longer have sufficient power to hold and guard the walls of faith and the morals of Christianity because our age is so different from their thinking. Therefore let us employ them [the Aristotelians][9] as supplementary troops and in a sense admit them to the class of theologians. But let us be very careful that the barbarians do not seize sovereign power. Let the Bible and the law of Christ always rule supreme in theology. Let those theologians of old, the most holy prelates, hold the provinces, and let the later generations aid them in everything, as if they had been born for this purpose, for they cannot in any way be compared with the theologians of old either in piety or in spiritual gifts or in the extent of their learning.

After pondering this for a long time, I was uncertain how to introduce

* * * * *

7 The sentence continues: *nisi id quod ingenii nostri graviore censura caruerit,* literally 'except that which is free of rather serious blame in our mind.' I suspect that the Latin is corrupt. The intended meaning is probably 'because to our mind it is not a serious flaw.'

8 I.e., exceeding due measure: Pliny *Natural history* 18.6, Erasmus *Adagia* 3.7.4.

9 I.e., the representatives of Aristotelian, or 'pagan philosophy.'

your relative[10] Hartmann von Hallwyl, a youngster of the most lively intellect, to the sublime study of theology, given that great assortment of useless books. I found it difficult to avoid what is most important to avoid: that so-called *white line, lest he embrace ignorant authors through lack of discrimination.*[11] Rather, I want him to read only the most illustrious authors, and read them with attention and (given his age) with judgment. Then, under my guidance, let him combine the rudiments of Hebrew with the study of Latin and Greek, to lay the proper foundations of his future erudition, for without them many retreat, defeated and in despair of conquering ignorance. He will find these rudiments sufficiently explained elsewhere, in our *Institutiuncula ad Hebraeam linguam.*[12] Let him attend to that goal, then go on to the rest of the disciplines. For first of all I believe Christ, whose pure philosophy he has learned from you long ago, should precede all other studies; the philosophy of our time is necessary as well, but can be covered compendiously. The best approach, however, in my opinion is through the commentaries of Conrad Summerhart, a most experienced theologian in this field, if I am not mistaken, who has treated the dark teachings of Duns Scotus,[13] the first among the recent theologians, and drawn from the great maelstrom of arguments clear conclusions, as they call them.[14] From this green pasture he may go on to any questions, however obscure, as he pleases, and under my tutelage he will receive his own food for digestion,[15] that is, briefly hear the responses to each; and that can be done within half a year, and they can be understood in greater depth later, through the practical exercise of disputations. For nothing is more conducive to this kind of philosophy. No discipline in all the universities better trains the intellect and sharpens and perfects it, like *iron sharpening iron,*[16] as long as it is a focused exercise and done without angry shouting and as far removed as possible from futile tenaciousness. For I do not wish disputations to be too quibbling and precise, blunting the mind with awkward and subtle ideas, and wasting time

* * * * *

10 On their relationship, see below, Ep. 11, note 2.
11 Aulus Gellius, *Attic Nights*, preface (cf. also Erasmus *Adagia* 3.7.4).
12 See above, Ep. 3, and below, Ep. 11, headnote.
13 Duns Scotus (ca. 1266–1308), scholastic theologian; the reference to 'darkness' is a pun on the name, which resembles the Greek word *skotos*, darkness.
14 'Conclusiones' is the scholastic term for magisterial pronouncements on questions.
15 Lit. 'that which makes honey.'
16 Prov. 27:17 and Erasmus *Adagia* 1.7.100.

which ought to be taken up with studies that are worthy of a man who wants to be counted among the erudite.

At the same time let him learn music, arithmetic, geometry and the remaining arts that are called liberal as preliminary exercises leading to true wisdom, and once he is imbued with the arts and philosophy as far as is necessary, we shall soon allow him to go on to scholastic theology. In two years' time he will overcome all difficulty on his own, for he is eloquent and gifted. We will go over non-essential, less important material either quickly or bypass it altogether, for such material can by itself occupy the life of an industrious man if you oblige him to learn everything. And while Hartmann is occupied with these things, he will not be taking a holiday from religion. Let him always ponder a passage from scripture, always be busy absorbing it into his thought. Thus a certain sublime and clearly divine element will be joined to literary studies and grow together in his mind. Once that is done, let him concentrate on the learned piety of the writers of old, although he should sometimes go back to the previously mentioned subjects, indeed take them in hand on purpose, lest he forget them through neglect. For everything is lost in time and the humanities, too, are forgotten within a few months, if you do not return to them daily. And the labour of reviewing will be small if it is done regularly. Those who take note of human nature, know its powers and its efforts and the difficulty of concentrating for a long time on one venture and the ease of casting one's thought over many areas. For the mind, when tired, is refreshed by pleasant variety.[17] When one task is completed, we begin anew, the tedium of the completed lecture is soon forgotten, and the mind is just as fresh in tackling the second round as it was before the race began. In one case the idle mind is weak because of disuse and slow even in the first round; in the other it is hot from continuous use, ready for anything, quick, impatient of delay, as it were. It hurries on and races and surpasses the expectation of the man spurring it on.

Let this be the form and the course of studies for our Hartmann, dearest Rudolf, supreme ornament of prelates. Let him apply his time to them and use it more diligently than others, who waste it on sleeping or dicing or empty talk or indeed on drawn-out parties – respect for your authority prevents me from calling them anything worse. This curriculum will be more pleasing, to the extent that these honourable studies are more helpful than boorish pleasures. Farewell, blessed in the Lord Jesus. Basel, 28 August, in the year 1517.

* * * * *

17 Paraphrasing Quintilian *Institutio oratoria* 1.12.4.

Letter 9: 6 December 1517, Louvain, Desiderius Erasmus to Capito

Printed in Allen 3:159–60, #731 and CWE 5, Ep. 731

[*Summary*]: Erasmus responds to Capito's critique of his polemic against Jacques Lefèvre, *Apologia ad Fabrum*, and what he regards as Ludwig Baer's irrelevant remarks concerning Erasmus's comments on hypostasis. He lets Capito know that he has sent a copy of the apologia to both Matthias Schürer and Capito for revision or annotation. He reports that the revision of his New Testament is almost done. Thereafter he will do research for his own benefit, since his efforts on behalf of other scholars are not appreciated.

Letter 10: 9 December 1517, Louvain, Desiderius Erasmus to Capito

Printed in Allen 3:163–4, #734 and CWE 5, Ep. 734

[*Summary*]: Erasmus defends his choice of the word 'composite' in explaining Christ's nature. He criticizes Lefèvre for not responding to his last two letters and is suspicious of his plans. He accepts the advice of Baer, who suggested that he frequently state his willingness to submit his works to the verdict of the church. He would never knowingly write anything that is not approved by the authorities, but recognizes that it is sometimes difficult to know the position of the church and avoid being criticized.

Letter 11: January 1518, [Basel], Capito to Hartmann von Hallwyl

This is the preface to Capito's *Hebraicarum Institutionum libri duo* (Basel: Froben, 1518), A2r–A4r. The work is dedicated to Capito's pupil, Hartmann von Hallwyl (1503–1573). Hallwyl matriculated at the University of Basel in 1518 and accompanied Capito when the latter moved to Mainz, spending the winter of 1520 with him there. From 1521 he studied in Leipzig. The members of the noble Hallwyl family had close connections with the city of Bern. Hartmann himself was active in its diplomatic service, representing the city in negotiations with the German princes of the Schmalkaldic League in 1546. By 1563 he was the city's administrator of the territory of Aargau, where he owned two estates and mining concessions.

Wolfgang Capito of Haguenau to the noble young man, Hartmann von Hallwyl, greetings:
It is obvious from your example, sweetest Hartmann, that it matters a

good deal and indeed a very great deal what formative precepts imbue the malleable mind of a boy from the very cradle, as they say,[1] before he draws on the errors of the common people. For the care of Johann Rudolf von Hall-wyl, the treasurer of our church and your truly great cousin,[2] has filled you, when you were still unformed, with good beliefs, instilled in you a sense of honour by praising virtue and vituperating vice, and tried every means, both admonition and gentle governance, to keep you in childhood, which is prone to evils, from developing the vices customary in nobles, that is, from luxury, ineptness, odious arrogance, and filthy love affairs.

The excellence of your morals and your mind prove that his attempt was not in vain, for you range happily and rapidly through every region of learn-ing and virtue, and after driving vice far off, you shine in studies that are no longer boyish. If you stay true to yourself you will soon not only match your industrious and respectable fellow students in learning and noble chastity but vastly outdistance them. Indeed, your modesty and gentle spirit are beau-tiful, and all the more admirable because they are so rarely found in our time in those who are of noble descent. The splendour of your birth does not make you mighty or proud, nor does it make your heart insolent. You show alike the nobility of your mind and the nobility of your family. You value personal integrity, constancy, and fortitude, you think highly of virtue, nothing or very little of waxen images and a long pedigree. Furthermore, the natural, as it were, authority of your wise and good cousin has strengthened that noble and upright mind of yours and fortified it. His way of life is reflected in yours; he implanted in you the best principles of life, so that one may behold, not without pleasure, his virtue reflected in you as in a portrait painting. The join-ing of like minds, especially of virtuous minds, gives wonderful pleasure, and most of all, if it joins together men related by blood. There shines forth in you, a youngster, your cousin's wisdom and his notably harmonious life.

But your cousin had no leisure, for his time was filled either with praying or saying mass or reading the ancient theologians or looking after the business of the church or his friends, which he did reluctantly, but nevertheless per-formed faithfully. Thus he recently gave up the provostship (as they call it) of this cathedral to live more fully for himself and his family and friends. But he

* * * * *

1 See Erasmus *Adagia* 1.7.53.
2 Johann Rudolf von Hallwyl (d. 1527) was an older cousin of Hartmann and took a close interest in the young man's education. See above, Ep. 8, headnote. Capito refers to him as 'patruus,' which usually denotes the father's brother, but in this case must mean 'cousin on your father's side.' I have rendered the word as 'cousin' throughout.

did not give it up to just any successor, but to the illustrious Johann Werner, Baron von Mörspurg,[3] noted as much for his noble descent as for the rare distinctions of his virtue and his exceptional love of learning and who does such justice to his office that he nobly recalls those ancient gifts of church prelates. You, Hartmann, free of care and ambition likewise are always making efforts on behalf of virtue and letters. You may be too young to serve your friends' interests, although you seem to serve their interests well even now, for you live a life that makes you a worthy offspring of your illustrious forefathers.

I shall be neither inattentive nor careless in aiding you on a journey so well begun, for you have come to me carefully recommended as the hope of your family. I promise I shall certainly be your teacher – I cannot say whether a suitable teacher, but a teacher, I think, who is lacking neither in attention nor in good will. For I shall, with one effort, train you in three languages that are reliable supports and a great help in the whole world of disciplines. Udalricus Zasius,[4] the Julianus of our time,[5] exemplifies these accomplishments. For many years, he has taught imperial law in a worthy manner at the University of Freiburg to young men of learning, good family, and noble fortune. For Zasius is fortified with Latin all round, as with Vulcan's arms, fearlessly engaging in battle the whole troop of legal scholars. He likes to cast doubt on matters and often gives a different verdict (truth being on his side), whereas all those hallucinating imitators, whom Horace rightly calls *slavish cattle*,[6] support the yes-side. Confident in his knowledge of pure Latin, he has earlier on revealed the genuine meaning of many laws, which the ignorance of barbarians had distorted and given an inappropriate meaning and encumbered with an awkward wordiness. Zasius collected his interpretations in a book which he entitled *The Distinct Meanings of Law*,[7] distinct, I say, not as one in a multitude, but as standing out from the multitude. The whole crowd of commentaries rightfully yields its place to that work as to the better book, although stubborn people still fight among themselves to the mad end, advocating their erroneous opinion with mutual ineptitude. By Hercules, Zasius shows how much one language – Latin – can contribute to legal knowledge. As a result everyone agrees that a man who lacks Latin also lacks legal knowledge.

* * * * *

3 See below, Ep. 41, headnote.
4 For Zasius see below, Ep. 15b, headnote.
5 Julianus Aemilianus, a second-century lawyer and a member of Hadrian's council.
6 Horace Ep. 1.19.19.
7 *Intellectus singulares* (Basel: Cratander, 1526).

In the same way, the three languages jointly aid theology, for in them the whole Christian tradition is contained: the Old Instrument,[8] as they call it, which Moses has handed down in the Hebrew language; the New Instrument which the apostles and evangelists have handed down to all the gentiles in Greek. And the age succeeding ancient and erudite Greece has expressed the meaning of both in Latin. You, who are a boy, will acquire a perfect command of these languages in a shorter time than we could learn one wretched, barbarian semi-language, who were languishing under indolent, or rather, ignorant teachers.[9] I shall open the doors to you, and you will enter into the mysteries of letters. Let me be your Mercury.[10] Take up the path indicated with confidence, and you will leave me behind, a man broken by lasting illness and cast down by countless waves of fortune, who has seen happiness too late. For I discovered the true beauty of knowledge only when I could no longer enter upon it, nor even had the will. I shall count myself very fortunate if I can duly point the way and show you and other more talented young people the straight path, so that you are not caught in the wilderness of Gothic disciplines, as I was, and grow old in them. They have imposed their fallacies on the world for some centuries now, so that religion itself, together with letters, has been tottering, no, has almost collapsed. But God took pity, and now people everywhere turn to a better harvest, everywhere embrace good literature and the tools aiding them in the study of learning classical languages. At the same time, I am confident that the virtues of the ancient and the pristine purity of Christian faith will return. To this purpose I wanted to spur the willing horse. Thereafter, listen carefully, when we carry on in our roles [as teacher and pupil], and these virtues will shine forth more pleasantly in their own light. This is the gracious service offered by our Erasmus,[11] who recently gave us an intimate

* * * * *

8 The common term is 'New Testament,' *Novum Testamentum*. Capito adopts the uncommon title of Erasmus's New Testament edition of 1516: *Novum Instrumentum*, 'New Instrument.' Erasmus reverted to the usual term in the second edition of 1519.

9 Capito echoes Erasmus, *Methodus verae theologiae* (151): 'minore paene negotio tres hae linguae discentur quam hodie discitur unius semilinguae miserande balbuties, nimium ob praeceptoris inscitiam.'

10 One of the roles assigned to Mercury in mythology was that of a guide.

11 Desiderius Erasmus of Rotterdam (1466–1536), foremost Northern humanist. Capito made his acquaintance in Basel, when Erasmus supervised the publication, and later the revision, of his New Testament edition. For some time Erasmus regarded Capito as his intellectual heir, but the two men fell out when Capito left the Catholic Church. See Ep. 516, headnote, for the preface to Capito's translation of Erasmus's *De ecclesiae concordia*.

glimpse of the elements of Greek with Erasmian smoothness,[12] unless you want to say that such grace and beauty arose from his incomparable eloquence, compared to which any language however rich its ore, would seem jejune and small and hardly worth a tenth of Syracuse's wealth.[13] Beatus Rhenanus,[14] the ornament of liberal arts, is another example. In the last two weeks he opened up [to you] the sources of grammar and offered from memory what is clearly useful and pleasant, given the subject.[15] With similar skill Johannes Oecolampadius put together a book of Greek grammar[16] redolent with uncommon learning. He composed it when he was staying at my house and received the licence in theology, as they call it.[17] He often taught you in a pleasant manner and in ready money, as they say, when he was at leisure, and so you mutually rewarded each other, he by teaching you and you by yielding intellectual fruit. Similarly, I keep admiring the

* * * * *

12 Erasmus's translation of Theodore of Gaza's Greek grammar had been published in Louvain in 1516 and was reprinted by Froben in Basel in 1518.
13 A proverbial expression, cf. Erasmus *Adagia* 2.4.45.
14 On Beatus Rhenanus, see Ep. 3, note 9. Perhaps Beatus shared with Hartmann a manuscript copy of Johannes Cono's Greek grammar. Cono (d. 1513 in Basel), a noted scholar, taught Beatus and the Amerbach brothers. After his premature death, Beatus edited some of Cono's papers, which were left in his possession. The Greek grammar, however, was never published. Cf. *Beatus Rhenanus: Lecteur et éditeur des texts anciens*, ed. J. Hirstein (Turnhout, 2000), 473.
15 The context (and therefore the meaning) of this sentence is ambiguous.
16 Johannes Oecolampadius (1482–1531) published *Dragmata Graecae Literaturae* (Basel: Cratander, 1518). He studied at Heidelberg and Tübingen and under Reuchlin in Stuttgart. He moved to Basel in 1515 and worked as a corrector for the Froben press. In 1518 he obtained a post as penitentiary at the cathedral of Basel, but moved to Augsburg shortly afterwards. He came under the influence of Reformation thought, fled the Brigittine monastery (Altomünster, near Augsburg), which he had entered in 1520, and became chaplain of the reform-minded knight and condottiere Franz von Sickingen. In 1522 he returned to Basel, began teaching at the university and preaching at St Martin's. In the following years he became the leader of the city's Reformation movement and, after the city's break with the Catholic Church in 1529, prepared the new church ordinance and served as head preacher (*antistes*) of the cathedral. After his death in 1531, Capito married his widow, Wibrandis Rosenblatt.
17 In 1518, Oecolampadius received a doctorate in theology from the University of Basel (the licence is the preliminary step). It was the prerequisite for taking up the post of preacher in Augsburg.

native philological skill of Bruno Amerbach,[18] who explains riddling expressions in Lucian or Euripides extemporaneously, whenever I question him. Indeed, I freely confess, these most learned men are refined by nature as well as art, whereas I am unlearned and of a crasser Minerva.[19] They, however, skilfully conceal their art and well deserve everyone's admiration. Yet embarrassment will never prevent me from sharing with this openhearted and talented man[20] my inadequate knowledge of Hebrew literature that was acquired, with the help of a teacher and not without great effort. For a resentful Jew[21] perfidiously tricked my industrious efforts, and taught me at great cost to know nothing of these things, until I boldly undertook to hunt down this exceedingly large material through *mute teachers*, as they say.[22] And I share my knowledge, although I had not planned on doing it, for I undertook to write this for you alone and intending to keep it private.

And so let this be the first rule: You will acquire the basic principles of Hebrew speedily, with nature as your guide; you will try to obtain it without a great number of commentaries, which frequently bring on tedium, that great plague of the mind, as we know. Therefore I too shall be brief here and offer my instruction without nonsense ...[23]

Letter 11a: January 1518, [Basel], Capito to Hartmann von Hallwyl

This letter is not in Millet's list. It is at the beginning of Book Two of Capito's

* * * * *

18 Bruno Amerbach (1484–1519) studied at Paris. He returned to Basel in 1508 without a degree, but with a good knowledge of the classical languages, and worked at his father's printing shop as an editor. He died of the plague in the following year.
19 I.e., simple. Horace *Satires* 2.2.3.
20 See below, Ep. 12, for Capito's plans to study Hebrew together with Bruno Amerbach.
21 A reference to the Spanish converso Matthaeus Adrianus, from whom Capito learned Hebrew (see below, Ep. 13). Erasmus reported that Adrianus was incensed about Capito's apparently derogatory remark (see also below, Ep. 18). Adrianus, who was a physician, published a Hebrew grammar in Venice in 1501. He moved to Basel in 1515, offering his services as a Hebraist to the Amerbach brothers. In 1517 he became the first professor of Hebrew at the newly founded Collegium Trilingue in Louvain. From there he moved to the University of Wittenberg in 1520, but quarrelled with Luther and left. Nothing is known about him after 1521.
22 I.e., books, an expression used by Gellius *Attic Nights* 14.2.1.
23 The body of Book One follows. The letter to Hartmann resumes on the last page.

Hebraicarum Institutionum libri duo (Basel: Froben, 1518), fols. P1r–2v, with the conclusion on fol. Ii 3r.

I decided to add an introduction to Hebrew (a guide not exceeding three ternions) to the *Psalter* recently printed by Froben.[1] There I recommended to students briefly and clearly the grammar of the sacred language, explaining the eleven letters[2] and putting together some information on the system of pointing. As I was writing it, my sweetest Hartmann, it occurred to me that I would do something worthwhile to pursue the same subject from another point of view, namely from the point of view of composition, so that an autodidact without an instructor would be able to see whenever he was far from what is correct. He would do so by comparing with the preceding material what the second book on the same subject offers anew according to the Latin usage or vice versa, if there was a good reason or if it was advantageous. Therefore I will outline rather than explain in full the case endings of nouns and verbs, the force and nature of the indeclinable words, as they call them, and the connectives, as necessary to the beginner. In this I shall as far as possible imitate the shrewd method of Theodore of Gaza.[3] That will be the contents of the second book. Thereafter, in a third book,[4] I shall

* * * * *

1 I.e., the psalter edited by Pellicanus, which was published in November 1516 (cf. above, Ep. 3). Capito's *Institutiuncula* filled thirty pages. A ternio comprises six leaves or twelve pages.

2 The sentence must be defective. The Hebrew alphabet has twenty-two letters (or consonants), as Capito explained on bb1r–bb7v. There are, however, eleven consonants with alternate forms.

3 The author of a Greek grammar published in 1495, which had recently been translated into Latin by Erasmus (Louvain, 1516; Basel, 1518).

4 The planned third book was apparently never published. A new edition of Capito's Hebrew grammar appeared from the press of Capito's relative and namesake, Strasbourg 1525 (see the preface, Ep. 238). The revised edition was dedicated to Ulrich Varnbühler. In the dedicatory letter Capito declared that he wished to consign the earlier edition to oblivion. It had been a 'premature birth' and useless (fol. Avi verso, Avii recto in the 1525 edition). Again he projected additions, speaking of two further books. Neither of them were forthcoming, however. Readers of the first edition of Capito's grammar apparently agreed with his own negative judgment. Wilhelm Nesen wrote to Bruno Amerbach in 1518 that Capito 'seems to obscure the grammatical usage of Hebrew on purpose and uses the most involved language exactly where his speech should have been quite pure and simple' (*Amerbachkorrespondenz* 2, Ep. 619, 121). Similarly, Otto Brunfels wrote to Beatus Rhenanus in 1520 that Capito introduced unnecessary difficulties ('multa intorquet,' *Briefwechsel des Beatus Rhenanus*, Ep. 182, 253).

describe the force of the root words and their range of meaning. The third book will however appear separately from the first two, to give the buyer the choice between buying those first two grammar books or the third which will offer a good supply of basic words (or roots, as they call them). Yet one part is not very useful without the other. But it is perhaps more convenient for buyers who often do not wish to lay out the money for both, but when they buy them separately, apparently not realizing what they are doing, they do not sense that they are paying twice as much.[5] This was the opinion of the good Hieronymus Baldung,[6] a man certainly who has not ceased to labour on behalf of literature. The Baldung family has brought forth learned and eminent men, and Hieronymus is the pride and leading light of the family. He is most learned in the law and he combines with knowledge of the laws a pure Latin style and in the most excellent manner evinces the force and spirit of rhetoric. His intellect is splendid and incomparably vigorous, indeed admirable beyond belief, quick of perception and *soaring like fire*, as Pliny says.[7] In a word: there is nothing he cannot do. Because of his wonderful discretion in handling affairs and his skill in administration he has some time ago been made councillor to His Imperial Majesty, Maximilian, and has been for some years at the provincial court in Ensisheim, being its very heart, and dispensing justice and right. Recently however he was, with the agreement of all good men, attracted to the most august court of the Austrian realm in Innsbruck, the seat and homeland of the dukes of Austria,[8] and made a councillor of the first rank with a respectable salary. Although he is almost completely overwhelmed with business, he shows nevertheless great concern for historical monuments, indeed he shines so sublimely in this field that one hesitates whether to give more credit to men of leisure who grow old in their sombre studies or to the man

* * * * *

5 *Nam ita fore emptoribus magis accommodum, qui saepenumero iunctim pro libris nolunt expendere, quod separatim, velut inopinantes vel dupliciter insumptum non perinde sentiunt.* The Latin sentence does not run. My translation gives an approximate meaning.

6 Hieronymus Baldung (ca. 1489–1539) studied at Vienna, obtained a doctorate in laws, and taught at the University of Freiburg. He then entered the service of the Habsburgs as an imperial councillor and lived at Innsbruck, the seat of the Habsburg government for Alsace and the Breisgau. Zasius, Zwingli, Erasmus, and the Amerbach brothers were among the friends and acquaintances he shared with Capito. He eventually became chancellor of Tirol, but continued to pursue his scholarly interests, which focused on collecting manuscripts.

7 Pliny the Elder *Natural History* 7.25.91.

8 See above, note 6.

whose time is divided among many obligations. You may add that he gives satisfaction all round: with courtiers he is urbane, witty, and authoritative, with philosophers and men skilled in literature he is literate and philosophical, but without being arrogant. I cannot but approve of the opinion of so great a man, my dear Hartmann, not only because he is a friend but because it appears to be expeditious. No one can believe what great benefit Hebrew letters bring to biblical studies unless he listens to the authoritative voice of experience. For this reason Hebrew, largely unknown and little-used, is regularly neglected. But I hope that Hebrew studies will insinuate themselves into the minds of young men gradually through these trifles of mine. As for the rest, enjoy these two books until the reader desires and obtains from Froben a third book.[9] He will, however, obtain it very easily, if he indicates that he finds the lack irksome and attests to his wish by eagerly buying these two ...

Up to this point[10] I have laid out the road leading to a knowledge of the holy language, which you will boldly acquire with virtue as your guide, my dear Hartmann; otherwise I will be sorry to have wasted my nightly toils which your sweet and noble nature has extracted from me. I have made the effort with all good will and in good faith, that my efforts may render you honoured and truly worthy of the venerable college of the first church in Basel,[11] distinguished by illustrious nobility and the most noble letters, in which you have recently enrolled as in a future campaign. May you be motivated by a desire for glory, which will redound to your lasting praise as long as you remain worthy of praise. Conversely, if you lower yourself and practise filthy vice, it will be like a lion skin covering a saffron-coloured robe,[12] and mirror your soiled image, proving to you the evil of a corrupted mind. Furthermore, I shall not deny to students a third book and complete it when I see that this, our labour, is not found displeasing. Farewell.

* * * * *

9 See above, note 4.

10 This paragraph, which continues and concludes the prefatory letter to Book 2 appears at the end of the volume, fol. Ii3v.

11 I.e., the University of Basel, founded in 1470 under the auspices of the cathedral (the first rector was the provost Georg von Andlau). Hartmann von Hallwyl matriculated there in the spring of 1518.

12 The proverbial expression denotes incompatibility. A woman's robe covered with a lion's skin was worn by Dionysius when he descended into the underworld. Cf. Erasmus *Adagia* 3.5.98.

Letter 12: [Beginning of March 1518, Basel], Capito to Bruno Amerbach

Printed in *Amerbachkorrespondenz* 2:105–6, #605

[*Summary*]: Capito asks Amerbach to obtain for him [at the Frankfurt book fair] the pages missing from his copy of Sophocles, and to buy for him a Greek Bible. Capito will reimburse him, or perhaps Adam Petri will donate them. He also asks Amerbach to buy Hebrew books other than the Bible and Agostino Giustiniani's *Psalterium*. Capito plans to study Hebrew together with Bruno during the summer. In the postscript he asks Johann Froben to send Oecolampadius a copy of Capito's *Hebraicarum Institutionum libri duo*.

Letter 13: 13 March 1518, Louvain, Desiderius Erasmus to Capito

Printed in Allen 3:252–3, #798 and CWE 5, Ep. 798

[*Summary*]: Erasmus thanks Capito for showing discretion and not sharing [Ep. 9 or 10] with Baer. He gave Capito's letter [enclosed with a letter to Erasmus?] to Matthaeus Adrianus, who angrily denied the claim that he was indebted to Capito and threatened to expose errors in the latter's Hebrew grammar.

Erasmus encourages Capito to spend more time on Greek than on Hebrew studies. The Jews, he says, are 'a nation full of most tedious fabrications' and do more damage than the scholastics. He wishes that Christians would not spend so much time on studying the Old Testament.

Letter 14: 18 March 1518, Weinsberg, Johannes Oecolampadius to Capito

Printed in *Briefe Oekolampads* 1:44–59, #35

[*Summary*]: Capito has reported that certain people are criticizing Oecolampadius's preaching on three counts: he is not entertaining; he is not severe enough; and he fails to take his departure from a biblical text, as the rules of preaching demand. Oecolampadius defends himself at length against the first accusation. He condemns the *risus paschalis*, the custom of delivering a humorous sermon at Easter, which often involves inappropriate practical jokes. He does not object to wit but doubts that the common people will understand subtle jokes. He also does not approve of priests being theatrical and scurrilous. Perhaps the people find it entertaining, but one must not use popular taste as a standard for evaluating the quality of a sermon. Joking does not earn a preacher respect; it earns him ridicule. Erasmus has expressed that very well in his *Folly* who is not foolish at all. Some people are critical of his wit. Why are they not critical instead of the filthy jokes of Poggio Bracchiolini, whose *Facetiae* are used by some preachers as source material? To support his views on humour in sermons, Oecolampadius quotes extensively from scripture, classical literature, and patristic writings. In view of such weighty testimony, Oecolampadius's critics must take care not to be considered heretics. He shares Johann Geiler von Kaysersberg's opinion on the *risus paschalis* and quotes his critical remarks. He then briefly answers the other two accusations brought against him. He does not want to be severe because the preacher should not be a tyrant; and he does not accept the rule that the preacher must begin with a specific biblical text. Sometimes it may be better to explain the import of a whole epistle than to spend an hour analysing a few words. He invites Capito to share with him his thoughts on the subject.

Letter 15: 19 April 1518, Basel, Capito to the Reader

Printed in *Briefe* 1:64–5, #37

[*Summary*]: This is the preface to Oecolampadius's *De risu paschali* (Basel, 1518). Capito advises Oecolampadius not to be discouraged by criticism [see Ep. 14]. He praises Oecolampadius for not being theatrical or scurrilous in his sermons and for not succumbing to the indecent humour of idle women. He warns the reader not to use popular taste as a standard for evaluating the quality of a sermon. Oecolampadius preaches sincerely and eloquently, and without pretence. Capito asks the reader to peruse his book carefully and not to give preference to a theatrical over a good preacher.

Letter 15a: Before 7 July 1518, Basel, [Capito?] to the Reader

This is the preface to *Contra D. Ioannem Eckium Ingolstadiensem, D. Andreae Bodenstein archidiaconi Wittenbergensis apologeticae propositiones pro Reverendo patre D. Martino Luther* (Basel: [Gengenbach], 7 July 1518), 226–7. The attribution to Capito is conjectural. Hermann Barge (*Karlstadt*, 137, n. 13) and, more recently, Thomas Kaufmann ('Capito als heimlicher Propagandist der frühen Wittenberger Theologie,' *ZKG* 103 [1992]: 81–91) ascribe the preface to Capito on the basis of literal and thematic parallels with the preface to his edition of Luther's works that appeared in Basel in October 1518. Karlstadt's *Apologeticae propositiones* and two other works mentioned in the present letter (Luther's *Conclusiones* and Prierias's *De potestate*) are also included in the October edition of Luther's works. Cf. also E. Freys and H. Barge, *Verzeichnis der gedruckten Schriften des Andreas Bodenstein von Karlstadt* (Nieuwkoop, 1965), 157.

Andreas Bodenstein Karlstadt (ca. 1480–1541) studied at Erfurt (BA 1502), Cologne, and Wittenberg (MA 1505, ThD 1510). He was archdeacon at All Saints from 1510 and in order to be promoted to the provostship obtained a doctorate in law at Siena (1516). He participated in the Leipzig disputation against Johann Eck in 1519 (see below, Ep. 31) and published several polemical pamphlets against him in 1519/20. He disagreed with Luther on certain doctrinal points and left Wittenberg for Denmark in 1521. On his return to Wittenberg six weeks later, he introduced radical changes and, in Luther's absence, played a leading role in formulating Wittenberg's church ordinance of 1522. When Luther returned, Karlstadt became isolated and moved to Jena. He was expelled from Saxony on Luther's initiative (1524). He turned to Strasbourg and Basel, but received little support from the leading reformers there. His preaching of iconoclasm caused unrest wherever he appeared. In 1525 he was permitted to return to Saxony after recanting his radical views. In 1529 he again became persona non grata and was driven into exile. He was expelled from Strasbourg, where he had fled, was unable to find employment in Basel, where he took refuge next, and finally secured a position as deacon in Zurich with the help of Zwingli. After Zwingli's death, he aided Bullinger in continuing the reformer's work. In 1534 he was appointed preacher at St Peter's in Basel and lectured on the Old Testament at the university there until his death.

To the Reader:

Eck, with his sophist's fang, has tried to gnaw at the *Conclusiones de virtute indulgentiarum* of the Reverend Father Doctor Martin Luther.[1] He has plucked them from the midst of the scriptural meadow, whereas Eck trusts too much in the opinions of Scotus, Capreoli, Durandus, Alfonso, Gabriel, and other modern doctors.[2] However, the Reverend Father Martin Luther deserves an aureole, as they say,[3] for being the first clearly to tear to pieces the abuse involving indulgences, at which so many thousand theologians have winked over so many years. It is criminal to mock the Christian peo-

* * * * *

1 See below, Ep. 19, headnote.
2 Duns Scotus (ca. 1270–1518), founder of Scotism; Johannes Capreoli (ca. 1380–1444), a pre-eminent Thomist; Durand de Saint-Pourcain (d. 1332), a famed nominalist; Alfonso de Spina (d. ca. 1491), author of *Fortalitium fidei*; Gabriel Biel (ca. 1425–95), a nominalist at Tübingen, perhaps mentioned because of his opposition to the realist Summerhart, whose work Capito had edited (see above, Epp. 1 and 8).
3 Cf. Exod. 25:25.

ple, for whom Christ has died, in such an impudent manner with things that have perhaps no foundation either in the gospels or in Paul, Origen and Jerome, or in Ambrose, Augustine, Hilary, Cyprian, and the other exegetes of old.[4] They may say: these are the opinions of theologians, even if they are modern theologians. Granted, but let them remain opinions and let them be nothing more than opinions, not a burden for Christians.[5] Let us not equate the opinions of modern theologians with articles of faith or the precepts of Christ and Paul. And, finally, scholars should be ashamed of the words they sometimes pour out in private among their friends:[6] 'This is what I would say in the classroom, but (let this remain between us) I think differently.' Also: 'This is what we say in the classroom, but (let this remain between us) these things cannot be proved on the basis of holy writ.' Rather, if they want to teach, let them not immediately compel people with threats (or else the condition of Christians is wretched!), but let them proffer testimony out of the sources, leaving aside the twisted interpretations they have made up themselves. Then the people will believe them. This was not done by the Master of the Sacred Palace, Brother Silvestro Prierias, who recently responded to Martin Luther in a way that made both theologians and non-theologians laugh at his 'essential, virtual, representative church.'[7] Everywhere the world is coming to its senses,[8] and every day lay people discover things concerning the Christian religion which they interpret differently, not only because they have read books (better books than we, the theologians), but because of the sagacity of their own minds – and what are we to do, who are far removed from the common herd? By our Lord Jesus Christ, open your eyes at last, o theologians, dismiss the scholastic opinions, let go of your childish wrangling, and approach the very springs of the scriptures. Let these words be regarded as written for the sake of admonition. They have certainly not been written without the tears and sighs of good men lamenting over that proud pertinacity and pertinacious pride.

* * * * *

4 For a similar list contrasting biblical and patristic writers with medieval exegetes, see below, Ep. 19. Karlstadt credited Capito with leading him away from the scholastics and encouraging him 'to follow in the footsteps of the ancients' (ut vestigia veterum imitarer; Barge *Verzeichnis*, 320–1).

5 The expression is echoed in Ep. 19, below: 'Scholastic opinions must not become a burden to Christians.'

6 The sentiments are echoed below, Ep. 19: 'saying one thing in the universities ... and another among their close friends.'

7 See below, Ep. 19, headnote. The expressions ridiculed here were criticized by Luther in his reply to Prierias, WA I, 656: 33–4.

8 The expression is repeated in Ep. 19 below.

Let Christ be my witness, who is blessed for ever. Let it come to pass. Let it come to pass.

Letter 15b: 13 August 1518, Freiburg, Udalricus Zasius to Capito

Udalricus Zasius (1461–1535) studied at Tübingen and became town clerk in Freiburg in 1494. He studied law at Freiburg, obtaining a doctorate in 1501, then taught at the university, while continuing to serve the town as a legal adviser. In 1508 he was appointed imperial counsellor. He published a number of influential legal works and had close ties to humanistic circles in Alsace. His student, Boniface Amerbach, brought him in contact with the humanists in Basel. There is a copy of this letter in the hand of Bruno Amerbach in Universitätsbibliothek Basel, Ki.Ar. C VIa 35II, fol. 19v.

Zasius to Wolfgang Fabritius, greetings.

They say that Poliziano[1] wrote letters infrequently, dear Wolfgang, most eminent man, because he would not send them unless they were polished and smoothly turned out. I see the same is true of you since your letters are rich in exquisite elegance. You rarely write unless you have an opportunity to prepare everything. I, on the other hand, write easily and frequently since I do not aim for neatness, being evaluated accordingly.[2] Nevertheless, even if you, a man of great renown, don't want to, I would like you to permit your servant to send a letter from time to time to me, who loves and genuinely embraces you. Our Melchior,[3] who has been appointed suffragan (if that's

* * * * *

1 Angelo Poliziano (1454–94), Italian poet and humanist, a friend and protégé of Lorenzo de' Medici, and one of the foremost classical scholars of the Renaissance. He was fluent in Greek, Italian, and Latin and was equally talented in poetry, philosophy, and philology. He published only one major work, the *Miscellanies* (1489), a set of brief critical essays on a varied list of textual issues. Ironically, Erasmus dubbed Zasius himself 'a second Poliziano.' Cf. CWE Ep. 408.
2 Rainer Bodenmann suggested correcting the word order of the Latin and reading, instead of *qui munditiam non quaero secutus qua nota expendar* (which is awkward): *qui munditiam secutus, non quaero qua nota expendar*, i.e., 'I have aimed for neatness and do not ask how I am evaluated.'
3 Melchior Fattlin or Vattlin (1490–1548) from Trochtelfingen. He matriculated at Freiburg in 1508 (BA 1509, MA 1513, Bac. Bibl. 1515, Lic. Theol. and ThD 1518). He was dean of the Faculty of Arts from 1516 to 1517, ordained priest in 1514, cathedral priest in 1517, and in 1518 he succeeded Balthasar Brenwalt as suffragan bishop of Constance. Leo X granted him dispensation from having to take up personal residence on account of the plague in 1518–19 and allocated to him one hundred gulden from the episcopal treasury on top of his income from the Zurich parish of Mettmenstetten. He remained a devout Catholic.

the right word) of the bishop of Constance, will move; there is still discussion over who will succeed him as preacher. Albert,[4] his colleague at the university,[5] has been made parish priest in Wolfegg and he too will move. The faculty of arts will keep its eyes open for good men. If those generous provisions had not made you happy, there would have been a chance of calling you back to us. For whoever is the senior preacher will in time also be put in charge of the parish. I have to say this, however: of course, the title 'parish priest' may be flattering, but the parish administration is a heavy burden weighing you down. I wish to know whether the business between your university and Gottesheim[6] has been safely concluded.[7] I would like to see that matter settled,[8] either by a friendly arrangement or some other outcome. Farewell and if it pleases you, at least drop me a line (if not a letter)[9] from the workshop of your elegancies. Recommend me to the great Erasmus and apologize for my lack of sophistication, or rather my faintheartedness, for when I was recently there, I did not make a very good impression.[10] Farewell from Freiburg. The Ides of August in the year of Christ '18. Your Zasius.

Letter 15c: 22 August 1518, Basel, Capito to Udalricus Zasius

> For Zasius see above, Ep. 15b, headnote. The manuscript of this letter is in Basel, Universitätsbibliothek, Ki.Ar. C VIa 35, fol. 53.

> * * * * *

4 Albertus Crus (or Kraus, d. 1538) registered at the University of Freiburg in 1504 (BA 1506, MA 1508, licence in theology 1517). He was prior in Güterstein (from 1515), parish priest of Wurzach, advanced to provost of Wolfegg, and was appointed suffragan bishop of Brixen in 1534.

5 The phrase 'ambo magister' is awkward. 'Ambo' is perhaps used in the sense of 'together with him' and, as the following sentence suggests, 'magister' must be used in the sense of 'magister noster,' the usual title for university professors.

6 Jakob Gottesheim of Ast matriculated at the University of Basel in 1507, was rector in 1510 as professor of civil law, and became involved in a dispute with the city council and university in 1517. He was suspended and replaced by Claude Chansonnette. In 1519 he left Basel for Strasbourg, where he served as episcopal official.

7 Lit. 'is in the harbour.' The metaphor is used by Terence *Andria* 480; Virgil *Aeneid* 7.598; cf. Erasmus *Adagia* 1.1.46.

8 Lit. 'in shallow water,' a proverbial metaphor meaning 'in safety,' 'out of danger.' Terence *Andria* 845; Plautus *Aulularia* 803; Erasmus *Adagia* 1.1.45.

9 Zasius puns on the similarity between a letter (*literae*), i.e., an epistle, and a letter of the alphabet (*litera*).

10 Zasius and Erasmus met during the summer of 1518, probably in Basel. Zasius described his first impressions of Erasmus in a letter to the Dutch humanist on 13 August 1518, cf. CWE Ep. 857.

Greetings. You have worked your charm on me with your very flattering criticism, dear Zasius, leader of all literature. Surely you have taken my measure up and down, as they say,[1] and have seen very clearly how worthless I am and how infertile my Minerva is.[2] Nevertheless, you see in me, with eyes sharper than Lynceus's,[3] the qualities of Poliziano,[4] although they are diametrically opposed.[5] His diction is very accurate, elegant, festive, happy, excellent both in judgment and intellectual ease, and he used to publish nothing (as you asserted), except what was polished and approved by all votes.[6] On the other hand, my very charming Zasius, you yourself are witness to how sloppy, barbarous, and stuffy[7] my diction is, how it displays no natural abilities, in fact, how utterly incapable of thought it is, of which there is none within me, unless you count sudden inspiration, as you repeatedly accused me when I was soldiering under your command.[8] But as I was trying to write and as my pen was being too playful, the result was a certain womanish and frail banter, while meanwhile I was practically drying up. Nature in her generosity often allows trifling things to blossom forth quickly, but if they do not reach their full glory as speedily as they have begun, they die while still being shaped by Nature's hand.[9] Just so my speech gushes forth in a turbulent rush, like a torrent, but held back by some barrier, it languishes, dries up and disappears. And so, you rightfully joke at the expense of your student, whom you prick gently with free-wheeling humour and made-up praise, but you encourage me in my torpor with these true delights, as food nourishes the mind, especially if given over and beyond the letter of the law. For you, truly the most experienced and likewise cultured man, very happily scatter scented flowers, pure pleasantries, and Attic witticisms[10] on the spur of the moment, with the Muses themselves dictating, as it were. Such is the power of your mind and your exceptional industry applied to many diverse pursuits.

* * * * *

1 Erasmus *Adagia* 1.3.85.
2 A variant on the adage *invita Minerva* (against the will of Minerva), Erasmus *Adagia* 1.1.42.
3 Lynceus's piercing sight was proverbial. Cf. Erasmus *Adagia* 2.1.54.
4 Cf. above Ep. 15b note 1.
5 Erasmus *Adagia* 1.10.45.
6 Erasmus *Adagia* 1.5.60.
7 Cf. Erasmus *Adagia* 2.8.59.
8 Capito matriculated at the University of Freiburg on 9 February 1505. He attended Zasius's lectures on imperial law for a period of four years (see below, Ep. 30).
9 Cf. Erasmus *Adagia* 2.5.32.
10 Cf. Erasmus *Adagia* 1.2.57.

For the rest, I sincerely congratulate Melchior[11] and Albert[12] on their increased honour and most splendid positions, as well as our university, which fosters men of this sort who merit such magnificent rewards and such great glory and readies them for the good life, although I, who prefer the quieter life, have avoided that type of fortune. For this reason, I won't leave Basel rashly except to change my position as preacher for another one in the same capacity. You will forthwith know about the commotion that is disrupting our life and the great turn of events. We have kept the truce on both sides for several months now, under the pretext of reaching an agreement.[13]

Finally, you are much more highly commended to Erasmus than you can be commended by my humble words. He read to me your letter,[14] which was to the point and notable for its erudite gravity, nodding his approval as he read, strongly applauding you, as it were. Our Oecolampadius[15] and your most dedicated disciple, Valentinus,[16] send their best wishes to you, a splendid man. Farewell. Basel. 22 August in the year of Christ '18. In haste through the hand of your Valentinus since I am fighting a cold.
Yours, Wolfgang Fab. Capito

Letter 16: 4 September 1518, Basel, Capito to Martin Luther

Printed in WBr 1:197–200, #91

[*Summary*]: In an earlier letter to Luther written from Strasbourg [now lost], Capito mentioned Erasmus's admiration and respect for Luther's *Sermo de indulgentiis*. Capito indicates that he too has read both that sermon and Luther's *Sermo de poenitentia*. Using military language he warns Luther that he is undertaking a fight against a powerful enemy. This enemy, he says, is guarded by a 'threefold wall': by papal authority, by the power of tyrants, and by the consent of scholars. Capito advises Luther to be more diplomatic in his criticisms. Using Acts 23:6 as an example, he recommends that Luther follow the example of Paul, who evaded a potentially incriminating question with a prudent response.

Capito mentions that he recently received a book by Silvestro Prierias, a

* * * * *

11 Melchior Fattlin. Cf. above, Ep. 15b note 3.
12 Albertus Crus. Cf. above, Ep. 15b note 4.
13 Cf. above, Ep. 15b note 6.
14 Cf. CWE, Ep. 857.
15 See above, Ep. 11, note 16.
16 On Valentinus Curio see below, Ep. 95, headnote.

response to Luther's treatise on indulgences. Capito advises Luther how to respond diplomatically to Prierias without angering him or offending the pope. He reminds Luther that he has supporters, including Andreas Karlstadt, Georgius Spalatinus, Johannes Sylvius Egranus, and Philip Melanchthon.

Erasmus approves of Egranus's *Apologetica responsio* and the latter would like to see it reprinted in Basel. Johann Eck has written against Andreas Karlstadt. Capito warns Luther that he will not be disputing before fair judges. Capito will write to Eck personally.

Letter 17: 4 September 1518, Basel, Capito to Johann Reuchlin

> This letter, printed in the *Illustrium virorum epistolae*, is the only extant letter between Capito and Johann Reuchlin (1455–1522), the German Hebrew scholar whose defence of Hebrew literature led to his condemnation by the papal court. He was tried for heresy (Judaizing) and initially acquitted, but the judgment was overturned after an appeal was launched by the Inquisitor Jacob van Hoogstraten. The controversy spread throughout Europe. Humanists everywhere rallied to support Reuchlin against the conservative theologians, who refused to admit the necessity of the three ancient languages for the study of theology. Reuchlin defended himself in part by publishing the numerous letters of his humanist supporters in two collections: *Clarorum virorum epistolae* (Tübingen, 1514; enlarged 1519) and *Illustrium virorum epistolae* (Haguenau, 1519).

Wolfgang Faber Capito to Johann Reuchlin, greeting.

Our Oecolampadius said[1] that the Greeks reported something or other about purgatory[2] against the Latin church at the Council of Basel. He himself copied [the passage] some time ago from a text belonging to some pilgrim, but lost it through theft, carelessness, or frequent moving. At this time, excellent Reuchlin, you can offer nothing more pleasing to both of us than to have it copied[3] at your house or share it with us for a little while. We will then most certainly return it, and with interest; that is, at a stroke you will

* * * * *

1 See Oecolampadius's letter to Reuchlin (beginning of September 1518), printed in *Briefe Oekolampads*, 71, #42.
2 Migne, PG 15, 61ff. includes this report under the title *Responsio Graecorum ad positionem Latinorum de igne purgatorio a Bessarione Nicaeno recitata die 14 Iunii 1438.*
3 He must be referring to a manuscript in Reuchlin's possession, which contained the passage in question.

create an even stronger bond, although we are already most obliged to you. Farewell. Basel. 4 September 1518.

Letter 18: 19 October 1518, Louvain, Desiderius Erasmus to Capito

Printed in Allen 3:414–16, #877 and CWE 6, Ep. 877

[*Summary*]: Erasmus recounts his experiences at Speyer. He met Franz Fritz (Irenicus), whose *Germaniae Exegesis* he finds puerile. He received a dull letter from Johannes Cellarius (Gnostopolitanus). Melanchthon said he would have criticized Erasmus's *Annotations* if Erasmus had not been a friend of Reuchlin. He received a visit from the poet, Helius Eobanus, who had come from Erfurt only to see Erasmus, as well as from Agostino Giustiniani, bishop of Nebbio, who had been favourably mentioned in Erasmus's *Apologia*. Hermann Buschius told Erasmus that a knight had threatened Hoogstraten, the prosecutor in the Reuchlin case. Hoogstraten is said to be looking for a safe house now. Matthaeus Adrianus is still annoyed with Capito [see Ep. 13, above]. Erasmus asks for another copy of Silvestro Prierias's book against Luther to replace the one that has been stolen from his bag.

Letter 19: October 1518, [Basel], [Capito] to the Reader

This is the preface to a collection of seven Lutheran tracts entitled, after the first item, *Ad Leonem X pontificem maximum Resolutiones disputationum de virtute indulgentiarum* (Basel: Froben, 1518). The volume also contains Prierias's *De potestate papae dialogus* and Karlstadt's *Contra ... Eckium ... apologeticae propositiones*. The text of the preface appears on folio a1v (= p. 2). On the history of the text and its reprints see WA 60, 431–50.

Capito began corresponding with Luther in the summer of 1518 and expressed his admiration for his writings (see above, Ep. 16). Capito may have coaxed Froben, who received the Lutheran tracts as a gift from Blasius Salomon, into reprinting them. Capito himself translated one of the pieces, Luther's *Sermon von Ablass und Gnade*, into Latin and provided shoulder heads. They sometimes go beyond the conventional purpose of providing summaries of the content and function as glosses supporting Luther's thought. For a detailed discussion of Capito's comments, see Stierle, 104–33. She concludes that Capito endorsed Luther's criticism of church abuses but did not fully understand the doctrinal implications of his writings.

The edition appeared anonymously (but cf. Capito's hints to Luther about his involvement, below, Ep. 24). At the time Capito did not want to run the risk of being labelled a Lutheran. When Johannes Fabri identified Capito as the author of the preface in 1526 (cf. WA 60, 433, n8), his support of Luther was no longer a secret. The book sold well, but a protest from Erasmus curbed any further publishing plans Froben might have had. 'I even used threats against the printer, Johann Froben, to prevent him from printing any of [Luther's] works,' Erasmus wrote to Leo X (Allen, Ep. 1143, 21–2). Other printers were not deterred. The collection was reprinted, with slight alterations and additions, in Strasbourg (1519) and by Cratander and Petri in Basel (1520).

To the fair theologians: Here are the theological works of the reverend father Martin Luther, whom many regard as a second Daniel sent by Christ. He has finally looked on us with merciful eyes and allowed Luther to expose some of the abuses that have arisen in his church, for the theologians neglect the gospel and Pauline theology together with the commentaries of old and busy themselves with amplifications, restrictions, appellations, and the nonsense of the (truly) Small Logics.[1] I only wish he could at last rouse all theologians from their lethargy, that they may disregard the dreams (summaries, I should have said) of the brethren,[2] and prefer the philosophy of the gospel to Aristotle, Paul to Scotus, and finally place Jerome, Augustine, Ambrose, Cyprian, Athanasius, Hilary, Basil, John Chrysostom, and Theophylactus ahead of Lyra, Thomas, Scotus,[3] and the other opinionated scholastic disputers; that they may refrain from drawing Christ into the world, as does the famous Thomas Aquinas everywhere, and instead instruct the world in the teaching of Christ; that they may stop saying one thing in the universities while acting out their comedies and another thing at home, one thing before the people, and another among their close friends; and that they may cease their attempts, regardless of their reasons, to call good men heretics for being unwilling to go along with their ineptitude. For they imitate certain theologians at the University of Paris, who wanted to condemn Jacques Lefèvre d'Etaples,[4] a pillar of erudition and integrity, as a

* * * * *

1 An allusion to the *Parva logicalia*, a standard medieval textbook of logic.
2 I.e., of Franciscan and Dominican authors.
3 Capito shows the typical preference of biblical humanists for the writings of the church fathers over those of the medieval scholastics Duns Scotus, Nicolaus of Lyra, and Thomas Aquinas.
4 Jacques Lefèvre d'Etaples (1460–1536) taught at the Collège du Cardinal Lemoine and published a number of editions and commentaries on Aristotle. Under the patronage of the reform-minded Guillaume Briçonnet, he devoted himself to biblical scholarship after 1507, publishing commentaries and, from 1523, French translations of the New Testament. He was attacked by the theologians of Paris and fled to Strasbourg in 1525. He was, however, recalled by Francis I, who appointed him head of the royal library and tutor of the royal children. In 1530 he moved to the court of the king's sister, Marguerite of Navarre, where he led a retired life.

heretic because he denied, with good reason, that that inept translation of the New Instrument is Jerome's.[5] Instead they have brought shame on the whole university, making their own ignorance, envy, and malice notorious before the whole world and perhaps all of posterity. Let them understand that scholastic opinions must not become a burden to Christians, let them understand that the world has come to its senses through the studies that are now emerging, that laymen are not as crass as they once used to be, that they love, breathe, and embrace Christ and Paul before all others, and that they will understand that some things are not as the quibblers have taught so far. Thus, brothers, the time has come to rise from sleep. Farewell, fair theologians.

Letter 19a: October 1518, [Basel, Capito] to the Reader

> This letter, like Ep. 19, comes from the Froben edition of Luther's works (for details see above, Ep. 19, headnote). The text, which appears on 302, is the preface to Luther's *De decem praeceptis*. For the attribution to Capito see WA 60, 434.

To the fair readers:
When you read the sermons of the reverend Father Martin Luther on the ten commandments, which follow below, you should remember that they were addressed to the people, who listen to the doctor as 'the ass listens to the lyre,'[1] unless the subject is taught with a 'rough Minerva,' as they say.[2] Therefore do not expect clever sentence structures or elegant words. Indeed, these sermons appear in a plain style matching the simple words used when they were delivered to the people in a sacred sermon, ex tempore and in German.[3] The purpose was not to delight learned readers but to benefit both untrained lay people and priests, who are the principal concern of the man who undertook this publication.[4] Therefore, fair readers, accept with good grace these sermons, however hastily put together, and love Luther whose

* * * * *

5 Jerome was commonly regarded as the translator of the Vulgate. Lefèvre, Erasmus, and other biblical humanists surmised that he merely edited or corrected the Latin New Testament version. Modern scholars support this view, but conservative theologians in the sixteenth century considered the idea blasphemous.

1 Erasmus *Adagia* 1.4.35.
2 I.e., in a simple manner, cf. Erasmus *Adagia* 1.1.37 ('crassa Minerva').
3 Luther preached the sermons in Wittenberg 1516/17.
4 A coy reference to Capito himself or a tip of the hat to the printer?

teaching of Christian piety is as pure and sincere as his life is blameless. Farewell.

Letter 20: [Fall of 1518, Basel], Capito to Bruno Amerbach

Printed in *Amerbachkorrespondenz* 2:131, #630

[*Summary*]: Capito's servant is gravely ill. Some think that it is the plague, but Capito thinks otherwise since the servant does not have any of the symptoms and complains only of a headache. Capito warns Amerbach not to visit him until the threat of contagion is past.

Letter 21: [December 1518, Basel], Capito to Johann Eck

The letter itself is lost. A passage is cited in Gerdesius 2:229 (also quoted by Stierle, 62, n.51): 'For I do not embrace everything of Luther's. I am now completely absorbed in Paul and can see every day from what sources he [Luther] has taken his new teaching.'

Letter 22: 13 January 1519, Basel, Capito to Caspar Amman

Printed in *Briefe Oekolampads* 1:81, #50, note 2. Amman (d. 1524), an Augustinian, studied Hebrew with Johannes Böschenstein in Ingolstadt after obtaining a doctorate in theology at Freiburg in 1500. He was provincial of Rhine-Swabia, but was prosecuted for his Lutheran sympathies in 1523.

[*Summary*]: Capito plans to publish a revised edition of his Hebrew grammar. He asks Amman to suggest corrections to the text. He writes that he has devoted the winter and early summer to the study of Greek theologians, but will return to Hebrew after that, relying on Amman's guidance. In the postscript he asks Amman to send his reply through Oecolampadius.

Letter 23: [Before 13 February 1519, Basel], Johannes Oecolampadius to Capito

The letter itself is lost. It is paraphrased by Beatus Rhenanus in a letter to Zwingli, printed in *Briefwechsel des Beatus Rhenanus* 136 and in Zwingli *Werke*, vol. 8, #59.

[*Summary*]: Oecolampadius has written from Augsburg informing him that

Luther was still in Wittenberg. He adds that Frederick III, elector of Saxony, has written a letter to Cardinal Cajetan on Luther's behalf.

Letter 24: ca. 14 February 1519, Basel, Capito to Martin Luther

Printed in WBr 1:335–7, #147

[*Summary*]: Capito informs Luther that he has very powerful supporters from the Rhine region to the North Sea. Upon hearing that Luther was in danger, Matthäus Schiner, Diebold III von Geroldseck, Christoph von Utenheim, and others have offered not only to cover Luther's expenses but even to find for him a secure place to live. Capito has seen a copy of a supportive letter from Frederick of Saxony to Cardinal Cajetan that makes the efforts of Schiner, Geroldseck, and Utenheim unnecessary, but they will nevertheless do whatever they can. Capito hints that he was involved in Froben's edition of a collection of Luther's works, which will disseminate his ideas throughout Italy, France, Spain, and England (see above, Ep. 19).

Letter 25: 15 February 1519, [Strasbourg], Otto Brunfels to Capito

On 13 January 1520, Otto Brunfels wrote to Beatus Rhenanus: 'I have written on the theme of reading the doctors of old, addressing it to Wolfgang Fabricius. The question I pose is: Which theology is preferable – scholastic or patristic? I shall send it during Lent ... If you think it worth publishing without offence to the theologians and without disturbing my peace, give it to a printer either in Sélestat or Basel.' The work was published as *Confutatio sophistices* (Sélestat: L. Schürer, 1520) with the letter to Capito on fols. a2 recto–b recto.

Otto Brunfels (ca. 1488–1534), of Mainz, entered the Carthusian monastery in Strasbourg and was active in humanistic circles there. In 1521, after failing to obtain a dispensation, he fled the monastery and became a parish administrator in Steinau. Driven out because of his Lutheran leanings, he accepted an appointment as pastor of Nauenburg in the Breisgau. In 1524 he moved back to Strasbourg, married, obtained citizenship, and opened a school. Brunfels was a prolific writer of pedagogical and religious/theological tracts. His interest in the sciences prompted him to resume studies at Basel (doctorate of medicine, 1532). In 1533 he was appointed city physician of Bern.

Otto Brunfels of Mainz to W. Fabritius Capito, preacher at Basel, greeting.
You once advised me, most learned Fabritius, that if I wanted to become as devout as possible and truly imbibe Christ, I should read Origen's commen-

taries. You said this not so much in order to guide me towards better values[1] as to draw me away from pagan literature. For you had been told that I was excessively devoted to them. With cunning you finally led me away from them, although at the time I myself did not recognize the trick. But, immortal God, how dutifully you got the better of me with your praiseworthy stratagem! I acquiesced and read not only Origen, but also Ambrose, Chrysostom, Nazianzen, Hilary, and Jerome, and to this day they continue to contain, fascinate, and consume all my attention. I read their grave and resounding opinions. Each has his special qualities: the one is compressed and concise, the other is more lengthy;[2] the one works his charm, like some Demosthenes, the other is more severe. Who could be more learned, more refined, more trustworthy, and more authoritative than Chrysostom? Who is more concise than Hilary? How great, do you think, is the trustworthiness and authority of his words? Who is dearer, sweeter, and more Christian than Origen? Meanwhile, leaving the others aside, I do not know if anyone is more learned than Jerome, for, in my opinion, he was not just an ordinary man, for literature itself and all the humanities seem to have made a trial in that one man alone. Cyril, not just a polished man, but altogether renowned and refined, writes openly and clearly, but fights bitterly. On top of that, he teaches, delights, influences, and attracts. There is none of the nonsense of the sophists, no Aristotle, nor the author of the *Six Principles*, who gives us Aristotle twice over again,[3] no childishness, and no wishy-washy distinctions. The same charm of speaking is altogether apparent in them all. Christ is everything and in everything. Everywhere they echo the apostle, sound of the gospel, and mirror the prophets. There is no battle of words amongst them, nor any dissension, except with the heretics and philosophers who strive to explain the mysteries of Christ based on human fallacies. They especially detest sects, and that is what convinced me to write, my Fabritius.

I wonder: either they were not theologians, or if they were, we do not treat theological wisdom sincerely enough; in fact, we treat it very coldly. Free me from such quibbling![4] Aristotle fills up the study halls of theologians and everywhere in the universities that most insolent and pugnacious [teaching]

* * * * *

1 Lit. 'to better fruit,' cf. Erasmus *Adagia* 4.5.27.
2 I.e., *adductiorem* is used here in the sense of *productiorem*.
3 A reference to Gilbert de la Porrée (Porretanus) (1076–1154), a scholastic logician and theologian who wrote *Liber sex principiorum* in which he explained the last six categories of Aristotle.
4 For the meaning of 'script(l)um' see Aulus Gellius 5.15.9, who uses the word to denote a minute examination or subtlety.

of Thomas, Scotus, Ockam, Hervaeus, and Durandus[5] is piled on, but no place is given to pure and pristine wisdom. Now one can hardly distinguish sacred from sophistical wisdom. I am afraid that if you take away from them Aristotle and the insoluble and obligatory *Summulae*, amplifications and restrictions of a certain Spaniard,[6] nothing sane will be left. Where did we get this plague from? Granted, Aristotle is an important philosophical writer and, if our philosophers would join him with Plato and Plutarch, no doubt they would discuss philosophy properly. But what business does he have with matters of faith? What agreement is there between Belial and Christ? What share does darkness have in light?[7] Why use as judge someone who is an enemy and foe of our religion when so many good authors have wracked their brains for us and when there is such a great supply of commentaries? Is the word of holy writ so insignificant that we must sully it with impure and sordid human reasoning? Is this how we mix holy with pure things?[8] Why send swine into our holy shrines? Did Christ not rebuke us about this? *Do not give what is holy to dogs.*[9] Why are we once again involved in a fight against giants?[10] Will that bearded sophist, that hairy and wanton chatterbox and mocker teach us Christ? A man whom even his teacher disparaged a great deal?[11] What if they turn everything into questions when they discuss the truth (for so they cavil)? How is Aristotle helpful with this? Will they expose the truth where truth is lost by more quarrelling? They should have tried another way. An answer to every question about scripture is known, in fact, only by the one who said, *I am the truth.*[12] It is necessary, as Chrysostom says,[13] to approach the issue with a godly purpose and in a spiritual sense with fear and trembling and to learn that if we ever find anything, we ought to draw conclusions within the limits of that blessed state and if we fail (for that is entirely in the hand of another) we are in no way to blame as long as we do what he commanded us to do and obey his precepts. Therefore if you come across a question or some difficult passage of scripture you should not have to uncover its mystery by relying on Aristotle, but

* * * * *

5 For a similar list of thirteenth- and fourteenth-century scholastic authors, see above, Ep. 15a.
6 I.e., the *Summulae* of Peter of Spain, a standard text.
7 Cf. 2 Cor. 6:14–15.
8 Cf. 2 Cor. 6:14–18 and Erasmus, *Adagia* 1.3.82.
9 Matt. 7:6.
10 Cf. Plato *Republic*, 378C, etc.
11 A reference to the reported disagreement between Plato and Aristotle?
12 John 14:6.
13 Cf. *Homily on John* 24 (23), 3 (Migne, PG 59:146).

instead be pure and undefiled. Next you should read the words assiduously and attentively and then you will find [the answer], for he who seeks will find.[14]

Even a man with a modest education, as long as he has a grasp of languages and a good background in grammar, can be a theologian because the better trained he is in the knowledge of rhetoric, poetry, history, and other humanities the better he will be equipped to approach theology. I do not see what else is necessary for a theologian than to be the type of person shaped by scripture and to meditate on the law of the Lord day and night.[15] He need not toil over it, as long as he reads it carefully. Darius said that he preferred to have one Zopyrus than a hundred Babylons,[16] likewise I would prefer a type of theologian who had read Jerome *extremely carefully*[17] than a hundred word-spinning sophists. Why is it necessary for a man to examine what is beyond him? As [Ecclesiasticus] says: *Do not be too concerned with superfluous issues and do not inquire curiously into his many works. For it is not necessary for you to see those things that are hidden from your eyes. You were shown a great deal that is beyond the grasp of man, but supplanted many of them with conjectures and only exercised yourselves in vanity. But always keep in mind that which God has commanded you.*[18] What does Paul say in order to deter some people from curious questions of this sort? *Do not become proud but stand in awe;*[19] and *So that you may not claim to be wiser than you are, brothers, I want you to understand that this is a mystery;*[20] and in the following: *For by the grace given to me I say to everyone among you not to think of yourself more highly than you ought to think, but to think with sober judgment;*[21] and more specifically, *Rejoice with those who rejoice, weep with those who weep. Live in harmony with one another; do not be haughty, but associate with the lowly; do not claim to be wiser than you are;*[22] and to the Colossians: *See to it that no one takes you captive through philosophy and empty deceit, according to human tradition, according to the elemental spirits of the universe, and not according to Christ.*[23] He did not want us to focus on examining subtle questions nor did he want the faith of Christ defiled by earthly

* * * * *

14 Cf. Matt. 7:7.
15 Cf. Ps.1:2.
16 Herodotus 3.160. The Greek text actually says 'twenty.'
17 Adage 1.5.90 ('ex amussim')
18 Ecclus. (Sirach) 3:21–4.
19 Rom. 11:20.
20 Rom. 11:25.
21 Rom. 12:3.
22 Rom. 12:15–16.
23 Col. 2:8.

philosophies. Nowhere do I see him mixing in Aristotle's convoluted words. I see citations from Aratus,[24] Menander,[25] and Epimenides;[26] I do not read sophistical nonsense. I read that Saint Athanasius, Jerome, and Augustine discussed questions, but not so ineptly, frivolously, and barbarously as the sophists. How does it show acumen, I ask, to discuss whether God is omnipotent, whether Christ's body can be at the same time both in heaven and on the altar? I am mentioning the notorious examples because they have been disputed for a long time. What is the point of this nonsense but to subvert the audience, to be applauded and puffed up? Who is so stupid and barbarian and foolish of mind that he does not believe that God is omnipotent and does not only believe that Christ is present in the sacrament, but even worships him? Nabal said, *There is more than one God*.[27] He was a fool to say so. Only a few are as insane. For just as consummate piety is found in few, so madness is exceptional. Do you not think that if a layman unexpectedly came across a sophist and saw him debating without reason, grunting and spitting, he would mock him under his breath, saying, 'Is he insane?' And yet there are books filled with such figments. And they scare off and ridicule anyone who does not know them as if he were not quite a theologian. They regard him as anything but a theologian if he does not teach such things everywhere he goes. But why am I going on, my Fabritius, asking that you solve this problem for me: whether ancient theology is preferable or sophistical? I am not saying this because I myself do not know this, but that you may persuade your students. The very learned Erasmus of Rotterdam has worked very hard in this matter. I hear that Maarten van Dorp, the theologian, has published an oration in praise of Paul,[28] on the harm caused by the sophists, on the usefulness of languages and correcting the holy scriptures on the basis of Greek manuscripts. But no effort is sufficient in this enterprise. Go on, for the foundations have now been laid and all that is left for us to do is to shut the mouths of those frogs and prevent them from holding forth to students in their impudent manner. I am sending you a collection of

* * * * *

24 Aratus (ca. 315 to before 240 BC), Greek poet best known for his only extant poem *Phaenomena*. He is quoted at Acts 17:28.
25 Menander (ca. 344–ca. 293 BC), the Greek playwright, is quoted at 1 Cor. 15:33.
26 A late seventh-century BC seer and poet from Crete who stated the well-known paradox: 'All Cretans are liars; one of their own poets has said so.' Titus 1:12 refers to the lies of the Cretans.
27 1 Sam. 25.
28 Maarten van Dorp (1485–1525), member of the Faculty of Theology at Louvain. He published an *Oratio in praelectionem Pauli* (Antwerp, 1519).

passages on the harm these sophists and their curious questions have caused in order to refresh your memory about what you yourself have read. I will send you more if you want. They will give you a starting point and even hearten you to inveigh against the sophists all the more bitterly. You will see the value the ancients put on dialectics and how, at that time, the scriptures had not been contaminated by sophistical dreams and perplexities. What would they now say if they saw all of theology sullied by nonsense of this sort? They, especially Origen in his *Homily XIV on Genesis*[29] and *Homily II on Exodus*[30] and likewise Jerome in a few passages, do not attack their knowledge in principle, but condemn those who attribute too much to pagan literature and who almost equate the decrees of the pagan authors with those of Christ. Since his philosophy is an octave[31] removed from the opinions of philosophers, it is most foolish to use the opinions of Aristotle to confirm or prove the laws of Christ. Farewell.

Michael Herr,[32] our brother extremely learned in Greek and Hebrew, greets you, as does Lambertus[33] the theologian. I am getting back to my Hebrew studies that were interrupted for nearly a year on account of my frequent illnesses. See that the Hebrew lexicon that you promised us gets published.[34] Greet Pellicanus.[35] Again farewell. Given on the 15th of February in the 1519th year from the birth of Christ.

* * * * *

29 Origen *Genesis Homily 14*, PG 12:237D.
30 Origen *Exodus Homily 2*, PG 12:306B-C.
31 I.e., a great difference or a very long interval. Erasmus *Adagia* 1.2.63.
32 Michael Herr (d. ca. 1550) received his BA from Heidelberg in 1510 and entered the Carthusian monastery at Strasbourg. There he became friends with Otto Brunfels, whose *Herbarum vivae icones* he completed after the author's death. While in Strasbourg he encountered the new evangelical ideas and fled the monastery together with Brunfels. In 1527 he studied medicine in Montpellier, but soon returned to Strasbourg and, in 1528, acquired citizenship. In 1534 he became physician of the civic hospital. From 1547 on he was involved in designing a new clock for the cathedral.
33 This may be a reference to Lambertus Pascualis, a fellow Carthusian, of whom nothing further is known; or to Lambertus Hollonius of Liège, who studied theology and was in the service of the Froben press in 1518. He died in Rome ca. 1522. The Franciscan François Lambert of Avignon (d. 1530) also comes to mind, but he was in the area of Lyon and Avignon at that time. He later left the Franciscan order and, after stints in Wittenberg and Metz, took out citizenship in Strasbourg in 1524. From 1526 he taught theology at the University of Marburg.
34 Cf. above, Ep 11a, note 4.
35 On Pellicanus, see Ep. 89, headnote.

Letter 26: 8 April 1519, [Basel], Capito to Desiderius Erasmus

Printed in Allen 3:526–7, #938 and CWE 6, Ep. 938

[*Summary*]: Capito asks Erasmus not to engage in a public controversy with Martin Luther. Avoiding a dispute with the reformer would give a younger generation the courage to continue the program of reform. He reminds Erasmus of the support Luther enjoys in Wittenberg and from Duke Frederick the Wise. Capito warns that a dispute with Luther would only please Erasmus's and Luther's enemies.

Letter 27: 7 May 1519, Basel, Capito to Antonio Pucci

This is the dedicatory letter preceding Capito's translation of John Chrysostom's *Homilia de eo quod dixit Apostolus, Utinam tolerassetis* (Basel: Cratander, 1519), fols. Aii recto–verso. The translation was reprinted in Cratander's 1522 and 1525 editions of Chrysostom's *Opera omnia*, in both cases without the dedicatory letter.

Antonio Pucci (1484–1544) of Florence held doctorates in philosophy and theology from the University of Pisa. He became a protonotary at the papal court and, in 1518, succeeded his uncle Lorenzo Pucci as bishop of Pistoia. In 1531 he was made a cardinal (Santi Quattro Coronati). He repeatedly went on diplomatic missions to France and Spain, and in 1517 was appointed legate for Switzerland. In 1521 he raised troops in Switzerland for Leo X, and when Pope Clement VII was taken prisoner by imperial troops in the Sack of Rome (1527), Pucci stood hostage for him. He also maintained close connections with the Medici in Florence.

Wolfgang Capito to the reverend father in Christ, Lord Antonio Pucci, bishop of Pistoia, greetings:
Every day we appreciate better the great authority you showed when you were present among us here, Reverend Antonio Pucci, as your reputation grows in your absence, for our simple minds do not allow us even now to appreciate your talents fully. Yet each man privately extols either your courtesy or your worthy morals or your friendly address or your incomparable efficiency. I, too, look up to your vigorous intellect and acumen and most of all your classical erudition, of which you gave an uncommon example to those whom you received at dinner. There you seemed to recall us to the sane judgment of the ancients, as you spoke authoritatively about letters. As we observed your greatness in part (for its entirety exceeds our grasp), we finally came to the conclusion that we must congratulate ourselves on the

favour of the holy pontiff. Hence you came to us as legate, a man not only well known, which you have perhaps in common with many others, but the kindest man and most honoured by everyone in France as well as in Spain. For you discharged your legatine duty splendidly in both places, and that honour you share with very few. Furthermore, we congratulate ourselves on having you on account of the close link between the Pucci family and the House of Medici,[1] on account of your loyalty and integrity which is renowned everywhere, and on account of your liberality and its readiness to do good. And we have high regard for the pontiff's majesty, who declared his good will and favoured the requests of the [Swiss] confederates by sending you as legate. Others will acknowledge the favour according to their abilities, I can only do so with a small intellectual gift, whose fruit, if there is any, I completely dedicate to the glory of Christ and the apostolic see. For this reason I have recently translated the short book of St Chrysostom, which he gave the title *Concerning the apostle's words, 'May you bide with my weakness for a while.'* The book lacks neither elegance nor learning and it brings us to the realization that an understanding of scripture is better derived from an accurate examination of the circumstances than from odious verbal sparring. This translation, whatever its worth, I eagerly commend to you, reverend father, hoping that you will not disdain it as too paltry. I commend it to you, not for your own instruction (you, no doubt, have already a good understanding of it and have pondered it assiduously), but merely to indicate my inclination towards you, for I am deeply attached to you, and you do not cease to oblige me every day more deeply still by your favours. If this return does not match my debt, it is my ability that is at fault, not my will, for even if I wanted my thanks to be great, it is with difficulty that I produce this small return. To such an extent does the task, which I proposed to accomplish, exceed my ability. But it is the characteristic of a generous mind to base his assessment not on the size of an offering but on the intention of the giver. Farewell and best wishes. Basel, on the Nones of May, 1519.

Letter 28: 17 May 1519, Wittenberg, Philip Melanchthon to Capito

Printed in *Melanchthons Briefwechsel* T1:61–2, #57

* * * * *

1 I.e., with the Medici popes Leo X and Clement VII, and with Alessandro de' Medici, Duke of Florence, whom Pucci was rumoured to have aided in his political intrigues.

[*Summary*]: Encouraged by Oecolampadius, Melanchthon attempts to gain Capito's friendship because they are both striving to revive Christian literature and fighting the same enemy, the 'deceived sophists.' He ranks the people involved in the revival of Christian literature: Erasmus has initiated the movement by casting the dice, Capito and Oecolampadius come next, then Luther and Karlstadt, and finally, Melanchthon modestly states: 'I follow them, but at a long distance.' He is sending Capito some of Luther's writing and plans to send some of his own as well. Luther and Melanchthon approve of Capito's theses [i.e., the leaflet *Sub Volphgango Fab. Capitone subscriptas conclusiones ex evangelica scriptura et veteri utriusque linguae theologia mutuatas in Basiliensium Gymnasio disputabit M. Caspar Hedio* (1519)]. Melanchthon writes that he would like to have his *Rhetoric* reprinted in Basel because the first edition (Wittenberg: J. Grunenberg, 1519) was replete with errors. Greetings to Erasmus, Beatus Rhenanus, Caspar Hedio, Johann Froben, Hartmann von Hallwyl. He assures Capito of Luther and Karlstadt's friendship.

Letter 29: 15 June 1519, Mainz, Capito to Georgius Spalatinus

> Georgius Spalatinus (1484–1545) studied law at Erfurt. He took holy orders in 1508 and, from 1511 on, was mentor to two nephews of the dukes of Brunswick-Lüneburg studying in Wittenberg. In 1516 he became court preacher and private secretary of the elector of Saxony, Frederick the Wise. He accompanied the elector on diplomatic missions and to the German diets. He was sympathetic to Luther and in 1525 became a minister in Altenburg. Spalatinus continued to play an active role in the reformation of Saxony. He took part in the religious colloquies of the thirties and forties as adviser to the Elector John and to his successor John Frederick of Saxony. This letter is printed in H. Barge, 2:544–5, on the basis of cod. Chart. 13187, 249, in the Forschungs- und Landesbibliothek, Gotha.

To his friend Georgius Spalatinus, excelling in the humanities, greetings. The third time I looked for you in vain, dearest Georgius.[1] Thus I had to go away without the benefit of a recent conversation which is always the sweetest. We shall make up for this loss by letters. Give my regards to Martin Luther, Karlstadt,[2] and the other theologian whom you called most Chris-

* * * * *

1 The meeting took place in Mainz. See below, Ep. 32.
2 For Karlstadt of Bodenstein see above, Ep. 15a, headnote.

tian.[3] Together with them I shall fight, like a pygmy[4] among athletes, using both my feet, as the saying goes,[5] on behalf of sound piety and against stubborn arrogance, that is, against those who are always introducing new doctrine. In this vein I wish to add the commentaries of the old authors translated by me as well as I could,[6] bypassing the sophistical nonsense. I congratulate myself on having seen, only in passing, the most illustrious prince, whose clemency protects Christian studies. Farewell. Mainz, 15 June 1519. Your Fabritius Capito. I shall write to Melanchthon[7] during my journey.

Letter 30: 30 July 1519, [Basel], Capito to Ulrich von Hutten

> This letter fragment is quoted by Gerdesius, *Introductio in Historiam evangelii* (Groningen, 1744), 1:116, note b. The humanist Ulrich von Hutten (1488–1523) was descended from a family of knights. For some years he was in the service of Albert of Brandenburg, the archbishop of Mainz (see below, Ep. 32, for Hutten's promotion of Capito's interests there). Motivated by German patriotism, Hutten supported the Lutheran movement and used both the pen and the sword to defend his ideas. His lawlessness and his association with the knight's revolt resulted in his being placed under the imperial ban in 1522. He was given refuge by Zwingli in Zurich and died in exile.

... Two reasons drove me formerly from Freiburg: in part, the snares of the sophists and the nauseating writings of Scotus, which I pounded into my

* * * * *

3 Kalkoff *Capito*, 1, suggests that this was Bartholomaeus Bernhardi of Feldkirch, who taught at the University of Wittenberg and was rector in 1518/19. He was a committed Lutheran, married in 1521, and wrote in defence of clerical marriage (*Apologia* 1521).
4 Cf. *Adagia* 4.1.90.
5 Lit. 'with every foot,' cf. Erasmus *Adagia* 3.1.34.
6 Presumably a reference to his translation of Chrysostom, cf. above, Ep. 27, headnote.
7 Philip Melanchthon (1497–1560) studied in Heidelberg (BA 1511) and Tübingen (MA 1514), where he taught between 1514 and 1516 and worked as a corrector for the printer Thomas Anshelm. In 1518, he was appointed to the new chair of Greek at Wittenberg (B.biblicus 1519). He was much admired for his accomplishments in both humanistic and theological studies and soon became Luther's right-hand man. When Capito fell out with Luther over the latter's radical methods, Melanchthon played the role of mediator, but like Luther he thought that Capito did not show sufficient fortitude in defending his principles. Cf. below, Ep. 120.

wretched listeners, for which I was hired and received a public stipend. Later my critical faculty was gradually enlightened by reading authors in snatches, but it was a weak light that dawned on me. In part it was the authority of Philip of Rosenberg, bishop of Speyer,[1] who invited me with fair promises to come to Bruchsal, where I held the office of preacher for three years.[2] The immense mountain of business drove me from there, as did my ardour for letters, a desire for freedom (for I had to obey the canons and devote a fair amount of time to their councils). I had to supply answers to any rustic fellow about the most profane nonsense, answers to old women concerning their superstition, and sometimes to members of the nobility concerning matters of law, which went beyond theology, although I attended the famous Zasius's lectures on imperial law for almost four years.[3] But I shy away from courts and litigation ...

Letter 31: 31 July 1519, Leipzig, Johannes Cellarius to Capito

> This is an eyewitness account of the Leipzig disputation between Eck, Luther, and Karlstadt. The author, Johannes Cellarius Gnostopolitanus (1496–1542), studied in Bologna and Heidelberg. He published a Hebrew grammar, *Isagogicon in hebraeas literas* (Haguenau: Anshelm, 1518). The following year he applied for a position at the University of Wittenberg. Negotiations failed, however, and he went to Leipzig. He taught Hebrew there until 1521, when he moved to Frankfurt an der Oder. He became a Lutheran and was a minister in Frankfurt am Main from 1529 to 1532. After being replaced by a Zwinglian, he moved to Dresden, where he was superintendent until his death. Cellarius's letter was published under the title *Ad Wolphangum Fabritium Capitonem Theologie Doctorem et Concionatorem Basiliensem, Ioannis Cellarii Gnostopolitani Lipsie Hebraice lingue professoris, de vera et constanti serie theologice disputationis Lipsiace epistola* (Leipzig: Landsberg, 1519). The letter was reprinted in Johann Eck's *Expurgatio ... adversus criminationes F. Martini Lutter* (Augsburg: Grimm & Wirsung, 1519).

Johannes Cellarius Gnostopolitanus to Wolfgang Fabritius Capito, professor of sacred literature, greetings.

* * * * *

1 Philip of Rosenberg (ca. 1460–1530) studied at Pavia (doctorate in canon law). He was the nephew of the bishop of Speyer, through whose patronage he received livings at Worms and Speyer. In 1490 he was appointed vicar-general to his uncle and, on his death in 1504, succeeded him as bishop of Speyer.
2 I.e., from 1512 to 1515, at the Benedictine house in Bruchsal.
3 In Freiburg; on Zasius see above, Ep. 15b, headnote.

If I allow myself to pass up even a small chance of demonstrating to everyone the most sincere and singular respect I have for you, Wolfgang, I may be
accused of the vice of ingratitude, which I regard as the source and first
beginning of all vices and have always thought most detestable. Lest I fall
into this error and be judged worthy of the chains of Hippocrates,[1] I wanted
to declare openly my feelings of love, charity, and respect for you, not only
on account of your personal merits, but also on account of your great zeal for
literature and authors and the uncommon love of excellence which we have
seen shining forth in you, in Latin, Greek, and Hebrew. You will ask: And
what is this occasion? Let me tell you briefly. You are aware, my Wolfgang,
when and how long that great and heated disputation went on between Dr
Johann Eck of Ingolstadt[2] and Dr Martin Luther and Andreas Bodenstein
Karlstadt of Wittenberg, regarding certain conclusions (if I am not mistaken)
recently published.[3] As a result, after the conclusions, without commentary,
had been disseminated throughout practically the whole world, they began
to be discussed in invectives and controversies. Since, however, that method
was not regarded at all conducive to bringing the matter to a good conclusion, unless the protagonists took up the battle in a public disputation, it was
announced with the consent of both parties that a public disputation would
be held in the flourishing and successful University of Leipzig. Permission
was granted by our illustrious Prince George, duke of Saxony, great president of Thüringen, margrave of Meissen, and most generous supporter and
protector of the University of Leipzig.[4] And although the university, famed
for its excellence, has most beautiful halls of learning, which we call colleges,
and in them likewise most capacious auditoria, he wished that theological
disputation to take place nowhere but in his own castle. If I relate the order in
which matters proceeded in true and organized fashion, I will, I think, please
you greatly and at the same time declare my feelings for you.

* * * * *

1 I.e., the tyrant of Gela (d. 491 BC).
2 For Eck see above Letter 1a headnote.
3 I.e., Karlstadt's *Apologeticae propositiones* (cf. above, Ep. 15a, headnote), which
  Eck answered in a series of publications, the last of which was published in
  March 1519. In May, Luther joined the fray with his *Disputatio et excusatio
  adversus criminationes D. Ioh. Eccii.*
4 George, Duke of Saxony (1471–1539) had originally been destined for the
  church and had an excellent grasp of theological issues. Ignoring the objections
  of the bishop of Merseburg and the reluctance of university officials, he permitted the debate between Eck, Luther, and Karlstadt to proceed. He later turned
  against Luther, but was unable to prevent the spread of the Reformation in
  Saxony. He was succeeded by his brother Heinrich, who was a Lutheran.

On 27 June,[5] then, at the second hour of the afternoon they went up to the castle. In the early morning the guests had been received by the wise and learned Simon Pistoris,[6] professor in the faculty of law; then they all went to the church of St Thomas to hear mass, which was held in honour of the saints; then they went to the place appointed for the disputation, where on the instruction of the most illustrious prince, the leaders of the disputation were counselled concerning the moderation they must observe,[7] and then, at the second hour in the afternoon, as I said, the disputation took its course.

First Dr Johann Eck proposed to dispute with Karlstadt about free will, saying that it actively collaborated with grace in doing good works, and that will and grace acted thus in conjunction and not separately; and Eck proved his point very well, citing Saint Bernhard. Karlstadt fought back for a long time on the basis of his notes, saying that free will was merely passive and receptive as far as good works are concerned, and was capable only of that, but moved by the authority of sacred scripture and the holy Fathers, he finally yielded and declared with Eck that the free will was active in doing a good work, and so they achieved agreement on this point. Here you could have seen Eck's ability, my Fabritius, the great, almost Demosthenic, skill, the great string of inductions which he most smoothly began and ended, whereas Karlstadt proffered arguments and solutions with the aid of books and notes. And when, in his reply, he wanted to read the whole course of the argument from a note prepared at home, Eck was unwilling to permit him to go on. He was willing to accept it up to that point, but for the remainder, [he said] Karlstadt must abstain [from written notes], except when citing the words of a holy Father or holy scripture. Let them dispute, not read, said Eck. The matter was thus laid before the presiding gentlemen, and it was decided that reading the whole argument from a note was not the form a disputation should take; Eck was right to object to reading, and Karlstadt had to decide by the next day whether he wanted to proffer his arguments from memory or yield the victory in the disputation.

Karlstadt therefore returned the following morning, observing the laws of disputation, but equipped with numerous books, and he expounded in

* * * * *

5 The debate was carried on over a number of days, from 27 June to 15 July.
6 Simon Pistoris (1489–1562) studied law in Pavia and Leipzig (doctorate, 1514), where he taught from 1519 on. In 1523 he became chancellor of Duke George of Saxony.
7 The oration was written by the humanist Petrus Mosellanus and published under the title *De ratione disputandi* (Leipzig: Lotter, 1519). For Mosellanus, see below, Ep. 62, headnote.

learned fashion that God was the whole source of good works; Eck admitted as much because grace and free will operated jointly in each good work; according to Bernhard they acted together, not singly or separately, and therefore one must not deny that the free will was active, for even if God brought it all about, he did not do so in totality [*totaliter*], excluding any other cause. Karlstadt forcefully objected saying that the holy Fathers had not used such terms. Eck disarmed him by saying that they should leave the question of terms to pertinacious people; it was certain on the authority of the holy fathers that the whole of the good work was God's, yet free will had some part in it. He smoothly explained this, using the terms *per totum* but not *totaliter*.

When the issue of free will was brought to an end and left to the verdict of the judges to be selected later, Dr Martin Luther took on Eck concerning the topic of the primacy of the Roman church.[8] He proposed to dispute the statement: the pope was superior to others, not by divine law, but by human consensus, nor was St Peter given primacy over the church of God and the other apostles; rather, one head, namely Christ, was sufficient for the holy church. Countering that, Eck proved with clear testimony that one vicar was the primate of the church by the divine law of that supreme head, Christ, who had built his church on that rock, that is Peter and his successors, according to the clearest testimony of Augustine, Jerome, Ambrose, Gregory, Cyprian, Chrysostom, Leo, Bernhard, and several popes, who testified to it expressly. But Martin did not value their authority, relying on St Paul's statements in the Epistle to the Galatians and in other places. Eck tried to show that those passages did not contradict him, but it is up to the judges to decide whether he was successful.

Eck, too, admitted that the apostles were equal as far as the priesthood was concerned and in their apostolate, according to Leo and Cyprian, yet Peter had been made the head to avoid any opening for a schism. Then Eck objected, saying that Martin Luther's pronouncement supported the heretical Hussites and was among the articles condemned by the praiseworthy and holy Council of Constance;[9] Dr Martin replied that not all articles condemned there were heretical, indeed some of the articles of Jan Hus were most Christian and evangelical; he therefore asked Eck first of all to prove

* * * * *

8 Luther first entered into the disputation on 4 July.
9 Jan Hus (1372–1415) was tried at the Council of Constance and executed when he refused to recant. Biblicism and communion in both kinds were the hallmarks of Hussite teaching. Luther frequently invoked Hus's memory, and Protestant propaganda made him a forerunner of Luther.

that a council cannot err. This earned Dr Martin the disapproval of many. Similarly, his claim that the Greeks, who do not obey the Roman Church,[10] lead a good and salutary life. But that is up to the judges. Eck, however, objected: if the pope does not have the primacy by divine law, who gave Dr Martin the habit he was wearing and on whose authority did his brethren hear confession? Certainly the parish priest disagreed, etc.[11] Dr Martin responded, among other things, that he wanted to do away with the mendicant order, and he relied especially on the *Register* of Gregory, who denied that he was an ecumenical bishop. Eck showed the reason for his denial, although the quotation from Gregory super c. decretum 2.q.7[12] was correct, and it was for that reason that he resisted the emperor and the patriarch of Constantinople, as Platina relates,[13] of whose truthfulness as historian Luther made so much. But let the judges decide which man offered the more correct interpretation.

Next, they began to treat of purgatory and whether punishment by purgatory was derived from the scriptures, and was it because the souls of the departed were imperfect in charity or to give satisfaction for the sins committed on earth. Dr Martin responded, saying that the existence of purgatory could not be proved out of scripture, however consistently it was asserted, and when Dr Eck cited the books of the Maccabees, he denied that they belonged to the canon. By contrast, Eck showed that they were part of the biblical canon of the church, on the authority of Augustine and Jerome in the prologue and because many holy doctors can be cited who interpret St Paul's words in the Epistle to the Corinthians as references to the purgatory, i.e., *Salvation will come through fire.*[14] Dr Martin learnedly proffered another meaning. But whether his interpretation departs from that of the fathers, the judges must decide.

Concerning indulgences they disputed with less contention, for both alike

* * * * *

10 I.e., after the schism and mutual excommunications in 1054.
11 Eck's words were: 'From whom do they have the authority to hear confession and preach and enjoy the numerous privileges lavished on them by the apostolic See, over the frequent objections of archbishops, bishops and priests' (O. Seitz *Der authentische Text der Leipziger Disputation* [Berlin, 1903], 111).
12 Gratian *Concordia Discordantium Canonum*, Part II, c 2 q 6. Cf. WA 2:289.
13 The humanist and Vatican librarian Bartolomeo Platina (1421–81) participated in the scholarly discussions hosted by Cardinal Bessarion and was active in the Roman Academy. He wrote a critical history of the popes *Liber de vita Christi et omnium pontificum* (1474). The reference is to L.A. Muratori, ed. *Rerum Italicarum Scriptores*, vol. 3–IA, 97, lines 24–6.
14 1 Cor. 3:15.

spoke out against the abuse of indulgences, and Martin was gentler than in his writings elsewhere. For he admitted that indulgences were useful, yet maintained the view that indulgences were in lieu of good works. Dr Eck, by contrast, said that they were in lieu of punishment incurred for one's sins. But if Luther did not believe that indulgences were a form of satisfaction, he had already been struck down as anathema in the most recent bull of Pope Leo X.[15]

Then they disputed about repentance and how it was to be achieved. Dr Eck rested his argument on the holy scriptures and the Fathers. He said that repentance rightly began with fear, even fear of punishment, and to this whole argument Luther answered that filial fear rather than servile fear of punishment was the beginning of wisdom. But Dr Eck cited Augustine, Cassian, and others to show that it referred to fear, even to servile fear, and Martin admitted that even servile fear was the beginning of wisdom, but through grace. Eck fought back, for then grace would come before the beginning of grace; he said that 'wisdom' in that passage was to be interpreted as charity according to Augustine and Bernhard. Whether his objection was correct or not will be up to the appointed judges' verdict.

Finally Eck objected to conclusions 4 and 5 (that punishment was not lessened when a sin was remitted), saying that the pope could substitute indulgences for a penalty imposed as satisfaction, and the priest could compensate for it with an injunction, so that the penitent gave satisfaction for the sin not only to the church by also to God. But Dr Martin fought against this, and for this reason the matter was deferred to the verdict of the judges. The lords, however, requested that the rather difficult conclusions should be dealt with more quickly. Hence it happened that much material remained untouched.

Eck faced Karlstadt once more[16] and tried to prove to him that the scholastic doctors do not disagree with the preachers, if he understood rightly what they said about the removal of an obstacle and about a man doing good as far as lies in him, in which case God helps him and he is saved. Eck furthermore defended himself on the point of predestination being not pertinent to the matter at hand. Karlstadt had argued wrongly when he said that the authorities on predestination did not pertain to works bringing eternal

* * * * *

15 Perhaps a reference to the papal bull 'Cum postquam' dated 9 November 1518, which noted that indulgences had been authorized by the Council of Vienne and reasserting the papal right to dispense merits of Christ 'by the power of the keys.'

16 On 14 July.

reward. He had well and correctly cited what he had read in Bernhard: *Take away free will, and there is nothing that can be saved.*[17] Karlstadt was indeed a corruptor of books if he wanted to read *quo* [how] for *quod* [that] in Bernhard. Karlstadt responded to this, and the matter was deferred to the judges.

In the end Karlstadt objected to Eck's second conclusion, claiming that the just man sins in every good work. This displeased Eck. [In that case, he said] St Lawrence had sinned on the rack, and St Paul on the cross.[18] And when Karlstadt cited Augustine and Jerome, Eck pressed him rather hard to identify the passage, for it could not be found in them;[19] rather Eck would prove the opposite on the basis of Jerome's work against the Pelagians, and after a great deal more was bandied back and forth, that matter, too, was relegated to the judges.

There remained the matter of repentance, which Dr Karlstadt had asked the lords to assign to him a long time ago, but because Dr Martin had left and he himself was in a hurry to go home,[20] he no longer wanted to oppose Eck. And thus the disputation ended as magnificently as it had begun, with a speech most eloquently delivered by that excellent man, Johannes Lang of Lemberg.[21]

* * * * *

17 Bernhard of Clairvaux *Liber de gratia et de libero arbitrio* 1.2.
18 I.e., when they suffered as martyrs. Eck, however, mentioned St Peter rather than St Paul (Seitz 230).
19 I.e., the statement that 'the just man always sinned in doing any good work' (Seitz 232).
20 In fact, Duke George needed the ballroom for a reception of his brother Joachim. The disputation therefore concluded on 15 July.
21 Johannes Lang of Lemberg (1485–1565?) obtained his MA in 1513/14 and was rector at the time of the disputation. His speech, entitled *Encomium theologiae disputationis* (In Praise of the Theological Disputation), was published together with Mosellanus's oration by Lotter in Leipzig (see above, note 7). Showing diplomatic skill, Lang gave equal praise to each of the three protagonists. Information about Lang's early career is confusing. Two men by the name of Johannes Lang, both of Lemberg, studied at the university. One matriculated in 1508 and obtained his BA in 1510; the other matriculated in 1498 and obtained his BA in 1499. A note on the matriculation register would suggest that the second man is the author of the *Encomium*. The note says that he obtained his MA in 1514 (but this is an unusually long interval between BA and MA!), was rector in 1519, and left Leipzig to study medicine in Pisa, where he obtained a doctorate in 1522. On his return he served as physician at the court of the Count Palatine until his death. Cf. O. Clemen, 'Eine Gelehrtenfamilie in den Leipziger Universitätsmatrikel,' *Neues Archiv für Sächsische Geschichte und Altertumskunde* 45 (1924): 149–59.

You want to know, most learned Capito, who will be the judges. And that too I will not conceal from you. For prior to the disputation Eck and Karlstadt met in the presence of the councillors of the most illustrious Duke George of Saxony, etc., and of the rector and council of the university. Eck said he was willing and prepared to dispute and would do everything according to the instruction of the lords, as long as Karlstadt consented to leave the judgment to the university or designated another judge. Karlstadt, however, was just as prepared to dispute, asking that trustworthy notaries write down what was said, to which Eck immediately agreed, if only Karlstadt agreed with him on a judge. Therefore it was decided by the lords that neither of them should leave until they had agreed on a judge. Father Martin, however, did not want to accept any university's judgment, although Eck gave him the choice of practically all universities in Germany, Italy, France, and England, excepting only two. Luther, in turn, proposed to hand the contents of the disputation immediately over to the printers for dissemination, so that each reader was free to pass his own judgment. But the most illustrious prince's counsellors, and the council of the university, did not want to admit him to the disputation on those terms. And so the day ended with Luther unwilling to dispute, but later he was induced by the counsel of friends to return and undertook to take Karlstadt's place in the disputation. When that business was finished, Eck suggested to the counsellors of the most illustrious prince that the judges should be selected while Duke George was still present (for the illustrious prince was often present at the disputation). Then Martin suggested Paris and Erfurt, which Eck, too, accepted, as long as the associates of Martin, the [Augustinian] Eremites in Erfurt were not among the judges. But after the duke had left, Martin expressed the wish that the whole council of the university should render judgment, whether they were in civil law, or medicine, or philosophy, and that the members of the Dominican and Franciscan orders be excluded. But it seemed unfair to Eck that physicians or members of another profession should judge about the most important theological issues, yet the matter was by mutual consent left in the hands of the illustrious prince.

These are the matters about which I wanted to inform you, and you can put your firm trust in them. No doubt people will not be lacking, who are solely motivated by the desire to win and will graft on a few things to make it appear that they have won, however great the damage is to the truth. You, however, can trust in this report, for these are the facts and this was the order in which they proceeded in the theological disputation held at Leipzig. I vow, moreover, that I have not written either out of inclination or hatred for any party, but have merely reported how things happened, and our most illustrious Prince George will vouch for it, and his most just and wise counsellors, and all will be confirmed by the council of our University of Leipzig. And when the disputation will be published in future, the truth of what I say will become manifest.

Farewell, best and most learned of men among our friends, and give my regards if you have an opportunity to Dr Johannes Oecolampadius,[22] who is uncommonly learned in the field of the three Muses, and to Beatus Rhenanus[23] and Bruno[24] and all our friends. At Leipzig, in my house, 31 July, in the year 1519. With grace.

Letter 31a: [Before August 1519], Basel, Capito to Christoph von Utenheim

> This is the significantly revised and polished version of Ep. 7, which appeared in the reprint of J. Clichtove's *Elucidatorium ecclesiasticum* (Basel: Froben, 1519), fols. a2r–a2v. The changes were presumably made in 1519 in preparation for that edition, although the date at the end of the letter remained unchanged. The preface is reprinted in Johann Erhard Kapp, *Kleine Nachlese größten Theils noch ungedruckter und sonderlich zur Erläuterung der Reformationsgeschichte nützlichen Urkunden* (Leipzig, 1733), Part 4, 496–500.

To the reverend father in Christ and his lord, Christoph von Utenheim, bishop of Basel and his clement lord, from W. Fabritius Capito, greetings.

In the last two years,[1] during which I held the office of preacher in your most splendid church in Basel, whose most meritorious leader you are, reverend father, I have often and seriously questioned the origin of such great vices in the clergy. It occurred to me that it lay in the carelessness of the leaders. For they are said to wink at any impious practices whatsoever and thus increase the licentiousness of the sinner. Such licentiousness is diminished whenever they fight back or certainly, if they are unwilling to do that, whenever they pretend to fight back against those evildoers. For sinfulness is contained when impudent people are not encouraged, when they are not applauded, when they are not admitted into the familiar circle and hospitality of the prelates. But perhaps they may be excused for not wanting to undertake a matter which they have no hope to complete successfully, even if they strain every nerve. For these vices appear to have grown robust

* * * * *

22 For Oecolampadius see above, Ep. 11, note 16.
23 For Beatus Rhenanus see above, Ep. 3, note 9.
24 I.e., Amerbach, see above, Ep. 11, note 18.

1 See above, Ep. 7, note 1.

through time and have grown roots too deep to be pulled up or killed off. However, I believe that one must nevertheless make an effort, for in any business more is achieved with attentive vigilance than with inattentive carelessness. Nor do I say this because I doubt the application and faithful attention of all bishops. I will not deny that many of them act like true bishops, Your Honour being one of them. There are indeed bishops adorned with apostolic gifts who unceasingly keep in mind the care of their flock and even more so when they see that it is plagued by an irremediable contagion. For who will cure them, if they lack even an understanding of their illness? Who will imbue a man with wisdom, who cannot see the emptiness of his ignorance? That is the state of a large part of our ordained clergy. They know nothing, either sacred or profane, but they claim for themselves a knowledge of all things. They define everything, they impose the rules of life on everyone, yet accept no rules themselves and seemingly aim at appearing rather than being pious. Indeed we have practically no idea of our office (for I must speak the truth) and are Levites, carrying like the sons of Cath[2] hidden burdens of mysteries. We do not contemplate Christ's grace hidden under the cover of figures, that is, we are ignorant of the goal of the Christian religion. We mouth solemn prayers without care or thought, we sacrifice without inner involvement, we bark thousands of psalms without noting their allegorical meaning. We are like the Euthetian heretics,[3] whom Saint Jerome rebuffs. That is the origin of our disdain for what is holy and our pleasure in what is harmful.

Josse Clichtove, a blameless and learned theologian, wishing to remove this worst of evils has written four books entitled, according to the contents *Elucidation of the Church*, in which he explains appropriately and lucidly the whole meaning of the divine song, citing relevant scriptural passages. For what can be more suited to reforming morals than an understanding of the holy things, in which we are engaged every day for so many hours? Without them the Christian religion is shut out, it seems, and a window opened up to impious thoughts bringing back the superstitious nonsense of the Jews. For common sense cries out against the errors that have been generally handed down, against the large number of empty ceremonies, in which we place

* * * * *

2 See above, Ep. 7, note 3.
3 Presumably a corruption for 'Euchitian heretics' (Massalians) criticized by Jerome in *Adversus Pelagianos* (PL 23, col. 518). Cf. Erasmus's scholia ad locum in Froben's edition of 1520, vol. 3, 140A: '... Massilians, called Euchitians in Greek because they pray incessantly' (Massilianis, qui Graece dicti sint Euchitae, quod indesinenter orarent).

stem and stern, as they say,[4] so many confraternities which are lucrative to priests, and two thousand other practices of the same kind full of absurd nonsense, so that it seems there is hardly any difference between denying God and acknowledging him in this manner.

It is my plan to dedicate the *Elucidation* to you, reverend father, as a gift. If you consider its usefulness it is not unworthy of your episcopal title, especially in our time, according to the Hebrew proverb, [Heb.] *tov aruchat yaraq*,[5] as they say, that is, fresh greens are a sweet meal to him whose *stomach is rumbling*, as the famous author says.[6] There is nothing more timely, nothing more necessary than these commentaries, which allow us to understand sacred ceremony, to cleanse our untoward feelings, to bring peace to our mind, to recall us to virtue. Once the reader understands them, he commits the sacred words to memory and digests their meaning, converting them into energy, nerves, and blood. Therefore I beg you, best prelate: deign to recommend these excellent commentaries to the multitude of priests that they may know the mysteries of the office they have accepted. In this manner you will open up the door, allowing piety to return to the clergy, and will place the earth at her feet, like Antaeus, as they say.[7] There is no one, if I am not mistaken, who can deny that reading the commentaries has made him a better man and given him more understanding of his duty and inspired him to look to salvation, unless he has hardened to stone, as did the obstinate Pharaoh,[8] or is like Gryllus[9] whom sorcery changed into a pig and who could not be persuaded at all by Ulysses to wish himself changed into a man again. But I predict better results for us. Farewell in Jesus Christ. May he long preserve you for the task of restoring piety and virtue. Basel, 11 August 1517.

Letter 32: 3 November 1519, Basel, Capito to Albert of Brandenburg

This is the dedicatory letter to Capito's translation of John Chrysostom, *Parainesis prior* (Basel: Froben, 1519). The text of the letter is on pp. 3–10.

Albert of Brandenburg (1490–1545) held a number of important church offices: archbishop of Magdeburg and administrator of Halberstadt (from 1513),

* * * * *

4 Cicero *Ad familiares* 16.24.1; Erasmus *Adagia* 1.1.8.
5 See above, Ep. 7, note 5.
6 Ennius *Ann.* 1.1.
7 See above, Ep. 7, note 6.
8 See above, Ep. 7, note 7.
9 See above, Ep. 7, note 8.

archbishop of Mainz (from 1514), and cardinal (from 1518). As archbishop of Mainz he was one of the German electors and, ex officio, arch-chancellor of the empire. Albert surrounded himself with humanists and was originally sympathetic towards a reformation of the church. Capito, who entered Albert's service in 1520, was seen by many as instrumental in shaping Albert's attitude towards Luther. He resigned in 1523 when his pro-Lutheran attitude made his position untenable. Albert subsequently turned against the Reformation. Nevertheless, he was active in attempts to negotiate religious peace until 1534. Thereafter his stand hardened and he firmly rejected compromise.

Wolfgang Fabritius Capito to the most reverend father in Christ and most illustrious prince, Lord Albert, cardinal of the Roman church of St Chrysogonus, bishop of Mainz and Magdeburg, prince elector of the Holy Empire, primate and administrator of Halberstadt, margrave of Brandenburg, etc., greetings:

Hail, most reverend father and illustrious prince, outstanding ornament of the most august college of cardinals! The favour your princely munificence has bestowed on me is commendable on two counts: its magnitude and its fortunate nature. For although anything, however paltry, is superlative when it is given to a man who does not deserve it, what shall we say when it is conferred on him who was not even known to exist earlier on. Your Highness recently gave an example of your memorable generosity when you bestowed a favour on me, who was entirely unknown and of whose existence you had known nothing a little while ago. Encouraged as well as aided by my friends and supporters, I came to Mainz[1] to seek what they call 'royal requests'[2] with respect to a benefice at the cathedral in Basel. I sought access first through Your Fatherly Reverence, that I may gain the favour of the newly elected king[3] through your favour or, if I had obtained my request by other means, to make sure that you would not be reluctant to confirm it with your approval – the validity of these things depends entirely on you, for you are in charge of the royal coffers according to the constitution of old.[4] Of course I never doubted your good will or the benevolence of

* * * * *

1 In June 1519. See his letter to Spalatinus from Mainz (Ep. 29 above).
2 By custom the newly elected ruler conceded to each elector the right to nominate candidates for a certain number of church posts (twelve in the case of Albert).
3 I.e., Emperor Charles V, elected in 1519; in theory he remained king until crowned emperor, in Charles's case, in 1530.
4 The Golden Bull of 1356; the archbishop of Mainz was arch-chancellor ex officio.

Your Most August Highness. It is well known to me: for the past six years[5] I have heard your praises sung, which acknowledge your munificence and your virtuous actions. This was not the least of the reasons why I was eager to come to Mainz. For virtue and excellence have their own attraction, and especially excellence in men who are of such an old family, illustrious for its royal fathers and forefathers. Well, I thought to myself, if nothing comes of it, it will be worth undertaking the journey to see that pillar of religion and nobility. And I will not regret the effort or the cost. Indeed, my bold enterprise succeeded. I went from the starting to the finishing line, finding not only a patron but the prince himself, not only a well-inclined man but a benefactor and the guarantor of the desired advantage. O newly prosperous fortune! Or rather, o incomparable princely benevolence! As soon as Your Illustrious Paternity had heard the request I made through Ulrich Hutten[6] and the physician Heinrich Stromer,[7] who took all this trouble on my behalf, the reverend father, Tommaso Cajetan, cardinal of St Sixtus arrived unexpectedly.[8] As you were leaving to attend on him, you answered my sponsors that you could easily approve their request, but this would hardly be in the interest of Capito; such requests merely yielded courtly promises which are usually 'windeggs.'[9] You had made up your mind to nominate me as courtier before the future king, and among the number of courtiers that no one could refuse. For custom or law allowed each elector to nominate twelve men, I believe. You nominated me not only for the benefice in Basel but also

* * * * *

5 I.e., since Albert's elevation to the see of Mainz.
6 For Hutten see above, Ep. 30, headnote. He was in Albert's service from 1517 to 1521. Albert dismissed him in the fall of 1520 under pressure from the papal court (see below, Ep. 60a), but kept him on his payroll until 1521.
7 Heinrich Stromer (1482–1542) studied and taught at Leipzig (MA 1501), then obtained a medical doctorate (1511). He became Albert's court physician in 1516 and served him until 1519. He resided in Leipzig for the remainder of his life. Sympathetic towards the Reformation, he travelled with Capito to Wittenberg in 1521 in an attempt to head off a confrontation between Albert and Luther over the former's sale of indulgences. When Saxony turned Protestant in 1539, Luther visited Leipzig and was hospitably received by Stromer.
8 The Dominican Tommaso de Vio, Cardinal Cajetan (1469–1534) studied and taught in Bologna. He advanced rapidly in the service of Pope Julius II and was made cardinal in 1517. In 1518 Pope Leo X sent him as legate to the imperial court. He examined Luther at the Diet of Augsburg in October 1518, returning to Rome in August 1519. Cajetan also went on embassies for Leo's successors, Adrian VI and Clement VII. He was an accomplished theologian and the author of numerous theological and philosophical treatises.
9 Proverbial expression for 'nonsense.' Cf. Erasmus *Adagia* 3.7.22.

another in the city of Mainz, to which I had never aspired. Moreover, you promised me a choice among the three best positions there.[10] When my friends reported this to me, I was astounded, uncertain whether such great men were making fun of my simple mind. Finally I collected from their expression, their mien, and their very words that there was no underlying conceit, that everything corresponded to the truth. Can you imagine the state your little protégé was in? What pleasure he experienced and, in turn, what great surprise took hold of him in his excitement? I silently asked myself: For what god (I am tempted to say) has sent this love for me[11] into the heart of a prince who is in every sense one of the great? Coming to my senses again, and considering the matter more closely I realized that it was no divine action, nor miraculous. For I know very well that I am not important enough to merit nature's course being disturbed on my behalf. Indeed, I am not overly generous in proclaiming miracles, to which others are too readily inclined, not to say, too insolent, when they say and assert with much ado that something surpasses the oracles of the prophets or surpasses the apostolic epistles, and assert it from the pulpit, where only the gospel should be proclaimed.

And to whom do I owe this great clemency of Your Reverend Paternity towards this unimportant man? For one thing, I would say, to the Muses and the Graces – not that they are my familiar companions, but they dwell in perpetuity in Hutten's heart as in a commodious home and often visit the beautiful lodging of Heinrich Stromer's mind, who has the foremost knowledge in medicine, as if it were a most beautiful lodging. The doors of the Muses are always open, and they generously received Fabritius as their guest and clothed him, it seems, in tailor-made kudos, lest my crudeness put me at a disadvantage. In this they embraced the fairness of Plato rather than the haughty Stoic severity of Augustine.[12] For the latter calls a little white lie on behalf of a dear friend a sin, whereas the former, who is more experienced in human affairs, calls a useful lie a duty indeed. Such great witnesses have easily convinced you, a prince who loves not only every man of learning such as your

* * * * *

10 See Albert's instructions to the papal notary Karl von Miltitz to see that 'Wolfgang Fabritius Capito and Baptista Johann Wesamer, our familiars, be created canons on account of their good character and singular industry: three for Capito and two for Wesamer, the choice of churches to be theirs' (the text of the instructions is in Kalkoff *Capito*, 139–40).

11 Capito is using poetic language reminiscent of, e.g., Virgil *Aeneid* 3.38 ('Quisnam deus ... oppulit').

12 Plato, e.g. *Laws* 735a; Augustine *Enchiridion* 18.6.

courtiers Hutten and Stromer, and Erasmus of Rotterdam, the ornament of
the Christian world, whom, I understand, you have invited many times to
come to you,[13] offering him the most generous stipend – you love not only
them but also anyone however unsuccessful in literary enterprises, such as
myself. For this is the peculiar characteristic of perfect virtue, especially intellectual virtue, that it measures others by its own stature. Our Hutten, who
was most successfully educated from childhood on, hunted down the beau-
ties of both languages when he was still a young man, and made a full assault
from the citadel of eloquence. He is most talented in all arts and conquered in
a short while the difficult study of both laws. And he measures Capito by his
own stature, the slender shoot, that is, against the fully grown oak, and rendering generous rather than true judgment he attributes to me erudition
together with knowledge of old and recent theology. For although I have
always been thirsting for elegant learning, I have achieved it least of all, nor
could I achieve it. For as a child I was given over to teachers who could teach
nothing except what had to be unlearned again and whom I exchanged for
still worse teachers. How much time did I give to authors such as Tartaretus,
Orbellius, Brulifer, and Bricot![14] How much time did I spend on the complexities of Scotus![15] How much on jurisprudence which contributes to theology
nowadays, that is, towards income. Nor would I regret the effort, if it had not
been so preposterous. Finally when I was no longer a young man (too late, I
fear) I attempted to learn what I should have known as a boy. The marrow of
my mind which should have been nourished by the fertile reading of authors
perished when I was confronted with thousands of arid, quibbling questions
and nonsense. As a sheep loses its fleece in the midst of thorn bushes, I lost my
natural talent, which was not completely without merit, amid the thorny conclusions, corollaries, propositions, and replications. I gladly acknowledge
[my shortcomings], to make known to all the good nature of those who have
clothed their naked friend and to show what motivated their gesture of good
will. For the friendly generosity that prompted their tribute will be the more
obvious the less I am worthy of the tribute. And Your Reverend Paternity will
be judged all the more generous for continuing in the patronage of a man who
has been unsuccessful in achieving literary skills, and doing so for the sake of

* * * * *

13 Cf. Allen, Epp. 614 and 661. The efforts were unsuccessful.
14 Standard medieval authors and textbooks, frequently made the butt of human-
    istic jokes and complaints; see, e.g., Erasmus, Allen, Ep. 1304:62: 'vix Holcot
    aut Bricot soloecisset crassius' or his *Ratio* (Holborn, 192): 'in Holcotis, Bricotis
    ac Tartaretis, in sophisticis cavillationibus.'
15 Duns Scotus. See above, Ep. 8 note 13.

literature, or rather for the sake of those luminaries of our age, such as the men who sang my praises. I am now and shall always be most willingly in their debt, for you deign to look on my worthless self and every day almost bury your old favours under new ones. For you wish to attract me to your inner circle which I am anxious and eager to join, for it is illuminated, as it were, first through the illustrious majesty of Your Highness, and especially through those flashes of your genius, from which even night could receive some light.

The venerable and noble lord, Dean Lorenz Truchsess,[16] a man whose mind is most skilful in handling affairs and at the same time refined, has brought me a message in which you recommended to him that I be given the office of preacher.[17] Although you know how much they themselves favour me, whose task it is to deliberate about appointing a preacher, you nevertheless asked that they invite me to accept the position for your sake. Konrad of Liebenstein,[18] canon of the cathedral chapter, as they say, a man of stout heart and faith, wrote to me, saying nearly the same thing. I believe he heard it from the most learned and most noble Dietrich Zobel,[19] the canon and supervisor of studies of your metropolitan church, who is in charge of the sacred responses at Your Reverend Paternity's court. Finally Hutten wrote about the higher stipend that goes with the office through your clemency, which provides me with more tolerable circumstances and peace of mind, and Hutten is in a position and usually does report what is certain, for you use him as your private secretary, and he is of all men least given to hypocrisy. Such was the powerful influence of men of probity and learning who persuaded Your Highness, spinning out their kind dreams about me or

* * * * *

16 Lorenz Truchsess of Bommersfeld (1473–1543), dean of the cathedral chapter at Mainz and holder of a number of prebends in Würzburg, Worms, and elsewhere. He was a powerful figure in Mainz, acting ex officio as representative (*Statthalter*) of Albert during the latter's absences. He eventually had a falling out with the archbishop over his financial administration and was forced to resign his deanship for a pension. In 1530 he left Mainz for Würzburg.

17 The text of Capito's official appointment as cathedral preacher, dated 10 February 1520, is in Herrmann, 207–8.

18 Konrad of Liebenstein (d. 1536), canon from 1517, succeeded Zobel (see next note) as supervisor of studies of the chapter on his death in 1531.

19 Dietrich Zobel of Giebelstadt (d. 1531) held canonries at St Thomas's in Strasbourg and in the cathedral chapter at Mainz. He obtained a doctorate in civil and canon law at Heidelberg (1500). He served as vicar-general to successive archbishops in Mainz and acted as their legal and political consultant. Zobel had ties with humanistic circles and advocated moderation in the religious debate.

otherwise decking me out to my advantage. Let them consider how good this was for their reputation; it was certainly good for me, for they gave me a most benevolent patron through their own limitless benevolence, a patron whom I had not even greeted in person before, an advantage that I thought was no small addition to my fortune.

While I was considering this, I was suddenly overcome by feelings of anxiety and helplessness. I was wondering how I could show myself worthy of the office. On the one hand, my crippling ignorance deterred me, for if I venture to write something, I shall make many people aware that my talent is weak and sterile, although on the surface at any rate it gives the impression of some fertility. On the other hand, I have no opportunity to show my gratitude and attention in any other way, and so I decided to risk my reputation, which is in itself puny and insubstantial rather than fail to return thanks. Indeed it is rather impudent to repay true favours with mere nonsense. But what could I do? I cannot repay it, I shall yield therefore whatever good is in me entirely to Your Amplitude. Thus, greatest prince and epitome of nobility and religion, accept the harvest of the poor field that is my mind, even if it bears little fruit and is hardly ploughed, for I have nothing else to give. I labour to consign the harvest, if it has any worth, to the memory of posterity, wholly in honour of Your Highness. But there will be no remembrance anywhere among the nations, for human effort dies with us, divine force survives beyond the allotted time; but my talent, I fear, is even sub-human. Thus when they called me, it would have been Capito's duty to obey your command and to become preacher there, but fate detains me at this time in Basel, although I do not refuse to make the effort I owe you in Mainz. I am merely putting it off[20] until a better opportunity presents itself to take a task in hand that is more suited to my powers. I know my powers cannot do what is perhaps easy for some, but almost impossible for others, that is, for common people: so great is the diversity of our natural dispositions, and everyone uses what talent he has. May Your Reverend Lordship fare well, great prince, and may you remain unharmed in Christ for the benefit of piety and letters. Basel, 3 November in the year 1519.

Letter 32a: 16 November 1519, Basel, Capito to Albert of Brandenburg

This letter is not included in Millet's list. It follows the preface (above, Ep. 32)

* * * * *

20 He was formally installed as preacher 10 February 1520 (by proxy, see text of protocol in Herrmann, 207–8) and moved to Mainz at the end of April 1520.

on 11–16 of Chrysostom's *Paraenesis prior* (Basel: Froben, 1519). Both the prefatory letter and the *Paraenesis* are included in the *Opera omnia* of Chrysostom published by Cratander in August 1522. The letter is omitted, however, in an expanded edition of 1525. See below, Ep. 109, for Cratander's request for additional translations from Chrysostom.

To the most reverend father and most illustrious prince Lord Albert, archbishop of Mainz, cardinal, etc. duke of Brandenburg etc.: W. Fabritius Capito's Preface to the *Prior Paraenesis* addressed to Theodorus the apostate.

I have translated the *Prior Paraenesis* of St John Chrysostom from a very old Greek manuscript. He addressed it to Theodorus who deserted the monastic life. In this piece our most eloquent author uses his wonderful force of persuasion as if he were declaiming before an audience in a school. This was very common among the ancient authors who combined in equal parts facility of speech with a knowledge of the scriptures, as is particularly evident among the Greeks in the example of Chrysostom, among the Latins in the example of Jerome. For both men imbued their works throughout with a rhetorical spirit. At times they pretended to deal with enemies and affected a hostile spirit, as if they were fighting for their lives in a battle line, or with needy friends, supporting them in their grief.[1] We find either exhortations to work or precepts to avoid error, or other things pertaining to Christ's doctrines, which they treat with closely structured arguments, with admirable copia and felicitous style, all but compelling the reader to feel spiritual joy or be industrious or follow the correct observances or whatever they had in mind. Because of these efforts, they kept their eloquence from flagging and weakening through disuse, for nothing dries up more easily than eloquence which must be maintained by continuous practice. Later they gave their skills honourable names to avoid the suspicion that adheres to that art and destroys faith in persuasive arguments. In this they were quite different from the professors of our age. For in the same measure that we are strangers to all rhetorical skill, we wish to create the appearance that we do nothing without skill. To a great extent everything is spoken according to rule, with many scriptural quotations piled up in a disorderly heap – quotations that have no relevance to the matter at hand. Many times we croak the name of Aristotle or Justinian,[2] many times we bring forth ques-

* * * * *

1 The structure of this and the following sentence is loose.
2 An allusion to the two principal authors taught at medieval universities. Capito here postures as a humanist criticizing the scholastic system.

tions, arguments, and replies, quoting doctors and doctors again, and two thousand bits of nonsense of that kind – as if we were moonstruck. They fight with both feet, as the saying goes,[3] contending that this is how it ought to be, as if Christ relied on human aid and the truth did not have its own force and charm by which it can insinuate itself unless it is infected with a spurious eloquence.

Those others [the church fathers] open up to us the apostles' mind in their published books, or they expound the scriptures in the spirit of Christ, or they explain our faith soberly and purely, or they range widely over the field of rhetoric and bring forth effective and substantial arguments. They speak of faith, piety, blameless morals, tolerance, and other such precepts of Christ, and they do it without impudently defining whatever pleases them. Sometimes, I admit, it is well to rouse hearers to fight against perfidious evils, but at other times these fights are only figments of imagination, and the writers build up some Antaeus[4] to defeat with Herculean fortitude, of course merely to exercise their style. For style develops language facility, and likewise is the best custodian of that facility once it has been acquired. Nor were the fathers hemmed in as we are in the narrow straits of Jewish tradition. They had freedom,[5] as long as the precepts of Christ were observed, to wander at large in any region that is open to a sane judgment. And these men of grave authority sparingly used their judgment. They did not wander off into strange territory, ineptly venturing into fairyland; they did not mix in bombastic and turgid stuff. On the contrary, they disguised their erudition, especially the Greeks. And as far as I know, the Latins, too, with two exceptions: Jerome and Augustine, who were, as it seems, at times rather fond of praise and permitted themselves to misuse scripture,[6] giving it their own preconceived sense, but they did so with great modesty. Hence they prudently made it a rule to distinguish between divine precepts and human decrees. For the latter are uncertain, while the former stand firm and are constant, and one must not believe even an angel who speaks against them. For the decisions of human beings are changing every hour, however strongly reinforced by the bulwarks of tyranny; what is God's, however, cannot be vitiated. The writers differ in their opinions, but they all cast their

* * * * *

3 Lit. 'with every foot.' Cf. Erasmus *Adagia* 3.1.34.
4 See above, Ep. 7, note 6.
5 Capito uses the slogans of the Reformation, in which Christian freedom is opposed to 'Jewish' legalism.
6 I.e., twist its meaning to their purpose. Similarly Erasmus in his *Ratio* (Holborn, 287).

vote for the truth. Each of them has his peculiar gift. They are not easily combined into one; thus anyone who attempts to harmonize them will be frustrated. Mixing them all up, he will put together a body of odd proportions that is barely hanging together, a monstrous shape. In the same way the centos of pagan authors are of help to those who put them together to aid their memory and group things in distinct categories, but of no use to others. For they often give men of little learning confidence, leading them to the harmful conviction that they are knowledgeable, as if they could have knowledge of all things, when they have touched nothing except *with the tip of their lips*, as the saying goes,[7] and as if that could properly merit the name learning. No one could understand, on the basis of Gratian's miscellany,[8] the force and ardour of Jerome, the vehemence of Chrysostom, the subtle mind of Hilary, the apostolic dignity of Cyprian; no one on the other hand could fail to understand the effort made by Gratian and Isidore.[9] But that industrious man put material together in compendious form, perhaps to aid his memory or, if he wrote it for public use, he did so without prejudice to anyone, even if his opinion is now placed at a par with the oracular words of Christ himself. Who will ever find in Peter of Lombard[10] the gifts of even one of the old writers except, perhaps, Augustine, if he does reflect Augustine. Indeed, the three or four words he has plucked from him draw their force from the context of the speech, whereas you can glimpse nothing definite from an arrangement of excerpts, except the merest shadow. After all, a limb plucked from the remainder of the body is bloodless and of no use. Add to this that writers sometimes play clever games. They speak clearly enough to the acute reader, but they often speak cautiously to avoid giving a handle to slanderers who are only waiting for an opportunity to inflict harm. Therefore these things escape the attention of readers who are not alert, indeed they are never understood except by those who are used to their mode of expression. Yet I am not afraid to promise that, for the most part, the divine talent of Chrysostom is clearly discernable in this particular work, the *Paraenesis*. For he perfectly balances two conflicting ideas: the

* * * * *

7 Lucian *Apologia* 6 and *Dialogi meretricii* 7.3; Erasmus *Adagia* 1.9.93.
8 I.e., the twelfth-century collection of ecclesiastical law *Concordia discordantium canonum* by Gratian. His work became the standard introductory textbook at law schools.
9 The best-known work of Isidore of Seville (d. 636) is *Etymologiae*, an encyclopedic work that became the principal sourcebook of the Middle Ages.
10 Peter of Lombard (d. 1116), author of the *Sentences*, a standard textbook for theologians.

severity of the punishment with the clemency of the judge, the atrocity of the crime with the abundance of mercy, all hell for a sin of which you have not repented with universal forgiveness if you repent. He allows no one to think of God as wrathful and an avenger ready to strike you down, or conversely, to think that sins will go unpunished that have not been wiped out by penitence.

I think I can guess why Ambrogio of Camaldoli[11] refrained from translating this piece, although he translated the second *Paraenesis* addressed to the same man and the other pieces that precede this one in the Greek codices. It is more difficult than the others because of the very complex argumentation, but that apparently is not what discouraged the learned Ambrogio. What deterred him in my opinion was the assertion of certain opinions which are at variance with doctrines as they are generally understood, to give you one example: releasing a man from the remaining debt, once his sin has been remitted – a debt which we exact mercilessly, as if God were not readier to forgive than some embittered women. For we see that even women are sometimes appeased by one word and soften their stand, especially if you yield to them and submit yourself to those who are angry. Likewise, a man who is generous does not take revenge for an injury in such an exacting manner.

I found that this *Paraenesis* has no patron and yet stands in need of a patron because of its dignified and liberal treatment which is hateful to certain carping men. It is in need of an uncommon patron who has the power to illuminate the obscure with his majesty and help those who are not in favour with his favour, and who can support the weak with his authority, and therefore I have dedicated it to you, reverend father, most illustrious prince, for no one is more suitable to receive this gift. Nature, the kind parent of the world, and fortune, which is often rather unfair, have, with a joint effort, shaped you to perfection. Nature gave you a most generous lineage, an acute mind, and a body that is elegant as well as unimpaired in strength; fortune has allowed you to rule over free men, to surpass princes in power no less than in prudence and splendid virtue. Your ecclesiastical dignity shines forth among the pillars of faith; the pope, vicar of Christ, is the only man whom you acknowledge as your superior on earth. And I shall be satis-

* * * * *

11 Ambrogio Traversari (1386–1439), a monk at a Camaldolese monastery near Florence, was a leading patristic scholar. He served as a papal legate at the Council of Basel in 1435 and also attended the Council of Ferrara-Florence (1438–9), which relied on his knowledge of Greek in efforts to heal the Greek schism.

fied that you have done your duty as Maecenas if you as much as scan my little work, for I make no inopportune demands and [hope you will inspect it] when you are at liberty and when Your Eminence, who is beleaguered by so many cares and overwhelmed by so many waves of business, has sufficient leisure to do so. May Your Reverend and Illustrious Paternity fare well and be an ornament to Capito's studies and continue to foster him, as you have begun. Basel, 16 November, 1519.

Letter 33: 23 November 1519, Augsburg, Johannes Oecolampadius to Capito

Printed in *Briefe Oekolampads* 1:102, #66

[*Summary*]: Oecolampadius begins by expressing his delight in his friendship with Capito. He is sending him, along with this letter, a copy of Jodocus Textoris's *Christiani poenitentis confessio* in an effort to have the work reprinted either by Johann Froben or Andreas Cratander. If they are unwilling, he would like Capito to send it back to him because he could easily find other printers willing to undertake the task.

Letter 34: [Mid-November 1519, Basel], Capito to Ulrich von Hutten

The letter itself is lost. A fragment is printed in *Hutteni opera* 1:315, #145. For Hutten, see above, Ep. 30, headnote.

... I will undertake to obtain a doctorate in pontifical law, as they call it, in order to establish my authority of course. You are aware that this is the most sacred of aims. There are people who consider it a vice to be a theologian and civil at the same time, as though it were necessary for a theologian to deprive himself of all that makes him cultured ...

Letter 35: [1519], Sélestat, Beatus Rhenanus to Capito

Printed in *Briefwechsel des Beatus Rhenanus*, 562

[*Summary*]: If Capito is dissuading Zwingli from editing his *Dialogus*, Beatus does not want to take the blame. He does not object to the publication of the other books which Capito has shown him, but they must not interfere with the printing of the Cyprian edition. He does not want to burden Froben with them since his schedule is already full. Beatus regrets that the edition of Cyprian is proceeding so slowly since Erasmus is expected to send some works shortly. He warns Capito not to betray the author of the *Ars et modus inquirendi et damnandi haereticos* [i.e., Crotus Rubeanus], a work which will be too caustic for the taste of the monks. Everyone would laugh if Erasmus's work were to appear with Capito's annotations (cf. above, Ep. 9). Greetings to Caspar Hedio.

Letter 36: [End of February 1520, Louvain], Desiderius Erasmus to Capito

Printed in Allen 4:198–201, #1074 and CWE 7, Ep. 1074

[*Summary*]: Erasmus informs Capito that Edward Lee has published his *Annotations* against Erasmus's New Testament. He uses abusive and violent language to describe his critic. Lee 'wormed his way' into his acquaintance at Louvain and learned Greek with the sole purpose of criticizing Erasmus's New Testament. At first, Lee submitted critical notes to Erasmus, but he found most of them useless, except for two or three that made him reread and compare some passages. Lee resented Erasmus's attitude and sent no more notes, but spread the rumour in England that he had found three hundred places where Erasmus was wrong. The vice-chancellor of the university, Briard of Ath, has refused to arbitrate between them. Lee then threatened to publish his work and circulated it among his friends, while refusing Erasmus the opportunity to read it. Finally the book was brought to the attention of some of Erasmus's friends, who strongly advised Lee to make his peace with Erasmus. Instead of doing so, Lee spread the rumour that his work was being published at Bonn, while it was in fact being printed at Paris. Erasmus predicts that Lee will be laughed at by learned and judicious English scholars.

Letter 36a: [End of February or beginning of March 1520, Basel], Capito to N

This letter (see Millet, appendix 1) is known only from a citation in Scultetus 1:67. For the date of the letter see below, note 2.

... Here[1] things are continuously improving. The theologians and monks are on our side. When I recently gave an exposition of Matthew, I had a large and attentive audience.[2] Some threaten Luther with dire things. But [his]

* * * * *

1 I.e., Basel.
2 On 17 March 1520 Hedio wrote to Zwingli: 'Capito now preaches daily on the gospel according to Matthew to a very large audience' (CR 94, 279; Zwingli *Opera* 7, #13).

view is now too well received and cannot be uprooted by any force. There are people who accuse me of favouring Luther, although I studiously conceal it ...

Letter 37: 5 March 1520, Lucerne, Oswald Myconius to Capito

Oswald Myconius (1488–1552) studied at Basel (BA 1514) and taught at schools in Basel and Lucerne, from where this letter is written. In 1522 he was dismissed on account of his sympathies with Zwingli's reform ideas and moved to Zurich, where he taught at the cathedral school until 1531. He then became minister of St Alban's in reformed Basel and Oecolampadius's successor as professor of divinity at the university. The manuscript is in the Lutherhalle, Wittenberg, #00124/I6/156/173.

To the excellent theologian W. Fabritius Capito, most skilled in the three languages, promulgator of the divine word in the main church at Basel, his most reverend lord.

Hail. How much I was saddened by your quick departure recently, most learned and humane Capito, you may judge by my great joy in your presence. For I have never had a more pleasant experience during my stay in Lucerne than the sudden sight of you as I came out of church. No doubt you saw that I was almost too stunned to greet you and that it was on account of joy not fear. But is my emotion surprising when no sight is more pleasing to me than the sight of learned men, when no conversation is more pleasing, no company more pleasing? And even if considerable embarrassment overcomes me on seeing such men, I suppress it completely out of the love I bear them. And that is especially the case when I encounter luminaries of learning, among whom you are not the least. Far be it from me to flatter you, a skill I have never learned and have no desire to learn, which indeed is so averse from my nature, that nothing can be more averse. I say what my mind, which is very simple, tells me to say. You are the only man who, next to our Erasmus, the restorer of all good studies and especially of Christian theology, sustains humane letters and wonderfully promotes that true Christianity. You are able to do so because you have the intellectual armour, you are equipped with a knowledge of languages, youth, courage, and innumerable other features that are absolutely necessary for that business. It was with good reason, therefore, that I took such great pleasure in your sight, because you are a great scholar. But to tell the truth, I was almost more affected by your kindness than by your erudition. You made inquiries from me: a learned man from a boor, a great man from a cipher, a truly wise man from an ignoramus, indeed a celebrity from an unknown man. For you were known to me by sight long ago and also on account of your erudition, through your preaching and your books. But what about myself? Even if you saw me in the past, you did not care, for I was not worth caring about. I could not become known to you on account of my learning, for in my opinion, so help me God, I don't have a bit of learning. And yet you questioned me as if I was learned, you talked to me as if I knew something. I cannot tell you how much I appreciate that. I have sung your praises to all my friends, especially Zwingli,[1] as indicated by his letter in which he asked me to greet you most cordially in his name. He thought you had not yet left, for I wrote to him in a great hurry telling him everything about our meeting. I have not forgotten about Chrysostom whom, you say, you have partly translated anew.[2] How I wish I had some influence over you in that respect! In that case my only order to you would be to finish what you have begun. And I would give this order not only because of the advantage to the public, but also because I know of nothing which could give you more merit in the eyes of God, not to mention that a new translation (in my opinion) would be easier for you than a revision of the old translation, which you had in mind then. But I am importuning you. I have written to let you know my feelings about you and ask you to take it in good part. Farewell for the sake of the Christian religion. I commend myself to you. Lucerne, on the Nones of March, 1520. I hope Hedio and Nepos[3] are well. I hear they are both learned and good men. Yours completely, Myconius.

Letter 38: 17 March 1520, Basel, Capito to Desiderius Erasmus

Printed in Allen 4:210–12, #1083 and CWE 7, Ep. 1083

[*Summary*]: Capito advises Erasmus to abandon the controversy with Lee. Lee's polemic will carry no weight and will not damage Erasmus's reputation. He notes that Lee has attempted to gain favour with him (see below,

* * * * *

1 Cf. Myconius's letters to Zwingli in January 1519 and March 1520 (*Opera* 7:102, 123).
2 Cf. the dedicatory letter, Ep. 32.
3 I.e., Caspar Hedio (see below, Ep. 47, headnote); Jacob Nepos or Naef (d. before 1527). In 1516 he was in the service of Erasmus on whose behalf he repeatedly travelled to Basel, Strasbourg, and other cities. In 1518 he accompanied Erasmus to Basel and there married the daughter of the printer Michael Furter. He taught Greek privately and at the university. He was often consulted by and collaborated with printers in Basel, especially with Cratander.

Ep. 54) and other German humanists but was unsuccessful in doing so. Hutten, Oecolampadius, and Zasius have expressed their displeasure with Lee's book. Capito feels that he cannot remain silent in this controversy, but will approach the subject in moderate terms. Capito will publish nothing until it has been approved by Rhenanus to avoid publishing anything too extreme.

Letter 39: 17 March 1520, [Basel], Capito to Martin Luther

Printed in WBr 2:70–1, #267

[*Summary*]: Capito praises Luther for what he has accomplished for humanity since only he can take a stand against the pontiffs and mendicants. So far he has protected Luther's interests [in Mainz]. Edward Lee has written against Erasmus. Luther's opponents in Louvain and Cologne have condemned some of his theses. Capito regrets being drawn into the dispute, but encourages Luther not to back away from the expected dangers. He sends greetings to Melanchthon, Karlstadt, and other theologians and asks Luther to direct letters for him to Mainz and to write to Hutten.

Letter 40: 14 April 1520, Basel, Capito to Ulrich Zwingli

Printed in Zwingli, *Briefwechsel* 1:299–300, #132

[*Summary*]: Capito informs Zwingli that Edward Lee has written a virulent attack against Erasmus. Capito intends to write a response on his way to Mainz. Erasmus has written and published an *Apologia* and has the support of scholars. Capito asks Zwingli to contact him via Johann Froben or Andreas Cratander. Greetings to Leo Jud. Capito is not disturbed by the affairs of the late Johann Liechtenburg. If he happens to meet his relative, he will offer an explanation. In an earlier letter to [Liechtenburg?] he spoke imprudently. He sends greetings to Oswald Myconius, from whom he has received a letter (see Ep. 37). He is too busy to reply at this time.

Letter 41: 15 April 1520, Basel, [Johann Werner von Mörsburg] to Capito

The writer comes from a noble family in Alsace (Mörsburg, Mörsberg, de Morimont) going back to the twelfth century. By the fifteenth century members of the family were in the service of the Habsburgs and acquired considerable property in the Basel area. Johann Werner (d. 1525), canon in the Basel cathedral chapter from 1500 and later its provost, studied in Paris and Freiburg. He was a patron of humanists but hostile towards the Reformation.

Thomas Murner dedicated two of his works to him. The manuscript of the letter, which is written in German, is in Ki.Ar. 25a, #7 in the Universitätsbibliothek, Basel.

To his most propitious [lord]: Dear Doctor, I let you know that I had two letters from you through Truchsess,[1] and I shall keep to your comforting and friendly message. I also ask to spare me any unnecessary costs, for I believe that there will be many *preces*[2] that will not be very useful. Baron Rudolf of Sultz,[3] my dear brother-in-law, has negotiated with Villinger[4] on my behalf. He is very willing that I should hire a solicitor for all, who might notify him when they are released, and that this solicitor be supplied with money to straighten things out in the chancery. That is the parting advice I had from him, when I took my leave. He is very favourably disposed towards my late father and well informed of his service to the house of Austria. He is well aware of that, and will, together with Paul,[5] be mindful of me. Therefore I ask this: would you go to Villinger and likewise tell him and say regarding the lawyer that he should be supplied with money to straighten things out in the chancery, and would you also hand over to him the letters that I sent you earlier and that are for him.

   Also, dear Doctor, there are 30 gulden outstanding. I beg you make them available to me by a safe and well-equipped messenger, but you may keep the 30 crowns and act in trust. I will requite it with complete loyalty. I commend you to God. Given on the Sunday of Quasimodo, in the year '20.

* * * * *

1 The Truchsesses were a prominent family in Basel. The reference is either to Lorenz Truchsess (see Ep. 32, note 16), the dean of the chapter, or Jakob Truchsess von Rheinfelden (d. ca. 1545), who is documented in the matriculation records of the Universities of Basel in 1513 and Dole in 1518. By 1520 he served as Capito's secretary. In the 1530s he served as a councillor to Duke Ulrich of Würtemberg.
2 'Requests,' see above Ep. 32, note.
3 Rudolf von Sultz (or Sulz; d. 1535) came from an old Swabian family with close ties to Schaffhausen and Zurich. He was at the time in the service of the emperor, trying to detach the Swiss from the French King. Later on he was in the service of Ferdinand and active on his behalf in the recatholization of the Tyrol.
4 Jakob Villinger (d. 1529), royal treasurer, an influential financial officer at the Habsburg court and chiefly responsible for financing Charles's campaign for the imperial crown in 1519.
5 Perhaps Paul von Armstorff (d. 1524), the imperial chamberlain, and a powerful voice at Charles's court at the time, although his influence waned after 1521.

Unfortunately our affairs are not going well.[6] We are in the greatest danger. I am worried that we may not be able to stand up for ourselves and will have to leave the city, and we are without solace, we know of no one who can help us, etc.

Hand on the remaining letters.

The provost of the cathedral in Basel.

Letter 42: 18 April 1520, Basel, Capito to Bernhard Adelmann

Printed in *Briefe Oekolampads* 1:114–16, #77

[*Summary*]: This is Capito's preface to Oecolampadius's *Index in tomos omnes divi Hieronymi cum interpretatione nominum Graecorum et Hebraeorum per Ioan. Oecolampadium theologum in ordinem digestus* (Basel, 1520). Though written in Latin, the *Index* includes Greek and Hebrew words together with the peculiar phrases and usages of each language. Capito praises Oecolampadius's modesty for desiring to have the work published anonymously. He criticizes the efforts of his scholastic predecessors, whose compilations show poor judgment. It took Oecolampadius less than a year to complete the index, thanks to his skill in Greek, Latin, and Hebrew. Readers who use the index will obtain easier access to Jerome's teachings. He thanks Adelmann for his patronage and asks for his continued support.

Letter 43: 30 April 1520, [Wittenberg], Martin Luther to Capito

Printed in WBr 2:93–5, #282

[*Summary*]: Luther begins with a modest disclaimer (see Capito's praise in Ep. 39). He wishes Capito could have joined the side of the reformers under more favourable conditions. Luther regrets that he became involved with Eck, who wants only to further his own glory. He considers Eck's response to Karlstadt to be mere nonsense. Luther has read Edward Lee's work, which has been inspired by the Louvain theologians. He is awaiting a reaction from the theologians of Louvain and Cologne to his *Responsio ad condemnationem per Lovanienses*. He has already written Hutten and would have

* * * * *

6 Perhaps a reference to the tensions between the city council and the ecclesiastical authorities. The struggle of the city to free itself from the influence of the bishop came to a head in 1521 (cf. *Eidgenössische Abschiede*, IV-1a, p. 8, February 1521).

written Oecolampadius, had a courier been available. Matthaeus Adrianus (see above, Ep. 11, note 21) has been hired to teach Hebrew at the university for a salary of one hundred gulden. Luther is amazed how sincerely Frederick of Saxony favours humanist learning. He recommends Egranus (see Ep. 47, note 7), the courier, to Capito.

Letter 44: [Before 28 April 1520, Basel], Gervasius [Schuler] to Capito

> Gervasius Schuler (1495–1563) studied in Basel and for a while was a teaching assistant to Paulus Phrygio in Sélestat. He held a number of clerical positions in Switzerland (Zurich, Bischweiler, Bremgarten, and Basel) and was parish priest of St Martin in Memmingen from 1533 to 1548. From 1548 to 1550 he stood in for Johann Haller at the cathedral in Zurich, then moved to Lenzburg where he was parish priest until his death. The manuscript of the letter is in Fr. Gr. I 19, #26 in the Universitätsbibliothek, Basel.

To the excellent Wolfgang Fabritius Capito, theologian and doctor, most famous both for the holiness of his life and his learning. Dearest friend:

Great love, loyal devotion and sincere good will urge me to write to you, fame-bearing Capito. I may have little talent for poetry, but these vapid lines should not displease you. I admit my poetry is bleak but my mind is candid and should be respected among friends. Your noble character gives you authority, you are affable, you are fair, you never spurn meeting anyone or hearing his requests. Skill in the three languages has made you a celebrity. You know the writings of Aristotle, the papal law, you are wise in holy writ, and in addition, your speech is in no way inferior to Cicero's. Why go on versifying?[1] Our triply-learned Erasmus wrote in his letter what I cannot express in verse.[2]

In a sudden burst of passion, I poured out rather than wrote, these verses, most excellent doctor. In addition I send you the orations of Cicero for which you asked me today.[3] I would send you all my books. Just command me, and it is right that I obey your commands. Write the name of Gervasius, your servant, in the list of Capito's clientele, even if I am unworthy of being included in that book. Farewell, true ornament of Germany and refuge of good letters.

* * * * *

1 The first paragraph is in verse, the second in prose.
2 See Erasmus's praise above, Ep. 4.
3 See also Capito's request to Cochlaeus below, Ep. 46.

Letter 45: [Beginning of May 1520, Mainz], Capito to Philip Melanchthon

Printed in *Melanchthons Briefwechsel* T1:76, #92

[*Summary*]: Capito reports with disapproval that Oecolampadius has entered a Brigittine monastery at Altomünster near Augsburg. He criticizes Oecolampadius for submitting himself to an unnatural yoke for the sake of religion and argues instead that it is better for a Christian to live in the world as an example to others than to live apart from the world in a monastery. He is also worried for Oecolampadius's health because he would be required to burden his body with absolute silence, vigils, and fasts. Above all, he objects to the Brigittine order itself, because women have authority over men, a preposterous order in Capito's opinion.

Letter 45a: 28 May 1520, Frankfurt, Johannes Cochlaeus to Capito

This previously unknown letter is in the Bayerische Staatsbibliothek, Munich, under 'Autograph Cochlaeus' (no shelf mark).

Johannes Cochlaeus (d. 1552) studied at the University of Cologne (MA 1507) and became rector of the grammar school in Nürnberg, a post he held until 1515. At that time he went to Italy as a tutor to three nephews of the city councillor Willibald Pirckheimer and himself studied law at Bologna. In 1517 he obtained a doctorate in theology at Ferrara. He was ordained and appointed dean of St Mary's in Frankfurt, where he settled in 1520. He seemed at first sympathetic to Luther but soon changed his position and became one of his most vocal opponents.

Many greetings. Nothing has pleased me more in a long time, dearest Capito, than your (albeit very brief) letter to me.[1] May God effect that the continuation of our friendship match the beginning of this affection in sweet pleasure, and increase it. I rightly offer you any friendly service I can provide in exchange for your kindness. I am well aware, dear Capito, how unworthy I am of your friendship, being, as it were, inferior to you in all gifts of nature, fortune, and virtue. But since you are kind enough to offer your friendship to me without prompting, I would clearly be not only boorish but a stupid blockhead, if I did not most eagerly accept it. I will try very hard indeed to ensure that you will not regret your kindness.

* * * * *

1 Not extant.

I have recently seen your Hebrew grammar. I read it eagerly, but nevertheless deferred buying it on account of your promise to add a third book.[2] This will be very useful and necessary, especially because copies of Johann Reuchlin's *Vocabulary*[3] are becoming rare. I brought with me from Rome several Hebrew writings, which I will gladly send you if you have the time to look at them. I am otherwise occupied and have put them away willingly because reading them is rather hard on my eyes.

I do not quite understand what you mean about the factions of the monks. It seems that Luther is rather troublesome not only to the brethren but also to the Pope and all of Christendom and that he is exceedingly pugnacious. Indeed I fear that he will not be able to sustain such a great load by himself in the long run. Erasmus is acting more wisely. He produces greater results, causing less tumult and animosity. Let me know some time what you think of Hutten. I believe he is not unknown to you, for he often stays there,[4] and indeed he must be known to you of old from his works. If he should be in your company, I ask that you kindly greet that most noble man in my name.

What happened recently in the great Reuchlin affair[5] is already known to both you and him, I believe. If not, let me know, and I will give you a full account, for I witnessed it myself. Farewell. From Frankfurt, 28 May 1520.

Letter 46: End of May 1520, Mainz, Capito to Johannes Cochlaeus

> The letter itself is not extant, but Cochlaeus reports on it in a letter to Willibald Pirckheimer (text in *Willibald Pirckheimers Briefwechsel*, ed. H. Scheible [Munich, 1997] 4: #698). Cochlaeus relates that he was present at an effort, initiated by Franz von Sickingen, to settle the Reuchlin affair in the papal court. Turning to the Luther question, Cochlaeus declares his support for the reformer. He then mentions Capito's letters (see Cochlaeus's reply to one of them above, Ep. 45a):

* * * * *

2 I.e., Capito's *Hebraicarum Institutionum libri duo* (Basel, 1518). The promised third book (see above, Ep. 11a, note 4) never materialized.

3 Cochlaeus is referring to Reuchlin's *De rudimentis Hebraicis* of 1506, which contained a dictionary.

4 I.e., in Mainz. For Hutten, see above, Ep. 30, headnote.

5 On Reuchlin cf. above, Ep. 17, headnote. After a lengthy appeal process, the trial against Reuchlin, who had been accused of Judaizing, was again going forward in Rome. Reuchlin was eventually found guilty. The official verdict was handed down in June 1520. Cf. also Cochlaeus's report to Pirckheimer below, Ep. 46.

... In the last few days Fabritius Capito wrote to me twice from Mainz.[1] His sermons are much praised here as well. In the second letter he asks me to send him all the works of Cicero in portable form, in an Aldine print. I have asked here [in Frankfurt], but in vain. I certainly know of no one who could oblige him in this matter more easily and readily than you. You have Venetian merchants at your command, who will not deny you anything. I beg you, if it is not inconvenient, to be of service to the man. I know that you like him. You will be reimbursed in full – I guarantee it, indeed I shall be your debtor. If the Aldine press does not have the orations of Cicero, [he asks for an edition] from another press, as long as it is portable.

Letter 46a: 13 June 1520, Mainz, Capito to Thomas Truchsess

> This letter (not in Millet) is printed in *Hermann Buschius, Hypanticon principi et clementissimo antistiti Spirensi Georgio Comiti palatino Rheni, super solenni suo in Spiram urbem introitu, dicatum* (Basel: Cratander, 1520), title-page verso. Buschius was likely staying with Capito at the time. Cf. a poem by Buschius at the end of Gertophius's *Recriminatio* (1520) [26], which is signed 'ex aedibus Capitonis extemporaliter' (at Capito's house, extempore). The present poem commemorates the ceremonial entry of the bishop, George Count Palatine, into the city of Speyer, which took place in 1519. The addressee is the Frankonian knight Thomas Truchsess of Wetzhausen (d. 1523). Truchsess studied at Leipzig and Bologna (doctorate in canon law, 1504) and obtained livings in Speyer and Würzburg. He was the vicar-general of the bishop of Speyer (from 1507 to 1513) and dean of the cathedral chapter (from 1517).

Wolfgang Fabritius Capito to the noble and erudite Thomas Truchsess, dean of Speyer, greetings.
Hermann Buschius[1] left with me a fine poem[2] about the most illustrious

* * * * *

1 Cf. above, Ep. 45a.

1 The humanist Hermann Buschius (d. 1534) studied in Cologne and taught in Münster and other cities in northern Germany. From 1502 he taught poetry and rhetoric at the newly founded University of Wittenberg. In 1507 he returned to Cologne, where his support for a humanistic curriculum and for Reuchlin made him *persona non grata*. Buschius, who also championed Luther's teachings, eventually ended up at the Lutheran University of Marburg, where he taught poetry from 1527. See also below, note 4.
2 I.e., the *Hypanticon*. For a summary of the contents see H.J. Liessem *Hermann van dem Busche: Sein Leben und seine Schriften* (repr. Nieuwkoop, De Graaf 1965), 65–8.

George, prince of the Palatinate, bishop of Speyer, being received into his city with great honour.[3] The poem, it seems to me, breathes a spirit more fortunate than one might expect from this age. Its theme is a happy one; the complex poetry hides the gravest philosophy. The Latin style is graceful, clear, and expressive, without any harshness or gaps. You might say it is the prose of a fertile mind or displaying the natural ease of Horace. It pours forth a continuous stream as from a golden fountain. I believe Buschius has a natural talent for invention and style. For how else could he compose all this so evenly and readily? He was about to dedicate it to you, worthy sir, as I heard from him at dinner, when he earnestly praised your wonderful hospitality, your candour, your love for men of letters, because (as he says, and I have proof) you are very much a man of letters yourself. Thus, most honoured Thomas, you are worthy of such a prince not only because of your illustrious forefathers but also because of your most splendid erudition, your virtuous character, your complete faithfulness in conducting affairs, and I beg you most urgently to receive this eulogy of the bishop and at the same time the eulogist himself. Applaud and look favourably on the eulogy and help and protect the eulogist, for he excels in letters and in leading a blameless life, but has so far suffered a fortune unworthy of him.[4] In this manner, lending an ear to your counsel, the best of princes will make his eulogist happy and appear truly worthy of such praise, when he exhibits an example of his liberality towards him.

As for the rest, it is a singular proof of Erasmus's goodwill towards Your Grace that he has presented you with a picture of himself that is true to life. You are right to make much of it, for it represents one half of Erasmus.[5] From

* * * * *

3 George, count Palatine (1486–1529) was elected bishop of Speyer in 1513. He presided over the trial of Johann Reuchlin, a cause célèbre in the sixteenth century. Thomas Truchsess (the addressee of the present letter) was delegated to examine Reuchlin's *Augenspiegel* for heretical pronouncements. As a result of Truchsess's findings, the bishop acquitted Reuchlin, but the verdict was appealed to Rome and eventually overturned.

4 Buschius was an outspoken supporter of humanism and the Reformation and often used provocative language in defence of the two movements. His career suffered accordingly. He encountered stiff opposition, not only at the University of Cologne (see above, note 1), but also during brief stints at Leipzig and Erfurt and as rector of the Latin school in Wesel. In each case his employment was terminated.

5 Erasmus repeatedly enjoyed Truchsess's hospitality, when passing through Speyer. The image mentioned here was a portrait medal made by Quentin Metsys in 1519. We know that Erasmus had a number of copies made as gifts for friends and patrons. Capito's words reflect the legend on the medal: 'An image true to life; a better image is found in my writings.'

his books you have already perceived the other half, that is, the image of his mind. Combining it with the image of his body, you will have Erasmus's true self. Whenever you please, you can see his physical outline with your eyes and the sentiments of that divine mind of his with your heart. Farewell, and love both Buschius and Capito, for each of us is equally striving to honour you. Mainz, on the day before the Ides of June, in the year 1522.

Letter 47: 23 June 1520, Basel, Caspar Hedio to Capito

Caspar Hedio (1494–1552) studied at the University of Freiburg (BA 1514, MA 1516) and from 1518 at the University of Basel, where he was a student of Capito. He completed his licence in theology in 1519. In October 1520 he followed his teacher to Mainz to serve as his assistant, and the following year succeeded him as cathedral preacher (see below Ep. 102, note 2). In November 1523 Hedio was appointed preacher of the cathedral chapter in Strasbourg, a position Capito had coveted as well. There was a falling out between them, but mutual friends succeeded in reconciling them (see below, Epp. 169, 170). Hedio was active in the reformation of Strasbourg and in historical scholarship. He published a number of German translations (of Eusebius' *Ecclesiastical History* and Platina's *Lives of the Popes*) and two chronicles. The autograph manuscript of this letter is in the British Library, ms. Add. 21.524, fol. 5, 2.

Hedio to his incomparable patron, the preacher Wolfgang Fabritius Capito in Mainz.

Hail! Yesterday, that is, on the feast day of Saint Alban, after I preached in his church, I gave your letter to the worthy Claude.[1] It was wonderful to see the pleasure with which he received it. Clearly, you could not have sent him anything more welcome, it seems. He said more than once that he would keep it like a treasure. At dinner, he showed it to his best friends, not without great praise for Capito. He was triumphant that, involved as you are in so much work, you did not begrudge writing to him. Privately he said a great deal to me that I shall soon tell you in person. He is your most sincere patron. He wants to make every effort to acquire a canonry for you in Basel, even if nothing comes through King Charles.[2]

Your letter also addressed the treasurer.[3] He will write back through Bern-

* * * * *

1 For Claude Chansonnette see below, Ep. 67, headnote.
2 For Capito's efforts in 1519 see above, Ep. 32, note 1.
3 Johann Rudolf von Hallwyl. See above, Ep. 8, headnote.

hard von Klingenberg,[4] who will shortly come to you. For the coronation obliges him to go there.[5] Hartmann[6] would do well for once to write his uncle. He asked me whether they do not have ink and paper in Louvain! He should make allowances for old affections.

The excellent Egranus[7] was staying with us for some days. We would gladly have received him as well as we could. If we neglected anything, you will make it up. He advised Jakob Truchsess[8] to go to Wittenberg, and me to make an effort to obtain a position in Augsburg. He asserted that mention was made of me there. I embrace your counsel. I shall not be mercenary, and I shall not do anything without your knowledge, whatever conditions are offered to me. It would take too long to write to you about the decision made these past days not to print any more of Luther's works.[9] The comedy was acted in the presence of Egranus, from whom you will hear about it. Your brother[10] is well. He is tongue-tied, but will

* * * * *

4 I have not been able to find biographical data for Bernhard von Klingenberg. The family was prominent in the Thurgau and traditionally in Habsburg service (cf. *Historisch-biographisches Lexicon der Schweiz*, ed. H. Tribolet [Neuenburg, 1931]). See also Ep. 49, where Bernhard is mentioned as the bearer of the letter.

5 Charles's coronation took place in Aachen on 23 October 1520.

6 For Hartmann von Hallwyl, see Ep. 11, headnote. The remarks suggest that he was in Louvain at the time, perhaps delivering a letter to Erasmus (Ep. 38 from Capito to Erasmus is dated March 1520). Erasmus sent his regards to Hartmann in December 1520 (Ep. 64 below).

7 Johannes Sylvius Egranus (d. 1535) studied in Leipzig (BA 1501, MA 1507) and became priest of St Mary's in Zwickau (Saxony) and later in Joachimstal. In 1520 he travelled by way of Wittenberg to Basel, where he wanted to meet with Capito. The latter, however, had already moved to Mainz. At the time Egranus was receptive to Reformation ideas or at any rate wrangling with Luther's teaching. See Bernhard Adelmann's remark in a letter to Pirckheimer: 'His speech, his behaviour, and his writings show an amazing inconsistency. How he will turn out, only God knows' (*Willibald Pirckheimers Briefwechsel* 4, Ep. 694). Egranus soon became embroiled in controversy and was viewed with suspicion by both Catholics and Protestants. Like Erasmus, he preferred reform of the church from within and remained Catholic.

8 Truchsess (see Ep. 41, note 1), who had been Capito's amanuensis in Basel, joined him in Mainz and is documented there until August 1521 (cf. Ep. 105). By 1523 he had returned to Basel (cf. Epp. 165 and 174).

9 See above, Ep. 19, headnote.

10 Either Capito's brother Heinrich (see below, Ep. 157) or, as Bodenmann suggests, self-referential, i.e., Capito's brother in Christ.

improve with the years, I pray. Von Rotperg[11] and Christoph[12] send you sincere greetings.

In the last meeting at Zurich the senate of Charles asked that the Swiss send delegates from each canton to the king,[13] and I hear from one of the representatives that it will be done. The rest is going very well. Farewell, Basel, 23 June 1520. Your Caspar Hedio.

Letter 48: 29 June 1520, Strasbourg, Jacob Sturm to Capito

> The manuscript of this letter is in Paris, Bibl. SHPF 756/1 (autographes Labouchère, vol. 1) fol. 155. Jacob Sturm (1489–1553) was a member of a patrician family in Strasbourg and destined for the church. He studied at Heidelberg and Freiburg (MA 1505), where he taught in the faculty of arts, then studied law under Udalricus Zasius. In 1517 he returned to Strasbourg and served as secretary to the provost of the Strasbourg Cathedral. From 1523 on he was a member of the city council and instrumental in supporting the reformation of Strasbourg. He also took a leading role in attempts to unite the Protestant forces.

Greetings, most honest Wolfgang. I hear that Dietrich Zobel, canon at Mainz, will resign the living he has here in the church of St Thomas for a yearly pension.[1] I am therefore writing to the royal secretary Jacob Spiegel,[2] asking him to attempt with your help or any other friends he might have in Mainz to persuade the said Dietrich to cede that living to me for an honest

* * * * *

11 Not identified. Members of the noble Rotberg family played a prominent role in Basel during the fifteenth century. Several members sat on the city council or held canonries in the cathedral chapter. Their ancestral seat was then Stammburg, which they sold to Solothurn in 1515. They retained estates in Bambach and Rheinweiler.

12 Perhaps Christoph Ewi[n]ger, to whom Ep. 174 is addressed and who was married to Kunigunde von Rotberg.

13 Cf. J. Strickler, ed., *Die eidgenössischen Abschiede aus den Jahren 1521–28* (Brugg, 1873) IV-1a, 6 for the delegates meeting with representatives of the empire in February 1521. By 'senate' Hedio presumably meant the *Reichsregiment*, a commission handling government affairs.

1 For Zobel see above, Ep. 32, note 19. In January 1521 Petrus Wickram made similar inquiries, but Zobel appears to have kept the canonry, to which Wolfgang Geuch of Strasbourg succeeded on his death in 1531.

2 For Spiegel see below, Ep. 134, headnote.

pension (if I may say so). Spiegel will give you more details. For this reason I beg and beseech you by the old friendship which we have now enjoyed for many years to aid Spiegel with your influence and counsel and undertake this labour for my sake. In doing so you will do me the greatest possible favour at this time, and you will find that you have not conferred this favour on an ungrateful man, for you know that I have long been your friend and will shoulder any burden on your behalf. Farewell, best of friends, from Strasbourg on the very day of Peter and Paul, in the year 1520. Your Jacob Sturm.

Letter 49: 2 July 1520, Basel, Laurentius Loss to Capito

> Laurentius was a chaplain at the cathedral. His name and position ('Schaffer,' i.e., administrator) appear in the list for the year 1525. See 'Verzeichnis der Kapläne des Domstifts' in *Aktensammlung zur Geschichte der Reformation in den Jahren 1519 bis Anfang 1534*, ed. P. Roth (Basel, 1937). The manuscript of this letter, written in German, is in Ki.Ar. 25a, #7 at the Universitätsbibliothek, Basel.

Respected and most learned sir, my goodwill is completely at your service. I doubt not that Your Honour remembers well and has not forgotten a prescription for a salve, which the knight H. Varnbühler[1] once gave you, and which you misplaced and lost, and then left with me. Could you obtain the prescription from him again, for you deserve especially well of him, and could you communicate it to me? That is my humble request of Your Honour: would you be so kind once again and do me the favour. Please consider that the only reason I ask is my pressing need, and you are in a position, on account of your acquaintance, to obtain the said prescription for the salve from the knight H. Varnbühler and send me his reply. Enclose it in a letter and send it to me, and you will have my goodwill and service forever. For I hope and wish that you will soon take up residence in Basel again, and will gladly be of service to you in this matter.[2] You have made a good effort and have left us with teachings such as have certainly not been heard in many years and will, I believe, make for a new and good beginning. The

* * * * *

1 Huldreich (or Ulrich) Varnbühler (1474–1545) studied law at Basel, Freiburg, and Vienna. He was a protonotary in the imperial Regiment from 1521 to 1523, and frequently travelled on court business. During the last years of his life he lived in Strasbourg. The prefatory letter to the second edition of Capito's grammar (1525) is addressed to Varnbühler.

2 See earlier efforts to get him a canonry, Ep. 47, note 2.

knight Bernhard von Klingenberg,[3] who brings you this letter, would be willing safely to convey your letter and the enclosed prescription to me. I commend myself to your pleasure. Given Friday after the Visitation of Mary, in the year of the Lord, '20.

Your well meaning Laurentius Loss, administrator at the Cathedral in Basel.

Letter 50: 17 [July] 1520, Rome, Peter Gebwiler to Capito

Peter Gebwiler (d. after 1557) looked after Capito's legal affairs in Rome. He came from an Alsatian family and, by 1525, was chaplain at the cathedral of Basel (cf. *Aktensammlung zur Geschichte der Reformation in den Jahren 1519 bis Anfang 1534*, ed. P. Roth [Basel, 1937]). He appears to have studied law at Dole and in the 1530s was in the service of the Margrave Bernhard of Baden and scribe of Röteln. Cf. *Amerbachkorrespondenz 2*, Ep. 1476, headnote. The manuscript of this letter is in Ki.Ar. 25a, #52, in the Universitätsbibliothek, Basel.

This letter contains the first notice of the difficulties Capito encountered in his attempts to obtain the provostship of St Thomas. His title was contested by two other candidates (for details see below, note 2). One of the contestants, Jacob Abel, a notorious pluralist, involved him in litigation for years to come. In 1539 an anonymous German report (printed in F. Herrmann, 249–50) summarized the affair as follows: 'Some twenty years ago a courtier, named [Jacob] Abel, expertly harassed Wolfgang Capito in the matter of the provostship of St Thomas in Strasbourg and cited him before the Roman court. When the said Doctor Capito was in the service of the cardinal and elector of Mainz, a settlement was reached between them under Pope Leo [X], and he was ordered to leave Capito in peace. But afterwards, when Doctor Capito went to Strasbourg to assume the provostship and began to teach the gospel, Abel, on the instigation of certain people, as was to be expected, reopened the suit against Doctor Capito, and when Doctor Capito refused to obey the citation to Rome and the legal process (for he knew what to expect in Rome, being now a preacher of the gospel), Abel alleged contempt of court and obtained a sentence of execution and other Roman actions, according to his desire. But since those actions are no longer obeyed in Strasbourg and Roman courtiers are no longer permitted there, Abel could not execute the papal judgment. He therefore laid a complaint against Capito and cited him before the court, invoking the secular arm of the law, in order to proceed with the execution of the judgment. But the

* * * * *

3 See above, Ep. 47, note 4.

honourable city council was unwilling to permit the business of the papal
court and the hawking of offices in their city and ordered Abel to abstain from
further action against Capito, since papal jurisdiction did not apply in Strasbourg.' Cf. the letter from the city to the imperial law court of 8 June 1534
(AMS IX, 2/4), noting that 'all legal proceedings of the pope at Rome, all the
business of his courtiers, and unlawful financial transactions are quite rejected
by our city and its authorities' (all römische bepstische process, curtisey und
unbilliche finantz in unser Stat und oberkeit gentzlichen aberkannt). For Abel's
actions in the thirties see *Die Reformationsprozesse der Stadt Strassburg am Reichskammergericht zur Zeit des Schmalkaldischen Bundes*, ed. R. Schelp (Kaisers-
lautern, 1965), 220–3.

On 28 June I first received a letter from your relative, the respected Friedrich
Prechter,[1] concerning the death of the provost of St Thomas in Strasbourg.[2]
After reading it, I immediately reminded the reverend cardinal of Santi
Quattro[3] and Paolo Bombace[4] to look after these matters once again. This has

* * * * *

1 The Prechters were a wealthy merchant-banking family from Haguenau, resident in Strasbourg from 1475 on. Friedrich Prechter senior (d. 1546) was an
  imperial councillor; his son and namesake (d. 1528) sat on the Strasbourg city
  council; his daughter Felicitas was married to Ulrich Varnbühler (see Ep. 49,
  note 1), who also belonged to Capito's circle of friends and acquaintances. The
  older Prechter was married to Susanna Pfeffinger (for Capito's acquaintance
  with the Pfeffingers see below, Ep. 157, note 8).
2 The twenty-five canonries of St Thomas were numbered. Number 13 was held
  by the provost Jakob Fabri von Reichshofen, who died on 6 June 1520. Capito
  had been confirmed as successor by the pope, but the papers had not yet
  reached him. In the meantime, the chapter elected Johannes Hepp to canonry
  13. Hepp had earlier on been evicted from his canonry (Number 14) on charges
  of rape. Number 14 was acquired in November 1520 by Jacob Abel, a papal
  protonotary and a well-known pluralist. He is said to have held more than a
  hundred benefices. In Strasbourg and environs he held a chaplaincy at
  Molsheim and vicarages at Old St Peter, Monswiller, Schwindretzheim, and
  Erstein. In addition to the canonry at St Thomas, Abel also claimed the provostship of the chapter (cf. AST 192, 1520, fols. 12–13). A third contender for
  that office was Sebastian Bender, another notorious benefice hunter, who sold
  his rights to Abel. After a prolonged legal battle, Capito replaced Hepp
  (evicted from canonicate 13) and Abel as provost on 25 August 1521 (AST 192,
  1521, fol. 6). For further developments see below, Epp. 55, 60, 175.
3 Lorenzo Pucci (1458–1531), a jurist, became apostolic protonotary in 1488. His
  career continued under Julius II and Leo X, who made him cardinal in 1513
  (his title was Santi Quattro Coronati). As cardinal penitentiary (from 1520), he
  was in charge of indulgence sales.
4 Paolo Bombace (1476–1527) held a lectureship in rhetoric and poetry at Bolo-

now been done through the pope. But Paolo and I were quite surprised that no letters have reached us informing us that you are in possession. For a brief has been sent through the Fuggers[5] around the first of May. Although Prechter wrote that he had not yet received it, it is hardly possible that he did not receive it a few days after the death. We have no doubt about your title. Unless Paolo and I are mistaken, the brief will take the wind out of the sails of your adversaries, who on hearing of the provost's death were nevertheless pressing on with the judgment obtained in their own favour. And they will extort letters executorial and send them as quickly as possible to Strasbourg, to demand that they be served on the holders, and when they find none, they will take possession on the basis of those same letters. Your Honour must hereafter beware of similar letters and any other lightning bolts insinuating or intimating possession, and be neither intimidated nor afraid. *The bow does not always strike the target it threatens.*[6] On the contrary, appeal this challenge to His Holiness, before a notary and witnesses, and send us the appeal. Duly appoint legal representatives in Rome, and if you are absent from Strasbourg, make sure to appoint representatives there, who will conduct your business loyally (but I suppose you have done that long ago already)[7] and who at least take possession in the name of Your Honour.

Eck prepares to depart for his homeland.[8] His Holiness, the pope, they say, has yesterday evening made him a present of five hundred gold ducats. Further pronouncements have been made against Luther and his followers,[9] but they have not yet been distributed in print. Farewell and continue in your affection for me, as usual. Given at Rome on 17 [July][10] 1520. Your P. Gebwiler.

* * * * *

gna, then taught at Naples, and in 1513 became Lorenzo Pucci's secretary (see preceding note). In 1517 he accompanied Lorenzo's nephew, Antonio Pucci, who had been made papal legate for Switzerland. He returned to Rome the following year and died in the Sack of Rome, 1527.

5 Financiers of the emperor, with branch offices throughout Europe.

6 Horace *Ars poetica* 350.

7 On 26 July 1521 Capito appointed Jacob Schmidthauser, Jacob Sturm, Thomas Vogler, Beatus Felix Pfeffinger, and Heinrich Eubel as his representatives (TB 1:175).

8 For Eck see above, Ep. 1a, headnote. Eck had been in Rome for some months and participated in the preparation of the bull condemning Luther. On 17 July he and Girolamo Aleandro were appointed papal legates. Eck was commissioned to publish the papal bull in the dioceses of Brandenburg, Meissen, Merseburg, and Saxony (i.e., in the territories of Frederick the Wise and George of Saxony).

9 I.e., the papal bull 'Exsurge Domine' of 15 June 1520.

10 The month is missing in the manuscript but may be supplied on the basis of the reference to Eck, who departed Rome around 18 July.

Letter 51: 25 July [1520], Leipzig, Christoph Hegendorf to Capito

The manuscript of this letter is in Ki.Ar. 25a, #54 in the Universitätsbibliothek, Basel. The year date is uncertain. Millet assigned the letter to the year 1520, presumably connecting it with a letter from Mosellanus (Ep. 62), which may have been written in response to the greetings conveyed by Hegendorf. However, there is also a copy of the present letter in the Simmler collection at the Zentralbibliothek, Zurich, marked '1521,' presumably because of the reference to Halle. Capito is documented in Halle in July 1521 (see below, Epp. 98, 99), but this does not exclude his presence there in the summer of 1520.

Christoph Hegendorf (1500–1540) studied at the University of Leipzig. In 1519 he wrote a poem in praise of Luther, commemorating the Leipzig Disputation. He taught school in Leipzig and wrote textbooks, including a letter-writing manual. By 1521 he had obtained his MA and began teaching at the university. Over the next decade he was engaged in legal studies. In 1530, the bishop of Poznan (Posen) invited him to teach classics at the university there, but he was obliged to leave five years later on charges of Lutheranism. He moved to Frankfurt, where he obtained a doctorate in law. From 1537 on he was a legal consultant of the city of Lüneburg and from 1539 the city's church superintendent.

Well, my most learned Capito, I am one of those who, once they have experienced a man's generosity, frequently return, expecting more of the same, not minding the proverb, *Go away, Carians, Anthesteria is over*.[1] Although I have been most generously treated by you, I am far from satisfied, so that when I, too, stayed in Halle[2] I called on you at your residence. And even though you were very busy with your studies, I began to bother you with clearly illiterate letters. Oh my Capito, what would you give for not having been so generous to a guest, who allows himself so readily to be invited. Then, I believe, you would not have been interrupted so often in your peaceful studies. But what can you do? I have decided to be insolent. Whether you want it or not, I come, and even if I am not always welcome, I suppose that my intention at least is welcome. And I am also consoled by that common saying *If he isn't glad to see me, he'll be glad to see me leave*.[3]

Well, here is your Christoph, that inopportune guest, thanking you from a

* * * * *

1 I.e., the Athenian feast during which people were permitted to act with greater freedom. Cf. Erasmus *Adagia* 1.2.65.
2 See above, headnote.
3 Source not identified.

distance for all but overwhelming me with good – an obscure man whom you had never met before and who, for all he is worth, gives himself completely into your hands. But even if he does not object to going into slavery or pledging himself to you, he will never be able to repay what he owes you. But enough of that. I have given your regards to Mosellanus[4] and Philipp Neukam.[5] By God, you should have seen the men jump with joy, and not without reason! For who would not jump with joy when he receives greetings from Capito, that is, the most learned and kindest of men? And because they cannot give you anything else, they greet you in turn. Farewell in Christ. I was obliged to be brief and write extempore because the courier hurried me on. We urgently desire your arrival here. Farewell again. Given at Leipzig, on 25 July. All my friends send greetings to you, especially Hieronymus Schutz,[6] a young man of wonderful talents.

Christoph Hegendorf

From the college of the prince.[7]

Hail, our leader, most learned Capito, live for Christ, live for learning! Write back, when it is not inconvenient.

Letter 52: July 1520 [Ebernburg?], Ulrich von Hutten to Capito

Printed in *Hutteni opera* 1:363–5, #181

[Summary]: Hutten again begs Capito for a copy of the papal letter to Albert of Brandenburg condemning Hutten's publication, and tells him to ask Tilman [Kreych] to help him. He asks whether Nikolaus Carbach has news from Frankfurt. Hutten's brother is at Franz von Sickingen's and will act as go-between. Hutten wants Capito to inform him of the reception of the German poem *Clag und vormanung*. He sends his regards to Johannes Alexander Brassicanus. Franz von Sickingen thinks that Charles V will support them.

* * * * *

4 See below, Ep. 62, headnote.
5 'Philippus Novenianus Hasfurdensis' (d. 1563) studied at Leipzig (BA 1515, MA 1519, B med 1525). He was a poet and the author of philological and medical works. From 1528, he worked as a physician in Halle. His connections with Mainz are evidenced in a poem in praise of Albert (1531).
6 Perhaps Hieronymus Schytz of Schneeberg, documented at the University of Leipzig in 1518, and from 1526 to 1529 in Bologna, or Hieronymus Schucz of Chemnitz, who registered at the University of Leipzig in August 1521.
7 The new college, built with the financial support of Duke George, was completed in 1515.

Letter 53: 8 August [1520], Gelnhausen, Ulrich von Hutten to Capito

Printed in *Hutteni opera* 1:367, #183

[*Summary*]: Hutten's life is in danger. He writes that Leo X has demanded of the archbishop of Mainz in two letters to have him apprehended and sent to Rome. He requests that Capito inform Erasmus and others about this. Hutten has written Frowin von Hutten to intercede on behalf of his printer.

Letter 54: 13 August 1520, Mainz, Capito to Martinus Gertophius

In 1520 Edward Lee (see note 1 below) published a critical review of Erasmus's edition of the New Testament: *Annotationum libri duo* (Paris: Gourmont, 1520). Erasmus immediately replied with an *Apologia nihil habens, neque nasi neque dentis neque stomachi neque unguium, qua respondet duabus invectivis Eduardi Lei* (Antwerp: Hillen, March 1520). This was followed by a longer apologia entitled *Responsiones ad annotationes Ed. Lei* (Antwerp: Hillen, April/May 1520). Among the reprints that appeared that year was an edition by Schoeffer in Mainz. It contains, on pp. 2–5, Capito's letter to Martinus Gertophius, parish priest in Dietenheim.

Wolfgang Fabritius Capito to the outstanding theologian Martinus Gertophius, parish priest in Dietenheim, his old friend and associate, greetings.

Most learned Martinus, while at dinner with learned men, I read out your letter in which you fume so angrily against the Englishman Lee and in which you also casually cast aspersions on me because he praised me.[1] For the most part, your letter raised a great laugh. You could have witnessed a merry dinner. Everyone teased me in his own way. When they heard what you write of Lee's book, that it contains, in your opinion, nothing but insults, someone interjected: 'Look at this sharp-witted patron of Lee's. How cleverly he dis-

* * * * *

1 Cf. Allen Ep. 1061: 196–209, where Lee hails Reuchlin and Capito as his 'teachers' and praises their genius. He calls Capito 'the most successful compiler of a Hebrew grammar, who generously passed on the rudiments and so skillfully reduced them to order that I need nothing further' (CWE Ep. 1061: 232–4). Gertophius's letter is not extant. Edward Lee (ca. 1482–1544) studied at Oxford (BA 1501), Cambridge (MA 1504, BTh 1515), and Louvain (from 1517 to 1520, without taking a degree). On his return to England, he served at the court of Henry VIII as almoner (from 1523) and was sent on diplomatic missions to Spain (1525–30) and Rome (1530). In 1531 he was incorporated as doctor of divinity at Oxford and elevated to the archbishopric of York.

guises the most odious thing with a softer term. For Lee's book does not contain insults: the man is an insult himself. Indeed he is a veritable crime, and an infernal, most harmful fury.' 'What?' I said, 'Does he not guard all of theology with those sacred annotations of his?' 'He guards it,' he said, 'like Sinon[2] the Greek, who destroyed Troy, for he disguised the truth and concealed his fraudulent purpose. Does a man, then, show his talent by lying?' 'It seems to be a talent,' said another, 'to have at his fingertips such a load of lies, but it isn't talent. It's corrupt nature, which knows how to make up on purpose what is convenient at the time, but doesn't know how to lie smoothly, connecting one point with the next.' Others said a great deal in the same vein and even wittier things, but at the same time more offensive, and so I refrain on purpose from putting them on paper. Otherwise I would seem to go on deliberately against the wretched man and diminish the praise he gave me, for you (please God!) make me out to be delighted with his praise.

But to reply to your letter briefly: I completely agree with you in everything. I have never seen any writing more insolent or more virulent; nothing that is so crammed full, and indeed crazy with insults worthy of women and containing more bold assertions that are beyond, and indeed contrary to, the truth. If you take away from his work, first of all, what is false, then what is slander, good gods, you have nothing left except what is jejune. In two pages you could cover what is left, and however short, it would be too much even for a generous reader because of its notable ignorance. There are men, who die laughing whenever they look at a page of Lee's work, because the stupidity of the man is so unexpected, and he is so vainglorious in his ignorance. I, however, read it and can find nothing amusing in it that would make me laugh, but perhaps I am too serious. Indeed, most of the book is morose, superstitious, and foolishly boastful, and quite of the kind that in itself usually raises a laugh. But it does not make me laugh at all, for this inept man deserves the greatest pity rather than ridicule. His mind is in such a stupor, that he does not see his own turpitude. Or else, he is worthy of the greatest hatred and seemingly must be detested and taken off to court to suffer the death penalty for his nefarious deed, his delirious arrogance and self-love (to which I have been averse from childhood on), which he betrays everywhere in that most inane book. For practically every paragraph breathes insolent vanity. For whatever he is worth, he is a Gnatho,[3] but he

* * * * *

2 Sinon pretended to be a deserter and persuaded the Trojans to bring the 'Trojan horse' into their city.
3 A character in Terence's play *Eunuchus*, who came to denote the flatterer and parasite.

flatters only himself and agrees only with himself and attributes everything to himself alone, and cannot bear anyone unless they admire and adore whatever falls from Lee's lips even if it is imprudent. If a youngster had blathered rather petulant stuff against a good man one might excuse him on account of a youthful lack of self-control. If he persisted in his madness and spewed out poison even in writing, you would say that he has lost his mind and there was no other cure for him except fisticuffs. But what, I ask, can you do with Lee, who has brought his lies together over a two-year period, who publishes such a hateful book against a man in whose debt he is? What can you do with a man whose errors have been demonstrated by Erasmus in these three books[4] and who still dares to show his face among men? You would assert that no madman in chains raves more than Lee. Indeed no prostitute prides herself more on her beauty than does Lee on his unheard-of erudition. He is so pleased with himself, as is apparent everywhere in his magnificent work and as scholars attest to me in letters, that he believes all must give up writing once he himself has begun to write and supply such perfect and useful arguments. Let learned Italy *give way*, then.[5] Yield, oh Germans! Yield, Frenchmen and Spaniards! Throw away your books and live a life of leisure. For that great Lee has suddenly come forth, like another Daniel sent to the world by God to bring assistance to humanity as it struggles, who can teach what he has not learned, who knows how to treat holy writ although he is an insignificant master of arts[6] and has taken up his task only recently, who acquired skill in the three languages in a few months and now, I believe, seized knowledge of all things conceded by God to him alone in his dreams. So certain and profound is his knowledge that *even Momus[7] could find nothing to criticize*, if Erasmus had corrected what Lee annotated. Indeed he himself attested to that among his friends and gave proof of it in his previous invective, saying that he wrote his annotations, which one great donkey calls 'sacred,' under divine inspiration, although there are others who call them truly 'sacred,' that is execrable in the sense in which the poet

* * * * *

4 Presumably counting the *Apologia ... qua respondet duabus invectivis* and the two books of the *Responsiones*.

5 The Latin expression 'dare locum,' which Lee used at *Annotationes*, 8r, was ridiculed as unclassical by Erasmus, LB 9:137.

6 See above, note 1, for Lee's academic career. Here Capito ignores his theological studies, but two sentences further on he calls Lee a theologian. Cf. Erasmus's *Apologia* (*Opuscula*, 292) on that point: 'To what extent is he a theologian? I cannot say.'

7 A mythological figure personifying fault-finding. Lee made this boast in his *Annotationes*, Aii verso.

calls *thirst for gold sacred*.[8] For desire for possessions breaks up concord
among men, and this type of sacred annotation, written by a man who is a
priest and a theologian (and one might add, a little bigot) has very much disturbed the peace of scholarship. Eris,[9] when she was passed over, threw a
golden apple among the assembled gods and caused a quarrel. Edward Lee
was able to destroy the tranquillity of scholars with his shitty little book. O
plague, o Furies! Have you no consideration for my stomach, which is quite
a bit more nauseated by the praise of that execrable rascal than by the mad
insults which certain pseudo-monks recently piled on me with both hands,
as they say.[10]

Finally, I too believe that the matter should be winked at, that one should
not reply even in one word to manifest slander, and especially that Erasmus
should not reply. For otherwise there will be no end of people to whom he
will have to reply in that way. There are so many two-legged donkeys, who
cannot bear living in obscurity, who would commit a similar crime, no
doubt, in an effort to obtain from Erasmus some response in writing as Lee
did. And to tell the truth, it seems to me that no answer would be enough for
Lee himself, that most loquacious frog. How can you suppress with reason
the insane and furious attempt of a man who pours out whatever comes into
his mind as if in a dream? For this sycophantic rascal took on the role of
slanderer, not in a rational or judicious manner, but with a certain boldness
and daring; starving for glory, he ventured anything to relieve his hunger.
Yet Erasmus, the most prudent of men, deigned to hold his own against him
and to support more thoroughly what is already firm enough through skill
and nature, that is through Erasmian skill and the force of the truth, so that
no one could overthrow it. But Lee continues as he did before, not knowing
how to recant, and he says perhaps other things in another form, although
the strongest proofs have been advanced from other sources, such that Calumny herself could find nothing to hiss at. Yet I see, as I have said earlier,
that nothing can satisfy Lee. He will always find something to croak back in
his stubbornness. For half his brain is dried out with ardour for glory which
burns in him immoderately, and it is apparent everywhere in his book that
he speaks without thinking, as if he were in a fever. Nor does he seem to

* * * * *

8 Virgil *Aeneid* 3.59.
9 In Greek mythology, the goddess personifying strife. The golden apple, which
   she threw among the guests at a party to which she was not invited, bore the
   inscription 'To the fairest' and caused a quarrel among the goddesses.
10 Cf. Erasmus *Adagia* 1.9.16 ('ambabus manibus haurire'). I do not know what
   incident Capito had in mind.

care whether what he says is appropriate, as long as it is a great deal, and he gives off an empty, senseless sound.[11] I will quite admit that he can grunt with the pigs, but he cannot bring objections in a learned and relevant manner. I do not deny that Lee gave Erasmus an opportunity to write those books of responses for the benefit of the public. For just as *good laws arise from evil behaviour*,[12] an opportunity of explaining the truth arose in this case from the most shameful sycophantic behaviour. Yet I wonder how they will bear it, whom nothing pleases except what displeases the best men.

As for the rest, it is nice of you to say that you were thinking how unwillingly Capito would bear your attack on Lee, Capito's eulogist, that is, but the man's crime and love for the truth won out over your friendship for me, so that you were less afraid of my anger, as if I would be pleased by the insidious praise of Lee, a man unknown to anyone so far. No, his praise was blameworthy and wicked and cast serious suspicion on me of having deserted the truth and formed a friendship with a slave to inane glory, who was so unlearned and boorish and stupid and so wonderfully confident, who had no scruples to do anything to make a name for himself, who *mixed up the sacred with the profane*,[13] as long as it contributed to his reputation, a man who for the sake of celebrity and hearing his name bandied about, chose to attack the leading light among all ranks of scholars, that is, Erasmus, the torchbearer of a reborn theology. For Lee knows nothing solid in any field and, correspondingly, would be equal to attacking all professions. Why hasn't he brought an action against Linacre or Guillaume Cop or Leoniceno, the restorers of medical science?[14] Why not against Udalricus Zasius or Andrea Alciati,[15] the restorers of jurisprudence? Because he believes that theology touches everyone, whereas the remaining disciplines

* * * * *

11 Reminiscent of Virgil *Aeneid* 10.640: 'dat inania verba, dat sine mente sonum.'
12 Macrobius *Saturnalia* 3.17.10; Erasmus *Adagia* 1.10.61.
13 Horace *Epistles* 1.16.54; Erasmus *Adagia* 1.3.82.
14 Erasmus (Allen Ep. 862: 16–19) mentions the same three men as the guiding lights of medicine. Thomas Linacre (d. 1524) who studied medicine at Padua, returned to London in 1499 and became the tutor of Crown Prince Arthur. From 1509 on he was royal physician to Henry VIII. He founded the College of Physicians in 1518. Guillaume Cop (d. 1532) obtained his medical training at Paris and became personal physician to successive French kings. Niccolò Leoniceno (1428–1524) lectured at Padua and Ferrara. He published translations of Galen and wrote a book on epilepsy.
15 On Udalricus Zasius see above, Ep. 15b, headnote. Andrea Alciati (1492–1550) studied law at Bologna and Ferrara. He taught at various universities in France and Italy. He was regarded by his contemporaries as the greatest interpreter of the Roman law. Today he is better known for his history of emblems.

concern only a few people. For everyone believes that any dispute about the gospel concerns him, and indeed it does concern everyone, whereas juris- prudence and the medical profession, as it is now, are not as broadly appli- cable and concern only a few. Therefore that idiot Lee believed that holy writ was a field that suited his plan. For his design was to come to people's notice by any means whatsoever. And for this reason he did not take aim at just anyone. Erasmus seemed to him the most suitable character for his tragedy. For he saw that the world had accepted Erasmus as her teacher, although he makes no such claims about himself. Nor does he readily accept such assertions from others or generally bear with good grace those who openly make such claims on his behalf. Our Thraso,[16] then, was certain, if he harassed Erasmus as odiously as possible, even if he did not deign to give him an answer, there would be no good man of letters who would not immediately attack Lee. For what did that loquacious Thersites[17] hope to achieve with the insults he hurled against the great Agamemnon, when there are many men like Ulysses? And Erasmus has many men like Ulysses enrolled among his troops. Did Lee hope that they would bear it with equa- nimity when they saw their general insulted? Look what thanks he gets from Capito. In return for his fraudulent praise, which he has deigned to give me in his hateful work, I shall reveal the truth about his fraudulent intent to make his name immortal. I shall do so in the preface to this fine book, which has no other flaw than that it commits Lee's name to the mem- ory of posterity. Yet, because it is candid and cutting in its criticism, it will condemn Lee who has acted with fraud and deceit, and convict him not only of ambition, but also of cheating, of fraud and ingratitude. Thus it would seem quite a bit more honourable to be without honour than to suffer eter- nal infamy and hatred on account of an inane reputation.

Next, you joke about Lee's eloquence and wittily prefer it to Cicero's. For Cicero's writings are always pleasant and never tiresome and indeed fill you with a great desire for more. The reader's mind is always intent on what follows, and the author's divine mind is revealed only on the tenth reading. In all aspects Cicero's writings seem rather august even if you have just glimpsed them once *through a lattice*,[18] as it were. Lee's writings, by contrast, satiate the reader, however eager he may be, even if he has merely tasted

* * * * *

16 A character in Terence's play *Eunuchus,* whose name became synonymous with 'braggard.'
17 A character in Homer's *Iliad* who railed at King Agamemnon until he was beaten into silence by Ulysses.
18 Cicero *De Oratore* 1.35.162.

them, whereas Cicero usually makes them more eager. If you persist in reading Lee and attempt to go further, you are seized by a wretched feeling of surfeit, and even what you have not read as yet, indeed what you have merely glanced at, shows you the author's ignorance, intention, and character. And how will you understand the subject matter, when you read the work more accurately? For many things cancel each other out, or they are so obscure that you need a Delian swimmer, as the old adage says.[19] In all of this you certainly have spoken for me. For I cannot get myself to read through nonsense of this kind, not only because it is common and trifling and has already been discussed frequently (for I have talked about these things at length with Erasmus in Basel), but because he draws out everything beyond the due measure, and twists everything into a calumny, because in his desire to reproach Erasmus, he sometimes criticizes what is well said, and soon, as if he had forgotten what he said, confirms the same things. Motivated by a shameful morosity he raises up a terrible, tragic storm everywhere about the ass's shadow and the goat's wool.[20]

You know Capito, you know how I dislike that womanish procacity. Nor do I see who among scholars would have the stomach to bear it and read the man's mad stuff without getting angry. As far as I know, I have come across only one fat-belly who approved Lee's book, but he was moved by envy more than led by judgment. He recently gave me the book and, laughing maliciously, said: 'Look at this learned and Christian author. He is the only truly pious and erudite man. He knows Greek, Latin, and Hebrew, so that Erasmus rightly envies him.' My dear Gertophius, you'll find that the old adage is true: *Like lips like lettuce*, as they say.[21] But that doesn't disturb me much. It cannot be changed: dung beetles will always be lovers of dirt, and men who are turncoats, inconsistent, and jumping from one profession to another, men who are ranters and a nuisance will always insult the best men. For they delight in such treasures, whereas we by contrast admire the divine talent of Erasmus even in these books of responses, in which he replies to Lee's insane insults, without being vengeful, however – a thing that not everyone can do. Who would not piously love the modesty of that Christian heart? I wish Lee had shown the same modesty. Then you would have no reason to blame me for being mentioned in his book.

I dedicate to you these books of responses which the author wrote in a

* * * * *

19 I.e., someone who can interpret an oracle; Erasmus *Adagia* 1.6.29.
20 I.e., about nothing. The expressions are proverbial: Erasmus *Adagia* 1.3.52 and 53.
21 I.e., There is a match for everyone. Eramus *Adagia* 1.10.71.

hurry because he did not think that they would be a lasting work. Armed with them you may reply to any fools in your region, although here we have one who is so stubborn that even Truth herself would not satisfy him. If you must bear in your region people of that sort, either bid them farewell as hopeless, or do as physicians do with their patients as a last resort: try the final remedy, that is, soften their backs with beatings everywhere.[22] For that type of demon cannot be driven out in any other way. Farewell, sweetest Martin, and always bring your authority to bear on me with such exhortations. Jakob Truchsess,[23] a most elegant young man and quite learned in the two languages, who recently interrupted a journey to stay with me, sends his regards to your brother Johann Gertophius.[24] Mainz, on the Ides of August, in the year 1520.

Letter 55: 24 August 1520, Rome, Peter Gebwiler to Capito

> For Peter Gebwiler see above, Ep. 50, headnote. The manuscript of this letter is in the Universitätsbibliothek, Basel, Ki.Ar. 25a, #56.

I beg and beseech you, as I began to do in my other recent letters to you (and I do so advisedly and with the endorsement of all your friends) that you attempt without delay to acquire possession of the provostship, lest he[1] should obtrude himself, for I very much fear that he will do so and compel the chapter of St Thomas to act with executorial letters and the threat of ecclesiastical censures. Nor is the chapter to be trusted, as Your Lordship perhaps thinks, for I fear that they have a secret understanding. I do not write anything rashly, as you know. Therefore you must put everything else

* * * * *

22 Capito is echoing Johannes Gertophius's *Recriminatio* (Basel: Cratander, April 1520), 11: 'opus est uno, fustibus et virgis, quibus tergum tuum ... inscribemus.'

23 See above, Ep. 41, note 1.

24 Johannes Gertophius was a corrector at the Froben press in 1518/19, as he relates in the *Recriminatio* (see note 22 above). He is documented in the records of the University of Wittenberg in 1522. Apparently he was not well known outside his own circle. On 8 December 1520 Johann Beham wrote to Althamer, who had inquired about the author of the *Recriminatio*: 'I know nothing about that Gertophius of Ulm ... It is an assumed name ... but what does it mean? It appears to be Greek. Write and tell me what it means' (J.A. Ballenstedt, *Andreae Althameri vita*, [Wolfenbüttel, 1740], 64).

1 I.e., Jacob Abel. For Capito's litigation against Abel and his efforts to obtain the provostship of St Thomas see above, Ep. 50.

aside and diligently seek to take possession, for I know that if you do otherwise the chapter will deceive you in this. I have no doubt that several from the same chapter are also striving for the provostship. It is not advisable to make arrangements for the case concerning the canonry until we are more certain about the possession of the provostship, so that the case can be heard by the same judge. However, it would be much preferable to enter on the provostship without a lawsuit. Your adversaries obtained a brief sent from Strasbourg (and, in my opinion, it was through Vogler)[2] before we had received any of the letters etc. I am grateful about what you write regarding the canonry and entitlement of Balthasar, provost of Waldkirch,[3] and I shall agree to any honest terms. Yet there is some urgency in this matter, lest he come to an agreement with his adversary, as they say; and whatever Your Lordship has done, I believe it has always been in my interest. But if you should meet at the emperor's court, you will be able to employ in this matter the efforts of our most reverend lord,[4] who is well acquainted with the same lord doctor Balthasar. Therefore, carry on and you will clearly realize that nothing you have done has been conferred on an ungrateful man.

Farewell. Rome. 24 August 1520.

P.S. A judgment on the *Augenspiegel* was recently rendered against Dr Johann Reuchlin and in favour of Jacob van Hoogstraten, O.P.[5] The matter of Dr Luther is well known to you from my other letters, etc.

Most obediently, P. Gebwiler.

* * * * *

2 Thomas Vogler (d. 1532), who had studied law at Freiburg, was from 1501 almoner to the cathedral of Strasbourg. He was a loyal Catholic, and in 1524 unsuccessfully tried to arrange a colloquy between Catholic and Protestant sympathizers. In 1525 he was a canon at St Stephen's but eventually withdrew from the city. Gebwiler's opinion not withstanding, Capito appointed Vogler one of his four legal representatives in the matter concerning his provostship (see above, Ep. 50, note 7).

3 I.e., Balthasar Merklin (ca. 1479–1531) studied at Paris and obtained a doctorate in canon law at Bologna (1500). He held canonries in the cathedral chapter of Constance, St Simon in Trier, St Thomas in Strasbourg, etc., as well as a provostship at Waldkirch. He served as imperial councillor at the court of Maximilian and Charles V, whom he accompanied to Spain. The present business may have been connected with his (upcoming) journey and the need to appoint a stand-in or legal representative for the period of his absence from Germany. In 1527 he was made vice-chancellor of the empire and bishop of Malta, and in 1529 he succeeded to the bishopric of Constance.

4 I.e., Albert of Brandenburg.

5 For Reuchlin see above, Ep. 45a, note 5.

Letter 56: 28 August [1520], Fulda, Ulrich von Hutten to Capito

Millet's summary is based on the notes of R.G. Richter in 'Ulrich von Hutten und das Kloster Fulda,' *Fuldaer Geschichtsblätter* 8 (1909): 49–57. Richter reports only that the manuscript of this letter was offered for sale in 1907. He (and Millet) were unaware that it was acquired by the Pierpont Morgan Library in New York. The text of the letter was published by R. Salomon, 'An Unpublished Letter of Ulrich von Hutten,' *Journal of the Warburg and Courtauld Institutes* 12 (1949): 192–6.

[*Summary*]: Hutten recommends to Capito the bearer of the letter, Crotus Rubeanus, who is on his way to Mainz. He asks Capito to help him obtain a living from the abbot of Fulda, a canon at the cathedral and residing in Mainz. He also asks him to enlist the help of Dietrich Zobel. Capito has urged Hutten to embrace peace and compromise, but he is unable to contemplate peace as long as the Roman 'arch-tyrants' are despoiling Germany. He is not afraid of Leo X, who is relying on the secular arm, whereas he himself is relying on God. Hutten asks Capito to continue supplying him with news and asks specifically about Erasmus and More.

Letter 57: 30 August 1520, Mainz, Capito to the Dean of St Thomas
[Nicolaus Wurmser]

This is a letter to the chapter of St Thomas, nominally addressed to the dean, Nicolaus Wurmser (1473–1536). Wurmser, who also held a canonry at Young St Peter's in Strasbourg, was educated in Italy (doctorate in canon law from the University of Siena, 1503). He was a staunch opponent of the Reformation and of Capito personally. He fled St Thomas in 1524, taking with him a reliquary, cash, documents, and the seal of the chapter. In 1529 he settled with the city and retired to a canonry he had acquired in the meantime at St Margaret's in Waldkirch. The autograph manuscript of this letter is in the Archive Municipale, Strasbourg, AST XVI, 5.

Capito to the Dean of St Thomas, greetings.

Venerable, noble, and most learned and most respected gentlemen: The last transaction between us makes abundantly clear how friendly and favourably disposed Your Lordships are towards me. For you seemed to congratulate me from your hearts on my successful accession to the provostship and prebend and to the canonry, etc. Your friendly disposition led me to abstain from pursuing in court my right against you worthy gentlemen,[1] for you decided at that time to act, promising through the most learned and noble dean that you would give no one possession except me, whatever claim was presented, and until I obtained possession, you would account to me alone concerning the income from the provostship (although the noble and excellent Wolfgang Boecklin,[2] provost of Young St Peter's, privately added more during dinner).

But rumour has it that Jacob Abel[3] continues to scoff at the law and play tricks. He has little claim on you nor, as I believe, is he popular with Your Paternities. And indeed it seems likely to me that he will make every attempt, as is his habit, to make whatever plans he can think of, going against the firm will of our Most Serene Lord[4] who favours me and trying to blunt the effect. But I shall easily evade his machinations. For the most reverend lords, Cardinals Giulio de Medici and Lorenzo Pucci[5] and His Holiness himself[6] guard my interests, even if I do not solicit their support. Yet I have not been idle on that account but have written to our Most Serene Lord and to the above mentioned most reverend lord cardinals. Furthermore the most reverend lord [the archbishop of] Mainz has written most effective recommendations on my behalf, that is on behalf of his councillor, to the same luminaries of the Roman court.[7] Nor do I have any doubts that our most serene Lord will declare in my favour, if only you reverend, noble, and

* * * * *

1 See Ep. 55.
2 Wolfgang Boecklin of Strasbourg (d. 1530) studied law at the universities of Bologna and Siena (doctorate of civil and canon laws, Siena 1501), became canon of Young St Peter's in 1505. In 1509 Pope Julius II appointed him provost of St Peter and canon of St Thomas, dispensing him from residence to allow him to remain at the Roman curia. From 1513 on he was also abbot of Klingenmünster in the Palatinate. He was a staunch Catholic and in 1529 represented the interests of the Strasbourg canons who had been obliged to leave on account of their confessional stand.
3 See above, Ep. 50, note 2.
4 I.e., Pope Leo X.
5 Giulio de Medici (1478–1534, later Pope Clement VII) lived in exile in Rome after the expulsion of the Medici from Florence in 1494 and was actively involved in Pope Julius II's campaigns in Italy. After the election of Pope Leo X (Giulio's cousin) in 1513 and the restoration of the Medicis to Florence, he rose rapidly. In 1523 he was made archbishop of Florence and cardinal of Santa Maria in Dominica. From 1517 on he was the pope's vice-chancellor. After his cousin's death he failed to secure his own election and left Rome for Florence. Leo's successor, Pope Adrian VI, died in September 1523, and Giulio was then elected as Pope Clement VII. For Lorenzo Pucci, see Ep. 50, note 3.
6 I.e., Pope Leo X.
7 Cf. Albert's letter below (Ep. 58), which was drafted by Capito himself!

excellent gentlemen will support me and pay no attention to the claim of my adversary, if he should proffer a claim. For you can easily help with the appeals and expose the malice of certain people. Otherwise my simple desire to oblige Your Paternities will put me at a disadvantage. Therefore, most generous gentlemen, I beg Your Excellencies to [spare] me troubles, etc. and join my legal representatives in the appeal made at my own risk, and I shall preserve you from any loss. It will not be difficult for the notary and my friends to find suitable reasons in that matter, namely: the apostolic brief given to me earlier during the [provost's] lifetime and conceding to me his rights after his death gave me accession through the method of regress in phrases that were worded in the customary manner. The appeal can be based on the fact that the chapter made the nomination without dealing with my legal claim and that Johann Hepp[8] obtained possession of the said prebend and canonry from you, although he had not yet been evicted by three definite sentences, in fact had not even been cited before the court. Therefore you were in no legal position to eject anyone from his rightfully acquired place. Later, however, when [Abel] used the law to displace Capito and Johann Hepp, you were willing to do your duty, protesting, etc. Then the censures with which he threatens will have no effect. Therefore Your Lordships will do the lawful and respectable thing, indeed your bounden duty, and you will put me and my supporters under obligation in every way to everyone of you. Even now I pledge myself to Your Reverend Paternities, to exert myself for you tirelessly either with my prince or my other supporters. Mainz, 31 August, in the year 1520. Wolfgang Capito.

Letter 58: 1 September 1520, Mainz, Albert of Brandenburg to Leo X

> Printed in Kalkoff, *Capito*, 133–4. The letter was composed by Capito on behalf of the archbishop.

[*Summary*]: The dean of the church of Halberstadt has consented that Valentin von Tetleben be confirmed as his coadjutor. Albert of Brandenburg asks the pope to reduce the administrative fees due for that transaction. He has been told that Leo X has conferred on Capito the provostship of St Thomas in Strasbourg at the request of the Swiss and the intercession of Lorenzo and Antonio Pucci. A certain Sebastian Bender, however, after he learned through witnesses about the death of Jakob Fabri von Reichshofen, the pro-

* * * * *

8 For Hepp losing canonry number 14 and acquiring number 15 under dubious circumstances, see above, Ep. 50, note 2.

vost of St Thomas, has claimed the position. Albert of Brandenburg begs Leo X to intervene *proprio motu* in Capito's favour. He expects to accomplish much through Capito's services for Leo X and the church.

Letter 59: 1 October 1520, Augsburg, Georgius Spalatinus to Capito

> For Spalatinus see above, Ep. 29, headnote. The manuscript of this letter is in the Staatsbibliothek, Munich, clm 10357, #17.

Many greetings. My dearest Doctor Capito, I would like you to have for yourself a keepsake of my most clement prince, Duke Frederick of Saxony, elector of the Holy Roman Empire.[1] Here is a silver coin with his likeness, so lifelike that you would say it is breathing. For I cannot and ought not to doubt that it will be dear to you for the sake of the memory of a man who kindly favours you. For when I asked for it on your behalf, he agreed with such goodwill that for that reason alone I could not be more devoted to a prince who deserves best in every way of the best studies and the best men, even of myself who am a nobody. Farewell and best wishes from all my friends. Hurriedly, from Augsburg, 1 October, 1520.

Letter 60: 24 October 1520, Rome, Peter Gebwiler to Capito

> For Peter Gebwiler and the lawsuit discussed in this letter see above, Epp. 50 and 55.
> The manuscript of this letter is in the Universitätsbibliothek Basel, Ki.Ar. 25a, 53.

Greetings with commendation etc. The reason why Your Lordship has received letters from me more infrequently perhaps than might be expected, is this: the case of the provostship and the canonry and prebend has not yet reached the stage we are aiming at. But we have vigorously contested the claims of your adversaries every day and in every way, so that nothing seems to remain short of coming to blows. In this battle the main issue has not been decided. We have not yet turned the corner in this business, so to speak. But the whole argument was about whether, after a general sentence was obtained after the death of Jakob Reichshofen[1] against all

* * * * *

1 Frederick the Wise (1463–1525), Elector of Saxony, founder of the University of Wittenberg, was a noted patron of the arts and protector of Luther.

1 The previous holder of the provostship. See above, Ep. 50, note 2.

and sundry, executorial letters by decree and execution of writ could be demanded on the strength of the same, or not. Your adversaries had in mind, with the matter having been adjudicated by virtue of the aforementioned general sentence, to compel the chapter to hand over possession before anything would be done by us in the principal matter. We have resisted this with all our strength and used many special writs to effect that the case will be taken away from the previous judge[2] before whom they obtained the decision they hoped for, and reassigned to another[3] for judgment so that we may more easily obtain the desired result. Immediately following the receipt of the notice, an appeal was launched on behalf of Your Lordship, and with that case of appeal committed, it now remains for us to make sure that the records of the case be transferred from the first judge, so that the deceptions and tricks of your adversaries may be seen from the legal proceedings. Without seeing them, there would be no point in initiating the process.

Sebastian Bender, another of your adversaries, had the pope's provision on the second day, unless I am mistaken, after the death of Johannes Schutz.[4] As for the claim of Jacob Abel, after viewing and reviewing the laws in detail and in accordance with the helpful advice of prudent and well-informed friends, we must devise another way, by which the weapons and arms prepared against us will strike their authors in turn. In this matter the most reverend lord cardinal of Santi Quattro Coronati,[5] now cardinal penitentiary, promised to make every effort, and also gave us no small hope which, as I believe, Your Lordship learned in part from Doctor Valentin von

* * * * *

2 Cardinal Antonio Trivulzio (ca. 1470–1520), auditor at the papal court. Abel submitted a copy of his judgment, dated 24 September 1520 (see below, Appendix 1), to the city council of Strasbourg in 1534, when he unsuccessfully tried to have it enforced through the secular authorities. The copy is in the Archive municipale of Strasbourg, AMS IX 2, #4.

3 The attempt to substitute Mercurio de Vipera for Trivulzio seems to have failed. Trivulzio confirmed his earlier judgment, and Abel took possession of the provostship by proxy on 14 November 1520 (see Appendix, Document 2).

4 Johannes Schutz (or Schütz) was the chapter's legal representative (*procurator*) at the papal court. He is documented in 1510/11 as canon and provost of St Peter and Michael. See A. Meister, 'Auszüge aus den Rechnungsbüchern der Camera Apostolica zur Geschichte der Kirchen des Bistums Strassburg 1415–1513,' in *Zeitschrift für die Geschichte des Oberrheins* 46 (1892), 104–51. Schütz died in the fall of 1520. For Bender see above, Ep. 50, note 2, and Ep. 58, summary.

5 I.e., Lorenzo Pucci. See above, Ep. 50, note 3.

Tetleben,[6] since he presented the letter sent to the cardinal by Your Lordship's patron of Mainz.

There is not one among all the others who does not play his part properly, especially Dietrich Spät,[7] who is circumspect and handles all cases that come up with careful diligence. He is tireless in his efforts and his labour, indeed he has extraordinary skill and experience in forensic cases, and we will use him in future as well. Hence I have no qualms to recommend him and his friends in Mainz who are not unknown to Your Lordship, and all of their affairs, although nothing is needed less than those most commendable persons being further commended by an unimportant man like myself. Yet I am fully persuaded that the aforesaid Dietrich, his friends and associates, will find that my insignificant recommendation, for whatever it is worth, did merit Your Reverend Lordship's attention.

Farewell. Given at Rome on the 24th of October 1520. Do not completely forget in your good fortune, Most Reverend Lordship, your insignificant client, your most obedient Peter Gebwiler.

Letter 60a: After 25 October 1520, Mainz, Albert of Brandenburg to Leo X

This letter is printed in *Hutteni opera* 1:363–4. It has not been included in Millet's list, presumably because the nominal writer is Albert and no draft exists for the letter. However, Gerdesius, who first printed the text (II-2, 12–14) stated that he took it 'ex manuscriptis Capitonis' (from the manuscripts of Capito), i.e., Capito composed this letter on Albert's behalf. Böcking in *Hutteni opera* wrongly suggests that the letter was written in July 1520, whereas an internal reference supplies 25 October as the *terminus post quem*.

[*Summary*]: The papal legate Caracciolo has delivered to Albert the pope's gift of a golden rose. Albert thanks Leo for the honour. He assures him of his loyalty. He has taken action against Hutten's libellous pamphlets and dismissed him from his service. Albert has issued commands to have Luther's works suppressed as well. As for publishing the bull against Luther, Albert has incurred a great deal of unpopularity on account of his loyalty to Rome. Further action is not advisable without the support of the secular princes. He will consult with the papal legates in this matter and do his best.

* * * * *

6 See below, Ep. 93, headnote.
7 See below, Ep. 175, headnote.

Letter 61: 11 November 1520, [Heidelberg], [Martin Bucer] to Capito

Printed in *Corr Bucer* 1:119–22, #18

[*Summary*]: Bucer praises Capito's role in single-handedly defending humanist culture in Germany. Jacob of Hoogstraten has taken offence at a remark Bucer made about him and denounced him as a partisan of Luther. He is threatening to prosecute him. Bucer is imploring the help of Hutten and Capito. He is ready to accept any situation whatever, provided that he can leave the company of those opposed to literature and true piety [i.e., the Dominican monastery at Heidelberg]. Thomas Murner has just published an anonymous pamphlet in German against Luther. At Maternus Hatten's house Bucer read Georg von Schwalbach's copy of the dialogue, *Hochstratus ovans*. He already suspects who was the author and who advised the author.

Letter 62: 13 November 1520, Leipzig, Petrus Mosellanus to Capito

Petrus Mosellanus (d. 1524) studied at Cologne, where he registered in 1512. In 1524 he moved to Freiburg (Saxony) and taught Greek at the local grammar school. In 1515 he matriculated at Leipzig, completed his MA in 1520, and began teaching Greek at the university. In the same year he became bachelor of theology and also taught in that faculty. He was attacked by Jacques Masson, a Louvain theologian, for praising language studies as a prerequisite for the theology student (*Oratio de variarum linguarum cognitione paranda* [Leipzig: Schumann, 1518]; Masson's criticism is entitled *De trium linguarum et studii theologici ratione* [Antwerp: Hillen, 1519]). Although Masson officially directed his criticism at Mosellanus, it was meant to include Erasmus, who had made similar pronouncements in his 1518 *Ratio verae theologiae*. Erasmus accordingly answered Masson in *Apologia contra Latomi dialogum* (Antwerp: Thibault, 1519). Between 1516 and 1521, Mosellanus published a number of textbooks and pedagogical writings. He also produced editions and commentaries on Aristophanes, Gregory of Nazianzen, Isocrates, Lucian, Aulus Gellius, Quintilian, and others. He was planning to visit Italy when he died prematurely at Leipzig in the spring of 1524, much regretted by his many humanist friends and correspondents, among them Jacobus Sobius, Richard Croke, Julius Pflug, and Mutianus Rufus. The manuscript of the letter is in the Universitätsbibliothek Basel, Kir.Ar. 25a, #50.

I cannot tell you, best Fabritius, how much I loved you even though you were known to me only by name. But after you wrote me a letter declaring your goodwill towards me, I began to burn with an even greater love for you, for I realized from the letter that my love was returned, and returned by such a great man. The reason why you now receive the letter I wrote some months ago together with the present batch[1] is this: one problem led to another, and there was no courier at hand, so that that letter was overlooked and, as it happens, was lying among other papers.

I do not know the state of scholarship in your part, whether studies flourish there or are persecuted by the sophists. Here at any rate we are superior to the enemy, and our party is victorious, and it is not only the better but also the more numerous party. Martin Luther's ferocity stirs up things somewhat. You can easily tell from the following how zealous our prince is on behalf of the humanities: in the last few days when our lord George[2] was in Leipzig, he mentioned and praised you more than ten times, showing that he was most concerned on your behalf.[3] Nor was that all. Indeed, he commissioned Caesar Pflug,[4] that efficient and industrious knight and principal figure at our court, to inquire in detail about you and your affairs. For this reason Pflug has now (and even earlier) several times approached me and Heinrich Stromer,[5] councillor of this city, who was known to him before. But we do not know what your attitude towards us is and whether you can be drawn away from Mainz under certain conditions, and therefore I could not make any definite pronouncements so far. You need have no qualms about the fairness of the city, the loyalty of many friends, the great eagerness of the young people, the constant good will of the prince. But here is what's relevant to the matter: you must reveal your feelings about Leipzig in a letter to either of us. Then it will be our business to see that the prince will write to you himself and invite you with a definite offer. You cannot imagine the quality of the intellectual life and the living standard

* * * * *

1 I.e., together with Stromer's letter to Hutten and Melanchthon's to Mutianus Rufus, mentioned below.

2 Duke George of Saxony. See above, Ep. 31, note 4.

3 On 11 November 1520, Petrus Mosellanus wrote to Conrad Mutianus Rufus: 'We are looking around here for a way to enable us to bring Fabritius Capito here. All the young people are eagerly inclined to the study of holy writ. More than three hundred people listen to me lecturing on Paul's epistles, and I'm certainly not the best teacher. See how much times have changed!' (*Briefe Mutians*, Ep. 596).

4 Caesar Pflug, official (*Amman*) in the government of Leipzig and councillor of Duke George. Mosellanus taught his son Julius, who studied at the University of Leipzig until 1517 and eventually succeeded his father as the duke's adviser.

5 See above, Ep. 32, note 7. Stromer became a member of the town council in February 1520 and advanced to the position of first councillor in 1526.

here, how splendidly we live, how honourable are the lives of the clergy. For you will not find here examples of actions similar to those done in Mainz with impunity. You understand what I am saying and what I am leaving unsaid.

The bearer of this letter is a Jew,[6] but truly turned into a Christian, and turned into a Christian through Luther's sermons. He is an upright and trustworthy man. I sent him, weighed down with letters and documents to my native city for the sake of completing a certain little business. You can write back through him about everything, even the most private matters. He would sooner die than betray his friends. I have had him stay in my house for one and a half years, and I know him as I know myself. I wonder what Hutten[7] is doing. It has been reported that an apostolic legate fell into his hands these days, who was equipped with many bulls.[8] Stromer has written a letter to Hutten; see to it that it is conveyed to him secretly. For that is his request. Give the man my respects, for I have no time at all to write to him, nor do I have anything to write.

The bearer brings some works of Luther, as you will see. I wonder how the matter will end, for Martin makes no concessions as far as his ideas are concerned, although many friends have counselled [moderation]. On the contrary, he rages every day more seriously against tyranny. May it turn out for the best. My prince George does not like the man as much as the Elector Frederick does.[9] Farewell. In haste, from Leipzig. And do write back. On the Ides of November, in the year '20. Your P. Mosellanus.

* * * * *

6 Bernhard Coppinger (before his conversion, Rabbi Jakob Gipher). He was the bearer of this letter as well as of letters to Mutian (see above, note 3). In 1519 he taught Hebrew at Wittenberg; in 1520 he lived in Mosellanus's house, then returned to Wittenberg, where he was Johann Drach's teacher. He is last documented in 1539.

7 See above, Ep. 32, note 6.

8 The report was false, but Hutten frequently made threats of that kind. In April 1521 he wrote a letter to Charles V (text in *Hutteni opera* 2:12–21), insulting the papal legates Aleandro and Caracciolo and threatening them with physical violence. He said the actions of the legates 'provoked him to seek their punishment' (ad ultionem et poenam nos ultro provoces; Böcking, 16) and he would give orders 'to draw the sword against them and to take up arms' (iubebo gladios expediri adversum et arma suscipi iubebo; ibid., 20). Aleandro's efforts to have Luther's books burned led to riots in Mainz on 28–9 November 1520, during which the papal legate was manhandled (see Beatus Rhenanus's report on 7 January 1521, *Briefwechsel*, 226f.).

9 See above, Ep. 59, note 1.

Letter 63: 4 December 1520, Mainz, Capito to Martin Luther

Printed in WBr 2:222–6, #357

[*Summary*]: Johann Eck has written a boastful letter to Hoogstraten declaring how much the business of Christ has succeeded at Leipzig. Luther [by his *An den christlichen Adel*] and Hutten have sounded the war trumpet, and a battle seems imminent. Although Luther and Hutten are not defenceless, their opponents seem to have the advantage. Most people side with Luther, but some support the Romanists. Someone in Cologne has written a dialogue entitled *Hochstratus ovans*, reproaching Eck and Aleandro for burning Luther's books, and has wrongly cast aspersions on Capito as well. Eck has replied. Aleandro is hiding his anger, but he is keeping a wary eye on Capito. Thomas Murner published two anti-Lutheran books: *Ein christliche ermahnung* and *Von Luthers Lehren und Predigen*. Capito reiterates his fear of the violence that accompanies war. Using scriptural references as examples, Capito advises Luther to be moderate and to make concessions for the sake of peace. 'I am not saying that Christ's business should be put aside, but one must indulge the common people in many things ... Do not preach the word of Christ contentiously but with charity.'

Letter 64: 6 December 1520, Louvain, Desiderius Erasmus to Capito

Printed in Allen 4:394–6, #1165 and CWE 8, Ep. 1165

[*Summary*]: The popularity of the Reformation in the Low Countries is apparent by the people's rejection of the papal bull *Exsurge Domine*. This is also evident in the ill treatment of Erasmus's critic Vincentius Theoderici by the people at Dordrecht. Erasmus denies Vincentius's accusation that he incited the people. The Louvain theologians Masson and Turnhout dare not publish their works against Luther. Erasmus has been sent a pamphlet criticizing his New Testament edition. He instructs Capito to find the author of an anonymous dialogue mentioning Cardinal Wolsey and to tell him to suppress the piece. The situation in Louvain is difficult. If Wilhelm Nesen publishes his *Vita S. Nicolai*, he must not do it anonymously and he must not mention Dorp. The theologians have been silently pressuring Erasmus, thinking that only he could vanquish Luther. Erasmus emphatically rejects the notion. He asks Capito to inform him of Albert of Brandenburg's attitude towards him. He sends greetings to Ludovicus Carinus and Hartmann von Hallwyl.

Letter 65: 28 December 1520, Speyer, Martin Bucer to Capito

Printed in *Corr Bucer* 1:133–5, #23

[*Summary*]: Bucer has reached the crisis point: he will either be ruined if the Dominicans gain the upper hand or celebrate the victory of truth together with his friends. He asks Capito to write letters of recommendation for him, should the need arise. A fellow monk, who was in the same situation as Bucer, advises him to obtain from Rome a release from his monastic vows. Maternus Hatten, whom Bucer consulted, reckons that Anton Engelbrecht, suffragan bishop of Speyer, would be willing to settle this affair. He sends his regards to Jakob Truchsess.

Letter 66: [1520, Leipzig?], Christoph Hegendorf to Capito

For Hegendorf see above, Ep. 51, headnote. The manuscript of his letter is in the Universitätsbibliothek Basel, Ki.Ar. 25a, #55. The text is written in Greek.

Hail Capito! I am very surprised that you write nothing. I do not think that you have changed. I am not unaware of your affability and kindness, unless the tribe of those who slander my good qualities and those of other good men and, heaping up abuse by the wagonful, have changed your attitude towards me.[1] What can I do? ... I do not have a sycophant's sting. It is not difficult to slander a man and speak against him and very easy to do so by word of mouth, but to make another a better man and improve on what we criticize is altogether laborious. Let them prattle against me all they want: I shall not move a finger.[2] Write to me and cast evil reports concerning my behaviour out of your heart. I am writing to you in Greek, taking a risk. By taking aim often, I may strike Aphrodite.[3] Farewell and love me as I write on the spur of the moment. Your Christoph Hegendorf.
You must make the best of my misshapen letters.

* * * * *

1 Hegendorf made the same complaint in a letter to Andreas Althamer (cf. below, Ep. 101, headnote): 'Capitonem [gr.] allellon gegenemenon thaumazo. Male sit quibusdam [gr.] kakoglottois, qui illum mihi [gr.] ellaxan' (I am surprised at the change in Capito. Damn those evil-speakers, who have changed his attitude towards me!; Ballenstedt, 79–80).
2 Cf. Erasmus *Adagia* 1.3.21.
3 I.e., succeed. The metaphor is taken from winning a game of knucklebones; cf. CWE 40, 899:3–4.

Letter 67: 1 January 152[1], Basel, Claude Chansonnette to Capito

Claude Chansonnette or Cantiuncula (d. 1549) was a native of Metz and the son of a notary. He studied law at Louvain and Basel, where he obtained a doctorate in civil law (1519). He taught at the university and worked in the municipal chancery as a notary. In 1522 he became syndic to the town council and was sent on an embassy to the French court. He published a number of legal textbooks and commentaries on legal sources and translated Erasmus's *Exomologesis* into French (1524). In 1524 he asked to be released from his duties and returned to Metz, ostensibly to look after his father, but actually to avoid involvement in the Reformation debate. At the time he sympathized with the reformers. He worked for the town council of Metz for some time until, in 1527, he became chancellor to Cardinal Jean de Lorraine, bishop of Metz, on whose behalf he served on diplomatic missions to the imperial court. From 1533 on he served at the court of King Ferdinand in Vienna.

The manuscript is in the Universitätsbibliothek, Basel, Ki.Ar. 25a, 64. It is erroneously dated 1520. The text is printed in A. Rivier, *Claude Chansonnette* (Brussels, 1878), 29.

Greetings! Believe me, my patron, fortune has hardly ever inflicted a more bitter wound than when I recently had to depart from Worms without seeing you and in uncertainty about my affairs.[1] But I had to keep to the arrangements made with my companions on the journey. I have no doubt that you have almost completed the matter in which you are acting on my behalf; therefore you will be able to bring it to a conclusion and completely free me from my cares and uncertainties. I am sending to the most reverend and illustrious prince the decrees of the council of Nicaea and other matters beside, but on the same conditions on which I have received them from the owner of the book, that is as a favour, for I would never have entrusted it to anyone except you (for it is entrusted to you as long as the prince has it).

You will also see a copy of my letter, which you will hand on if you think it will be useful or help the matter at hand; I leave this up to your judgment. At any rate make sure to let me know through the present courier on what ear you want me to sleep.[2] For there is another matter in the wings but, in my opinion, less worthy than the plan you promote. And even if that prospect were better than your plan, I would nevertheless prefer to have you as

* * * * *

1 Capito accompanied Albert of Mainz to the Diet of Worms. As indicated in the letter, Chansonnette was hoping to enter Albert's service.
2 I.e., whether I need to worry or not, a proverbial expression, cf. *Adagia* 1.8.19.

my patron; for whatever I may accept or comes my way in future, whether your object eludes us or is successful, I will in any case always be very much in your debt because of your benevolence towards me. But I cannot believe that anything will come to pass contrary to your wishes, for everything that is the prince's affair is in your hands. On account of your incredible benevolence I am under obligation to you for your many favours, an obligation I could not repay or escape even if I put myself up for auction. Nevertheless I beg you, my support and sweet ornament, and beseech you by your obliging and clement heart: tighten the bonds between yourself and your Claude ever more, at this very hour. And yet I owe everything to you already. I shall be grateful like a young stork,[3] and I shall not allow the memory of the favours you have done me to wither in my breast.

Farewell: I shall fare better if I am worthy of receiving Your Eminence's letters, in which you either call me to your prince under a definite offer, or indicate that I need cherish no further hopes. It is for this reason that I have sent the present courier to you at my expense. I have directed a letter written in the vernacular to your amanuensis Jakob Truchsess,[4] that it may be shown if necessary. Effect the promotion, my patron, and I shall effect that you will never regret it. Basel, on the Calends of January 1520 after the incarnation of our Lord. Claude Chansonnette, forever at Your Eminence's service.

Dearest Wolfgang, I ask that you let the courier go as soon as possible, while you are writing or looking after my business in the court of your prince or indeed, as I hope, while you have my business in hand, for he cannot remain long, hardly a day or two; by all means write what you want me to do, for you can write within an hour what you have found out from your prince.

Letter 68: 5 January [1521], Basel, Konrad Heresbach to Capito

> Konrad Heresbach (or Hertzbach, 1496–1576) studied at Cologne (MA 1515), then travelled in France (taking a degree in law, perhaps in Orléans). From 1520 on he was in Basel, working as a corrector for the printer Johann Froben. In July 1521 he registered at the University of Freiburg as MA and bachelor of law. In the fall of 1522 he left for Italy, where he obtained a doctorate in law from the University of Ferrara. He taught at the University of Freiburg in 1522 and again on his return from Italy in 1523. On being refused a raise in salary, however, he resigned and became tutor to the son of the Duke of Cleves.

* * * * *

3 Storks were proverbial for their gratitude, cf. *Adagia* 1.10.1.
4 See above, Ep. 41, note 1.

Appointed councillor, he undertook diplomatic missions for the Duke and was rewarded with ecclesiastical prebends. He resigned them in 1536 and married. He continued in the service of Cleves and was involved in peace negotiations between the religious factions. In 1562 he retired to his estate on an island in the Rhine near Wesel and devoted himself to scholarship. He produced editions of classical authors, wrote a manual of farming, and left a *Diarium seu quotidianae preces*, published at Basel in 1574. The manuscript of the letter is in the Archive Municipale, Strasbourg, AST 40, #58, fol. 435.

Greetings. I recently wrote you, most learned Capito, a letter that was perhaps more friendly than accurate, for I was far from licking my letter into shape as a she-bear usually does with her cubs. Indeed I could not even rewrite it. On his return,[1] Claude affirmed that the letter had been conveyed to you in good faith. I cannot be very angry with you for not replying, for you are involved in too serious business to take time out for my nonsense. But in writing again, I want to urge one thing on you: if you find out anything about my affair, could you immediately inform me? Philipp Engelbrecht[2] brought some news back from Freiburg, but everything was vague and doubtful. I shall not pay cash for hope, but your Honour may easily venture guesses in a letter. Unless I obtain something definite before April, I shall go to Italy to N. and apply myself again to those things which long ago ceased to appeal to me[3] on account of my Greek studies.

There is nothing new here that isn't old news in your place. I would consider myself fortunate if you took the time to write even one word to me.

Farewell, my support and sweet ornament. Basel, on the day before the Feast of the Magi.

Your Konrad Heresbach. I beg you not to begrudge me the favour of transmitting the enclosed letter to Adam Weiss,[4] who will convey the remaining letters to Cologne.

* * * * *

1 Presumably Claude Chansonnette had delivered the letter when he visited Worms. See Ep. 67.
2 On Engelbrecht see below, Ep. 79, headnote. The vague news presumably concerned an appointment at the university (see above headnote).
3 I.e., law. He delayed his journey to Italy for a year (see above headnote).
4 Adam Weiss of Crailsheim (ca. 1480–1534) had the lectoral prebend at Liebfrau in Mainz and from 1516 to 1520 taught theology at the University of Mainz. In 1521 he moved back to Crailsheim, where he was instrumental in introducing the Reformation.

Letter 69: 6 January 1521, Basel, Claude Chansonnette to Capito

> On Chansonnette see headnote to Ep. 67. The manuscript is in the Universitäts-
> bibliothek, Basel, Ki.Ar. 25a, #65. The text, like Ep. 67, was published by Rivier,
> 30–1.

Greetings. My most learned patron, I am awaiting the return of the courier whom I sent to you with the [decrees of] the Council of Nicaea.[1] And I expect nothing but that the affair has been concluded according to my expectations and your goodwill towards me, for you can do anything at the court of your (and as I hope now my) prince.[2] Have no doubt. I shall be at your service and act on your nod. As long as we are together, you will always find that I am a man whom you can give any command and in whom you can put your complete trust. If I did anything else, I would be most ungrateful. But the matter will always remain under cover, as long as I am with you, for I have not said a word to any mortal man.

As for the rest, there is at your place a certain royal secretary by name of Remaclus.[3] If you are on familiar terms with him, you may want to find out from him whether he wants to write to me. For I know he would write to me about the matter of a privilege concerning my native Metz. For I have seen to it that those who are in charge of it should go to him. I do not write to him, because he was not yet at Worms when I was there. Farewell, anchor of my hope, and I pledge to you everything I can do physically or mentally. Basel, on the day of Epiphany, 1521. In haste. Nothing, if not yours, Claude Chansonnette.

Letter 70: 13 January 1521, Wittenberg, Felix Ulscenius to Capito

> It is clear from Ulscenius's letters that he studied at Wittenberg with financial
> support from Capito. There is no trace, however, of his enrolment. Hartfelder,
> who first published this letter, notes that only one 'Felix' appears in the matric-
> ulation records of the university for the years in question: Felix Beyer of

* * * * *

1 See above, Ep. 67, for the loan of the book.
2 See above, Ep. 67, for Chansonnette's hope to obtain a position at Albert's court.
3 Remaclus Arduenna (d. 1524), an Italian poet, who studied at Cologne. For a while he lived in Paris, supporting himself with teaching. He eventually entered the service of Margaret of Austria as secretary and, in 1520, was named court historian by Charles V.

Zurich. The Ulscenius (or Ulsenius) in question is, however, more likely a relative of Dietrich Ulsenius of Kampen in Overijssel, who was for a time city physician of Nürnberg, then taught medicine at the universities of Mainz (1502–4)
and Freiburg (1504–5). The younger Ulscenius was a supporter of the Reformation. In 1525 he was arrested in Ensisheim on account of his confessional stand.
Capito interceded on his behalf with the Ensisheim pastor, Petrus Wickram
(see Ep. 254).

The text of the letter is printed in K. Hartfelder, ed., *Melanchthoniana paeda-
gogica* (Leipzig, 1892), 112–15.

Ulscenius to Capito, greetings. Since ingratitude is regarded by far the
most absurd of all vices, I have at any rate the intention of giving you
thanks. For the man must have a very kind heart who overwhelms with his
favour someone from whom he can hardly hope a good deed in turn. How
much do I deserve from you, sweetest teacher? Not a single stick! O how
fortunate I am to have you as my patron! What more could I ask of the
gods than a loyal father in this world, such as I have now, who excels the
rest in every way. I hope the thought will never enter your mind that you
have bestowed your favour on an unfeeling person. In future, when fortune favours me, I shall repay you most generously. In the meantime
it adds not a little to the mountain of Capito's praises that, apart from
your admirable knowledge of the languages, everyone says that you are
adorned with uncommon kindness, and are so ...[1] sincere and open to
everyone, although a certain man of note (as he regards himself) who was
recently received kindly by you,[2] traduced you and even Erasmus in conversation with people in Erfurt, saying that you were too much of a time-
watcher. Drach of Erfurt told me when I passed through. He and Eobanus[3]

* * * * *

1 Illegible.
2 Perhaps Justus Jonas. Cf. below, Ep. 121, in which Capito objects to Jonas's in-
   fighting, and Jonas's Ep. 126, in which he counsels Capito to stop prevaricat-
   ing.
3 Johann Drach or Draconites (1494–1566) studied in Erfurt (BA 1512, MA 1514)
   and became a canon at St Severus. In 1521 he resigned his canonry and went to
   Wittenberg, where he obtained a doctorate in theology in 1523. Appointed
   preacher in Miltenberg, he was driven out because of his Lutheran leanings,
   and eventually became a professor at the University of Marburg and (from
   1551) Rostock. He frequently visited Wittenberg to work on a polyglot edition
   of the Bible, parts of which were published between 1563 and 1565. In Erfurt,
   he was a close friend of Eobanus Hessus (1488–1540), who graduated from the
   university BA (1506) and became headmaster of the school of St Severus. In

defended you when they heard the slander, saying that it was great prudence on your part and must not be ascribed to hypocrisy. The fact that
Philip[4] was very kind to us is a sign of his standing faithfully by you and
being most zealous for your name.

The great Luther, so vigorous in treating sacred scripture, to whom I diligently listen, has now finished the second decade of the complete psalter.
He immediately undertook to lecture on the Sunday gospels according to
the holy year. He gives other sermons very freely. Melchior Zobel and Reinbold,[5] my most congenial housemates, never miss even one of them. They
live felicitously in agreement, happy to live in an age that allows them to see
Luther and listen to his gospel teaching.

At present we three inhabit a small house and attend Philip's private and
public lectures, which are: on Paul to the Romans, Virgil, Aristophanes'
Clouds, and sometimes Ciceronian orations. I believe Zobel and Reinbold
will receive a visit from Philip right away, although there is no need to fear
danger if it does not come to pass. For Philip often obliges his pupils to visit
him. By God, they rarely show themselves outdoors, thinking, according to
Mercury's saying to the tortoise: *It is better to stay at home, because it is harmful
outside.*[6]

For there is nothing to call the students away from their studies. The
place is not beautiful, the people are boorish, food is not splendid, and
Bacchus, who is most likely to keep students away from the Muses, is
unknown. Even if these things were freely available, they would be
scorned by them (believe me), after the example of the rest of the nobles as
well as other respectable young men. That is how attractive the humani-

* * * * *

1509 Eobanus was promoted MA. By this time he had become renowned for
his poetry. From 1514 on he lectured at the university. Confessional strife
nearly closed down the university during the twenties. Eobanus was, like his
friend Drach, a supporter of Luther, and in 1536 accepted an appointment at
the University of Marburg in Lutheran Hesse.

4 I.e., Melanchthon.
5 Melchior Zobel of Giebelstadt matriculated at the University of Wittenberg in
July 1521; for 1521/2 he is documented at Leipzig. He probably made Capito's
acquaintance through his relative (?) Dietrich Zobel of Guttenberg (ca. 1500–8),
canon at St Thomas in Strasbourg and at the cathedral chapter in Mainz, where
he resided. The latter had a successful career in the church, and in 1544 was
elected bishop of Würzburg. 'Reinbold' is Johann Remboldus of Haguenau, a
student of Capito's at the University of Basel, where he registered in the spring
of 1518. He later became the head of the city council of Haguenau.
6 Hesiod *Op.* 365.

ties are to the Wittenbergers. They are extravagant in the house of the erudite and honourable doctor, where they usually have wonderful literary
competitions. I, however, live as frugally as possible, so as not to involve
you in great costs on my behalf. It would be to the general good, if you
recommended me to them. A dialogue has appeared here, entitled *Hoch-
straten and Leo*,[7] in which you are criticized,[7] but Philipp ...[8] dialogue.
Farewell, venerable teacher, and greet in my name Marquard of Hattstein,
that man famous for his forefathers and his learning, and Ulrich Varnbühler, that man of most acute judgment.[9] At Wittenberg, from our common lodgings, 13 January, 1521.
Totally yours, Felix Ulscenius

Letter 71: 16 January [1521], Ebernburg, Ulrich von Hutten to Capito

Printed in *Hutteni opera* 2:5, #221

[*Summary*]: Franz von Sickingen has asked Capito to approach Albert of
Brandenburg to help in the cause of Reuchlin. They have invited him to join
them at the Ebernburg. Hutten is annoyed that Capito has not written to his
friends in a while and inserts only brief messages to them in letters to others.
He suggests that Capito is distancing himself from him.

* * * * *

7 I.e., *Hochstratus ovans*, published anonymously in 1520. 'Leo' should perhaps
   read 'Leus.' Edward Lee (see above, Ep. 54, headnote) and the Dominican
   inquisitor, Jacob van Hoogstraten, are the main speakers in the dialogue.
   Hoogstraten refers to Capito (Böcking, Suppl. I, 480): 'Verum de Capitone
   scias, quod nebulo cautissimus sic rem attemperat, quod eum et humanitatis
   periti iuxtaque sophistices antesignani patienter ferant, summus tamen Pontifex, quo minus forte cum caeteris latret, ei offam obiecit, imo autoramento in
   suas partes conduxit, nam Praeposituram donavit sancti Thomae Argentinen-
   sis ecclesiae; magis itaque mutus erit quam piscis' (But you should know that
   Capito is a most cautious rascal and arranges matters such that both the
   humanists and leaders of the sophists bear with him patiently. And the pope
   threw him a sop so he would not bark with the rest and brought him over to
   his side with a decree, for he gave him the provostship of St Thomas in Strasbourg. He will be more silent than a fish). Lee replies, complaining that Capito
   repaid his compliments with recriminations (see above, Ep. 54, note 1).
8 The phrase is blacked out and illegible.
9 Marquard of Hattstein (1488–1522) studied at Erfurt, Paris, and Bologna. In
   1519 he became canon at the cathedral chapter and at St Alban's in Mainz. For
   Ulrich Varnbühler see above, Ep. 49, note 1.

Letter 72: 26 January 1521, Strasbourg, Petrus Wickram to Capito

> Petrus Wickram (d. 1540) of Turckheim, who studied at the University of
> Freiburg (BA 1502, MA before 1505, doctorate in theology 1511), was a nephew
> of Geiler von Kaysersberg and, like him, preacher at the Strasbourg cathedral
> (1512–22). He became a canon (summissarius, i.e., stand-in) at St Thomas in
> 1517. In 1522 he became chaplain in the convent of Sts Margaret and Agnes in
> Strasbourg and furthermore succeeded his brother Conrad as parish priest of
> Ensisheim. In 1528, after Strasbourg had turned Protestant, he resigned the
> canonry at St Thomas and accepted a pension. Cf. J. Bücking, 'Die Ensisheimer
> Pfarrer Conrad und Peter Wickram,' *Archives de l'Eglise d'Alsace* 17 (1964): 57–
> 70.
>
> The manuscript of this letter is in the Universitätsbibliothek Basel, Ki.Ar.
> 25a, #46.

Greetings. The bearer of the present letter, Vincentius Wickram,[1] my relative, has been commissioned by my brother the suffragan bishop[2] to speak
with you, excellent man, and I ask that you lend him a favourable ear. You
have repeatedly promised your help in word and deed. Give us your help
now. My brother resigned the parish of Ensisheim[3] and wishes to obtain a
canonry, preferably in the church of St Thomas of which you are provost.
Dietrich[4] has two canonical prebends in his hands which he will in the next
days resign for a pension. You who are the man's superior will do us an
immense favour if, through your assistance, my brother the suffragan
bishop, could come into possession of one of them in exchange for a pension. Do this favour to your friends, and you will have us more readily at
your service than ever.

* * * * *

1 Vincentius Wickram (d. 1532) was a member of the city council of Colmar and
  represented that city at diets in Worms and Nürnberg and at other meetings
  between 1521 and 1523.
2 Conrad Wickram (d. 1535), who studied at Paris and Freiburg (DTh 1511),
  taught at Freiburg, was parish priest of Ensisheim from 1503 to 1522, and suffragan of Wilhelm of Honstein, bishop of Strasbourg. He obtained a canonry at
  St Thomas only in 1532.
3 Conrad Wickram's resignation, the result of drawn-out litigation over his non-
  residence and financial arrears, took effect only in August 1522. Petrus Wickram became his brother's successor at that point. His failure to take up residence as promised remained a point of contention and led to his resignation in
  1527.
4 I.e., Dietrich Zobel. For a similar inquiry see above, Ep. 48.

As for the rest, I hear that you have been made a counsellor of your prince.[5] I am pleased that such a great prince is guided by the counsel of learned men and men of good conscience, and I wish all princes had such men at their side. Then the interests of the Christian commonwealth (which has now been cast into the depth and barely exists any more) could easily be looked after. I know you are a man who fears God and has regard for what is honest rather than what is useful. This has given me hope for great spiritual progress in your prince (unless you become a different man among the courtiers). Let me give you a brotherly warning, however. You have found favour in the eyes of your prince. Make sure that you do not lose favour in the eyes of the Highest. You stand above the rivers of Babylon;[6] walk with care lest you be suddenly drowned. You know how hard it is to preserve peace and quiet of the mind in such a great whirlpool. Conduct your business carefully, that that most cruel and pestilent plague be driven out.

No good man favours that fellow Abel,[7] who is more iniquitous than Cain. Only a few rascals of his own kind are able to put up with this monster, and their patience is wearing thin. Accursed is the land in which not even Abel could remain uncorrupted. Such thorns and thistles is this promised land[8] of ours bringing forth. But we deserve the wrath of God because of our sins, so that we are not worthy of a prelate that is more learned and better than we, for like flock, like shepherd,[9] and to understand the condition of either, ponder what I shall write:[10] On the day on which the idol of Baal was erected among the Babylonians, a certain Babylonian, the prince of the priests of Baal, prepared a great banquet in the temple of St Thomas and called together the priests of Baal that they might adore him. And those who adored him devoured behind closed doors the

* * * * *

5 Capito was appointed in the fall of 1520 (see below, Ep. 102, note 2). The council was chaired by the chancellor (Hofmeister) and had representatives from the cathedral chapter (the dean of the chapter was a member ex officio and regent during Albert's absence), the nobility and the city, as well as two scholars (Capito was one of them). The council had far-reaching decision power. Albert reserved for himself only business with Rome. See H. Goldschmidt, *Die Einsetzung der kollegialen Regierung im Kurfürstentum Mainz und ihre Entwicklung bis zum 30 jährigen Kriege* (Göttingen, 1908).
6 Cf. Ps. 137:1.
7 See above, Ep. 50, note 2.
8 Cf. Deut. 9:28 etc.
9 Similarly Petronius *Satires* 58.4: 'Qualis dominus, talis et servus.'
10 The following appears to be a cryptic reference to Abel's instalment as provost by proxy on 14 November 1520. See Appendix 2.

food placed before the idol, calling out: Great are you, Baal, and there is no falsehood in you. But Daniel, who adored his true God together with his children, did not deign to bend his knee before Baal and was ejected from the place of the idol, and made a stranger. On the following day Daniel called the followers of the true provost to a banquet in honour of his God, where they ate the *bread of affliction*[11] in the bitterness of their hearts and drank a measure of tears, and for this Daniel and his children were cast out from the face and eyes of Baal and his priest. And he sits among them, like Daniel among the lions in the den.[12] It is up to you, brother, to take care that that serpent is ripped apart, that Baal is destroyed and we are brought out from the den of lions and dare to speak with a free voice: Great is the provost of Daniel. Farewell and remember me well, from Strasbourg on the 26th day of January, in the year 1521.

Your Petrus Wickram, fellow-priest.

Letter 73: 29 January 1521, Frankfurt, Johann Cochlaeus to Capito

> For Cochlaeus see above, Ep. 45a, headnote. The manuscript of this letter is in the British Library, Add. Ms. 21.524, fol. 7, #3. The text is published in Kolde, *Beiträge*, 197–201.

I shall diligently guard the message our most illustrious and most reverend prince wrote to me, prompted by you (I immediately guessed that). It is your endeavour, most honoured Capito, faithfully to promote with your counsel and effort and for the common good of the whole church my plan which is in itself clearly paltry and weak. A man must have a heart of stone if he does not risk his reputation only but also his life in this public emergency. You are already suspect in the eyes of the Lutherans. Take care that you will not become suspect to the other party as well by any tergiversation. You cannot stay neutral any longer. I remember that a caution was given in some public matters prohibiting that anyone remain neutral in a rebellion. I am not demanding that you cast your good name in the maw of those biting dogs without cause, but I warn you from the depth of my brotherly heart: do not be lame in both legs.[1]

* * * * *

11 Deut. 16:3.
12 Cf. Dan. 6.

1 I.e., be consistent; cf. *Adagia* 3.3.56.

What about my pages? What if they fall into the hands of the Lutherans?[2] If that has happened, it must be blamed on my rashness and your failure to guard them faithfully. But you are too prudent and responsible to allow that to happen. Here I am sending two additional quaternions, all of them written in haste and without preparation and still hot from the first burst. Soon I shall attempt something more authoritative. I wish I could in the next month write a response to [Luther's] two books, one in German of which you have seen the beginning, and the other in Latin about *The Babylonian Captivity*. For these are the two weightiest of all of Luther's publications. However I shall first attempt to respond concerning the second proposition, on sin, grace, and free will, which he shores up with the largest bulwark of arguments.[3] I do not yet have all his books and those I do have are on loan. It bothers me that I must respond to such difficult matters in such hurried fashion, when I am as yet an obscure, unimportant man, practically a youth. But faith in the truth sustains me and the example of David's fight against Goliath. Farewell.

Commend me to the prince and write back, and write often and copiously. I have not much leisure now for letters, even if I wish for it. From Frankfurt on the 29th of January, in the year 1521. Your J. Cochlaeus.

Letter 74: 30 January 1521, [Speyer], Martin Bucer to Capito

Printed in *Corr Bucer* 1:136–8, #24

[*Summary*]: Bucer is embarrassed to bother Capito again, but he has nowhere else to turn. He informs Capito that he is hiding at Maternus Hatten's while waiting to find out how he can be released from his monastic vows. He met with Jakob Spiegel who felt that Bucer himself should go to Rome, but he is reluctant to do so. An unnamed former monk from Sélestat said that he already wrote Johann Man, a papal guard, in order that Man obtain a commission addressed to the suffragan bishop of Speyer, Anton Engelbrecht, and the vicar, Georg von Schwalbach. Hatten is going to Worms to advise Capito and Spiegel about this matter.

* * * * *

2 The 'pages' mentioned here were perhaps part of Cochlaeus's *Antwort auff Martin Luthers freueliche Appelation vom babst uff ein zukünfftig Concilium* (1524), which had been composed in 1520, as indicated in Cochlaeus's preface: 'It is four years that I have written this response, and it was my first attack on Luther' (quoted by Kolde, *Beiträge*, 199).

3 I.e., the second article mentioned in the papal bull of excommunication.

Letter 75: 5 February [1521, Wartburg?], Ulrich von Hutten to Capito

Printed in *Hutteni opera* 2:113, #278

[*Summary*]: Bucer has not yet responded to Hutten's many letters that Capito was supposed to relay. [These letters are not extant.] Franz von Sickingen is annoyed that Bucer does not maintain contact with him. Hutten asks for clarification of Capito's recent statement that Hutten has not been excommunicated, nor should he be. Hutten is concerned about Albert's health. He asks Capito whether the rumour that Aleandro is a Jew is true or not. He also wonders how Luther is doing and wants to be kept informed about Bucer's case.

Letter 76: [Before 6 February 1521, Frankfurt?], Wilhelm Nesen to Capito

Wilhelm Nesen (1493–1524) obtained his BA from the University of Basel in 1515. He worked as an editor and proofreader for the Froben Press, where he made the acquaintance of Erasmus, whose devoted admirer he became. During 1518/19 he was in Paris supervising the studies of the sons of Nicolaus Stalburg of Frankfurt. During that time he visited Erasmus at Louvain and later moved there. A diatribe against the Louvain theologians, published under the name of his brother Konrad, in 1519 (*Dialogus bilinguium ac trilinguium*) may well have been a collaboration between Erasmus and Wilhelm Nesen. Not surprisingly, the university refused him permission to lecture in the faculty of arts. In 1520 he became involved in a controversy between Erasmus and the English scholar Edward Lee. He may have been the editor of a collection of letters directed against Lee (see Capito's contribution to the affair, Ep. 54, above). As the reference to Erasmus in the letter below indicates, tensions developed in their relationship when Nesen openly supported Luther.

The manuscript of the letter is in the Bibliothèque SHPF in Paris, ms 756/I, col. Labouchère, t. 1, p. 58.

Nesen to the most learned Capito, greetings. The last few days I have been very ill with a head cold.[1] The place where the jaws open and close was so painful that it almost killed me. You spend your days among laws and princes. I congratulate you with all my heart on your good fortune and pray that it will always remain that way and never desert you. I have written to

* * * * *

1 'Seminarium' may refer to the septum.

you through the common priest at Steinheim,[2] but you have not yet written back what you are doing. Please give this task to the noble young Truchsess, who is your amanuensis,[3] and let him reply in your name lest the long and perhaps fruitless hope does make me more anxious than necessary: What are my hopes concerning those imperial *preces*?[4] I have heard nothing concerning Luther that I did not hear with pleasure. Erasmus in his grand way says nothing to anyone, fearing that his letter may be intercepted. Farewell, most learned Capito. Allow me to commend myself to you.

Letter 77: 7 February 1521, Constance, Johannes Alexander Brassicanus to Capito

Johannes Alexander Brassicanus (d. 1539) studied at the University of Tübingen (MA 1517) and was crowned poet laureate by Emperor Maximilian in 1518. He entered the service of Maximiliaan van Bergen, lord of Zevenbergen, a ranking diplomat. Brassicanus accompanied his employer to Switzerland, passing through Constance when he wrote this letter. He also seems to have accompanied Bergen to Italy, where he received a doctorate in law in 1522. After Bergen's death in 1522, Brassicanus returned to Germany and taught first at Ingolstadt, then held the chair of rhetoric at the University of Vienna. He published editions of patristic writers, poems, and a book of proverbs.

The manuscript of the letter is in the Universitätsbibliothek, Basel, Ki.Ar. 25a, #42.

Brassicanus to Capito, greetings. I have not yet forgotten, dearest Capito, your most generous generosity in Mainz when you received me into your house and embraced me with great good will.[1] By the Muses, let me tell the truth: you showed me a neat trick.[2] For you were overwhelmed with wagonloads of business and received your dutiful friends more gladly than others,

* * * * *

2 Johann de Indagine (also called Rosenbach, ca. 1467–1537), astrologer, priest of Steinheim from 1488. In 1514 Albert sent him on several missions to Rome. He became canon of St Leonhard in Frankfurt in 1515, and dean of the chapter in 1521. He had Lutheran leanings but remained a Catholic.
3 For Truchsess see above, Ep. 41, note 1.
4 On *preces* see above, Ep. 32, note 2.

1 Probably in July 1520, when Hutten sent his regards to Brassicanus in a letter to Capito (above, Ep. 52).
2 Brassicanus transliterates the Greek word *kinabeuma*, a knavish trick. Cf. Aristophanes *Frogs* 699. It does not seem to be an appropriate use of the word.

who are dreaming away the day,[3] receive unwillingly those who come at the most opportune time. We therefore owe you, that is, a man no less upright than of notable erudition, whatever duty piety prescribes and whatever plain and sincere gratitude commands. I have no doubt that you will love your Brassicanus with equal warmth. If you consider his humanistic learning, his name is not worth mentioning even over dinner, but the special effort he has made to be of service to humanistic learning makes him, for many reasons, a man worthy of your trust. That licentiate, who comes to you,[4] need not be ashamed of his learning and his life. If you can do anything to help him in the affair of our Fabri,[5] I beg you earnestly, strike up the lyre well. Whatever effort you make on his behalf, consider it done on behalf of the humanities. Smith is known to smith,[6] and he comes too well-recommended to need my praise. Farewell, prince of men, most famous and most dear, and bear life at court patiently. Perhaps fate will allow you shortly to emerge from that ocean as well.

Give a thousand greetings from me to Caspar Hedio, the best theologian, Ludwig Carinus, the delight of the Muses, and my sweet Hartmann von Hallwyl, a truly noble young man, twice dear to me in everything.[7] I beg you to respond for the sake of our friendship, even if it is only in a few words. Constance, in the year 1521, on the seventh day of the month of February. Johannes Alexander Brassicanus, devoted to your excellence.

Letter 78: 9 February 1521, [Speyer], Martin Bucer to Capito

Printed in *Corr Bucer* 1:138–9, #25

[*Summary*]: Bucer thanks Capito for his concern and good advice, but he did

* * * * *

3 Lit. 'are Lotus-eaters.'
4 Unidentified.
5 I.e., Johannes Fabri (cf. Ep. 114, headnote). Brassicanus was staying with Fabri in Constance. The unknown licentiate was presumably aiding his efforts to obtain a canonry in Constance. Fabri himself went to Rome on that business in the late summer of 1521. See Albert's letters of recommendation for him: Epp. 110a, 115.
6 Cf. Erasmus *Adagia* 1.2.25, a metaphorical expression indicating shared interests and a pun on Fabri's and Capito's names (i.e., his middle name, Fabritius) since the Latin word for 'smith' is *faber*.
7 For Hedio and Hallwyl see above, Epp. 47 and 11, headnotes. Ludovicus Carinus (d. 1569) was canon at Beromünster and studied at Basel (BA 1514) and Cologne. He eventually left the Catholic Church and was deprived of his canonry. After moving to Strasbourg, he was made a canon at the chapter of St Thomas in 1546.

not have the time to write the apostolic notary, Johannes Corycius, before the departure of the courier for Rome. Meanwhile a friend of Maternus Hatten sent to Rome the request in writing and promises that within two months Bucer will receive the papal brief granting commission to Anton Engelbrecht to absolve him from his monastic vows. He regards Engelbrecht as his patron. Bucer sends his regards to Jakob Truchsess and the poet Tilmannus Conradi Philhymnus.

Letter 79: Before 23 February 1521, [Freiburg], Philipp Engelbrecht to Capito

Philipp Engelbrecht (ca. 1499–1528) matriculated at Wittenberg with Luther and in 1512 attained an MA. In 1514 he matriculated at Freiburg where, in 1516, he became professor of poetry on the recommendation of Ulrich Zasius. In 1521, he attended the Diet of Worms. His public support for Luther created difficulties for him on several occasions. Among his literary achievements is a poem in praise of Freiburg (1515). In April 1521, he was crowned poet laureate at Worms.

The manuscript of this letter-poem is in the Universitätsbibliothek Basel, Ki.Ar. 25a, #34. It was delivered to Capito together with Ep. 80, a note from Bucer to Capito. The metre is a glyconic followed by an asclepiad, an arrangement often used by Horace.

From the first book of poems[1] by Philipp Engelbrecht

Ode 4 to Wolfgang Faber Capito: that liberty is an incomparable thing.

When you advise me, Capito, to apply myself to jurisprudence more industriously, and to acknowledge the names of ancient jurists like Scaevola,[2] Alfenus,[3] Proculus,[4] Catus,[5] Celsus,[6] Atilius,[7] and likewise Aelius,[8] I believe

* * * * *

1 The poem seems to have remained unpublished.
2 Quintus Mucius Scaevola (d. 82 BC), called *Pontifex*, an eminent lawyer and orator; he published the first systematic treatise on civil law, providing the foundation for many later commentaries.
3 P. Alfenus Varus (fl. 39 BC – AD 2), a former pupil of the jurist Servius Sulpicius Rufus, many of whose *responsa* were published by Alfenus in his *Digesta*, a work in forty books.
4 Proculus, a prominent Roman jurist of the first half of the first century AD.
5 Sextus Aelius Paetus Catus, consul in 198 BC, Roman jurist and author of the *Tripertita*.

that you are telling a story to a deaf man.[9] For Jupiter unfortunately has moved them from their order and, not without nausea, has replaced them with a common lot: Baldus,[10] Trinacrius,[11] Cino,[12] Andrea,[13] Butrio,[14] and then Bartolo[15] too, and others who smear the insipid volumes of canon law with their nonsense. How can I prate about such feeble stuffers[16] who unfortunately distract the mind with cunning tricks and Sicilian deceit?[17] The renowned Stoic school did not discuss such things in the Cecropian lands.[18] Hardly anyone will cast these warnings out of my mind to make me forget the good lessons that I have learned. The person surrounded by the noise of the city does not know how pleasant it is to live in good leisure with the Muses and Apollo. The golden mean tempts me, a cultivator of the busy life of the forum, not to hazard, to my detriment, my frail boat in these fierce

* * * * *

6 Publius Iuventius Celsus, a distinguished Roman jurist, praetor AD 106 or 107, legate in Thrace, twice consul, proconsul of Asia, member of Hadrian's *consilium*.

7 L. Atilius, one of the earliest Roman jurists from the sixth century BC (see, e.g., Cicero *De amicitia* 2).

8 Aelius Marcianus, one of the last Roman jurists, active in the period after Caracalla (AD 211–17), author of voluminous manuals, such as the *Institutiones* and *Regales*, and some monographs, chiefly in the domain of criminal procedure.

9 Cf. Erasmus *Adagia* 1.4.87.

10 Baldus de Ubaldis (1327–1400), a famous medieval jurist who taught law at Pisa, Perugia, and Padua.

11 Nicolaus de Tudeschis (1386–1445), a Sicilian jurist more commonly known as Panormitanus, one of the foremost Decretalists of the post-classical canonists and a papal delegate to the Council of Basel.

12 Cino da Pistoia (1270–1337), Italian jurist and poet; he studied law in Pistoia, received a doctorate from Bologna in 1314, and was a well-known judge, professor of law, and author of numerous legal texts.

13 Andrea Barbatius (ca. 1400–79), teacher of both canon and civil law in Bologna and Ferrara.

14 Antonius de Butrio (1338–1408) held doctorates in canon and civil law; taught in Bologna, Perugia, Florence, and Ferrara, and wrote a *Commentarium in Decretales Gregorii IX*.

15 Bartolo da Sassoferrato (ca. 1314–57), considered one of the foremost civil law jurists of the Middle Ages; he held the chair of law at Perugia from 1343 onward.

16 *Fartores* (from *farcio*), fatteners of fowls; in this case, 'stuffers' of nonsense.

17 The Sicilians were proverbial for practising deceit. Cf. Erasmus *Adagia* 2.4.10.

18 I.e., in Athens. Cecrops was the mythical first king of Athens and regarded as the archetypal ancestral figure.

storms. Neither the discovery of Hercules' dog[19] on the shores of Tyre, nor the purple conch of the Red Sea, nor the gold mined from the middle of the mountains renders me so stupid and irresponsible that I would fetter my free life. It is sufficient for me to separate the golden mean from evil things.

Philipp Engelbrecht

Letter 80: 23 February [1521, Speyer?], [Martin Bucer] to Capito

Printed in *Corr Bucer* 1:140, #26

[*Summary*]: Bucer is attaching this note to a poem by Philipp Engelbrecht dedicated to Capito (see Ep. 79). Philipp's brother, Anton Engelbrecht, the suffragan bishop of Speyer, sends his regards to Capito and is favourably inclined towards him.

Letter 81: January/February 1521, [Worms], Albert of Brandenburg to the Archbishop of Capua

This letter is addressed to Nicolaus of Schönberg (1474–1537). Descended from a noble family in Meissen, Saxony, Schönberg went to Italy, entered the Dominican order and made a rapid career, advancing to the position of procurator general. He enjoyed the favour of the papal court, especially of Cardinal Cajetan, and taught theology at Rome from 1510 on. He went on missions to France and Hungary on behalf of Leo X and was made archbishop of Capua on 12 September 1520. The manuscript of Albert's letter, drafted by Capito, is in the city archive of Strasbourg, AST 40, page 4 of #36, fol. 565.

Reverend father in Christ and dearest friend, kind affection and obedience. I congratulate Your Most Reverend Paternity on obtaining the archbishopric of Capua. It was given to a most deserving man and clearly shows the kindness and goodwill of His Holiness towards his friends. I am moreover thankful that Your Reverend Paternity so often offers his help in my affairs and indeed gives useful assistance, and I give my holy pledge that [the

* * * * *

19 According to the myth, one day the dog of Tyro, a Phoenician nymph loved by Hercules, ate a purple shellfish and came back to her with its nose coloured scarlet. Admiring this hue, Tyro told Hercules that she would no longer love him unless he gave her a garment of the same colour. Hercules obediently went off to search for the purple dye and found it near Tyre.

goodwill] is mutual; for whatever effort you make in my affairs, I shall in turn gratify Your Reverend Paternity wherever I have an occasion. I therefore commend to Your Reverend Paternity the matters which Valentin von Tetleben will discuss with you as with our singular friend. By the same effort Your Reverend Paternity gives us more reason for showing ourselves grateful, and we have obtained for ourselves a trustworthy patron. [Given at Worms.] The Cardinal of Saint Peter ad vincula.[1]

Letter 82: 3 March 1521, Augsburg, Bernhard Adelmann to Capito

Printed in *Briefe Oekolampads* 1:142–3, #98

[*Summary*]: Adelmann begs Capito to respond to his letters. Oecolampadius's *Iudicium de Luthero* is being circulated in Latin and in a German translation, but he does not know by whom. Johann Eck attempted to harass Oecolampadius on account of this. Oecolampadius is showing more determination than ever to resist him. Adelmann admires the erudition displayed in Oecolampadius's *Paradoxon, quod non sit onerosa christianis confessio*. He asks Capito to write back and to include information on Erasmus. Oecolampadius sends his regards.

Letter 83: 4 March 1521, Basel, Nicolaus Michael Araelunus to Capito

The writer, a native of Arlon in Belgium, registered at the University of Louvain in February 1515. The nature of the favour for which he thanks Capito here is unknown. The manuscript of the letter is in the Archive Municipale, Strasbourg, AST 40, #55, fol. 431.

I see from personal experience, kindest of men, that there cannot be anything more unpleasant or bitter for a grateful heart than lacking the opportunity of making even a modest return. That is what happened to me in your case: I embrace your divine merits in my heart, and do so frequently, and I look anxiously for a way of somehow repaying your kindness towards me, if not fully (which I cannot hope to do), at least partly. Often I am angry with my fate and curse it because it wanted me to be born in this station, in which I can experience your kindness but cannot repay what I have received even in the smallest degree. In that one respect I feel the grave injustice of fortune,

* * * * *

1 In November 1520 Albert exchanged the cardinalate attached to the church of St Chrysogonus with the more prestigious one of St Peter ad vincula.

and a great desire has arisen in my heart, and my mind, too, is burning to pay back your favour. At the same time I recall how small are my means, how little I can do in my weak position, and how immense is my obligation towards you, who treated a man, who was unknown to you and on whom you had never set eyes on before, so kindly that you could not be more dutiful to a brother. Looking at my debt to you, I can hardly conceive of it properly, not to speak of verbalizing it. How will I repay your kindness considering that my little fortune is so paltry and indeed amounts to almost nothing, when the favour you bestowed on me exceeds perhaps what Croesus himself could do if he spent his whole wealth? Even if I laid down my life for you, I could only partly repay your kindness. Yet I know that you have as little need of my gratitude as I lack the means of conferring it, but as Seneca says,[1] *to have said thanks well is to return thanks*; and Aischines obliged Socrates more with his grateful and modest speech than the wealth Alcibiades offered him with a most generous heart.[2] I also acknowledge that I am no match for these men, because your meritorious deeds on my behalf are so great that, whatever abundance of words I could muster, no one could make so grand a speech that it would not seem paltry in comparison with your kindness. I am so tongue-tied, moreover, that I would not even be a match for a mediocre subject, and you are so elegant, acute, and perspicacious that nothing could satisfy you except the most polished, perfect, and exquisite composition. Since, then, I suffer defeat on both fronts, the only thing I can do is never leave off remembering you, loving you, and striving with all my might not to appear ungrateful. Farewell most prosperously. Basel, in the house of our Cratander, on 4 March, in the year 1521. Nicolaus Michael Araelunus, totally yours.

Letter 84: 10 March 1521, Augsburg, Bernhard Adelmann to Capito

Printed in *Briefe Oekolampads* 1:143–4, #100

[*Summary*]: Adelmann is enclosing a letter he has received from Oecolampadius. The latter wanted Capito to know that Johann Eck has threatened the city council of Augsburg and Oecolampadius himself with excommunication unless they suppress the *Iudicium de Luthero*. Oecolampadius is con-

* * * * *

1 Seneca *De beneficiis* 2.17.
2 On Alcibiades' relationship with Socrates cf. Plato *Symposium* 218 C-D; Socrates reportedly said of Aischines that he was 'the only one who knows how to praise me' (Diogenes Laertius 2.60).

cerned for his monastery's reputation [i.e., the Altomünster]. Adelmann begs Capito to reassure Oecolampadius. In the postscript, Adelmann adds that Oecolampadius apparently thinks that Capito circulated the *Iudicium* in order to free him from his monastic vows.

Letter 85: 23 March 1521, [Ebernburg], Martin Bucer to Capito

Printed in *Corr Bucer* 1:142, #28

[*Summary*]: Bucer asks Capito to deliver a letter to Jakob Spiegel, in which he requests his intercession with the bishop of Speyer or one of his councillors. Bucer's opponents know that he has received a papal bull absolving him of his monastic vows, but are striving to prevent its execution.

Letter 86: 28 March 1521, Ebernburg, Martin Bucer to Capito

Printed in *Corr Bucer* 1:142–4, #29

[*Summary*]: Bucer is anxiously awaiting a response to the many letters he wrote about his desire to be absolved of his monastic vows. Franz von Sickingen informed him that Capito had promised to come to the Ebernburg during the Easter season. Bucer begs him to keep his promise so that they can discuss his situation. Ulrich von Hutten has time for religious matters [cf. *Corr Bucer*, 1:#6 suggesting that this is a reference to Hutten's plans to complete his invectives against the clergy]. Bucer requests Capito to respond by way of one of the servants of Schweickard von Sickingen and sends his regards to Caspar Hedio.

Letter 87: 29 March 1521, Wiesbaden, Capito to Girolamo Aleandro

Printed in Kalkoff, *Capito*, 134–5

[*Summary*]: Capito thanks Aleandro for recommending him to Cardinal Giovanni de Medici. He mentions a recent encounter with a partisan of Luther in Frankfurt who reproached Aleandro for opposing Luther and for trying to destroy Reuchlin, Erasmus, and humanist learning. Capito defended Aleandro by pointing out that Aleandro appreciated Luther's intellectual powers, but not his radicalism and their consequences and that the English are now ambivalent towards Luther. Aleandro and Erasmus are in agreement, and Aleandro is protecting humanist scholarship, as he demonstrated by helping Capito in the affair of the provostship of St Thomas.

Capito reports meeting with Johannes Cochlaeus, whose work for religious peace he praises warmly. He warned Cochlaeus not to share his plans with anyone except Aleandro and to give the impression of fairness in his writings against Luther.[1] Capito recommends Cochlaeus to Aleandro.

Letter 88: 30 March 1521, Augsburg, Bernhard Adelmann to Capito and Conrad Peutinger

Printed in *Briefe Oekolampads* 1:144–5, #101

[*Summary*]: Oecolampadius and Adelmann are wondering what happened to the [reading] glasses that Capito had promised. He asks Capito to send a pair to them by way of Peutinger, and Adelmann will cover the expense. Oecolampadius is annoyed that the daily routine at the Altomünster is impeding his studies and reading and blames himself for the troubles arising from his monastic vows. He asks for Capito's advice. Luther's case is in God's hands.

Letter 89: [March 1521], Basel, Conradus Pellicanus to Capito

The Franciscan Conradus Pellicanus (1478–1556) studied at Tübingen, where he came under the influence of Paul Scriptoris. In 1499, he began to study Hebrew and soon established personal contact with Johann Reuchlin. He took holy or-ders in 1501 and in the same year finished his Hebrew grammar, *De modo legendi et intelligendi Hebraeum* (Strasbourg, 1504). In 1502, he became a lecturer in theology in the Franciscan monastery of Basel. In October 1512, he interrupted a trip to Speyer to spend a night with Capito in Bruchsal and discussed with him the question of transubstantiation. He continued to pursue his humanist interests and allowed his convent to become a centre of Reformation propaganda. In 1516, he published a Hebrew psalter, to which Capito added a brief introduction to Hebrew (see above, Ep. 3). In 1523, the city council of Basel

* * * * *

1 Cochlaeus was ambivalent about Capito at this time. A few months earlier (Ep. 73, above), he had warned Capito that he was suspected of being a Lutheran. In a letter to Aleandro of 11 May 1521, he asked the legate to keep Capito in the dark about their correspondence, 'although I know nothing bad about him' (quamquam nihil scio de eo mali). He continued, however, with pointed remarks about the moral blindness of certain people and in general lamented the dishonesty and deceit he encountered everywhere (mira item fraus et industria in technis). The text of Cochlaeus's letter is in W. Friedenberg, 'Beiträge zum Briefwechsel der katholischen Gelehrten Deutschlands im Reformationszeitalter,' ZKG 18 (1898): 112.

appointed Oecolampadius and Pellicanus to professorships in theology at the
university. Three years later, however, Pellicanus accepted Zwingli's invitation
to move to Zurich, where he taught Greek and Hebrew until his death.

The manuscript of this letter is in the Universitätsbibliothek, Basel, Ki.Ar.
25a, #71. The year date is given in the address on the outside of the letter.

Salvation and grace. I can hardly believe that you are as fully occupied with
the very pressing business of the most illustrious court of your prince, most
learned Capito, as I am with the small flock of my brethren. Thus it is neither
man's fault that we stopped writing to each other, although in your frequent
communications with Basel, you have neglected to greet your friend even by
letter. But I blame this too on your hectic schedule, unless perhaps you have
come to value me less due to my monk's habit.[1] But *the gods also dwelt in the
forests*[2] and yet the form of my dress does not take any of my humanity away,
even if it gives me no privileges. All of us friars, to a man, are giving great
attention to the gospels and Paul. Our preacher[3] seems to me a changed man
and preaches the gospel excellently and in a fully occupied lecture room not
without traps being laid for him, which he scorns. Otherwise, few people are
living up to the obligations, which you successfully preached, recommending
the most Christian teachings to the people of Basel before you left.[4] Many
clamour against them, others pretend not to know them.

May God look after Luther. It is by divine dispensation that our attempts
seem to have been directed until now and by divine grace alone this dangerous affair may turn out well at last. You are, I hope, another Mordecai,[5]
a patron of piety. My brethren and I are working hard at substantial
concordances[6] of the Old Testament according to the Hebrew original, with

* * * * *

1 In 1493, Pellicanus entered the Franciscan monastery at Rouffach; in 1502, he
   became a lecturer in theology in the Franciscan monastery of Basel, and in
   1519, he was elected warden of the Basel monastery.
2 Virgil *Eclogues* 2.60.
3 Tilmann Limperger (ca. 1455–ca. 1535), appointed suffragan bishop of Basel in
   1498. He was suspended from all his ecclesiastical functions by the end of 1525
   for his Protestant sympathies, but reappointed preacher at the cathedral in
   1529 after the Reformation triumphed in Basel.
4 I.e., before the spring of 1520, when Capito moved to Mainz to take up the
   position of cathedral preacher.
5 Esther 2:5ff.
6 The work was finally published as *Commentaria Bibliorum* (Zurich: Froschauer,
   1532–9), 7 vols. Pellicanus originally offered the manuscript to Froben, who
   was reluctant, however, to assume the financial risk (see Pellicanus's preface to
   the Zurich edition, B2v–3r).

the many variants in our translation[7] noted on the facing page accompanied with a great variety of annotations. The work will be finished in July and, in my opinion, will be useful for many purposes. It will offer an incomparable lexicon, a Hebrew grammar, a corrected edition of the Bible, annotations on the Old Testament, a most fitting collation of scripture, and interpretations of proper names. If you obtain any Hebrew material, keep us sometimes in mind. Indeed you know well that I have never denied you anything requiring my efforts.

Farewell in Christ and, although you are entangled in secular labours, see that you do not cease to be a soldier for God. I cannot write more; you will still have me as a friend even if you are as silent as a rock. I know that you are overwhelmed by greater affairs. May the Lord be with you and guard you always from evil. Basel. Written in haste, as you can tell.

Letter 90: 13 April 1521, Rome, Paolo Bombace to Capito

Printed in Kalkoff, *Capito*, 136–8.

[*Summary*]: Bombace explains why he did not reply to Capito's inquiries. He had nothing concrete to report about Capito's efforts to obtain the provostship of St Thomas in Strasbourg. At last Capito's agents in Rome have supplied the necessary papers. Four papal briefs are being prepared and would already have been executed had the matter of Hieronymus Schulz, bishop of Havelberg, not delayed the pope. Valentin von Tetleben can attest to Bombace's eagerness in pursuing Capito's affairs at the papal court. Bombace is asking for further instruction. Pucci is prepared to write on his behalf and Bombace is prepared to cede part of his rights to Nerlius, and will write at greater length on the matter. He sends his regards to Albert of Brandenburg.

Letter 91: 13 April 1521, [Ebernburg], Franz von Sickingen to Capito

This letter has been printed by P.C. Molhuysen, 'Een onuitgegeven brief von Frans von Sickingen,' NAKG 3 (1905): 93–5; the text is on 94–5.

* * * * *

7 I.e., the Vulgate; cf. Schiess I, Ep. 64 (Pellicanus to Thomas Blaurer, December 1523): 'e regione ascripsimus vulgatam translationem, cuius nimia varietate, ut nosti, licet equivocatio ingens emergat' (on the opposite page we have added the Vulgate translation, which, as you know, has too much variety [i.e., different translations for the same word] and creates much equivocation).

[*Summary*]: Sickingen offers his services to Capito. He reports that Bernhard Spiegel's vicarage at the cathedral of Speyer is being claimed by the papal courtier Johann Rastoris. He feels sorry for Spiegel, who is supporting a mother and several sisters. He asks Capito to intercede on Spiegel's behalf, who is ready to appear before an unbiased judge. He suggests either the archbishop of Mainz or of Worms or the bishop of Speyer.

Letter 92: 23 April 1521, Mainz, Hartmann von Hallwyl to Capito

On Hallwyl see above, Ep. 11, headnote. This letter is printed in Herrmann, 211–12.

Hartmann von Hallwyl to Wolfgang Capito, greetings.

I praise your magnanimity, most illustrious Capito. Your conscience is clear, you do not deserve ill of the Christian commonwealth.[1] *Let this be your wall of steel: to be conscious of no evil, and to blanch not because of guilt.*[2] Only now do I understand your most prudent counsel, when you said that you did not want to be involved with any faction, especially because there is blame on both sides. You will never escape unpopularity. That has not been granted to any mortal, for envy follows men like their shadow, and especially those who aspire to praise. The next best thing is to bear it with equanimity. You are so involved in these affairs that you cannot easily extricate yourself from them. You are in the same position as a man who boards a ship for his amusement, to look around or walk around on it, but suddenly it weighs anchor and is carried out to sea, and he feels sick and vomits, looking in vain for a way out. You too have entered on the business of princes for the sport of it, so to speak, now you are overwhelmed by the waves of business and are dragged along against your will. But do not allow even that to torment you, my dear Capito, for what cannot be changed must be borne with equanimity. *Man's life is like a game of dice: if a throw does not produce what you needed most, you must correct with skill what the throw has produced by chance.*[3]

If the Luther affair becomes tumultuous, what good and truly Christian man would favour his party, when Christ himself teaches his people nothing more earnestly than peace and charity towards one's neighbour?

* * * * *

1 Hallwyl is referring to Capito's unsuccessful efforts to obtain clear title to the provostship of St Thomas in Strasbourg.
2 Horace *Epistulae* 1.1.61.
3 Terence *Adelphi* 739–41.

Indeed, when Christ entered a house he used the providential greeting: Peace be with this household. What harm is there in Luther yielding some of his rights and showing regard for public peace? In that respect a man does not act prudently, in my opinion, who wants to go on as before; rather, it is the characteristic of a prudent man to strive for what is best and outstanding, for in this manner he will reach the average mark. We must aim at the top to achieve at least a modicum of success.[4] For somehow it often happens that the outcome falls short of our hope and the goal we set for ourselves. You warn me rightly and faithfully, when you counsel me to put away party monikers such as 'papist' and 'Lutheran,' and I will diligently try to do so. I prefer to be a spectator rather than an actor in this comedy, or rather, this tragedy.[5]

Caspar Hedio sends you his regards. Yesterday he made a truce with the fever and even dined with us in the house of Eberbach.[6] But today he is at war again. I do not know when he will be restored to his former health. We hope for the best.

Farewell, best of teachers. If you are not able to write back, ask Jakob[7] to reply, that I may know how your affairs are going, for I wish you all the best. Again, farewell.

Mainz, April 23, in the year 21.

I shall defend you as modestly as I can, but if they cast insults at you, I will not bear it. For piety towards my teacher demands as much.

Letter 93: After 22 April 1521, Worms, Albert of Brandenburg to Valentin von Tetleben

> This letter was drafted by Capito; the text is printed by Herrmann, 209–11, who dated it incorrectly December 1520. A *terminus post quem* is given by a reference in the text to a letter of 22 April 1521 dealing with Albert's efforts to obtain the title of apostolic legate (see below, note 2). The manuscript of Capito's draft is in the Archive municipale, Strasbourg, AST 40, #36.
>
> Valentin von Tetleben (d. 1551) was at the time Albert's legal representative

* * * * *

4 Cf. Erasmus *Adagia* 2.3.25: 'Summum cape, et medium habebis.'
5 The wording is reminiscent of Erasmus, Allen Ep. 1155:8 'ego huius fabulae spectator esse malim quam histrio.'
6 On Hedio see above, Ep. 47, headnote. Johannes Stumpf von Eberbach (d. 1533) matriculated at the faculty of theology at the University of Mainz in 1509, became cathedral preacher in 1515, and cathedral priest (*Dompfarrer*) in 1519. He taught theology at the University of Mainz.
7 I.e., Truchsess, Capito's amanuensis. Cf. above, Ep. 41, note 1.

and man of business in Rome until 1522. Tetleben, who studied in Erfurt and had a doctorate in both laws from Bologna (1511), entered Albert's service in 1513. He was the type of simoniac about whom the reformers complained. He had canonries at Halberstadt and Mainz, provostships in Lebus and Aschaffenburg, and other livings in Hildesheim and Erfurt. He became Albert's vicar-general in 1523 and ushered in a new anti-Lutheran phase. In 1537 he was elevated to the bishopric of Hildesheim.

Dear Sir: After your last letter, which I received three days ago, Girolamo Aleandro brought us the bull for Halle,[1] and I send you the letters from His Imperial Majesty concerning the matter of the legation[2] and the title of St Peter ad vincula.[3] Rely thereafter on the patronage of de Medici,[4] the most reverend cardinal of Santi Quattro,[5] the archbishop of Capua,[6] and the imperial legate,[7] but attempt if possible, to get the appointment for more than one year. If that is denied, however, go back to a one-year appointment. Furthermore, you have already received earlier on our letter concerning the title of St Peter ad vincula, which we wrote from Mainz, and no doubt still

* * * * *

1 The papal bull delivered by the legate granted Albert the right to sell indulgences in connection with the Neue Stift, his new foundation in Halle, and prompted Luther to compose a sharp invective against the 'Abgott of Halle.' See below, Ep. 120.

2 Albert was at this time attempting to be named papal legate ('legatus a latere') but had to wait for this dignity until 1531, from which point on he calls himself 'legatus natus,' i.e., legate in perpetuity. The letter mentioned here, from Charles to Leo X, is dated 22 April 1521 (printed in Kalkoff, *Quellen und Forschungen aus italienischen Archiven und Bibliotheken* [Rome, 1906], 120–1).

3 Albert was named cardinal in 1517. His cardinalate was originally associated with the church of St Chrysogonus. In 1520 he exchanged it for the more prestigious St Peter ad vincula. Cf. his letter, dated 17 November 1520, in which he offered to relinquish the premises and income associated with St Peter: 'Nam de emolumento et domo nihil angor, quin ea lubens retento titulo Sancti Petri ad Vincula illi concedam' (Vatican Archive, Arx Angeli Arm. I- XVIII, 750).

4 I.e., the papal vice-chancellor Giulio de Medici. Cf. above, Ep. 57, note 5. Albert wrote to him on the same day (22 April 1521), concluding 'you will hear about the matter from Valentin Tetleben' (text partly edited in Kalkoff, *Quellen und Forschungen aus italienischen Archiven und Bibliotheken* [Rome, 1906] 121–2). Although no draft survives, it is likely that the letter to the vice-chancellor was (like the present letter) composed by Capito.

5 Lorenzo Pucci, see above, Ep. 50, note 3.

6 Nicolaus of Schönberg, see above, Ep. 81.

7 Don Juan Manuel (d. 1543), Spanish emigré at the Burgundian court and Charles's emissary 1520–2.

reached the reverend Cardinal de Medici in Rome. But you rightly warn that there is need for a faster response, and I have given that task to my people now; but the reply would have been in time if the letters have arrived within the normal timespan.

Concerning the church of Havelberg, the case is still in favour of Hieronymus, bishop of Brandenburg,[8] although we fervently espouse the cause of our relatives,[9] to whom the most illustrious Margrave and Prince Elector Joachim, our dearest brother, appears to be as much attached through the bond of nature as I am and promotes their advantage as vigorously as he can. But [the bishop of] Brandenburg has so often been agreed on that one cannot change it in a rush now. Furthermore, the bishop of Havelberg is in a way serving at the court of my brother, and the German princes are not in the habit of having courtiers and servants from their own family, so that our objection does not so much concern Gumbert himself[10] as it concerns his high standing.

You add that the lord of Capua[11] ended up saying that just as we serve the pontiff and the apostolic see, His Holiness in turn will oblige us in the matter of that legation and in other concerns. We would very much approve of that, for in all our actions we aim to serve him zealously and to good purpose, so that we have no doubt of attaining anything we wish from His Beatitude if the clemency of His Holiness corresponded to my goodwill. However, since the words [of the bishop of Capua] appear to cast doubt on my diligence, they disturb me. Therefore remove whatever suspicion has by chance arisen in this matter, although it is quite unlikely and could not come about easily.

* * * * *

8 Hieronymus Schulz, bishop of Brandenburg and chancellor of Joachim of Brandenburg (who had the right of nomination). Schulz succeeded to the bishopric in 1520 after Georg Blumental, who had been elected, withdrew in return for compensation and the promise of other benefices. See also below, Ep. 116.

9 The candidate favoured by the papal court was Albert's cousin Gumbert. See note 10 below.

10 Gumbert (1503–28), son of Frederick V of Brandenburg, had canonries in Würzburg and Bamberg and was papal chamberlain in Rome. Albert and Joachim generally promoted their relatives, but in this case preferred Schulz and sought a more exalted position for Gumbertus. The wording here is discreet, but cf. Joachim's more explicit letter to Leo X (Kalkoff, *Quellen* [see above, note 2] 136), in which he rejects Gumbert's nomination to the bishopric and asks 'for a much greater provision for our relative.'

11 See above, note 6.

I shall arrange with the Fuggers[12] about the thousand gulden being paid to you in Rome for expediting the position of coadjutor of Halberstadt. And we shall attempt to return the favours of the reverend Cardinal de Medici and the bishop of Capua as far as it is in our power, although we could not obtain possession on account of the difficulty of accession.[13] Since we are forcibly prevented, we shall attempt in the following days to assert ourselves forcefully. Similarly we shall do our part in the case of the reverend cardinal of Santi Quattro or his nephew with regard to the preceptory in Hoechst, and if it does not suit him to accept it, I shall not object to legal steps being taken. I fear, however, that there will be complaints in the current meeting of princes, and they can hardly pay out more at this time.[14]

I am displeased about what you write regarding the letters of the French king in favour of [the bishop of] Brandenburg. What displeases me most of all is that his representative,[15] an imprudent man as it seems, is trying to cast suspicion on me, as if I had such close relations with the French king.[16] Although there is no danger that anyone believes such an absurd story, I have written a response and addressed letters to him, but because I have not received mail from my brother in the meantime, I could not post them.

Expedite the indult for Dietrich Wenck[17] and also the third sentence

* * * * *

12 The famous Augsburg banking firm.
13 Albert was administrator of Halberstadt from 1514 and coadjutor from 1521, but he never became bishop. Halberstadt remained, however, linked with the bishopric of Magdeburg.
14 Hoechst was one of the archbishop's residences on the Main. The transaction presumably involved Lorenzo Pucci's nephew Antonio, who was at the time recruiting mercenaries for the pope. A document in Albert's *Ingrossaturbuch* 52, 105v, shows that he was negotiating with the preceptor of Hoechst, Heinrich Mayrspach, whom he promised money for his resignation once the necessary paper work had been completed ('uff Bebstlicher Heiligkeit revocacion aller negocia oder petitorien').
15 Alberto Pio. See below, Ep. 134, note 3.
16 Both Albert and his brother Joachim had initially favoured the French king in the imperial election, but Albert changed his mind after being bribed by the Habsburg candidate, Charles.
17 Dietrich Wenck (d. 1531) studied law in Bologna. He was dean of St Victor (from 1517, provost from 1528), canon at St Stephen's, and vicar of St Martin (1519–22) in Mainz. The indult may be for pluralism or for prolonged absence from his spiritual duties. As Albert's notary (*Kammerschreiber*) Wenck looked after legal and financial business, which included the collection of indulgence fees.

against the abbot of St Egidius in Braunschweig.[18] I have decided to procure
the *preces* for you even before the bishop of Trent[19] asked me and I have
given the same task to Capito, asking that he inform us in time of this matter. As far as Camillus is concerned,[20] however, I make no promises, as matters stand now. Later we shall see how matters stand and do what we can to
suit his wishes, on account of your petition. In another letter you write,
among other things, that Guilelmus Cassiodorus Berchmonensis,[21] who has
served us well and justly, commends himself to us. Please give our regards
to him in our name.

Let His Holiness read the pamphlet of Martin [Luther] in your translation.
In the meantime that obstinate man is raving more and more and writes
more atrocious things every day in both languages. Indeed His Imperial and
Catholic Majesty is acting in a pious and saintly manner, and, as I hope,
towards the complete extinction of the fire that has been lit.

I have started inquisitorial proceedings against the abbot of Saint Peter[22]
of the Benedictine order through the suffragan bishop of Erfurt.[23] He main-

* * * * *

18 Dietrich Koch, who protected the prior Hermann Boeckheister, a supporter of
   Luther, and allowed Gottschalk Kruse, later reformer of Celle, to preach at St
   Egidius (cf. U. Faust, *Die Benediktinerklöster in Niedersachsen, Schleswig-Holstein
   und Bremen* [Munich, 1979], 40).
19 Bernard of Cles (1485–1539), who studied at Bologna (doctorate in civil and
   canon law 1511) and was elected bishop of Trent in 1514. He was a councillor
   of Emperor Maximilian and active in bringing about the election of Charles V
   to the imperial throne. In 1521 he was involved in determining the powers to
   be assigned to Charles's brother Ferdinand and remained at the latter's court
   as his chancellor. From 1531, he was governor of the Hapsburg lands on the
   Upper Rhine.
20 Not identified; Millet suggests Giulio Camillo (d. 1544), later patronized by
   Francis I. He was in touch with the Strasbourg reformers; cf. Sturm to Bucer,
   8 September 1533, with an enclosure from Camillo (TB 6:220).
21 Guilelmus Cassiodorus Barcinonensis (d. 1528) was auditor in the Roman
   court 1511–23. He became bishop of Sardinia and was the author of a collection
   of legal papers relating to the papal court (cf. *Nomenclator literarius theologiae
   Catholicae* II, ed. H. Hurter [Innsbruck, 1906]).
22 Johann (II) Hottenbach von Siegen (abbot 1501–25, d. 1526). The situation in
   Erfurt was volatile. There was an uprising in June 1521 in which some sixty
   houses of clergy were destroyed. The tumult centred on St Mary and St Severin. The situation remained tense. The city council supported the reformers
   and in 1524 directed the abbot to permit his monks to marry. Hottenbach
   resigned his post in April of 1525.
23 Paul Hutten (d. 1532), suffragan bishop resident in Erfurt. Albert had established an inquisitorial board headed by Hutten and Jodocus Trutfetter in 1517.

tained his equanimity throughout the whole visitation, but when it came to the execution, the chapter of the order assembled there interfered and appealed together with the abbot. Therefore keep the matter under careful observation in case they try to achieve something in Rome, in which case you should at least succeed in having the case remitted to the parties, as is the custom.

Letter 94: [May 1521, Worms], Capito to Albert of Brandenburg

> The text of this memorandum, which discusses the Habsburg-Valois rivalry and lists the advantages of an imperial expedition into Italy to recover Genoa and Milan, is printed in P. Kalkoff, *Festschrift* 11–12. It is cast as a contribution, of Albert to a discussion of these matters at the Diet of Worms. The manuscript of the draft (in German) is in the Universitätsbibliothek, Basel, Ki.Ar. 25a, #154. It sums up in German the content of a Latin memorandum from the papal legate Marino Caracciolo to Albert of Brandenburg (see TB 1:128–30).

The most reverend lord in his capacity of archbishop of Mainz. Firstly, because my Most Kind and Gracious Lords are members of the Holy Empire and it is appropriate in this imperial diet[1] to command and sufficiently ensure that peace and law be maintained, the interests of the empire be promoted, and a reduction of its power be prevented, one must guard against the following: the Swiss who favour the French,[2] Duke Ulrich of Würtemberg[3] who is influenced by the French, and the duke of Gelderland.[4]

It follows that the imperial cities take this as an opportunity to make connections and seek relief: France will skilfully use all sort of tricky practices to make the empire serve her purposes. And if there were nothing else, the

* * * * *

1 I.e., the Diet of Worms.
2 Cf. below, Ep. 109, note 11.
3 Ulrich of Würtemberg (1487–1550), who became duke in 1498, originally supported Emperor Maximilian in the Swiss War of 1499/1500, but changed sides in 1512, when he left the Swabian League. When the League defeated him in 1519, he went into exile. In 1520 Charles took possession of Würtemberg for payment of war debts to the League. It was governed for him by his brother, Ferdinand I. Ulrich attempted to regain his title with the help of the French and eventually (1531) was reinstated.
4 Karel van Egmond, duke of Gelderland (1467–1538), was a client of the French king and caused considerable problems for the Habsburgs. He died without heir, and Emperor Charles negotiated with his successor, William V of Cleves, who surrendered his claim to him.

activities surrounding the dispute about the articles of faith would bring much disadvantage, which cannot be fought with any other means. Therefore the ecclesiastical princes should pay attention to the fact that their wealth creates more resentment than Luther's goading.

Rebels must be driven from the country; those who further this goal ought to be given feudal lands. That would disrupt the tricky practices of the French king and reduce his profit, then he would not have so much money to give to the Swiss confederates. The income of the empire would be raised and the money could be used to administer and maintain the law and to pay a salary to those who execute the plans discussed and keep the mercenaries from going over to France. Offer pay to the impoverished nobles, who now are most attached to Luther, [consider] the pope and the Venetians, [and those] who in all pertinent matter were on the side of the empire.[5] The Swiss would stay home, for if they wanted to start a war, the imperial mercenaries would make sallies on them and that would be unpopular with the common man, and they would not obey the authorities. This would be most useful to the empire and could be done without great risk. The Milanese detest the autocratic rule of the French; help them.[6] The French lack German soldiers without whom nothing can be done. Nor are the Italians confident enough without external military support. The Spaniards will help on account of Naples,[7] if a hundred thousand crowns are made available. His Imperial Majesty would prefer to remain at home four months longer and it would be useful if the enemy were overwhelmed in short order, while he is as yet unprepared. Speed is very effective in war.[8] With the expenses the emperor would incur on the journey to Spain, half the expedition could be completed. The princes would be compensated for whatever they spent, with the wealth of Germany increased through booty (apart from other possible benefits). Let it be done immediately to prevent the adversaries from making preparations.

* * * * *

5 'Pope' and 'Venetians' appear as cuewords in the margin. No further context is provided.

6 I.e., the Sforzas; the French laid claim to Milan, and the city state became a battleground on which the Habsburg-Valois rivalry was played out. In 1525 King Francis I was captured by imperial troops in the battle of Pavia and became Charles's prisoner. The Sforzas maintained their rule with Habsburg support until Francesco II Sforza's death in 1535, when Charles assumed the rule.

7 Aragonese Naples was occupied by the French in 1494. In 1503 Spain expelled the French troops and installed a viceroy, but the kingdom remained a target for the French.

8 Cf. Erasmus *Adagia* 5.1.85 ('celeritas in malis optima').

Letter 95: 8 May 1521, Basel, Valentinus Curio to Capito

Valentinus Curio (Schaffner) of Capito's hometown Haguenau, documented
1516–32, studied at Freiburg and moved to Basel in 1519. He married the
daughter of the printer Meyer zum Hirzen, took out citizenship, and took up
the book trade himself. In 1519 he produced a Greek lexicon, jointly financed
by him and Capito and printed by Cratander. He set up a printing press in
1521 and later litigated with Cratander over the reprint rights of the lexicon.
He continued in the book trade and travelled frequently to collect manuscripts.
His quest for manuscripts is the subject of this letter, the manuscript of which
is in the municipal archive of Strasbourg 40, #57, fol. 434.

Salvation in the Lord. I am most grateful to you, my teacher and most kind
saviour, for recently commending me to Spalatinus[1] in a letter. It had the
desired effect. In the friendliest spirit he gave me three or four manuscripts,
as pious as they were erudite, very popular with buyers and easy to sell. For
they are keen on this type of work, and practically nothing can be palmed off
on buyers by any stratagem, except the writings of Erasmus and Luther. Furthermore, I had a magnificent reception from Hutten, but I don't know
whether I made any progress with my request. He made considerable difficulties about lending me Quintilian,[2] telling me that he himself must check
some chapters, but finally we came to an agreement: if he wanted the work
published, he would give it to me for a short time. Thus I departed, with
access to the book civilly denied (I believe). I cannot say whether he will send
it or not. I would very much want fair volumes to appear from my press right
from the beginning, so that I would acquire a name (as they say) from the
start, and the favour of learned men would follow, especially because I have
already made a new typeface for myself. No doubt you will approve of it, and
I would have sent you a specimen by the present courier, if he could have
stayed here two days longer. Today I have finished the 'Ironies of Hessus,'[3]

* * * * *

1 On Spalatinus see above, Ep. 29, headnote.
2 On Hutten, see above, Ep. 32, note 6.
3 I.e., a satire entitled *Argumentum libelli Symon Hessus Luthero ostendit ...* (in German *Symon Hessus zeigt an ...* Zeringen, 5 January 1521), published anonymously by Urbanus Rhegius, with a dedicatory preface addressed to Nepos.
   On the verso of the title-page a letter to the Reader refers to the book as 'ironias
   Hessi' (the Ironies of Hessus). Cf. Otto Clemen, 'Das Pseudonym Symon
   Hessus,' *Centralblatt für Bibliothekswesen* 17 (1900): 566–92. Liebmann, *Urban
   Rhegius*, 366, does not mention Curio's edition.

elucidated by my Nepos and by Beatus[4] with some scholia and references,[5] but it was done in secrecy. The printing has recently been completed and turned out rather nicely. Please accept a copy from the present bearer. I have nothing else that I could give to you, my saviour. For the rest I would do anything in your favour, as I ought to. Finally I beg and beseech you in your benevolent and kind feelings towards me, that you continue to seek my salvation, for as long as you are there and favour my affairs, I cannot but hope for the best. Please forget that I have sometimes erred on the side of incivility. I have *put off the old man*[6] and, according to the most friendly counsel you imparted to me a little while ago, I shall be entirely a new man, etc. Assuredly yours. Farewell, my support and sweet adornment, and when my press is idle, I ask you to aid me with manuscripts, if you have any. I have commended myself to our friend Spalatinus on account of that matter, and have no doubt that he will send something. In that matter I shall willingly acknowledge your reminder about what I owe him in turn. Given hurriedly at Basel, 8 May, in the year 1521.

My father-in-law, who is devoted to you,[7] sends his greetings together with the whole family, except my wife Anna, who now lives in God. I sorrow and grieve about her death. Who can doubt that I have lost the apple of my eye.[8] Let us pray that she will live in Christ forever. Amen.

Letter 96: 29 May 1521, Worms, Capito to Georgius Spalatinus

> For the addressee see above, Ep. 29, headnote. The manuscript does not appear to be extant. The text was printed by Johann Friedrich Hekelius, *Manipulus Primus* (Groningen, 1695), 59–61.

To the most upright man, Georgius Spalatinus, chaplain and private secre-

* * * * *

4 I.e., Jacobus Nepos and Beatus Rhenanus (?). See above, Ep. 37, note 3.
5 Curio is presumably referring to the shoulder heads, which contain caustic comments such as 'Dolet Romanis quod Germani resipiscunt' (It irks the Romans that the Germans are smartening up) or 'Laici in rebus fidei doctiores hodie episcopis' (Lay people are more knowledgeable today about matters of faith than bishops).
6 Eph. 4: 24, Col. 3:10.
7 Jacob Meyer zum Hirzen (1473–1541), a prosperous cloth merchant, member of the city council, and from 1530 burgomaster. He supported the Reformation and was a close friend of Oecolampadius.
8 Lit. 'one of my two eyes.' They were married in 1520.

tary of the elector, Prince Frederick of Saxony, his lord and venerable friend, greetings in Christ Jesus.

Balthasar Hawer,[1] the bearer of this letter, is a forthright and, as far as I know, good man, and quite a good Latinist. Indeed he is the son of an excellent man, with whom I was once in close contact. He is now about to approach the court of your prince, attracted perhaps by the very solid reputation of the prince and his most incorruptible courtiers. Thus, if there is a suitable position for him, please have him appointed to it, as far as he can be of use to the best of princes. Do so for my sake, at least. Whatever happens, please let him know casually of our friendship, for the sake of which you wish him well.

Today the books of Luther will be burned, as a most certain report has it, in the public market place. My prince has gone away. He is cautious and wants no part in this tragedy. They will show the imperial mandates, as they call them,[2] which show more spirit than prudence. Things will calm down after a while unless (and there is that risk) matters come to a head on both sides and the verbal sparring ends in bloody armed combat. I can think of no worse calamity. May our Christ give it a favourable turn. I accept fate however bitter, as is the will of God. That is what we deserve, I believe, for our sinful life. Farewell. Worms, on the 29th day of May, in the year 1521.

Wolfgang Capito.

On the 27th of May, between ten and eleven, the marquis Guillaume Chièvre died.[3] It seems that the Spaniards and courtiers are not overcome by grief! On Friday the emperor will leave. In the next letter I shall write at great length.

Letter 97: 21 June 1521, Höchst, Capito to Girolamo Aleandro

Printed in W. Friedensburg, 'Beiträge zum Briefwechsel der katholischen Gelehrten Deutschlands im Reformationszeitalter,' *Zeitschrift für Kirchengeschichte* 16 (1896): 496–7

* * * * *

1 Not identified. Perhaps a son of the notary Johann Hawer of Bruchsal, where Capito was preacher until 1515. Cf. J. Rott, *Investigationes Historicae* (Strasbourg, 1986), 1:198.
2 The edict banning Luther was signed by the emperor on 8 May. It was promulgated together with other decisions made at the Diet of Worms on 26 May.
3 Guillaume de Croy, lord of Chièvres (1458–1521), councillor of Philip the Handsome of Burgundy and lieutenant-general of the Netherlands from 1505. He became chamberlain and mentor of his son Charles, the future Emperor Charles V, and an influential voice at the young prince's court. He advanced to the position of chief treasurer and was created marquis of Aarschot in 1518.

[*Summary*]: Constant, yet inconclusive, rumours keep reporting that students at Erfurt attacked the officials and servants of the archbishop of Mainz. Ulrich von Hutten has declared war on all priests supporting the pope, and has given his own supporters signed and sealed letters granting them the right to rob priests. Capito warns Aleandro to be on his guard against attacks. He hopes that the emperor will take action. He entrusts him the case concerning the provostship of St Thomas to Aleandro and asks him to send the four papal briefs confirming his nomination through Matthäus Schiner.

Letter 98: 13 July 1521, Halle, Capito to Girolamo Aleandro

Printed in W. Friedensburg, 'Beiträge zum Briefwechsel der katholischen Gelehrten Deutschlands im Reformationszeitalter,' *Zeitschrift für Kirchengeschichte* 16 (1896): 497–9.

[*Summary*]: On 4 July Capito and Albert of Brandenburg arrived at Halle and received confirmation of the rumours of the disturbances at Erfurt. The counts of Mansfeldt, who till then supported Luther, have begun to intervene. According to Johann Voigt, placards announcing that three hundred brave young men have joined arms to defend the Gospel were posted at Magdeburg. Violence ensued. Albert of Brandenburg sent Capito to the city council of Magdeburg to persuade them to track down the instigators of the riots through nightly patrols and undercover investigations. Capito, however, suspects that the violence was caused by students from Wittenberg. A master of arts was apprehended and jailed. Albert of Brandenburg has assembled his counts and vassals to repress the growing violence. Capito supports his efforts 'for they can be led with words where force would not easily drive them.'

Karlstadt held a disputation at Wittenberg against monastic vows and auricular confessions. Although Karl von Miltitz explained that the Elector Frederick had prevented the publication of a tract on confession, Capito has found out that it is for sale. Miltitz brought a copy for Capito but took it away again when he did not encounter him in person. Melanchthon has written a response to the condemnation of Luther by the faculty of theology at Paris.

Albert of Brandenburg was informed that on 25 May four briefs were sent concerning the case of the provostship of St Thomas. He asks Aleandro either to send them on to Friederich Prechter in Strasbourg or give them to Laurenz Nachterhofer. Given his situation, Capito cannot abandon his duties at Albert's court. Valentin von Tetleben anticipates continuing litigation in Rome over the provostship of St Thomas.

Letter 99: 15 July 1521, Halle, Capito to [Nicolaus Wurmser], the Dean of the Chapter of Saint Thomas

For the dean, Nicolaus Wurmser, see Ep. 57, headnote. The manuscript of the letter is in the Strasbourg city archive, AST 16 (13,1) #9. It concerns Capito's claim to the provostship. On the background see Ep. 50.

Reverend, noble, and most learned sirs, my most humble commendation. Our Most Holy Lord has sent four briefs[1] to the men who act as his legates at His Imperial Majesty's court. They concern the provostship together with a prebend and canonry, which, they say, has been fully bestowed on me. And at the same time I had a letter telling me that there is no legal obstacle to keep you (as is your obligation) from granting possession to my legal representatives unless you do so out of ill will towards me. But I do not at all suspect that that is the case, indeed I rather trust that the venerable chapter congratulates me sincerely on finally enjoying the fruit of justice, when I lay claim, with the best right, to the title which has so often been promised me. I therefore trust that you will act in your kindness, and no doubt you will do so, and voluntarily concede me the possession that is mine by right, and I shall faithfully acknowledge your good will towards me. For that will foster concord between us, and there can be nothing more pleasant for me and more convenient for your church, which we shall easily preserve with our joint efforts, when we show to each other mutual good will.

Given at Halle, from the castle of St. Maurice, 15 July, in the year 1521. Wolfgang Capito, most devoted to Your Reverend Paternities.

Letter 99a: 15 July 1521, Mainz, Sebastian Rotenhan to Capito

This letter is #107 in Millet's list. It has been renumbered to reflect the date given at the end of the text.

Sebastian Rotenhan (1478–1532), a Frankonian knight, studied law in Italy (doctorate from the University of Siena, 1503) and eventually became assessor at the imperial law court at Speyer. He travelled widely through Europe and the Near East, visiting Palestine in 1514 and becoming a knight of the Holy Sepulchre. After his return he entered the service of Albert of Mainz (1519–1521), then joined the household of Konrad of Thüngen, bishop of Würzburg.

* * * * *

1 See above, Ep. 98.

In 1530 he attended the Diet of Augsburg as imperial counsellor. Rotenhan's scholarly interests focused on geography. He published an annotated list of geographical names and the first map of Franconia (printed in Ingolstadt, 1533). This letter appears at the end of his edition of the *Chronicon* of Regino of Prüm (Mainz: Schöffer, 1521), fols. [59v–60r], which was dedicated to Charles V.

Sebastian Rotenhan, Franconian, German, jurist, golden knight, to Wolfgang Fabritius Capito, professor of holy writ, greetings.

Lest the status of this author remain concealed from the keen reader, my erudite and likewise most amiable Capito, I thought it would be worthwhile if I commented briefly and as it were in passing on his blameless life, his laudable enterprise. Our Regino Prüm was a monk of wonderful sincerity and simple innocence, who flourished in the monastery of Altrip under the emperors Louis III and Arnolf.[1] For a long time he lived under the rule and the order of his superiors and, as they say, also a little while under obedience[2] until he was elected abbot by the agreement of the brethren and assumed the title of father and leader. For a while he fulfilled these duties in an honourable manner and without any suspicion of evil adhering to him, then he was forced to suffer treachery, which usually dogs outstanding virtue, and to bear it either because it is instituted thus by nature that human fortune is most unstable and fallible when it appears most firm, or because fortune's favour is never apportioned less fittingly (drawn from the jar of Jupiter, as they say)[3] than in the case of a man meriting the best, for good fortune is more likely to befall the wicked and immoral.[4] For thus fortune is *cruel* and savage *in playing with us,*[5] as can be seen in the example of our Regino, who was a man of obvious integrity, never harmed anyone, and never bothered anyone. However, he suffered a certain Richarius with ill grace, and through his trickery and deception was cast out of his high office, not without loss of reputation, as if his supervision of the monastery had been corrupt. It happened through divine agency, I believe, which permitted that

* * * * *

1   Regino of Prüm (ca. 845–915), a Benedictine monk, was born at Altrip in southern Germany and became abbot of Prüm in the Eifel, then moved to Trier. He composed three works: a catalogue of liturgical chants, a collection of canon laws, and the *Chronicon*, which covered the period from AD 1 to AD 906. It was the first book of its kind written in Germany.
2   I.e., an official such as a sacristan, cellarer, cantor, etc.
3   Cf. Erasmus *Adagia* 2.1.87.
4   I cannot identify the Greek quotation.
5   Cf. Horace *Odes* 3.29.49.

excellent mind to be freed of the cares of an abbot for the benefit of the public and allowed him to devote himself completely to the innermost recesses
and arcane secrets of philosophy. For we must acknowledge that that was
the case when he devoted himself to various writings, as if he had been
returned to his calling, and especially to reading history, the knowledge of
which, he thought, had a civilizing effect on us. Yet in our age there are
some religious who either out of zeal or conscience, as they say (although
that seems to me often a pretence and quite vain), touch nothing at all that
has the slightest taste of the old integrity or recalls or reflects it. They are
very cautious men indeed, and of course most circumspect about how they
spend their time. Indeed, they believe that any time spent on the humanities
is a waste, as if anything recovered from the old authors for the purpose of
developing character were *windeggs*;[6] as if one could earnestly praise the
convoluted and unfounded homegrown commentaries they bring forth (or
rather, abort) and as if they did not waste their time, often abandoning
themselves to wealth and leisure;[7] for the majority is corrupted by indolence
and emasculated by the temptations of luxury. By contrast industry and zeal
is cheated and shortchanged. O topsy-turvy piety, oh most mordant hypocrisy! But our Regino lived by another rationale and judged differently. He
did not only peruse the ancient monuments or content himself with rephras-
ing the texts, which were too sophisticated for his time. In those times, when
individual dioceses were governed by diverse laws not at all in agreement
with the laws of the Roman pontiffs, he furthermore brought together the
ecclesiastical laws of Germany, expending effort and learning on them in
equal measure. He dedicated the manuscript to the archbishop of Trier,
copies of which can now be seen in Mainz and Wangen. Nor was he the
only monk in Germany who undertook this, others among our forefathers
worked with equal zeal. Helmold Wagirensis (also called Holsatius) wrote
on the Teutons and Slavs,[8] Hermann Count of Veringen[9] and Bruno,[10] both
of the Reichenau, Rupert (or Robert), who wrote perhaps more on the

* * * * *

6 Erasmus, *Adagia* 3.7.21.
7 Cf. Cicero *De Oratore* 3.32.
8 Helmold of Bosau (ca. 1120–77), author of the *Chronica Slavorum*, a major
    source for history of the German colonization of East Europe, lived in the ham-
    let of Bosau in Holstein (thus named 'Holsatius').
9 Hermann von Reichenau (1013–54), a Benedictine monk, German chronicler,
    poet, composer, astronomer, and mathematician.
10 Hermann's contemporary, the learned abbot Berno of Reichenau.

French than on the Germans,[11] Widukind of Corvey on Saxony,[12] Gregory on universal history,[13] and Hermann on selected periods in history,[14] all monks, vied to hand down German history to posterity. Their output can in no way be compared to the inertia of our time.

If I find that this book pleases the public, I will perhaps publish their works. There is one thing in which I ask the reader to be indulgent with our Regino: a certain Cirrhenian tract, where Germans now live, has many centuries ago discarded the name of 'Belgian Gaul,'[15] as I shall explain elsewhere more fully, but he could not stop his pen from ascribing to the Gauls the shores of the river he mentioned and sometimes also fortresses. But we must bear this error of his with equanimity especially since anyone is permitted to denote provinces either by their old medieval or by their more modern terms, as long as periods are kept distinct and it is done without prejudice to anyone and without raising an argument. Farewell, my Capito, and continue to work valiantly on the Greek and Latin works with which you are able to serve the interest of the republic. Given at the court of Mainz, the arena we two share, on the Ides of July, in the year of salvation, 1521.

Letter 100: 26 July [1521], Leipzig, Petrus Mosellanus to Capito

> On the writer, Petrus Mosellanus, see above, Ep. 62, headnote. The manuscript of the letter is in the Universitätsbibliothek, Basel, Ki.Ar. 25a, #59.

Let us not make a big deal about which of us initiated our friendship since it does not matter much, even if it were appropriate for an insignificant person like me to take the initiative and especially to precede Fabritius, a theologian excellently skilled in three languages, not to mention the other talents in

* * * * *

11 Robert the Monk (of Rheims) who rewrote the anonymous *Gesta Francorum* in the eleventh century.

12 Widukind of Corvey (ca. 925–73), whose history of the Saxons is an important source for the history of Henry I and Otto I.

13 Gregory of Tours (d. ca. 593) wrote *Historia Francorum*, a universal history in ten books.

14 Hermannus Minorita (fl. second half of the thirteenth century) was the author of *Flores temporum*.

15 In Roman times, 'Belgian Gaul' (Gallia Belgica) was one of the three administrative regions of the province Gallia, covering the area between the Seine and the Rhine. Around AD 12, the area along the Rhine became a separate administrative unit, called Germania. Erasmus, who came from 'Gallia Belgica,' was ambivalent about whether to call himself a German or a Frenchman. On the whole question see A. Wesseling, 'Are the Dutch Uncivilized? Erasmus on the Batavians and His National Identity,' ERSY 13 (1993): 44–67.

which you excel me. A certain Tilman,[1] the master of ceremonies of the most reverend cardinal of Mainz and a man both learned and most devoted to you, brought your letter[2] to me and said that you, through the splendid and generous favour of the most reverend cardinal of Quattro Coronati,[3] I suppose, have been endowed with the benefice of a provostship at Strasbourg. How fortunate! May Christ Jesus the Almighty bless your appointment. When good things happen to you, they do not happen only to you, but we all reap the rewards. For how else can I interpret that you call me, an insignificant person, to share in your fortunes if my position here were not favourable? But, if I knew Fabritius intimately, I would, at any rate, not be surprised at that new generosity on your part, a generosity that few men practise, although at present I am not even known to you by sight. To whom will you not seem quite marvellously kind?

Not to mislead you about me, excellent brother (for I call you brother in as much as you have the attitude of a brother to me): first, I have a reasonable income here such that my annual salary for teaching Greek[4] publicly has been set by the prince[5] at 70 florins. Then, quite recently, when someone[6] here from the faculty of theology died, the most illustrious prince substituted me in place of the deceased. Now, the income from being a member of the college is more or less 100 florins a year.[7] And yet whatever it is, it does

* * * * *

1 Tilman Kreych (fl. 1518–21), chaplain of the archbishop of Mainz.
2 This letter is lost.
3 Lorenzo Pucci, see Ep. 50, note 3.
4 Mosellanus succeeded Richard Croke as lecturer of Greek at the University of Leipzig in 1517.
5 George, duke of Saxony. See Ep. 31, note 4.
6 Cf. *Matrikel Leipzig*, 2:25–6, which records that Mosellanus was admitted to lecturing in theology in August 1520. Mosellanus replaced Matthaeus Dameravius of Bohemia, who taught at the Collegium Maius from 1491 to 1520 (see Zarncke, *Urkundliche Quellen*, 592).
7 Cf. Mosellanus to Conradus Mutianus Rufus, 11 November 1520: 'I had to approach the court at one time, the council at another, in order to obtain the prebend of the Collegium Maximum, with its generous provision of a hundred gulden per annum. The duke conferred it on me against the will of all the sophists, as it is against custom and the laws of the university. I obtained it, however, partly through the favour of some great men and partly through a kind of exceptional skill' (Ambiendum fuerat iam in aula, iam apud senatum, ut contingeret haec praebenda collegii maximi cum summa libertate in annos centum aureos praestans. Hanc princeps, invitis sophistis omnibus, in me contulit; cum tamen obstarent mihi et consuetudo, et scholae huius leges. Evici tamen, idque partim magnorum hominum favore, partim exquisita quadam arte; *Briefe Mutians*, Ep. 596). Cf. Mosellanus to Julius Pflug, 1 March 1520 (*Pflug Corr.*, vol. 1, Ep. 9, and J. Schilter, *De libertate Ecclesiarum Germaniae* [Jena, 1683], 812–55).

not accrue to me without hard work. For this appointment brings with it the inconvenience that at some later time it will be necessary that I become the administrator of the entire college. Since this duty will call me away from my studies, I loathe it very much. And here is a new spot of trouble: by order of the prince, I am canvassing for a degree in theology, but our theologians will hardly permit this since, as they say, till now I treated them less than reverently, especially in some letter to Erasmus published in the middle of the *Farrago epistolarum*.[8] As well, they are afraid that I will not live up to the oath of obedience to the Roman Church (that is, to the Romanists), which I must swear. You see with what skill they are beginning to protect their own tyranny. There is a suspicion among the time-wasters (and this is a fact) that the prince will give me, once I have the doctorate, a canonry at the church of Meissen,[9] while the older men are passed over meanwhile. They also suspect that if at a general council there is a dispute between scholars and sophists, it will go poorly for them if many men of our kind, distinguished by titles, defend the opposing side. But, as I hope, they will not succeed. For my first protection lies in the favour of the prince[10] and then in the support of our entire university, to which that sort of man is hateful for many reasons. But, enough about that oak.[11]

I hear that you are planning your departure, even though you have the best of men as your patron.[12] The unbelievable integrity of your Prince

* * * * *

8 *Farrago nova epistolarum* (Basel: Froben, October 1519). Mosellanus complained to Erasmus about the publication of this letter (cf. CWE Ep. 1123:3–4, July 1520), in which he had lampooned the Leipzig theologians as sophists and 'word-spinners' and shown a decidedly Lutheran bias (CWE Ep. 911:58–64). The passage was omitted in later editions of the letter. Cf. a stern letter from George of Saxony (28 May 1520) in which he insisted on Mosellanus's appointment over the protests of the theologians. They had complained that Mosellanus maligned them 'especially in a letter to Erasmus of Rotterdam.' George accordingly demanded that Mosellanus refrain from negative remarks about the theologians or the university in future. For the text of George's letter see Felician Gess, ed. *Akten und Briefe zur Kirchenpolitik Herzog Georgs von Sachsen* (Leipzig, 1905), 122–3.

9 This canonry was one of the six prebends in the Saxon bishoprics (Meissen, Naumburg, Zeitz, and Merseburg) set aside by popes John XXII and Martin V specifically for theologians and canon lawyers. In order to obtain one of these prebends, Mosellanus had to acquire a doctorate in theology.

10 Duke George gave orders to Julius Pflug to silence critics within the faculty and to admit Mosellanus to the Collegium Maius (Fürstenkollegium). See Pflug Corr., vol. 1, 93, n4.

11 Cf. Erasmus *Adagia* 1.4.2.

12 Capito remained in Albert's service for another two years. See below, Ep. 164.

Albert will not allow you to do this. He will not easily permit you to depart (so Stromer[13] told me). I myself do not see where you can find a more distinguished place to stay. See to it that you promote the rebirth of letters in the sight of this hero, for you can, since he thinks very highly of you.

Farewell and send my reverend regards to Doctor Christoph von Gabelentz, whose pleasant company I enjoyed over the last months of winter.[14] Likewise, when you get the chance, recommend me to your friend Dietrich Zobel,[15] that unrivalled Maecenas, the beloved patron of letters. From our college at Leipzig on the feast day of Anne, mother of Mary.

Letter 101: 31 July 1521, [Halle?], Capito to Andreas Althamer

> Printed in J.A. Ballenstedt, *Andreae Althameri Vita* (Wolfenbüttel, 1740), 75–6
>
> Andreas Althamer or Palaeosphyra of Halle (ca. 1500–1539) studied in Leipzig under Petrus Mosellanus. He became chaplain of Schwäbisch-Hall, but was dismissed in 1524 on account of his Lutheran leanings. In 1525 he matriculated in Wittenberg, and from 1528 he was deacon of St Sebald in Nürnberg. He wrote a commentary on Tacitus, a catechism, and theological tracts in defence of Luther, and generally promoted the Reformation in the Hohenzollern territory. When Capito addressed this letter to him, he was an assistant teacher in a school in Schwäbisch-Hall.

Wolfgang Capito to Andreas Palaeosphyra, respected friend and rather felicitous scholar of good letters.

Here is the youth whom I have recently recommended to you. He has an uncommonly lively mind, but as yet unformed. You may make him an example of your industry and proof of your good teaching. If you take him under your wings and shape him according to his understanding and my expectations, you will make a firm friend of Jost Buchheimer, an outstand-

* * * * *

13 Heinrich Stromer, see Ep. 32, note 7.
14 Christoph von Gabelentz (d. 1535), matriculated at Leipzig in 1474 as 'Christoferus Gabelentz de Lewben,' then at Bologna in 1480 and at Siena in 1482. He was a canon at Mainz from 1498 and cantor from 1518, a benefice which he accumulated along with others at Naumburg and Meissen. He was doctor of both canon and civil law. In 1517 he represented Duke George at the Diet of Mainz. On 1 December 1531 he became vicar-general of the archdiocese of Mainz. Mosellanus may have met him while living in Meissen during the winter semester of 1519/20, when the entire University of Leipzig was forced to relocate to Meissen on account of the plague.
15 See Ep. 32, note 19.

ing physician,[1] and of Capito who is keen on doing his friends a favour and deserving well of them. I enjoyed the taste you gave me of your works;[2] it is a most pleasing attempt, for I usually take note of works that benefit the public. Practise your style and it will become smoother and will be more effective and powerful. Wesamer[3] will reply to you concerning the performance of *Eunuchus*.[4] Farewell, 31 July, in the year [15]21.

Letter 102: [Summer 1521, Halle?], Capito to Bonifacius [Wolfhart]

Bonifacius Wolfhart matriculated at the University of Basel in 1517 (MA 1530) and studied Hebrew under the direction of Capito and Oecolampadius. He was chaplain of St Martin in 1522 and taught in the faculty of arts. In Lent of 1522 he participated in a provocative dinner of pork and was suspended by the university. The outcome of an appeal is unknown, but in 1524 he still occupied the position of chaplain. From 1525 on he was active in Strasbourg, preaching the Reformation. In 1531 he was sent to Augsburg to further the Reformation there.

The letter appears to be part of a campaign by Capito to depict Albert as a prelate mindful of his spiritual duties. This was the image Capito wished to convey, especially to the reformers in Wittenberg, in order to persuade Luther to bear with Albert and to suppress his diatribe against the archbishop, *Wider den Abgott von Halle*. Cf. below, Epp. 103, 126, and 141, containing similar messages and his correspondence with Melanchthon and Luther on the same subject: Epp. 110, 120–2, 131.

There are two copies of the manuscript in the Universitätsbibliothek, Basel, Ki.Ar. 25a, #145 (draft) and #130 (neat copy). The text used here is that of the neat copy. Both versions are incomplete and undated, but the reference to the

* * * * *

1 Jost Buchheimer was Albert of Brandenburg's physician. His employment contract is in the Staatsarchiv in Würzburg (*Ingrossaturbuch* 52, 172 4–v). He was hired for four years in 1520, at an annual salary of 120 gulden. The 'youth' to be taught by Althamer may be Philip Buchheimer, documented as Albert's physician in the period 1528–36 (cf. *Briefwechsel des Beatus Rhenanus*, #274).

2 A reference to the commentary on Tacitus (*Scholia in Tacitum* ... [Nürnberg, 1529]) which Althamer also sent to Melanchthon. Like Capito, Melanchthon politely counselled Althamer to revise and improve his work (see *Melanchthons Briefwechsel*, Ep. 148 of June 1521).

3 In a letter of instruction to Karl von Miltitz (see above, Ep. 32, note 10) Albert requests a canonry for Wesamer, his 'familiar.' Nothing further is known about him.

4 A play by the Roman playwright Terence.

Diet of Worms serves as a *terminus post quem*. The text is partially printed in J.V. Pollet, *Martin Bucer: Etudes sur la Correspondance* 2:267–8.

Recently, when I went through my desk and cleared out the many notes I received from friends in Worms and for which I had no more use,[1] I came by chance across your letter. I recognized your elegant and polished handwriting, quickly unfolded it and read it for pleasure's sake, as if conversing with an old friend. Good gods, how dignified you express yourself, how gently you show up my cowardice! How friendly the spirit in which you rebuke me for having deserted the office of preacher![2] It was a great shame (you say) to waste such great talent, experience, and training in sacred preaching on a life in court, that is, on a workshop for hypocrisy. It was absurd for such a grave and upright man (as you think I am, whether you are serious or making it up, which is more likely) to give himself up to tricks and fraud and to pursue such insolent business at my age. But it was even more inept to do away with truth, authority, and constancy which should have been exemplary, and to live in this new and inauspicious manner, among fools clad in purple, among flatterers and false men. In that vein you run through everything, but you stray from the course, pretending that I am somebody, as if a good man could hardly survive at court (according to the old saying: *let him who wants to be godly leave the court*).[3] Indeed, either this is friendly chafing of your Capito, who is insignificant and ignorant and has innumerable vices, or you say this to exhort me and in your kindness make up something that you know is not in me, hoping to spur the laggard.[4] For I am usually frank with friends.

After I had read your letter, I felt a sharp pang of nostalgia and was overcome by the memory of your former counsel, of studies given up, of an office resigned. I recalled before my eyes the frequent conversations I had with the most reverend and illustrious cardinal of Mainz, my prince, which were not entirely different from your letter. For he is most humane and

* * * * *

1 I.e., when Capito attended the Diet of Worms, April-May 1521.
3 Capito became cathedral preacher in February 1520, but soon became too involved in court business to fulfil his obligations. Caspar Hedio substituted for him from October 1520 and officially became his successor as cathedral preacher in January 1521. Cf. his letter to Zwingli on 15 October 1520: 'I am the preacher until Capito returns from the coronation ... Capito will resign his office now that he has been made councillor (*a consiliis*) to the lord of Mainz' (*Hutteni opera* 1:421).
3 Lucan *De bello civili* 8.493–4.
4 Erasmus *Adagia* 1.2.47.

pious, and has no qualms to speak with me on familiar terms. He often talks about faith and religion, not infrequently asking what moved me to leave the office of preacher. He sometimes spurs me on with his own example, saying: 'If I did not have a problem with my voice (you know how thin and rough it is) and was afraid on account of my weak memory, I would preach Christ with great spirit! I would not be loath to preach the gospel, as indeed I am not loath to do anything that I know pertains to a true bishop – saying mass, consecrating churches, ordaining new priests – in sum, I perform all ceremonies and all devotional practices, and I do not shy away from any effort or expense or from anything that might serve as an inducement to simple minds and bring them to true worship. I only wish I could do what I see is best. The task of preaching would be most welcome. I regard it as pious and I would gladly preach to the people. How devoutly I would speak in that holy place!' And to say the truth, hearing from him that kind of exhortation and admonition made me somewhat uneasy. I acknowledged that it roused in my insignificant self considerable envy[5] of his lofty spirit, or rather, a loathing of myself. For I find in him the consummation of all natural talent and fortune, and yet he has not compromised his morals on account of his wealth, indeed he has humbled himself and has not spurned the lowliest task. On the contrary, he looked for it and voluntarily took it upon himself. I, by contrast, am of lowly birth and obscure as far as my life and fortune are concerned. I present the aspect of an unfortunate and embarrassed man, and am being regarded in that light by many. And it appears to others that I spurn the part of the preacher as it is completely spurned everywhere in our time by the leading men. In the eyes of many I too am such a man, deserting the post of asserting the truth, a man whom neither your strong letters nor the ample generosity of my prince has so far been able to recall to the task. In a renewed attempt to motivate me to take up that office, he will make every allowance and of his own accord confers everything on me that he thinks might honour or benefit me and satisfy my desire. Indeed I have been convicted and condemned tacitly by general opinion, not only by your verdict and that of my prince, of being lazy and inconstant (not to give away an even worse suspicion, for every man prudently disguises his own shame). But they are surprised that I have exchanged honourable terms, the highest success, rare felicity, and the most

* * * * *

5 'insignificant self ... envy' are supplied from the rough copy. The words are missing in the neat copy but appear in an interlinear insertion in a different ink.

desirable leisure for these burdensome and inferior duties at court.[6] But if some god, as they say,[7] were to arouse your benevolence and make you read these lines without prejudice (for I am mostly concerned with your opinion), I shall see to it that you will understand my reasons. I have the best excuse, or if not an excuse, the best reason to keep away from the most turbulent and raving sermons (for that is what they are in our time), for I am a man made for peace.

Preaching seems a tranquil and modest occupation if you look at the face of it, or certainly seemed like that to me when I was young. And in my zeal for preaching, I thought it was an excellent thing to ignore not only the wishes of my contemporaries, but also overlook the instructions of my relatives and parents. For on his deathbed my father begged me at length not to enter the priesthood precipitously and rashly. It seemed hardly safe and it was very rare to find a priest who excelled in life and learning and who controlled his harsh and violent temper, who was truly a priest and superior, according to our profession. He said that a chaste marriage was much preferable to sinful celibacy and gave me other fatherly advice of that kind. I clearly remember the last counsel of my dying father and have often reflected not only on his words but also noted his intention and his judgment. And yet the business of the gospel seemed to me most important. I quietly thought about its majesty and held its messengers in the greatest honour. On their account I all but venerated the pulpit as something sacred. Such was the attraction of an honest and upright life that turned me towards cultivating religion until that inclination was spoiled by the treacherous experience of things. Ah, how often I have prayed devoutly for the eloquence needed by a preacher, how often I have sighed over the Scotist commentaries with their deceptive complexities, how often I have laboured over the remaining heap of theological disputations and exerted myself to no effect.[8] I laboured even though I had an inkling that [such training] was all

* * * * *

6 Cf. Cratander to Boniface Amerbach, 13 November 1520: 'I worry about Capito getting too involved in the business of the court, which is the worst bane for all scholarly and honest minds' (*Amerbachkorrespondenz* 2:265). In his reply (ibid., 271), Amerbach expresses similar fears and speaks of the 'fraud, hypocrisy, lies, and flattery ... which are totally alien not only to the humanities but also to all honest scholars.'

7 Capito's phrasing is reminiscent of Cicero *Pro Cluentio* 3.7: 'Sed si qui mihi deus vestram ad me audiendum benivolentiam conciliarit, efficiam profecto ut intelligatis ... (But if some god will make you benevolent listeners, I shall see to it that you will understand ...).

8 For similar complaints about scholastic authors see above, Epp. 19 and 32.

really ludicrous and that my mind would be worn out by the material that was thorny rather than polished and that it would not increase my piety but make me more stubborn, for it practically instructs a man to fight and impudently assert what he does not know. Nevertheless I bravely suffered all the boredom of barbarity, *against Minerva's will* (as they say),[9] in the expectation of better things and future benefits. I saw in my imagination a man great in years and authority, teaching with honesty and vigour of the great gentleness of Christ, while the people attentively listened to his voice and hung on his lips. From time to time I exclaimed: Fortunate the man, who succeeds in kindling with his own fire a love of immortality in the people, a desire to embrace a pure and innocent life, to suffer evil, to live among themselves without sinning, without hurting one another, and without avenging a hurt. Therefore ...[10]

Letter 103: 4 August 1521, Halle, Capito to Ulrich Zwingli

Printed in Zwingli *Briefwechsel* 1:465–6, #185

[*Summary*]: Given the growing disturbances, Capito is pleased that Zwingli is acting in a truly Christian manner in the religious dispute. He speaks favourably of Albert of Brandenburg for urging people not to clamour against Luther. Even when a provincial of the Friars Minor sought permission from Albert to preach against Luther, Albert refused the request in order not to exacerbate matters. Instead he advised the provincial to concentrate on preaching the gospel truth, without slandering others. Indeed Albert will listen only to preachers who foster a sincere image of Christ. Luther's followers are arguing among themselves and introducing a new kind of sophistry. The nobility is beginning to fear the growing civil unrest in their dominions. Capito encourages Zwingli to retain his moderate stance. Though Capito is no longer court preacher, the growing Reformation dispute consumes much of his time. He believes that the church ought to be reformed and not overthrown. He wishes he could speak with Zwingli in person.

Letter 104: [ca. 26 August 1521, Halle], Capito to Albert of Brandenburg

In the following report, Capito advises Albert to reject an offer to become papal legate, an appointment he had coveted but which now involved the

* * * * *

9 Cicero *De officiis* 1.31.110; Erasmus *Adagia* 1.1.42.
10 The letter breaks off at this point.

unpopular task of enforcing the Edict of Worms against Luther and his followers. Over the past year Capito had done his best to persuade Albert to be
lenient towards the Lutherans. In this report, he forcefully argued against
acceptance of the legation, which would have ended that policy. He dwells on
the cost of the mission and on its inherent unpopularity, a theme already
present in Albert's letter of 22 April to Giulio de Medici, which may well have
been drafted by Capito. In that letter Albert noted the odium adhering to the
position, and cleverly portrayed it as a duty he was willing to assume rather
than a favour conferred on him by the pope: 'It takes exceptional daring to
draw down on my person the wrath of evil men of whom there is a rich crop
everywhere. They will be provoked by the title *legatus de latere* which I am
asked to accept, not so much for my sake as for the sake of the Roman church ...
People think I may be able to give the office a favourable aura. And so I have
once again decided to take the risk ... I ask that that task be assigned to me
quickly, before the meeting of princes [i.e., the Diet of Worms] is adjourned'
(text in P. Kalkoff, *Quellen und Forschungen aus italienischen Archiven und Bibliotheken* (Rome, 1906), 121). He soon changed his position. In May the papal
legate Aleandro reported that Albert was reluctant to publish the edict against
Luther because 'he feared to attract the grim hatred of all Germans.' He specifically objected to being the only prelate named inquisitor in the papal bull.
This gave him a prominence 'which he regarded as embarrassing' (Kalkoff,
Depeschen, 200). In the end Albert declined the legation and delayed publication of the Edict until 1522.

The autograph manuscript, written in German, is in the Universitätsbibliothek Basel, Ki.Ar. 25a, fols. 2–4. It consists of two versions. The text published
by Herrmann, 212–18, which I translate here, is a conflation of the two texts.
Sections I–III follow Ki.Ar.2 and agree roughly with Ki.Ar.3 up to I, 8. From
that point to II, 3 the texts of the two manuscripts differ considerably in wording, but not in contents. Section IV, 1–6, is based on Ki.Ar.3, which ends at that
point. The next section up to XII, 1 returns to Ki.Ar.2, which ends at that point.
The remainder comes from Ki.Ar.4. For details on the variants see the notes to
the electronic text at www.wolfgang-capito.com.

The text of Ep. 104 is also printed in J.C. Hoffet, *Esquisse biographique sur Capiton* (Strasbourg, 1850) 77–81, who vaguely indicates his source as 'Mss. Arch.
Eccl. Bas., vol. I.' That text appears to be an inaccurate version of Ki.Ar. 25a, 3.

Counsel, whether my Most Gracious Lordship, cardinal, archbishop, and
elector of Mainz, should accept the legation, etc. in the year 21.

In deliberating whether my Most Gracious Lordship should accept the
legation at this time, one should consider the burden, difficulty, labour, and
cost such a commission would entail and what honour and benefit one may

perhaps expect to accrue to His Grace, the elector, from the acceptance of the said legation.

[I] Firstly,

1: within recent memory Rome has never given to Germany a more dangerous commission than this one. Until now, legates were put to no great trouble to execute important tasks; they gained much money and honour on account of the prestige and authority of the holy see in Rome, but now those who accept it are generally ruined and disgraced.

2: The Luther affair, as is evident, is so entrenched in the whole world that one cannot hope to disparage it even with the greatest possible effort on the part of the whole clergy, although my lords, the prelates, have perhaps better hopes. For everyone tells them what is pleasant rather than the hard facts before us. They prefer to listen to what is cheering rather than what is necessary, etc.

3: Luther's enterprise is reinforced by the manifest abuse, deceit, and oppression practised by the legates sent from Rome;

4: similarly on account of other complaints of the German nation, especially concerning annates and acquisition of benefices.[1]

5: And perhaps it is the will of God the Almighty to reduce vice through such upheaval.

6: Although until now there was no effort to deal with Luther in a dignified manner rather than through forceful suppression, one may observe that his movement has grown and flourishes before all the world.

7: Thus there is no hope for peace and quiet in this matter, even if Luther and Saxony did not exist or were prepared to negotiate with us, for there are many others [like them], and even common sense may partly support points made by Luther.

8: Therefore, in my opinion, there is no other solution than giving the German nation less cause for complaint and interpreting several articles in the bull[2] or disregarding them altogether and no longer maintaining them. Neither solution, however, can be hoped for, as things are now.

[II] Secondly, even if Luther's view could be completely silenced once and for all, it is very awkward for my gracious lord of Mainz to undertake this and very difficult for His Grace to execute.

1: Everyone is of the opinion that Luther rose, maintained his hold, and

* * * * *

1 Cf. the 'Grievances of the German Nation' presented at the Diet of Worms (DRA, Jüngere Reihe II [Gotha 1896], 670–704).

2 I.e., the papal bull 'Exsurge Domine,' which excommunicated Luther.

was strengthened contrary to Your Grace's will at first; likewise, that no one was harmed at first except Your Grace, and that even today no one's interests are harmed.

2: The result will be that people suspect Your Grace, the elector, of looking not after the interests of the church and of faith, but after his own affairs and of vindicating himself. In any case there will be talk, and my gracious lord will be blamed for any actions that have been taken against Luther, as if Your Grace, the elector, had been their sole author.

[III] Thirdly, a legate absolutely must know the whole affair, all articles and fine print and their basis, in order to counter arguments, so that one really needs a specialist, who has been trained from youth on in dealing with documents and official correspondence.

1: Then, although it is appropriate for discussions to be carried out through agents and paid servants, it is nevertheless necessary in this case, as everyone is in the know and in a position to discuss it, and usually does so, that Your Grace's public statements be consistent with those made earlier on by your servants. This will be a great deal of work, for Your Grace will be involved in frequent and intense discussions since not everyone will be of the same opinion.

2: Furthermore, the business along with my gracious lord will be deprecated, despised, and driven into the ground, for the author of an action that commands no respect, is less respected himself.

3: Special care must be taken lest the servants, if the master does not look after the business himself, soon anger other people, as is unavoidable in such a matter, even if the servants always act as gently as possible, although they have been instructed to be strict. *The eye of the master fattens the horse.*[3] To look after the cultivation personally, makes for a fertile field.[4] To be present at important transactions makes for obedient servants. A good man is more highly motivated when he knows that his master pays attention and is aware of his faithful service; a useless man does or omits a great deal on account of his master's presence, whereas if the master does not look after his own affairs, he would butter his own bread and put money into his own pocket.

4: Industrious men are discouraged, for they always have to worry and fear that their actions and labour be disturbed and frustrated, as often hap-

* * * * *

3 K. Wander, *Deutsches Sprichwörter-Lexikon* (Leipzig, 1867–80; repr. 1987), 1. col. 171.
4 Cf. ibid. 3. col. 1332, 'Wer bei dem Pflügen reich will bleiben, muss selber entweder fahren oder treiben.'

pens, when the master does not observe their actions and is informed only after the fact.

5: Such a situation discourages us and makes us fearful, for no one dares to bite the fox,[5] especially in such great matters.

[IV] Fourthly, it is not desirable that my gracious lord [after accepting] the commission, ask for a nuncio to deal only with the Luther affair and to look after it together with other Italian scholars to save Your Grace, the elector, the work involved. It would not be desirable, even if they were paid by His Holiness, the pope, and directed to act according to the will and command of Your Grace, the elector, even if they swore obedience to no one but Your Grace, for the following reasons:

1: If they faithfully observed their oath, agreement, and orders and never acted without instruction and direction from my gracious lord, the above objections would still be valid,[6] and in my opinion, would certainly not slay the dragon.[7]

2: And even if the nuncio resided with my gracious lord and received his pay from Your Grace alone, one could not prevent him from writing to Rome. And if there were anything awkward, such people would understandably make polite excuses and all the embarrassment would be laid at the feet of my gracious lord, while they insinuated themselves into the favour of His Holiness, the pope, and obtained his gratitude and something useful for themselves. No vow or oath could prevent that.

3: If, however, there is a clause in their oath obliging them to pursue the Luther affair diligently and to indicate to my most gracious lord their findings and give him their considered counsel, they would make proposals and voice opinions according to their own customs, not having any experience in this country, and if their ideas are not accepted, they would always have an excuse, saying that their advice was not followed, for no nuncio from [Rome] shows great respect for my most gracious lord, except with flattery and hypocritical words.

4: Furthermore, they will say that they have sworn an oath of loyalty to the pope, as is generally required by law, which cannot in any way be restricted and will therefore openly state how my most gracious lord must act in accordance with His Imperial Majesty's promise that my most gracious lord would certainly destroy Luther and do away with him, which is impossible in these days.

* * * * *

5 Meaning 'venture to do something' (ibid., 1. col. 1256).
6 I.e., that it would be a heavy burden and involve Albert personally.
7 Lit. 'stab the bear to death.'

5: For if my most gracious lord would act as bluntly as the nuncios wanted him to act, it would result in hostility, war, and persecution, together with other disadvantages. This is a point that needs to be considered further: how could Your Grace, the elector, execute such measures, who would assist him, etc.

6: Finally[8] I cannot help thinking that the nuncios, whether they were paid by the pope or appointed and paid by my most gracious lord, would reap all the honour, benefit, and thanks, whereas Your Grace, the elector, would take on himself all the labour and great risk, effort and work, but not get anything here or in Rome except mockery, disgrace, and loss. That is how the matter stands, and anyone who looks into it will only come to the conclusion that this conflagration, the Luther affair, will not cease or be extinguished in the near future, or at any rate will leave behind smoke that will asphyxiate many. That becomes more obvious every day.

And if my most gracious lord acted in a more friendly and measured way, to avoid disadvantages, the Roman nuncios would accept it and know how to twist it and make it appear in their messages to Rome that Your Grace, the elector, was on Luther's side and disloyal to the Roman see. For the more learned, the more foolish men are,[9] unless they have experience as well. They will want the world to observe their bleak command. Should anything go wrong, not only the nuncios, but all the ecclesiastical princes of Germany would slip their heads out of the noose and leave my lord alone in the lurch.

[V] Fifthly, a legate must work long and hard on his reports of the affair and gain insights by reading about it; he must not shy away from riding a great deal to take counsel and be in good physical condition, and hold lengthy hearings and give replies himself, for Luther is entrenched not only here and in Magdeburg,[10] but even more so in several other places that cannot be directed by means of messages, nor would it satisfy the pope if Your Grace, the elector, did not knead the dough with his own hands.[11]

[VI] Sixthly, the legate must be hard-headed in such a matter and must not be easily diverted from the plan he has made and the counsel he has taken.

* * * * *

8 I.e., this is the last point in Ki.Ar. 25a, 3.

9 Proverbial wisdom, cf. Wander, *Sprichwörter Lexikon* (see above, note 3) 1. col. 1532.

10 In the summer of 1521, young men heckled the cathedral preacher, posted defiant pamphlets on the doors of the cathedral, and attacked the houses of priests. See above, Ep. 98.

11 Proverbial, cf. Wander, *Sprichwörter Lexikon* (see above, note 3) 2. col. 317: 'Die Hand in den Teig, so wird er fein' ([Put] your hand into the dough; thus it will become smooth).

1: For, if they encounter a mild, trusting, and quiet man, the opposition party will be all the more stubborn.

2: One must also consider how much that goes against the friendly nature of my most gracious lord and good prince.

[VII] Point Seven: My most gracious lord cannot expect honour or glory from this legation, but rather disgrace and general unpopularity.

1: For among these prattlers no Turk, no Saracen is more hated or despised than His Papal Honour and his servants.

2: One must think of the mockery, the satirical pamphlets, and the disrespect a legate has to suffer.[12] One might disdain them, but it nevertheless hurts an honest man to hear shameful slander.

[VIII] Point Eight: I do not know what good can come out of this, but I can certainly see that expense and damage cannot be avoided.

1: It is known how expensive it is to hire well-known scholars, and one needs at least four or five, or more, learned theologians, who know how to write and speak, not only on the basis of books, but who know history and have experience.

2: In addition, one needs a number of jurists, secretaries, and others, who are familiar with Roman usage. These are all people who are expensive to keep.

3: The licences and concessions do not yield sufficient profit, especially not in these times, and even if they were a going concern, they would not yield here and now a third of the profit they would yield in Rome.

And one must assume that the Luther affair will perhaps turn out like this: a number of people will be promised a salary for a year – paid as long as there is a reason or as long as it is our pleasure. That is obvious and undeniable.

[IX] Point Nine: It is easy to see what wars and hostilities can arise for my most gracious lord from such a legation.

1: In any case the knights, against whom neither government nor force nor prosecution will help us,[13] now follow Luther in many respects, as do the secular princes.[14]

2: The legation will increase ill will against my lord among many who will

* * * * *

12 Cf. the anonymous pamphlet *The Power of the Romanists* (*Dialogus de facultatibus Rhomanensium*, text in *Hutteni opera*, 4:363–406), published in 1520, in which legatine powers are derided and the legates' mercenary approach is lambasted.

13 The following spring Franz von Sickingen led a coalition of knights against the archbishop of Trier. See below Ep. 142, headnote.

14 Most notably, Saxony's Frederick the Wise, in whose jurisdiction Luther lived.

say: We have driven off the pope and the Romans. Does the lord of Mainz think he is the man to take over their business? Especially when my lord uses the licences to give out dispensations and offices, etc. and it is discovered that the legation is partly a commission against Luther.

·3: The situation is not improved by the fact that some among the opposition party are willing to join us, for a reconciled enemy cannot be trusted. Old hatred is soon renewed.[15]

4: There is also the trick of two princes agreeing on many good things, and one has no quarrel with the other, yet permits a nobleman with evil intentions to cross his territory and harm the other prince, and I will say nothing about what we know about the goodwill of our neighbours towards us and those who have had a hand in this. We can judge by their actions how much trust they deserve.

5: But [one might object]: We are assured of much help, from His Imperial Majesty and other allies. But that will be done valiantly through briefs, which command little attention. If we had money, of course we would not lack help.

6: Another concern is our own subjects, who may not be very keen on protecting us, especially in such a business.

[X] Point Ten: His Holiness, the pope, will take no pleasure in the actions of my most gracious lord; rather he will look with disfavour on my lord.

1: If there is only little action taken against abuses, my most gracious lord will be suspected of tolerating them or not working very hard to end them.

2: The writings of my most gracious lord concerning the German nation would suffer in their credibility.

3: The Roman nuncios will say and voice the opinion that they would have long finished the business and done a better job.

[XI] Point Eleven: One should not advise even the emperor to give his full support, for one may well conclude from past action in Rome how confident one may be in this matter.

[XII] Point Twelve: My most gracious lord could be a more effective agent and more useful in the matter, if he did not take on the legation.

1: In that way Your Grace would not be alienated from the other princes and estates, as might happen if the legation is accepted. For once the matter is official, Your Grace the elector will be regarded as having taken sides. And when there is talk of the complaints of the German nation, my most gracious lord would be isolated.

* * * * *

15 Cf. Erasmus *Adagia* 1.7.13 ('Ira tardissime senescit').

2: And the nuncios sent from Rome, if my most gracious lord stood back, would surround themselves with scholars, who will be determined to do as little work as possible and be uncommunicative to the Germans. On account of their impudence, they will be the more forward, while the Lutheran party will hang back somewhat, for by nature we respect foreign things, and the Roman nuncios are in such high repute on account of their skill, as if they alone were learned.

[XIII] Point Thirteen: One must find ways, after this tempest is over, for my most gracious lord to be made legate and be head of the legation with great honours, benefit, in peace, and without all the work, etc. It is likely that means can be found to achieve this.

On that account and for all the above reasons my most gracious lord would be advised to keep his counsel and go slowly in dealing with the unrest in Halle[16] and elsewhere,[17] that he safeguard his health and energy, his goods and his life for that work is risky on account of the cares and fears it brings with it, and the other difficulties I have indicated. And this will be advantageous to himself, his lands, and also to the Roman see. Thereafter, at an opportune time, Your Grace will likely find an opportunity to obtain the post of legate, when it will yield eternal praise and honour and an increase in faith, God's praise, etc. But I beg my most gracious lord to deign most graciously to accept my report and to do as Your Grace the elector thinks best, for the matter is Your Grace's decision alone, and I do not have the ability to serve both parties. May God bless, etc. W.C.

Letter 105: 27 August 1521, Neumarkt, Martin Bucer to Capito

Printed in *Corr Bucer* 1:169–73, #37

[*Summary*]: Bucer complains about the court of Frederick Count Palatine, which is dominated by drunken clergymen opposed to the gospel and learning. He has found only one priest who has avoided the depravity of the courtiers who influence both the priests and the people of the area. The

* * * * *

16 In January 1521 the provost of the new foundation in Halle, Nikolaus Demut, complained to Albert of Lutheran preachers inciting the people. Ironically, Demut himself went over to the Lutherans in 1523. Cf. W. Delius, *Die Reformationsgeschiche der Stadt Halle* (Berlin, 1953), 26.
17 I.e., in Magdeburg and Erfurt, where riots broke out in May and June 1521 (see above, Epp. 97–8). Albert removed the cathedral preacher, Andreas Kauxdorf, in September 1521. Johann Drach (Draconites) at St Severin was excommunicated. Cf. WaBr. 2:339 and above, Ep. 70, note 3.

Edict of Worms has not been published yet in Neumarkt. More learned people are embracing the gospel. Influenced by the Dominicans, Frederick
believes that it is wicked for the laity to interpret and preach the gospel.
The excerpt on confession from Erasmus's *Apologia qua respondet invectivis
Eduardi Lei* is being circulated in a German translation, adding to the impression that Erasmus supports Luther's teaching. Bucer thinks that Erasmus's
arguments are very effective. He hopes to see Capito in Nürnberg, and if
not, to receive news about Erasmus in writing. He expects to remain in
Nürnberg with the count. After their return, Bucer will seek other employment. He regrets having left Franz von Sickingen, who offered him a congenial place to lie low. He does not torment himself with self-pity, though, and
realizes that his current position is better than his previous one as a monk.
He asks Capito to send his regards to Jakob Truchsess.

Letter 106: End of August 1521, [Halle], Albert of Brandenburg to [Charles V]

Printed in P. Kalkoff, *Capito*, 140–1. The letter was drafted by Capito. A marginal note in the manuscript wrongly identifies the letter as addressed 'to King
Ferdinand.'

[*Summary:*] Albert expects to receive the Edict of Worms. Before publishing
it, he would like Charles's advice. Only a small number of delegates have
ratified the edict, whereas the number of opponents is growing. Publishing
the edict will have no effect; on the contrary it will exacerbate matters.
Albert believes that the Luther affair should not be settled by force. He is
awaiting Charles's guidance.

Letter 107: 15 July 1521, Mainz, Sebastian Rotenhan to Capito

This letter now appears as Ep. 99a.

Letter 108: 14 September 1521, Mainz, Caspar Hedio to Capito

For Hedio see above, Ep. 47, headnote. The manuscript of this letter is in Paris,
SHPF, ms. 756/2, fol. 61.

Greeting. I congratulate you on your honour, dearest patron.[1] You are pro-

* * * * *

1 The chapter of St Thomas accepted Capito's claim to the provostship on
  25 August 1521 (AST 192, 1521, fol. #6).

vost and canon of St Thomas. The attempt of those rascals has been frustrated, especially those who pretended to offer you obedience in the most
amiable manner, imitating Sileni, but in reverse.[2] Your relative, Friederich
Prechter,[3] asks you to be careful with them and circumspect. He discovered
their clever machinations in this business. For the day before yesterday he
described them to me as men of that sort, in whom one must not trust.
Indeed the proverb applies to them, which says: *They show you bread in one
hand, and have a stone in the other*.[4]

Furthermore I hope you will complete certain things that are still lacking
for your peace and quiet. For they say there is imminent danger, if by
chance, as human affairs go, Pope Leo dies.[5] Those who favour Capito
rejoice heartily that you have obtained an opportunity to achieve peace, a
thing you cannot even dream about among the affairs of the court.

There is a report that the people in Wittenberg have written an invective
against you;[6] I have already looked around everywhere at the Frankfurt Fair
but did not come across anything directed against Capito. If I discover anything, I will not keep it to myself. I know this also from the letter of Hutten
to Carbach.[7]

Others, whose names are kept dark, write that the prince of Mainz is in a
surprising rage against the priests everywhere, with Capito fuelling the
flames of this tragic conflagration.

I send you the books that you wanted. Eberbach[8] and I present you with
two berets, which I hope you will accept. There was nothing better for sale.
Beatus has worked diligently on Tertullian,[9] which I also send you, that is, a
theologian for a most perfect theologian. Erasmus will shortly be in Basel.[10] I

* * * * *

2 Sileni figures were ugly on the outside and had beautiful images on the inside.
  Cf. Erasmus *Adagia* 3.3.1.
3 See above, Ep. 50, note 1. Hedio met Prechter at the Frankfurt Fair.
4 Plautus *Aulularia* 2.2.18; Erasmus *Adagia* 1.8.29.
5 I.e., if Leo died, any incomplete transaction had to be approved by his successor. As it happened, Leo died in December 1521, and Capito's opponent did
  renew the lawsuit under Leo's successor, Adrian VI.
6 Perhaps the anonymous *Passio*. See below, Ep. 164.
7 Nikolaus Carbach (ca. 1485–1534) taught history and poetry at the University
  of Mainz. In 1518 he published a revised edition of Livy on the basis of manuscripts he found in Mainz, together with a revised German translation. Hutten's letter does not appear to be extant.
8 Johann Stumpf of Eberbach. Cf. above, Ep. 92, note 6.
9 His edition of Tertullian appeared from the Froben press in July 1521.
10 He arrived on 15 November (see Allen, Ep. 1242, headnote).

send you his *Letters* as well.[11] He will have the annotations on the New Testament printed. The text is almost ready.[12]

I have been restored by the favour of God and am well.[13] I ponder the letter that you wrote to Eberbach,[14] for it is very useful to me as well. I embrace your counsel with open arms, as they say.[15] I greatly detest lack of modesty and calumny.

I wish you good health in Jesus Christ. Very hurriedly from Mainz, 1521 on the day of the raising of the cross. Your friends send you greetings, etc.

Forgive a tired man. I wrote the letter en route.

Your Caspar Hedio.

Letter 109: 20 September 1521, Frankfurt, Andreas Cratander to Capito

> Andreas Cratander (d. 1540) was a graduate of the University of Heidelberg (BA 1503) and lived in Basel from 1505 to 1512, then moved to Strasbourg, where he worked as a compositor for the printer Matthias Schürer. In 1515 he returned to Basel, worked for a while for the printer Adam Petri, then set up his own business. He sympathized with the reformers and received a number of them in his home, among them Conrad Grebel and Joachim Vadianus, both mentioned in the letter below, as well as the Anabaptist Hans Denck. He was at the time the principal publisher of Oecolampadius (see the works mentioned in the letter). The manuscript of the letter is in the Universitätsbibliothek, Basel, Ki.Ar. 25a, #48.

Andreas Cratander to Capito, greetings. I congratulate you heartily on your position with the cardinal of Mainz, yet I cannot but welcome most joyfully your return to us from the commotion of the court, as I gather from your letter, for I owe everything I have to you. I have given Prechter[1] 100 florins in your name. I have given the bookseller Johannes Lor[2] some texts which he is

* * * * *

11 *Epistolae ad diversos* (Basel, 1521), published by the Froben Press in August.
12 I.e., the third edition, which appeared in 1522. The text and the annotations were printed in separate volumes. The text, as Hedio reports, was almost done. The annotations were completed in February 1522.
13 See above, Ep. 92.
14 The letter is lost.
15 A conflation of two adages, 'obviis ulnis' (with an open heart; Erasmus *Adagia* 2.9.54) and 'ambabus manibus' (with both hands; Erasmus *Adagia* 1.9.16).

1 See above, Ep. 50.
2 Johannes Lor was a publisher in Magdeburg. Basel printers (for example, Adam Petri) sometimes worked for him. Cf. Wackernagel, or 3:173.

to convey to you. Their titles are: *On confession, On the joy of resurrection, On praising God in Mary, On moderating disputations*, written by our friend Oecolampadius.[3] Also *On the Life of Moses* by Gregory of Nyssa.[4] Froben sent you Tertullian and the index to Jerome by a messenger.[5] I could not find the repertorium of Bertachini, nor are the works of Ovid from the Aldine press available.[6] Erasmus's letters have not yet been completed.[7] As for the rest, I am on good terms with Froben so far, except that he is not totally pleased that I am so friendly and intimate with Johann Koberger, Franz Birckmann, and Lucas Alantsee,[8] those great names among the booksellers. He fears for his own share, for this winter I shall print Saint Chrysostom, financed by the abovementioned gentlemen, and that bothers Froben. My wife and Polycarpus,[9] who is dear to you, are, I hope,[10] very well. In Basel there is fear of civil war, for every day great plots are hatched. One part wants to give aid to the emperor, the other to the king of the French.[11] I do not know what will hap-

* * * * *

3 *Quod non sit onerosa confessio, De gaudio resurrectionis sermo, De laudando in Maria Deo ... sermo, De moderandis disputationibus* (by Gregory of Nazianzen, translated by Oecolampadius), all published in 1521.

4 *Mystica Mosaicae vitae enarratio*, trans. Georgius of Trebizond.

5 I.e., Beatus Rhenanus's edition of Tertullian, see above Ep. 108, note 9; the index to Jerome's *Opera omnia* was published by Froben in 1520.

6 I.e., the *Repertorium iuris* of Giovanni Bertachini (Venice, 1488 and 1494) and the Aldine edition of Ovid (Venice, 1516).

7 The volume of the *Epistolae ad diversos* had in fact appeared, and Hedio secured a copy for Capito (see above, Ep. 108).

8 Johann Koberger (d. 1543) of Nürnberg, cousin of Anton Koberger, the founder of the Nürnberg printing firm. After Anton's death in 1513, Johann was largely responsible for the direction of the firm and expanded its connections with Italy and France. Franz Birckmann (documented 1504–30) was the manager of a large book selling and publishing firm that maintained agencies in Antwerp, Cologne, Paris, and London. In 1521 his headquarters were in Antwerp. He had close connections with the Froben press, whose books he distributed. Lucas and his brother Leonard Alantsee were prominent booksellers in Vienna, where they were active until 1551.

9 Polycarpus is Cratander's son. The printer was married three times, to Christina Lienhardt, Irmel (last name unknown, d. 1511), and Vronecka Renner (the marriage took place before 1522; she survived her husband).

10 They are in Basel; Cratander is at the book fair in Frankfurt.

11 After the battle of Marignano (1515), in which the Swiss troops suffered a defeat, parties developed for and against an alliance with France. Basel concluded an alliance on 7 May 1521, which provided for France paying pensions to individuals as well as to the city council. The alliance remained controversial, however, and was again the subject of discussion in council meetings in October (see Wackernagel 3:405–6).

pen. I have Ursinus Velius,[12] the most celebrated poet and learned Graecist staying with me, also Conrad Grebel,[13] a young man of outstanding talent, whose sister has married Joachim Vadianus.[14] Thus my workshop becomes more prominent through the conversations of learned men of this sort and will be better equipped in the future. Finally, I ask you to send me as quickly as possible anything you may have of Chrysostom that is worth printing and is not in the previous edition, for I would like this saintly bishop to be published adorned with a preface by you.[15] Farewell and continue to return your Andreas's affection, as you do. Our friend Valentinus[16] wishes you all the best. From Frankfurt, 20 September, in the year 1521.

Letter 110: End of September or beginning of October 1521, [Halle?], Capito to Martin Luther

Printed in WBr 2:393–4, #433

* * * * *

12 Caspar Ursinus Velius (d. 1539), a Silesian poet, was in the service of Bishop Matthaeus Lang and accompanied him to Italy, where he stayed from 1510 to 1514. He took lessons in Greek from Scipione Fortiguerra (Carteromachus) in Bologna. After his return to Germany he was crowned poet laureate by Emperor Maximilian I and taught Greek at the University of Vienna until 1521. He also obtained a canonry in Wrocław in 1518. He stayed with Cratander from August 1521 and moved on to Freiburg in 1522. After travels to Italy, he returned to Vienna, where he obtained the chair of rhetoric in 1524.
13 Conrad Grebel (ca. 1498–1526), the radical reformer, at the time a supporter of Zwingli. He studied at Basel (1414–15), Vienna (1515–18), and Paris (1518–20), but earned no degree, and was briefly in Basel in the summer of 1521 before joining Zwingli in Zurich.
14 Joachim Vadianus (1484–1551) of St Gallen was a graduate of the University of Vienna (BA 1504, MA 1508) and taught rhetoric there from 1516 on. Grebel was his student. Vadianus was crowned poet laureate in 1514. In 1518 he returned to his native city and in 1519 he married Grebel's sister, Martha. In addition to his humanistic studies, he also pursued medical studies at Vienna and became the town physician of St Gallen in 1520. He collaborated with Cratander on an edition of Pomponius Mela, published in 1522. Soon, however, his scholarly interests were overshadowed by the Reformation debate, and he became instrumental in establishing the Reformation in his native city. From 1525 to the end of his life he was mayor of St Gallen.
15 Cf. Capito's earlier translations of Chrysostom, Epp. 27 and 32, headnotes. Cratander included them together with Capito's prefaces in his 1522 edition of Chrysostom's *Opera omnia*. In a new edition of Chrysostom's works (1525), Cratander omitted the prefaces.
16 Valentinus Curio, who worked for Cratander at this time. For Curio see above, Ep. 95, headnote.

[*Summary*]: Luther has attracted the support of the common people because he has undertaken his work out of love of piety. Capito fears, however, that his radical approach will cause many of his followers to desert him. It has been reported that Luther is exacerbating matters by explicitly naming the church leaders whose vices he exposes. Capito cites the examples of Christ and Paul who criticized discreetly, which demonstrate that the spirit of Christ is gentle. He urges Luther to act more moderately in the future, expressing fears that Albert of Brandenburg may turn against him.

Letter 110a: 1 October 1521, Halle, Albert of Brandenburg to Leo X

Printed in Herrmann, 218–19 and there dated 23 October. The draft bears the date 1 October. The date 23 October (i.e., the date of despatch?) appears on the reverse of the page. This letter and Ep. 115 are letters of reference for Johannes Fabri. The drafts, now in the Strasbourg city archive (AST 40, #35a and b), are in Capito's hand.

Johannes Fabri (1478–1541) was born in the Allgäu the son of a smith. Not much is known of his life before he entered the University of Tübingen in 1505 to study theology and law. He was ordained priest and moved on to the University of Freiburg, where he obtained a doctorate in civil and canon law in 1510 or 1511. He served in a number of administrative positions (1511 vicar to the parish priest in Lindau, 1514 parish priest in Leutkirch) and was at one time in Basel, serving as official of Bishop Utenheim. A copy of Valla's *Opuscula* ([Basel: Cratander, 1518], now in the Houghton Library at Harvard University, shelf mark Phil 5771.2.5), which Capito presented to Fabri as a gift, is evidence of their good relations at that time. In 1518 Fabri became vicar-general of Constance, and in 1521 he was appointed suffragan bishop of Constance. In a book of sermons, published in 1520, he praised Capito and Oecolampadius as model preachers. He was initially sympathetic to Luther, but abandoned this view after the Leipzig Disputation of 1519, when Luther began to attack traditional doctrine. In 1522 he published a moderately worded polemic against Luther. An acerbic answer from Justus Jonas, who replied on Luther's behalf, hardened Fabri's stand. In 1523 he entered the service of Ferdinand of Austria, whose hard line against the Lutherans he supported. In 1530 Fabri was elevated to the bishopric of Vienna. He conscientiously fulfilled his ecclesiastical duties and was a respected patron of learning. He continued in his vigorous opposition to the Lutherans and published numerous polemics against them, as well as against the Anabaptists.

Albert furnished Fabri with the two letters of reference when he set out for Rome. He remained in Italy until the spring of 1522. The purpose of his jour-

ney was, among other things, to secure his title to a prebend and canonry in
Constance that had been challenged in court.

Most blessed, etc. I have been informed by Fabritius Capito, my familiar,
that a certain Johannes Fabri, a doctor of canon law from the diocese of Constance, is an admirably diligent partisan of the church, defending it in his
daily conversations not only in gesture and words, but also with action and
eloquence, for he is a better than average stylist. He has written a very good
book against the Lutheran faction, but as far as I know he has not published
it yet,[1] for he believes that there is no place for his talent on account of the
insane opinion which keeps the people from obedience. The attempt in itself
is excellent, even if he has had no practical success. For this reason I have
begun to patronize the man on the strength of his reputation, although I do
not know him in person, for we must show appreciation for those who have
ample good will towards us in turn. Furthermore I have heard that he has
earlier on obtained through the clemency of Your Holiness a prebend and
canonry in the chief church of Constance, but he very much fears a lawsuit
and therefore has decided to go to Rome, there to pursue his case against his
adversaries.[2] I cannot but commend such a well deserving man to Your
Holiness, although it would appear that he himself will easily gain your
respect and is his own best recommendation. I am all the more willing to
commend him to Your Holiness, to let you know that I too take note of men
who act in a honest manner and sincerely support Your Holiness, even if
they live at a distance. And Fabri is among a very small number who have
such a reputation, for the desire to fight the ancient laws has now invaded
everything.

Therefore I earnestly beg Your Holiness to deign to maintain him in the
prebend that he has obtained, on account of my pleas, for he is deserving
and every good man wishes it; in your usual clemency you will make it
known to him that my service has contributed in part to your favour. May
Your Holiness fare well and live a long and blessed life for the general benefit of the world. I commend myself most humbly to your most blessed feet.

Given at my castle at the city of Halle, 1 October, in the year, etc.

* * * * *

1 The *Opus adversus dogmata Martini Lutheri* was published in Rome, 1522.
2 Fabri's claim to a canonry in the cathedral chapter at Constance was challenged by Kaspar Wirt, provost of St Pelagius in Bischoffszell. The lawsuit was
   decided in Wirt's favour, but while Fabri was in Rome, another canonry
   became vacant, and in that instance his claim (which was also contested) was
   successful. On the litigation see I. Staub, *Dr. Johann Fabri, Generalvikar von Kon-
   stanz (1518–1523)* (Einsiedeln, 1911).

Letter 111: 5 October 1521, Wittenberg, Felix Ulscenius to Capito

> Printed by N. Müller in ARG 6 (1908–9): 172–4, #2. For Ulscenius see above,
> Ep. 70, headnote.

[*Summary*]: On Capito's invitation, Ulscenius poses an exegetical problem.
He has heard Capito state in a sermon on Romans 7 that less responsibility
ought to be imputed to children because they are ignorant of the law.
Melanchthon argued that Philippians 4 offers a different interpretation. On
4 October there was a disputation between Karlstadt and Johann Dölsch on
the worship of God and angels. Dölsch argued that temples should not be
built for angels nor masses be said to the saints. Karlstadt said that if this
were true, how ought one to interpret the passage in Genesis 19, which
states that Lot 'worshipped' the angels. Dölsch, unable to explain this, was
forced to resort to Augustine and Bede, whose authority Karlstadt did not
recognize. Karlstadt finally decided that Lot had sinned. Although he has
lived frugally, Ulscenius is in debt to Johannes Remboldus.

Letter 112: 6 October 1521, Wittenberg, Felix Ulscenius to Capito

> Printed by N. Müller in ARG 6 (1908–9): 174–5, #3

[*Summary*]: Ulscenius will continue to send newly published writings of
Luther to Capito. He asks Capito to greet Hartmann von Hallwyl on behalf
of Johannes Remboldus and himself. That day Gabriel Zwilling preached a
sermon strongly exhorting the audience no longer to attend or to assist with
the Mass. He affirmed that the flesh and blood of Christ are nothing but a
sign of the remission of our sins and of our reconciliation with God. This is
confirmed by the words of institution spoken by Christ at the Last Supper.
Neither the disciples nor their followers worshipped Christ's body and
blood. He reminded them that since God forbids the worship of signs or
images in the Old Testament, there is all the more reason in the New Testament for the sign [i.e., of Christ's body and blood] not to be worshipped.
God wants only himself to be worshipped. It is a mockery to insist that
Christ's death on the cross was insufficient for our sins. Zwilling will no
longer say Mass and made them feel guilty about attending Mass and
thereby condoning idolatry.

Letter 113: 14 October 1521, [Halle?], Capito to Desiderius Erasmus

> Printed in Allen 4:596–8, #1241 and CWE 8, Ep. 1241

[*Summary*]: Capito describes the aggressive campaign of the Lutherans. He wishes they were less virulent in defending their cause and more respectful of Erasmus. Burning Luther's works, however, is of no avail. Capito informs Erasmus that local authorities have acquiesced or connived with married priests. Albert of Brandenburg is reading the scriptures and has begun to introduce some reforms. Capito asks Erasmus's advice on how to proceed while he has Albert's ear. He advises Erasmus not to engage in polemic with Aleandro.

Letter 114: 1 October 1521, Halle, Albert of Brandenburg to Leo X

This letter now appears as Ep. 110a.

Letter 115: 18 October 1521, [Halle], Albert of Brandenburg to Lorenzo Pucci

This is another letter of reference for Johannes Fabri (see Ep. 110a, headnote). For the recipient, Cardinal Lorenzo Pucci, see above, Ep. 50, note 3. The manuscript, a draft in Capito's hand, is in the Strasbourg city archive (AST 40, 35b). The text is printed in Herrmann, 219–20. The draft is dated 18 October, but as in the case of Ep. 110, the reverse of the page is marked '23 October.'

Most reverend, etc. There is in Constance an experienced and renowned doctor of canon law, Johannes Fabri, a man of good faith, of Catholic belief and Christian zeal, for he asserts the authority of his Holiness, our lord, and of the universal church before everyone, straining every nerve, as they say,[1] and as you can see from the book he wrote in that sense.[2] As I hear from Capito, Fabri now fears lawsuits concerning a prebend in the church of Constance, which he obtained through the clemency of His Holiness, our lord. Therefore because I gladly make an effort on behalf of such men and regard it as my duty, I beg you, most reverend father, to interest yourself in his cause and ascertain, as is right, that he suffer no prejudice. For it will be very welcome and pleasing to see men of good will supported. Conversely, neglect makes them unpopular, for the general run of man looks to their own profit, and many hearts are won by noble generosity and patronage. For everyone returns the affection of one who shows affection and treats good men well. May you, most reverend father, look favourably on these

* * * * *

1 Erasmus *Adagia* 1.4.16.
2 Cf. above, Ep. 110a, note 1.

requests, as is the customary attitude towards devout men in your see, and if I am not mistaken, you will not regret the favour you confer on him.

Farewell, most reverend lord, I commend myself to you most diligently. Given 18 October.

Letter 116: 23 October 1521, [Halle], Albert of Brandenburg to Leo X

> This is a draft written by Capito for the archbishop of Mainz. The manuscript is in the Universitätsbibliothek, Basel, Ki.Ar. 25a, #141. The letter concerns the appointment of Hieronymus Schulz, bishop of Brandenburg, to the see of Havelberg. Joachim, the elector of Brandenburg, and older brother of the archbishop of Mainz, claimed the right of nomination. The matter had been pending for some time (see above, Ep. 93, of April 1521).

Most gracious, etc. Recently I explained at great length to Your Beatitude our great desire to see the reverend Hieronymus, bishop of Brandenburg, made bishop of Havelberg through your Holiness. At the same time I begged you to fulfil our wish, for the most illustrious Joachim, margrave of Brandenburg, elector, etc., and our most Christian friends and relatives demand this with all their energy. For they assert that the constitution of the margravate and of the Brandenburgians demands as much and there is no other man whom they either can or want to have as bishop in his place, and Your Beatitude has the highest authority to grant our petition on the following grounds: The [chapter] neglected to call two canons of the chapter who were not very far from Havelberg. They were tricked by a certain Georg of Blumental[1] who claims to have been elected, so there can be no doubt that a manifest fraud has taken place. For this reason we are wondering very much what has happened to prevent us from obtaining our request, which is fair or rather compelling, as things stand now, and the nature of the case is such that nothing can be more in the interest of the Catholic Church than what such great princes desire and expect, and it concerns such a man of whom we know that he has deserved very well of the holy apostolic see. Nor are there any grounds for anyone suggesting to Your Beatitude that this petition goes against the right, custom or even

* * * * *

1 Georg of Blumental (ca. 1490–1550) studied law at Frankfurt/Oder and was the secretary of the bishop of Lebus from 1507. He was elected to the bishopric of Havelberg and obtained papal confirmation, but was persuaded to yield to Albert's candidate. In exchange, Albert supported his election to the bishopric of Lebus in 1524. See above, Ep. 93.

concordats with the German nation. For what can be more evident than that the authority rests with Your Beatitude to provide for the church if the chapter does not provide for it in a timely manner or does so in a manner disregarding due process? And it is quite clear that they passed over two of the canons, leading and powerful canons at that, for one is a doctor of theology, the other a professor of law, indeed that they hastened to complete the sham election having been tricked by the sham candidate, as those in the chapter who are motivated by the love of truth have said in a document recently published. And such are the times now that, if there was a point at variance with the law or our concordats, nevertheless, as times are now, one ought to oblige the illustrious Joachim, the elector, etc. our dearest friend. He would not tolerate another man to become bishop in his [Schulz's] place, whoever he may be. Nor does he expect anything else, just as we ourselves stand firm in our belief that Your Beatitude will oblige us both in a matter that is so easy and fair, etc.

To the envoy: Magnificent, etc. I have once again written to His Beatitude, the pontiff, as you can see from the enclosed copy, on behalf of the venerable Hieronymus, bishop of Brandenburg, that he may be appointed bishop of Havelberg as well, according to the wish of Joachim, margrave of Brandenburg, elector, etc., my relative and friend. It will be your task to transact the business about which we have written and repeat the arguments orally, over and over again, if necessary. For there is no reason to delay, if only His Beatitude wishes (as he is very well able) to gratify us. For on the basis of law and tradition, given that the two canons, who should principally have been called, were not called, the power to appoint a bishop for the church has freely devolved on His Beatitude, and to appoint a man who is dear to the dynasty of Brandenburg and brings honour to the holy apostolic see and is able to serve it. The bishop of Brandenburg is the one and only man for this business. Act to the best of your knowledge, and we put our trust in you. Given, etc.

Letter 117: 23 October 1521, Wittenberg, Felix Ulscenius to Capito

Printed by N. Müller in ARG 6 (1908–9): 206–9, #18

[*Summary*]: Gabriel Zwilling recently preached a sermon against the Mass. On 23 October the Augustinians suspended the celebration of Mass in their own monastery. They disagreed with Karlstadt about how to proceed. Karlstadt wanted them to preach about the abuses of the Mass and abolish it only with the consent of the people, but they argued that the Mass was a danger to faith and must be rejected. The matter, therefore, was brought to

Melanchthon. He noted that Paul did away with circumcision. Why not do away with the Mass, he asked? Johann Femel, who was present at the discussion, lamented that the Reformation movement was so divisive and wished that they had all followed Erasmus's advice. To that Karlstadt responded that there is only room for moderation when all problems have been solved. Justus Jonas now ardently inveighs against the Mass and has decided to celebrate Mass only once a day in his church, obliging the congregation to take communion in both kinds. Ulscenius will communicate any new development that may concern either Capito or Albert of Brandenburg. Johannes Remboldus is attending all of Melanchthon's lectures. Ulscenius is sending Capito some treatises composed in the past few days by the theologians at Wittenberg.

Letter 118: 16 November 1521, Wittenberg, Felix Ulscenius to Capito

Printed by N. Müller in ARG 6 (1908–9): 264–5, #29

[*Summary*]: In response to Capito's query, Ulscenius acknowledges that he received half a gulden less than the ten gulden which Capito had sent him from the Frankfurt Fair. Recently he received four gulden, which he desperately needed. Ulscenius does not know what Capito or others wrote to Melanchthon, but the latter does not approve of men shying away from unpopular actions. Martin Luther, he writes, is facing opposition because he is not afraid to speak out on issues such as the papacy, human traditions, and the Mass. No one should be afraid to profess one's faith in God before others. The plague is abating in Wittenberg. Johannes Remboldus gives his regards to Capito. Ulscenius is sending Capito a copy of Johann Bugenhagen's *Epistola de peccato in Spiritum sanctum* and Melanchthon's *Positiones de missa*. He will also send Capito Melanchthon's soon to be completed *Loci communes*, if he wants them.

Letter 119: 30 November 1521, Wittenberg, Felix Ulscenius to Capito

Printed by N. Müller in ARG 6 (1908–9): 266–8, #31

[*Summary*]: Ulscenius has received Capito's letter [now lost] and read it to Melanchthon, who regretted that Capito did not list any passages in Luther's writings which in his opinion are at variance with scripture. Melanchthon will write to Capito himself [letter not extant, but cf. MBW, Ep. 179]. Ulscenius assured Melanchthon that Capito agreed with Luther's teaching and only desired that he were more moderate. Melanchthon responded that there is nothing immoderate about calling the enemies of Christ by their real name. Luther was right to attack the enemies of the church by name. Melanchthon will write to Hutten to desist from his attacks on Capito. Fifteen monks have left the priesthood under the leadership of Gabriel Zwilling. There has been no word on Luther's return [from the Wartburg]. Melanchthon is lecturing on 2 Corinthians in Latin and will procure various Christian writings in Greek for his students. Johann Bugenhagen, author of the *Epistola de peccato in Spiritum sanctum,* which Ulscenius recently sent to Capito [see Ep. 118], is lecturing on the Psalms and frequently citing the commentary of Felix da Prato. Ulscenius cannot comment on the future plans of the theologians at Wittenberg, but in many places Mass is no longer said. Justas Jonas and Georg Mohr will celebrate Mass only if there are people present willing to take communion in both kinds, as Christ instituted. The fund for the poor, instituted by the magistrate on Luther's advice, is daily growing because what was formerly donated to the church for vigils is now being added to the fund. Many citizens of Wittenberg are giving practical demonstrations of their fervent love for God and their neighbours. Ulscenius will send Capito his notes on Melanchthon's lectures. Ulscenius cannot depart from Wittenberg without disadvantaging himself. He has not yet achieved his goal.

Letter 120: 11 December [1521], Wittenberg, Philip Melanchthon to Capito or Nikolaus Demut

Printed in *Melanchthons Briefwechsel* T1:410–12, #189. The letter is addressed to Capito or 'in his absence, to the provost of the Neue Stift,' i.e., Demut.

[*Summary*]: Melanchthon is sending Capito a copy of Luther's letter to Albert of Brandenburg [from 1 December 1521]. He urges Capito to speak with Albert in private and to be supportive of Luther. Citing the New Testament, Melanchthon says that if Luther was divinely sent to reform the church, then people must not ignore or reject either God's messenger or his message. Luther has been much more moderate than Elijah, Elisha, or Christ ever were. He clarifies that all who are divinely sent to preach the gospel are prophets. The people need to be 'salted' by the restored message and worship of God. Melanchthon need not explain this in more detail to a theologian like Capito. He warns that Luther will publish [*Wider den Abgott zu Halle*], if Albert does not respond in the right way. He notes that the archbishop has already disparaged indulgences. It should therefore be easy to do away with them altogether. Capito will no doubt appreciate the fact that Luther has restricted his criticisms to the matter of indulgences. Melanchthon has made every effort to prevent the publication of Luther's criticism and will continue to do so, if Capito does his share.

Letter 121: 20 and 21 December 1521, Halle, Capito to Martin Luther

Printed in WBr 2:416–20, #447

[*Summary*]: Capito has not written Luther in a while because he recognizes that he and Luther completely disagree about the best approach to reforming the church. Erasmus, whom he met in Cologne, has been advising a conciliatory approach to the issue. Capito has been urging Albert of Brandenburg not to act against Luther in the wake of the Diet of Worms. Capito even cherishes hopes of Albert becoming a supporter of Luther. He praises Albert's handling of affairs and highlights his own efforts to aid Luther's cause. After returning to Halle, Albert seemed to be backsliding. He attempted to reinstate indulgences, but was opposed by Capito. Luther's advice will benefit Albert [see summary of Ep. 120 above]. Capito expects that Albert's support for reform will increase with his reading of evangelical writings. Capito therefore urges Luther not to ridicule or discourage the archbishop. Albert has commanded that sermons on the gospel of Matthew be preached and has forbidden the monks at Halle to speak out against Luther, though commanded otherwise by papal bulls. Heinrich Stromer can attest to Albert's open-mindedness. Capito himself desires nothing but the spreading of the gospel, the well-being of Albert, and an end to all invectives. He fears the threat of war and the accompanying bloodshed. Capito has many reservations about married clergy. He fears that some, after a few years of marriage, may seek an annulment, disregard the authority of their superiors, and thereby turn the people against the reformers. Balthasar Zeiger married a woman from Switzerland in Vaterrode, but the counts of Mansfeld, who disliked Zeiger, excluded her from their dominions. Zeiger insisted that he was lawfully married and so the matter was brought before Albert. He was eventually released from prison and abjured all vengeance, with Laurentius Zoch and Capito acting as witnesses. Unless the Spirit enlightens Albert, Capito will quit his court within four months. He asks Luther to respond via Melanchthon. In the postscript, written the following day, he mentions that Albert has responded prudently to Luther's letter. Again Capito stresses the need for moderation in order not to incite turmoil. He has written at greater length to Justus Jonas.

Letter 122: 21 December 1521, Halle, Capito to Philip Melanchthon

Printed in *Melanchthons Briefwechsel* T1:412–14, #190

[*Summary*]: Capito appreciates Melanchthon's discretion. Albert of Brandenburg read Luther's letter (of 1 December 1521) several times and said only
that he did not deserve such sharp words, especially since he had forbidden
the Franciscans at Halle to speak out against Luther and had stalled the
implementation of the Edict of Worms. Capito argues that Albert is not
opposed to the spread of the gospel; on the contrary, he is a more zealous
preacher than Capito. He believes that Luther will approve of Albert's
response, which is almost pleading and was written without prompting.
Capito beseeches Melanchthon to act prudently in order not to provoke
Albert. He continues to praise Albert's commitment to reform. Capito mentions how he admonished Justus Jonas in a letter to consider those elements
of their faith that they hold in common rather than to wage an internecine
war. He ends urging Melanchthon to continue speaking out on behalf of the
gospel.

Letter 123: [1521, Halle?], Capito to N.

The manuscript of the letter is in the Universitätsbibliothek, Basel, Ki.Ar. 25a,
#124. The letter may be addressed to Andreas Karlstadt, whose letter (Ep. 124,
below) appears to be a reply and contains literal parallels.

Capito to a brother, against the Antinomians.[1]
Many greetings. I have always wanted to travel to you that we might talk in
person about our common concerns, but business keeps me back against my
will. I was greatly pleased about the rebirth of the church and the bitter
struggle of so many young talented men against the pestilent superstition of
barbarity, but I now see a different development. For there are meddlers who
have the audacity of rejecting the Old Testament and denying it as if it were
the work of an evil, seducing demon, a damnable sin and an abomination
leading the world astray. There are others again who want the law re-established everywhere, and a third group who are excessively zealous and are
carried along like a clear torrent. They deny that the force of the law is conducive to salvation and at once turn upside down all divine law, without

* * * * *

1 I.e., those who equated the Old Testament with a legalistic approach that went
against the spirit of the New Testament.

realizing that the *law is given not only to the just but also to the unjust and adul-*
terers.[2] These people show little concern for salvation and God's glory.
Indeed in their fury they slander even whatever laws secular princes have
given. Can anyone approve of such people? Laws are necessary for public
order and the Christian commonwealth. Everything will be full of bloody
tragedies, if you give everyone the right to assert in public whatever he
pleases. I report with sadness that ill-advised men of this sort are aiding the
obscurantist sophists by foolishly interpreting that which has not yet been
clearly laid down and clearly disturbing public order.[3] It is salubrious with
the help of laws to drive out bad morals; it is godly to straighten out piety
gone awry or to be against the harmful author of contentious doctrine. Charity is the goal and end of instruction in the gospel as well. It originates in a
pure heart and in good conscience and in genuine faith.[4] They may praise
charity however much they please, but if it is not sincere, if the heart of
impure men mixes it with their own passions, desires, and dismal vices, they
err when they vaunt themselves. They are obeying their own desire. They
either want to make trouble or be held in high repute, but they do not teach
Christ nor do they attempt to recall good morals, and in the end no doubt
suffer shipwreck as far as their faith is concerned. Why do I say all that? The
reason is of course to make you, who are in the very citadel and at the pinna-
cle of erudition, look out as from a watchtower and prevent the incursion
and threat of the enemies who spoil the true harvest of the gospel with a
mock version that imitates the truth, who disturb the true, Christian peace
with their virulent passions, who infect the simple minds of their listeners,
who irritate the authorities and provoke them into condemning our studies,
our piety, and our inclination to religious duties. I think I have taken good
counsel for myself if, aware of my shortcomings, I keep to myself[5] and will
not join anyone's party. For I see no suitable leader and people everywhere
are carried away by insane passion rather than wise and pious moderation.
Farewell and peacefully seek the glory of Christ according to your vocation.

Letter 124: 1521, Wittenberg, Andreas Karlstadt to Capito

This letter is printed in C.F. Jäger, *Andreas Bodenstein von Carlstadt: Ein Beitrag*

* * * * *

2 1 Tim. 8:10.
3 The Latin sentence does not run, leaving the meaning of the sentence open to
   conjecture.
4 Echoing 1 Tim. 2.
5 Lit. 'I keep inside my skin,' a proverbial expression (Erasmus *Adagia* 1.6.92).

zur Geschichte der Reformationszeit aus Originalquellen gegeben (Stuttgart, 1856), 506.

To Wolfgang Capito, leader in sincere theology, his friend and respected patron:

I am sad, my most learned patron, about your indifferent health, and as sad as if my own health were affected. Next, I hear you saying that someone was overheard rejecting the Old Testament. This is far from true at the university here; on the contrary, we contend in public lectures as well as in disputations that there is nothing in the New Testament that Moses does not teach. That is what we think of Moses and likewise of the prophets (all of whom Christ has proved true). For the rest, since you complain about our remarkable liberty and the rascals who twist the best of everything to its detriment – we share your sentiment. I attest by the living God that I am greatly angered by that man's procacity.[1] But I believe the philosophy of Christ will be found to be immune against it; he averred that he was the cornerstone,[2] over which the ungodly would stumble, indeed the stone that was placed for the ruin of many,[3] which we owe to ungodliness.

Every day I am in need of the Hebrew lexicon and need it very urgently. If you wish to keep it with you much longer, allow me to have it copied at my expense. It is our desire to see you here in person, and safe. Farewell and allow me to commend myself to you. Wittenberg, etc. 1521. Your Karlstadt.

Letter 125: [January?] 1522, [Wittenberg], N to Capito

> This letter is printed in Kolde, 327–9. The original is lost. Kolde's text comes from the transcription in TB (1: 257–8), which states that the original was written *manu Capitonis*, in Capito's hand. Kolde suggests that the report, perhaps a broadsheet, was supplied by Ulscenius (see above, Ep. 70, headnote) or another of Capito's correspondents in Wittenberg. The provocative sermons mentioned here prompted widespread reaction. The affair was discussed in the sessions of the *Reichsregiment*, the governing body established in 1521 to handle problems arising after Charles's departure for Spain. Albert attended the sessions in Nürnberg and chaired them from April to June 1522 (cf. Planitz's report to the Elector Frederick, #29). It is likely therefore that

* * * * *

1 Jäger suggests that this is a reference to Gabriel Zwilling (on whom see Ep. 125).
2 E.g., 1 Pet. 2:6.
3 Cf. Luke 2:34.

Capito requested this report and copied or summarized it for Albert's information.

What Gabriel Lonicerus[1] preached in Eilenburg.
A fugitive Augustinian monk from Wittenberg, named Gabriel, travelled to Eilenburg on Christmas Eve and said he had been told and urged to preach. The chief official of Eilenburg, Johann Müller,[2] asked the parish priest[3] to do him a favour and allow the said Magister Gabriel to preach. The parish priest did not want to deny him the favour and gave his permission. The same request had been made of him also by Hans von Taubenheym,[4] *Rentmeister*[5] of the Elector Duke Frederick. He too asked that the said Magister Gabriel should be allowed to preach. On the morning of St Stephen's day the parish priest wanted to stop it because, he said, he and his congregation were in great danger on that account. He could not permit it without the knowledge of his archbishop and prelate, but the said Hans von Taubenheym responded that he would settle any problems if Duke Frederick asked about the archbishop of Magdeburg, the provost, or the parish priest.[6] And so the parish priest was obliged to permit the above mentioned preacher to

* * * * *

1   Not Johannes Lonicerus (d. 1569), an Austin friar who was driven out of Freiburg in 1522 after a public attack on the Franciscans, but the Augustinian Gabriel Zwilling (1487–1558). Zwilling, like Lonicerus, studied at Wittenberg (MA 1518) and was a supporter of Karlstadt. At Christmas 1521 he preached at Eilenburg, a small town in Saxony, and in January 1522 participated in iconoclastic violence. He moderated his approach, however, and became preacher at Torgau in 1523, where he helped to establish the Reformation.
2   Johann Müller of Rellikon in the canton of Zurich (d. 1542), studied at Cracow and Wittenberg (1522–4). In 1528 he became the first professor of Greek at Bern. From 1538 he taught in Zurich, and from 1541 until his death he was pastor of Biel.
3   Perhaps Heinrich Kranach (or Kranich), who is repeatedly mentioned in the documents demanding compensation for the damage done to his property during the riots incited by Zwilling's preaching. There were, however, three parish priests: Johann Schenckel, Johann von Melwitz, and Heinrich Kranach. Cf. K. Pallas, 'Der Reformationsversuch des Gabriel Didymus in Eilenburg und seine Folgen, 1522–1525,' *ARG* 10 (1913): 63–4, 68.
4   Hans von Taubenheym of Meissen was in the service of Frederick the Wise, Elector of Saxony. In 1528 he became visitator of the Saxon church, and in 1530 attended the Diet of Ausgburg.
5   I.e., a financial officer.
6   Frederick did inquire into the events, as directed by the imperial Regiment. Melanchthon, Justus Jonas, and Karlstadt defended Zwilling's actions in a joint letter to the Elector in October 1522.

preach, and he said during High Mass on Christmas Day in his sermon: We have prepared for Christmas during advent, with many prayers and fasting. But that means nothing. We haven't celebrated Christmas day correctly in eight hundred years. Singing, reading, praying, Mass, and all that happens in church is just balderdash. It is devilish. The devil made the pope, cardinal, bishop, priests, monks, and nuns. And then he preached that one must have faith, which would lead to charity, and charity would lead to works, and therefore one should leave everything alone. Leave the Mass, when the priest says Mass, [he said,] and don't go to communion if he does not want to give you communion in two kinds. Let go of man-made laws. All the prayers, fasting, and other commands of the pope and monks and priests are lies. They do it out of avarice – and much more of the same sort.

On Christmas Day after vespers, the aforementioned preacher preached again in the church of Eilenburg and was harsher than before and said one should not keep any holy days except Sunday, which had been commanded by God, and one shouldn't care about the precepts of the parish priest. It was the command of the devil and the Antichrist to carry around the sacrament in procession. One must not take it to the sick. If the priest didn't get a gulden for it, he would stay away from last unction and the sacrament.

On St Stephen's Day[7] at High Mass he preached similar things, especially about the Mass, that it was the devil's work. Remember I warned you [he said], stay away from it, and if anyone preaches differently, tell him openly: Priest, you lie. He also mentioned that masses for the dead, vigils, anniversaries, and confraternities were nothing but vanity and tomfoolery invented by foolish monks and priests.

On St John's Day[8] he likewise preached of the Mass, the monks, and the priests, the pope and the bishop and the devil's cap: It's all the same and one mustn't obey them. Christ has delivered us. We are all free, we have no obligations. We are free to eat meat during Lent. And indeed, he did eat meat that same day. The priest of Eilenburg and his preacher were invited on that day to go to the castle. In the evening they were served a meal of cooked bacon. The priest and his preacher did not want to eat it, but the fugitive monk, the *Rentmeister*, the chief official, Jorg Schonichen, a cobbler of Eilenburg,[9] and

* * * * *

7 26 December.
8 27 December.
9 O. Schmidt, *Petrus Mosellanus. Ein Beitrag zur Geschichte des Humanismus in Sachsen* (Leipzig, 1867), 73, n.8, reports that Schonichen wrote an open letter to Mosellanus, then rector of the University of Leipzig, urging him to support such actions.

the other guests at table in the castle, ate those 'fish' and said Christ had not forbidden it. Finally the aforementioned preacher said from the pulpit: Tomorrow I won't preach. Work all day and don't any of you go to church or Mass. Next Sunday I'll preach again.

On the Sunday after the feastday of the Innocents,[10] the holy preacher stood up to preach: I have preached as you heard me in the hope that the priest and his chaplains would stop saying Mass, but that did not happen. Abandon them. On New Year's Day after my sermon I will give you the Eucharist in two kinds. Follow me and I will say Mass in the castle and will give it to all who ask for it. And he explained why the Eucharist is displayed. There was no need to confess; one should make no distinction between days; one day was as good as the next.

On Sunday after the feast of the Innocents, at nine in the evening, two men threw rocks at the window of the priest's house in Eilenburg and broke the windows and stuck up a letter on the door of the priest's house, which said: Priest, this is to let you know that now that the omnipotent eternal God has given us here in Eilenburg a pious Christian and true preacher, who showed and taught and instructed us in the holy writ of God alone, and leads us to the very teaching and precepts of Christ, because we felt a great burden on our conscience while you, as we were told, had the cure of our souls, we want to know from you immediately: Let us know what you intend and are willing to do with regard to your preaching[11] and let us hear what you have to say publicly before the whole congregation, so that we can find out what your thinking is, but if that doesn't happen in a few days, look out what's going to happen to you. Be warned. May God the Almighty deign to enlighten you in the faith together with your people. 1522.

If we Christians want to follow Christ, we must all turn away from the teachings of the Antichrist and help to confess the true Christian faith. Thus I commend you to God.

Letter 126: 1 January 1522, Wittenberg, Justus Jonas to Capito

> Printed in Kawerau 1:79–82 (#73)
>
> Justus Jonas (1493–1555) studied at Erfurt (BA 1507, MA 1510), then Wittenberg, where he took up legal studies. In 1515 he returned to Erfurt (licentiate in civil and canon law, 1518), where he had close connections with the

* * * * *

10 30 December.
11 The reading and meaning of this clause is uncertain.

humanistic circle around Mutianus Rufus and maintained contacts with both Erasmus and Luther. In 1518 he obtained a canonry at St Severin's and began teaching at the university. In 1521 he accepted a provostship and a teaching position at the University of Wittenberg, although he was a reluctant lecturer and more interested in public affairs. He accompanied Luther to the Diet of Worms and returned via Erfurt in May 1521. He was now fully committed to the Reformation, but did not resign his canonry at Erfurt. In September 1521 he received a doctorate in theology at Wittenberg and the following year he married. He was present at the Marburg colloquy in 1529 and the Diet of Augsburg in 1530. Eventually he became superintendent of Halle, where he carried on the reform. As a result of the Interim (1547) he was forced to leave Halle and eventually settled in Thuringia, where he took over the parish of Eisfeld.

[*Summary*]: Jonas is pleased to hear from Capito that Albert is preaching in person rather than using a substitute and hopes that Capito will follow his example. The Italians are only interested in obtaining money from the Germans, not in providing spiritual leadership. The obtuseness of the German prelates, who offer no resistance, is amazing. Jonas denies the primacy of the pope. There was no good reason why the archbishop of Mainz had to pay huge fees to the Roman see in connection with his appointment. There must be an end to the tyranny of Rome. He is pleased to hear from Capito of Albert's efforts to fulfil his episcopal duties and prays that God may support his efforts. Melanchthon reports that Luther, too, is hopeful of Albert. Jonas deplores celibacy as a cover-up for maintaining concubines. He reports that Karlstadt and other priests have married. He himself is considering this option. Many people in Wittenberg now receive communion in both kinds. He urges Capito to continue his work on behalf of the gospel.

Letter 127: 1 January 1522, Wittenberg, Felix Ulscenius to Capito

Printed in ARG 6 (1908–9): 390–1 (#62)

[*Summary*]: Ulscenius mistakenly reports that Karlstadt married on 26 December [see correction in next letter]. On 25 December he celebrated an evangelical mass at the chapel of the castle, offering communion in both kinds. The Zwickau prophet, Markus Thomä, is staying at Melanchthon's house. Ulscenius will oblige Capito, once he understands what he is after. Remboldus asks Capito to send him money. They are both in great need of funds. He asks Capito to buy him a hat.

Letter 128: 1 January 1522, Wittenberg, Felix Ulscenius to Capito

Printed in ARG 6 (1908–9): 391–2, #63

[*Summary*]: Karlstadt preached twice on the Eucharist. The parish priest, Simon Heins, allowed the people to take communion in both kinds. Karlstadt will reportedly marry in two weeks [the marriage took place 19 January]. Melanchthon is at the court of Frederick the Wise. Karlstadt and Thomä vaunt themselves as prophets. The situation is tense. Remboldus and Ulscenius are in need of money; Ulscenius needs a hat. Melchior Zobel will travel to Leipzig on 5 January.

Letter 129: Mid-January 1522, [Halle?], Capito to Martin Bucer

Printed in *Corr Bucer* 1:182–4, #41. The letter is written in Greek.

[*Summary*]: Capito agrees with Bucer concerning the corruption of the courts. He himself wishes to retire from Albert's court and settle in Strasbourg. Capito disapproves of the radicalism of the reformers who preach civil disobedience. Conversely, he prays for a change of heart in the secular rulers and hopes they will listen to the evangelical preachers.

Letter 130: 16 January 1522, Halle, Capito to N

This manuscript is in the Universitätsbibliothek, Basel, Ki.Ar. 25a, #25. A copy by Simmler in the Zentralbibliothek Zürich identifies the recipient as Claude Chansonnette, but there is no supporting evidence. Cf. Ep. 67 above for Chansonnette's hopes to enter the service of the archbishop.

Greeting. The archbishop instructed me to ask you to take this young man, Wendelin, a relative of Peter Scher,[1] and give him special consideration beyond the others. For, as you know, he is skilled in both Latin and French. You have useful experience in these languages. You will have someone with whom you can practise. Make sure that he does his reading, for lack of practice brings on oblivion of letters. You know how fragile memory is, how

* * * * *

1 Peter Scher (Scherer, d. 1557), private secretary of Franz von Sickingen. After Sickingen's death, he entered the service of William of Nassau, then moved to Ferdinand's court in Vienna. He eventually bought the fief of Nambsheim near Colmar.

light-headed young people are and how prone to pleasures. Impose a limit on those things. Your diligence will be appreciated by the prince, for he has decided to take him into his service and allow him to handle even the most confidential matters. I wish you happy years, pleasant success in everything without anxious concern to which you appear liable. Bitter fate makes us work in the sweatshop day and night, too much perhaps, but it is all in the public interest. What can I say? Shall I allow the inconstancy of others forever to play on my simplicity? I shall shortly say goodbye to all cares, but *I shall not flee beyond the threshold of the house.*[2] Oh unheard of upheaval, from which I keep away as much as I can! Indeed I shall take care that it doesn't swallow me up as well. Given at Halle, 16 January 1522. Wolfgang Fabritius Capito.

Letter 131: 17 January 1522, Wittenberg, Martin Luther to Capito

> Printed in WBr 2:428–35, #451. The letter, which answers Capito's Ep. 121, was printed without authorization in Strasbourg by Hans Schott. It was included in a collection entitled *Iudicium D. Martini Lutheri de Erasmo ...* (1523). The letter was also published on its own in two prints that appeared without date or publisher's name under the title *Epistola Lutheri ad Wolfgangum Fabricium Capitonem Theologum utilissima.* Cf. WBr 2:428, for the suggestion that one appeared in Basel, the other in Erfurt, perhaps from the press of Matthes Maler. German translations of the letter issued shortly afterwards from Schott's press as well as from the press of Sigmund Grimm (Augsburg) and Adam Petri (Basel). The letter reveals Capito as a covert Lutheran who had been trying to influence Albert's policy. The publication forced Capito's hand. He tendered his resignation to Albert in July 1523. Capito himself first mentions the publication in a letter to Erasmus (below, Ep. 164 of 6 July, and cf. Ep. 165).

[*Summary*]: Luther regrets that Capito differs with him over the correct approach to spreading the gospel. He cannot accept Capito's advice to connive with princes and overlook their misdeeds for the sake of peace. In Luther's opinion this is 'flattery and the denial of the Christian truth.' He would rather imitate Christ, who was not afraid to give offence. One must never make excuses for sinful behaviour, although one may show charity to the penitent sinner. It is important to make a clear distinction between right and wrong. Capito's approach camouflages the truth and is ineffective. If Albert's letter to Luther was written from the heart, it was commendable; if,

* * * * *

2 I.e., not far; Erasmus *Adagia* 1.5.3.

however, he played the hypocrite under Capito's direction, as Luther suspects, it will have no effect. He protests in particular Albert's treatment of married priests. He does not believe that Albert wrote from the heart and accuses Capito of engaging in rhetorical tricks. He will not reply to Albert, leaving explanations to Capito.

Letter 132: 24 January 1522, Wittenberg, Felix Ulscenius to Capito

Printed in ARG 6 (1908–9): 427–8, #74

[*Summary*]: Ulscenius and Remboldus thank Capito for the five gulden he sent them. They are glad to hear that Capito plans to look more carefully after his financial affairs because lack of care has cost him dearly. Karlstadt's marriage has taken place. Next Sunday he will preach against images and ask that they be burned. Gabriel Zwilling has already done so in his monastery. Cristannus Beyer will be installed as mayor. The local brothel has been closed and prostitutes are being driven out of Wittenberg. Radicalism is driving away students and professors, for example Matthäus Aurogallus, who left for Prague. There is open disagreement between Zwilling and the reformers Justus Jonas and Nikolaus Amsdorf. The reformers meet daily with the city council to discuss changes in the church order. Melanchthon is most active in this matter.

Letter 133: 9 February 1522, Wittenberg, Felix Ulscenius to Capito

Printed in ARG 6 (1908–9): 442–3, #90

[*Summary*]: Ulscenius reports that Berlinus [unidentified] has praised Capito's sermons. Remboldus has heard that Capito will shortly depart for Nürnberg and asks for six gulden. He stands in great need of money and has no one from whom he could borrow. Justus Jonas is about to marry. The city council is acting in the interest of the Reformation. Melanchthon spoke out against an unnamed person who deliberately misinterprets 1 Kings 8:11. He may have had Capito in mind.

Letter 134: 1 March 1522, Strasbourg, Jacob Spiegel to Capito

Jacob Spiegel (1483–1547) of Sélestat studied at Heidelberg (BA 1500) and Freiburg, where he studied law under Udalricus Zasius. He obtained a post in the imperial chancery in 1504, but resumed his studies and from 1513 was professor of law at the University of Vienna. He again served in the imperial chancery under Charles V, then entered the service of his brother Ferdinand in 1523. In the wake of a fraud scandal at court that led to the downfall of the chancellor Gabriel Salamanca, Spiegel resigned and retired to Sélestat. He received a pension and practised law privately, devoting his leisure time to scholarship. His *Lexicon iuris civilis* (Strasbourg, 1538) was frequently reprinted. In 1536 he was given the honourable title of Count Palatine. Spiegel was sympathetic to the Reformation. The *Grievances of the German Nation* were published under his auspices; he aided Bucer in obtaining a release from his monastic vows.

The manuscript of this letter is in Paris, Bibl. SHPF, manuscript 756/1 (Collection Labouchère I, fol. 155).

Hail, dear provost, for I do not call you 'theologian' because you have stayed and lived too long in the court of the prince, who has attracted the hatred of all scholars in all of Germany. I know that you have a bad reputation with many people because you set aside the honour you gained for yourself through letters and are working in such a lowly office. I beg you by the immortal God to extricate yourself as soon as you can and fly here to your friends. Believe me, you will be received with open arms.[1] Whenever I go to our dear Prechter,[2] he complains about your delay. On his request, I write this letter in both of our names. There are people of standing here who are worthy of your consideration. There are people who are your avowed friends, and I am here doing what I can. They do not think that you risk losing your reputation, which would happen if you served at court much longer. You do not know, my dear Capito, how much I did for Albert, sticking out my own neck when he was after the cardinalate. I have ample testimony (for example, the letters of Carpi).[3] Let his majordomo Laurentius[4] attest to the great labour and diligence I have continuously expended on his business and the business of his churches. My purse can attest to the loss I suffered in return for my faithful service. It was then that I first found out from experience that it is true: *one must not trust in*

* * * * *

1 Erasmus *Adagia* 2.9.54.
2 See above, Ep. 50, note 1.
3 Alberto Pio, prince of Carpi (1475–1531), the imperial legate in Rome, 1513–19. Cf. above, Ep. 93.
4 Laurenz Nachterhofer, who was repeatedly involved in financial transactions with the imperial court on Albert's behalf; Paul Redlich (*Cardinal Albrecht von Brandenburg und das Neue Stift zu Halle, 1520–1541* [Mainz, 1900], 79) calls him Albert's 'special emissary' (*ausserordentlicher Gesandter*) at the imperial court.

princes ...; there is no safety with them.[5] Let my rustic and primitive learning be my solace, as you, a prince of erudition, will take solace in that truly golden learning, when you return to it. Take care, however, that you depart with greater favour and a greater reward than I who could not obtain my due,[6] for which I have begged you so many times to intercede. If Jupiter[7] is angry with me, I do not want you to say anything more to him on my behalf, but please answer at once or answer through your secretary, if you will ever return to your people and to your true dignity, which comes closest to the other[8] in this quite renowned city. Your friends know how much I love you, how much I value you, even if many people here, who are too favourably inclined towards Luther's name and his doctrine, say things about you – but it would not be safe to entrust their names to a letter. Yet I know that all indignation against you will soon abate, once you have said farewell to that court.

If your prince had been fairer to me, I would have dedicated to him my commentaries on the 12 books of the *Austriad*,[9] which is proceeding well and is approved by my literary friends. In future you will see how true their judgment is, for you are deservedly praised by one who is undeservedly praised. I am now working on the tenth book. Farewell and accept my letter with a sincere heart, for you know that my heart has always been open to you. Hurriedly, from Prechter's house in Strasbourg, on the first of March, in the year of the Lord, 1522.

Letter 135: 17 March 1522, Wittenberg, Felix Ulscenius to Capito

> The text of this letter is published in K. Hartfelder, *Melanchthoniana Paedagogica* (Leipzig, 1892), 122–3. For Ulscenius see above, Ep. 70, headnote.

Ulscenius to Capito, greeting.

* * * * *

5 Ps. 146:2.
6 Aleandro denounced Spiegel as a hypocrite and crypto-Lutheran (Kalkoff, *Depeschen*, 120). Of the moneys he received from Rome to pay for services rendered, he gave Spiegel only fifty of the hundred Rhenish gulden allotted to him (ibid., 163).
7 I.e., Albert.
8 The antecedent is unclear.
9 *Richardi Bartholini, Perusini, Austriados libri XII ... cum scholiis Iacobi Spiegelii* (Strasbourg: Schott, 1531). Spiegel eventually dedicated it to Ferdinand in a prefatory letter dated 31 January 1531 (fols. A2–3).

When I returned home yesterday from escorting [you],[1] I found Luther's gospel commentaries,[2] which I send on to you. Martin [Luther] together with his associate Philip [Melanchthon] were away[3] this past week because they had to restore order to those changes rashly initiated by Master Gabriel.[4] While they were absent, Amsdorf[5] presided over a disputation on the proposition 'That the pope is indeed the true Antichrist because he prefers himself to everyone else,' which issued into a resounding pronouncement against the pope. The man who lectures on the Psalms[6] opposed Amsdorf by saying that they could not prove that the pope is the Antichrist, for he called himself the servant of servants; but that's nonsense. For the rest, he took passages from Daniel 7[7] indicating that the kingdom of the Antichrist would last only three and a half years, and thus argued against the position that the pope is the Antichrist. But then some Augustinian[8] came up with this solution: Daniel is speaking about the revealed Antichrist, to which the present lecturer agreed, yet he asserted nothing, for (he said) he was no prophet. Already one and a half years have passed since the Antichrist condemned the gospel truth, an action that ought to have revealed him; there are two years left. In this way they interpreted the matter simply,

* * * * *

1 Ulscenius accompanied Capito who had come to Wittenberg on 12 March 'in order to reconcile himself, they say, to Luther, whom he had sometimes offended in his letters; they say that Martin had called him a virulent beast, etc. (reconciliaturus se, ut dicebant, Luthero, quem nonnihil offenderat suis epistolis; ita ut a Martino virulentam bestiam appellatum dicant)' in *Briefwechsel des Beatus Rhenanus*, 303.

2 I.e., Luther's *Enarrationes epistolarum et evangeliorum quas postillas vocant* (Wittenberg: Grünenberg, 17 March 1521).

3 I.e., did not lecture.

4 Gabriel Zwilling. See above, Epp. 112, 125.

5 Nikolaus von Amsdorf (1483–1565), a graduate of the University of Wittenberg (licentiate in theology, 1511) and a lecturer in theology and philosophy there. He was one of Luther's closest associates. In 1524 he went to Magdeburg and was instrumental in introducing the Reformation in that region. In 1542 he became the first evangelical bishop of Naumburg. After the Schmalkaldic War he was forced to withdraw and settled in Eisenach.

6 Johann Bugenhagen (1485–1558) taught school in Trzebiatow, took orders, and privately lectured on the Bible. In 1521 he moved to Wittenberg, where he was appointed pastor in 1525. He drew up ordinances for a number of towns in northern and eastern Germany and introduced the Reformation in Copenhagen (1537–9). He had obtained a doctorate in theology in 1533 and, on his return from Denmark, became superintendent of Saxony.

7 Dan. 7:25.

8 Not identified.

entrusting it to God, however. For who could affirm something as certain when the Son of God himself did not know it?[9]

Farewell, most kind instructor. I eagerly desire the grace and peace of Christ for you. At Wittenberg. The 17th of March in the year '22.

Felix Ulscenius

Letter 136: 23 April 1522, Ottmarsheim, Capito to Heinrich Cornelius Agrippa

Agrippa (1486–1535) studied law, medicine, and theology at Cologne and Paris. After military service in Spain, he moved to Dole in 1509, but left when he was attacked by the Franciscans as a Judaizer on account of his interest in the cabala. From 1511 to 1518 he was in Italy, first attending the schismatic council of Pisa as a representative of Emperor Maximilian, then lecturing in Pavia and Turin on hermetic literature. He made the acquaintance of the Italian humanists and philosophers Pico della Mirandola and Marsilio Ficino and composed theological and hermetic works, which remained unpublished however until 1529. In 1518 he went to Metz where he was appointed public advocate. When his theological views aroused suspicion, he moved to Geneva (1522) and Freiburg (1523), practising medicine. He became physician to Louise of Savoy, the queen mother (1524–6), then physician and court historian to Margaret of Austria. From 1532 to 1535 he lived in Cologne at the court of the reform-minded Archbishop Hermann von Wied. His philosophical works (*De incertitudine et vanitate scientiarum*, 1530; *De occulta philosophia*, 1531 and 1533) involved him in polemics. Although Agrippa was hostile towards the monastic orders and the scholastics, he remained a Catholic.

The text of this letter is printed in Agrippa's *Opera omnia* (Lyon, 1600), 2: 789–90 under the heading 'Amicus ad Agrippam' (A friend to Agrippa).

I was en route, when this good man[1] began to speak of you in complimentary terms. He described to me a man who was of all men the most erudite, by profession a physician, of encyclopedic learning and knowledgeable about everything, but especially strong in disputation, so that he could fight off a sophistic attack with his left arm. I asked his name. Agrippa, he said. He is from Cologne, was educated in Italy, has experience at court, that is, he is courteous, urbane, civil. I was almost transported by the unexpected

* * * * *

9 Cf. Matt. 24:36.

1 Not identified.

joy and interrupted: What, I said, does that physician think of the German heresy? Does he oppose Luther and does he support the most learned Parisians? Nothing like that, he said. He can precede Luther, but he cannot go against him, as the famous Luther realized.[2] Moved by his words, I wanted to write this to you, as we sit here drinking in a tavern, so that you may realize how mindful your Capito is of the kind treatment he had of you when you received him as a guest in Cologne.[3] There are, however, some points about the state of things in Germany that will be of interest to you. This is what the Lutherans have been teaching in Wittenberg: firstly, they declare openly that their interpretation of the scriptural text must be accepted. I shall give you a few examples: anyone, they say, who does not eat meat and eggs and that sort of food on Friday cannot be a Christian; anyone who does not take and hold in his hands the sacrament of the Eucharist should not be regarded as a Christian; anyone who confesses in Lent cannot share in the mercy of God; anyone who attaches value to works of piety shuts himself out from the path of salvation; and many other matters of that kind. They have incited the inexperienced multitude.[4] There were tumultuous meetings; the houses of the priests were stormed; violence was used against citizens; hence the verdict of the people has been reversed, and as a result the common cause of faith, as maintained by Luther and his followers, has become unpopular. Learned men have written to Luther. They have urged him to make his position known. Therefore he is now in Wittenberg.[5] He preaches daily; he criticizes his followers; he reproaches those who introduce bold innovations, who have no regard for the simplicity of the people; yet he does not cease to assert what he has previously asserted. Now the people come in droves, and with patience they will proceed to the freedom of Christ; if only the leaders realized how simple and easy the Christian faith is, and furthermore, what great difference there is between a seditious innovator and a patient Christian. There are people who cannot bear it when they are forcefully coerced to accept the gospel. Nor do we men of the papal party try to coerce them, unless some fools or flatterers have tried the opposite. Some people are obliged to recant quietly. The people are restless and

* * * * *

2 The phrasing is vague.
3 Presumably in November 1520, cf. WBr. 2:416.
4 A fiery sermon preached by Justus Jonas on 1 November 1521 resulted in tumult. On 3 December stones were thrown at the window of priests' houses and missals were snatched from altars and desecrated. Turmoil continued under the leadership of Karlstadt.
5 Luther returned from his refuge at the Wartburg in March 1522, on the invitation of the city council and with the approval of Frederick the Wise.

chew on the bit. But everyday people stand up and openly declare themselves for Christ. And who will attempt to hinder Christ in his course? No pope, I believe, has had that in mind. For if the pope were truly the Antichrist and the adversary of faith, as Luther everywhere makes the Roman pontiff out to be, why, most knowledgeable sir, does he not turn you away from the gospel? But I am happy to hear that you keep away from the daring of imprudent men. Indeed you continue doing what you do, displaying Christ's meekness, even in familiar conversations, so that no one can slander that pious intention. Then, if there are things that seem to require a generous interpretation, I would not want you to condemn it arrogantly or with malice. For does Christ ever sound bitter anywhere? And where, I ask you, does he show a reproachful spirit? Does he not everywhere appear benign? And we barely keep from raging. O preposterous piety, so morosely pious, that it can almost obliterate the image of piety, and certainly does not move anyone towards piety.

Farewell and reply when convenient. I shall write a more thoughtful letter when I have leisure. I have written this at the tavern in a desultory manner. Farewell again, from Ottmarsheim near Basel, on the 23rd of April, in the year 1522.

Letter 137: 5 June 1522, Nürnberg, Capito to Desiderius Erasmus

Printed in Allen 5:73–4, #1290 and CWE 9, Ep. 1290. Capito was in attendance on Albert at the first Diet of Nürnberg.

[*Summary*]: Capito comments on the contents of Zúñiga's *Erasmi Roterodami blasphemiae et impietates*, in which Erasmus is accused of being the principal inspiration of the Lutheran party. Capito declares sarcastically that Zúñiga is helpful to Erasmus because he will endear him to good men. He has heard a rumour that Erasmus has published a book against Luther, but gives no credence to it. Capito furthermore beseeches Erasmus not to respond to Zúñiga, which is also Albert of Brandenburg's opinion.

Letter 138: 17 June 1522, Geneva, Heinrich Cornelius Agrippa to Capito

On Agrippa see headnote of Ep. 136. The text of this letter is printed in Agrippa's *Opera omnia* (Lyon, 1600), 2:791–2.

I have received your letter, most learned Capito and at the same time most deserving of my respect, which you wrote to me on the 23rd of April, while you were on the road. I received it after quite a few days at my house in the city of Geneva from an unknown courier (for I was absent at the court of the duke of Savoy).[1] I cannot live up to such kindness. I can, however, forgive that good man, who spoke so kindly to you of me, although he spoke in jest. If I knew the man, I would thank him heartily for his service. If only I could become the man he described to you! What you have written to me concerning Luther was most welcome. Even though you have given me much material to reply with a long and copious letter, I am still awaiting more material before replying, since you promised you would write more fully when you had leisure. Furthermore, I commend to you this good father, the bearer of the present letter.[2] Do give him your advice and help, and commend him earnestly with letters of reference to some of your friends, whom he might need to approach. He is a good man and diligent minister of the word of God. You will see that easily yourself when you consider the man. Whatever kindness and good deed you confer on him, I shall reckon to be conferred on myself. As for the rest, this is what I most desire from you: reply whenever there is a trustworthy courier. Commend me and endear me, moreover, to all of your friends as a friend you have in common with them. Farewell most prosperously. From the city of Geneva, on the 17th June, in the year 1522.

Letter 139: [Between 12 June and 1 July 1522, Nürnberg], Gallus Korn to Capito

> Gallus Korn (or Gallus Galleus), a Dominican from Nürnberg, aroused controversy because of his criticism of church abuses. In 1522 he was forbidden to preach. He left the monastery and in 1524 found refuge with Johann of Schwarzenberg, a jurist in the service of Kasimir of Brandenburg. The manuscript of the letter is in the Universitätsbibliothek in Basel, Ki.Ar. 25a, #9. It has been published by F. Herrmann in *Beiträge zur bayerischen Kirchengeschichte* 11 (1905): 227–8.

Hail in our Saviour, dearest teacher of the truth, etc. I have no reason to overwhelm you with my insignificant letter: no favour, no friendship, not even an acquaintance. But there is a reason that is more potent than those: I speak the truth, which makes me bold and, I hope, will make you, excellent man, a kinder recipient. Your sermon has earned you the highest favour

* * * * *

1 Charles III (1504–53). Agrippa had hopes of obtaining a post at his court, but nothing came of it.
2 Perhaps François Lambert of Avignon, as suggested by Herminjard I, 101, n.2.

with the city council and our people, and so has your (and indeed our) most blessed prince and prelate, who beyond all hope nurses such a doctor of evangelical truth at his court. May I die, if there was not a great stir yesterday. Tell me, what can those people say now against our archbishop of Mainz and our prince – people who for a long time now have been complaining that he oppresses the gospel? We have heard a different message today. Glory to God and peace to our prince! But since difficulties are never touched on without complaint, I have no doubt that you too have fallen victim to the Pharisees' leaven of malice,[1] but one must pay no attention to them. They are a race of hypocrites. They will melt away like the snow and then their nakedness and their confusion will become apparent. These are good enough reasons, I believe, to justify my approaching you with a nuisance letter. The Lord knows, I have been persecuted by that kind of people for some ten years, and they have found no way to confound me. These days they spew their poison on account of two sermons. You will learn the facts of this affair from the enclosed note. I ask and beg in Christ's name that you read it. I am staying with my father, who is hosting the courtiers of our most reverend and illustrious prince of Mainz, etc.[2] I am safe by the decree of the city councillors. But I am not free to go about and say Mass or preach, on account of the tyranny of those wreckers of truth and killers of Christians. I have sent a letter to the Roman curia. I am not, and I do not wish to be, under their jurisdiction forever. And now, my most candid and at the same time most reverend father in Christ and doctor of the Truth, I adjure you by Christ and Christian piety: give counsel to the ignorant, bring help to the wretched, move all means to effect that our most benign prince, who holds that distinction by tradition, is as kind in lending an ear and helping those who are unfairly harassed as he is angry with all oppressors and violent men. See to it, I say, that so great a prince provide relief for me and give me his blessing on his departure so that I in turn need no longer keep away from the public, but may safely do my duty as priest, where it seems opportune, until the Roman verdict on that matter arrives. You will do this, I believe, for the sake of the truth, for the true and best and greatest God, for it is a matter that will be pleasing and well received among our entire people, and this single accomplishment will accrue to the immortal glory of our most illustrious prince.

Gallus Gallaeus, priest, your insignificant servant in Christ.

* * * * *

1 Cf. Matt. 16:11.
2 I.e., the retinue of the archbishop, in town for the imperial Diet.

Be kind enough to read at least the twelve axioms[3] and judge, and likewise the verdict of my people marked by this sign.[4]

Letter 140: 20 July 1522, Wittenberg, Felix Ulscenius to Capito

> For Ulscenius see above, Ep. 70, headnote. The text of the letter is printed in
> Kolde, 37–8, from the manuscript in the Universitätsbibliothek, Basel, Ki.Ar.
> 25a, #80.

Greetings. Congratulations, respected teacher, on your prince beginning to breathe Christ, and that almost against all hope.[1] Melanchthon and indeed all good men are happy that your efforts were not wasted in this matter. May God, to pray with the prophet, confirm what he has worked in him.[2] May it be to his glory alone. I have received two gulden, which you sent from Nürnberg through Magister Sebald.[3] Thank you, I hope to show my gratitude.[4] Martin [Luther] has attacked the king of England in a surprising manner,[5] and he does not even spare Charles, even when speaking from the pulpit in public. For we hear he takes a dim view of the Luther affair.[6] The people of Christ consider that significant. Indeed Martin shows himself a strong preacher, and our magistrate spoke up severely against those who are a scan-

* * * * *

3 I.e., a summary in twelve points of a sermon he gave and the judgment passed on it by fellow monks. The summary was enclosed with the letter and is now part of Ki.Ar. 25a, #9. It is entitled 'Apologema Galli Gallei in eius abitionem a coenobiis praedicatoriis, anno Domini MDXXII, Iunii 12. A German version, *Eyn handlung wie es eynem Prediger Munch ... gangen ist,* was printed in 1522, without place or publisher's name.
4 A corresponding sign appears in the margin of the enclosed 'Apologema' (see note 3 above).

1 See the preceding letter and Capito's report to Erasmus, Ep. 141, below.
2 Ps. 68:28.
3 Millet suggests that this might be the engraver Sebald Beham of Nürnberg, but it is more likely Sebald Münsterer (d. 1539) of Nürnberg, who studied in Leipzig (BA 1516, MA 1518) and matriculated in Wittenberg in 1520. He taught at the university after obtaining a doctorate in law in 1527.
4 Lit., 'cherish you in turn, like a stork.' Storks were proverbial for gratitude; cf. Erasmus *Adagia* 1.10.1.
5 He answered Henry VIII's *Assertio septem sacramentorum* first in German (*Antwortt deutsch* [Wittenberg: Schyrlentz, 1522]), then in Latin (*Contra Henricum Regem Angliae* [Wittenberg: Grünenberg, 1522]). The latter contains a preface dated July 15, 1522.
6 Charles V, then absent in Spain.

dal to the gospel. Yesterday three women, who are not leading an honest life, and a noble youth, who had broken into houses, were ejected from the town. His friends interceded many times with Melanchthon on his behalf but he would not hear them. Martin and Melanchthon want to see adulterers and blasphemers put to death, though not thieves. I believe you were of the same opinion. Melanchthon now tries to see that humane letters command greater respect in our community than they have until now, a matter, as you know, which is most necessary. He has completed his lexicon in the last few days,[7] and will send it to Anshelm[8] within a week or so. Setzer[9] has seen to it, who has recently come to Philip and is going to apply himself to the [study of] medicine. Johann Bugenhagen,[10] presently lecturer, has married a very decent young woman who is a citizen of Wittenberg. Wetzsteiner[11] from Nürnberg, who was with Martin at the Diet of Worms, has likewise married a young woman. As for Erasmus, who is rumoured to be about to write against Luther,[12] I found out that Martin said: even if Erasmus shamefully errs in some places concerning the teaching of Christ, there can be no doubt that he will recover from his error and come to think correctly about it. For until now he has merely shown himself to be a teacher of the law, and that according to the judgment of our friends, very purely and most elegantly.

Johannes Rembold[13] sends you greetings. Wittenberg, 20 July 1522.

Your Felix Ulscenius

Philip Eberbach,[14] a most eloquent young man, has recently come here.

* * * * *

7 A Latin-Greek dictionary, which was however never published.

8 Thomas Anshelm, printer at Pforzheim (where he published most of Reuchlin's works) and Tübingen. Melanchthon worked for a while as his corrector. From 1516 on he had a print shop in Haguenau, where he is documented until 1522.

9 Johann Setzer (d. 1532) was the brother-in-law of Anshelm (see note 8 above) and took over his business in 1523.

10 For Johann Bugenhagen see above, Ep. 135, note 6. On his marriage cf. WBr. 2, 592, n19.

11 He must mean Johann Petzensteiner, the Nürnberg Augustinian who accompanied Luther. He was a graduate of the University of Wittenberg (BA 1509, MA 1515). Cf. WBr. 2.297, n9.

12 Erasmus was urged to write against Luther, but refrained from doing so until 1524 when he published his *Diatribe de libero arbitrio*.

13 For Rembold see above, Ep. 70, note 5.

14 Philip Stumpf von Eberbach (d. 1529) matriculated at Wittenberg in the summer of 1521. In 1522/3 he lectured on Quintilian at the university. From 1523 to 1525 he was in Joachimstal, 'teaching the gospel,' as Melanchthon reports (CR, 1:592); from 1527 on he was at Coburg.

Melanchthon likes him a great deal because of his honesty and wonderful wit. He likes his company more than anyone's, so that he is like a brother to him. He will reply to Melanchthon in a public disputation on Saturday, and he usually disputes only with the closest friends. The topic will be the use of the sword. I would have sent it to you if he had completed it. He sends you his best wishes and has every goodwill towards you because he heard such salutary counsel from you once.

Letter 141: 17 August 1522, Mainz, Capito to Desiderius Erasmus

Printed in Allen 5:115–17, #1308 and CWE 9, Ep. 1308.

[*Summary*]: Capito warns Erasmus that his attempts to maintain the goodwill of both papists and Lutherans will only earn him the hatred of both parties. Hoogstraten has condemned Erasmus's writings in Cologne. Capito is also concerned that Erasmus's letter to Duke George of Saxony will make him the target of many attacks. Luther has written a most abusive answer to Henry VIII's *Assertio septem sacramentorum*. Capito identifies himself with the papist party, and expresses fears that the Reformation is moving from verbal to physical violence. Christ is the pretense used to justify political machinations. Capito finds himself unable to mediate between the Lutheran and papist parties. Albert asks Erasmus to send him his paraphrase on John. He was moved by the paraphrases on Matthew. Oecolampadius and Caspar Hedio send their greetings.

**Letter 142: 2 October 1522, Mainz, Albert of Brandenburg to the Elector
Richard, archbishop of Trier, Ludwig Count Palatine,
and Philip of Hesse**

This is a draft in Capito's hand (in German) now in the Archive Municipale in Strasbourg, AST 40 #47, fols. 404–5. The subject is Albert's responsibility to compensate the archbishop of Trier for the losses suffered as a result of Franz von Sickingen's unlawful expedition against Trier. The knight and condottiere Franz von Sickingen (1481–1523) was a son of the steward of the Count Palatine. Using his ancestral castle, the Ebernburg, as a base, he hired mercenaries and between 1514 and 1518 embarked on a series of private military exploits in Worms, Lorraine, and Hesse. He was placed under the imperial ban, but the emperor lacked the means of enforcing the judgment. When Sickingen engaged in negotiations with France, the newly elected Emperor Charles V preferred to make use of his military prowess himself and appointed him captain and councillor in 1520. The papal legate Aleandro acknowledged Sickingen's military power when he referred to him as 'the only real king of Germany' (Kalkoff, *Depeschen*, 178). In the aftermath of the Diet of Worms, Sickingen, who was one of the first secular leaders to declare his support for the reformers, offered asylum to Luther at his castle. He also extended his protection to Bucer and Oecolampadius. He supported Ulrich von Hutten's idea of a *Pfaffenkrieg*, a war on the Catholic clergy, and in particular on the ecclesiastical princes, but took no active steps as long as service to the Habsburgs seemed to offer him opportunities for advancement. When his hopes were disappointed, he formed a league of knights in 1522 and led them against Richard of Greiffenklau, the archbishop of Trier. The campaign failed and a second ban was imposed on him (October 1522). The combined troops of Trier, Hesse, and the Palatinate then attacked him in May 1523 at Landstuhl, where he made his last stand. He died of wounds received in that engagement. The Ebernburg was razed in June 1523. Albert was implicated in the affair when it became known that men in his service had given material and ideological support to Sickingen.

Albrecht, Archbishop of Mainz to Trier, Palatine, and Hesse.

First, my friendly obeisance, respected and noble count, dear friend, cousin and uncle! This morning at seven o'clock I was given a letter from Your Dear Lordships to our bailiffs, mayors, judges, councillors, and communities of our Rheingau. A second letter came in the afternoon, also from Your Dear Lordships, addressed to us, with much the same contents, that is, that we had substantial knowledge of the violent and deliberate feud and action undertaken by Franz von Sickingen in defiance of His Imperial and Royal Majesty, our most gracious lord, and contrary to the peace and order established in the Holy Empire. It concerns his recent attack on my dear lord Richard, archbishop of Trier and elector, which was undertaken without commission or authority, using military force against your land and its people and inflicting damage. [The letter stated that] Johann Hilchen,[1] a perpetrator of hostilities himself, and others who participated in these actions, had at times dwelled in our principality and our land. Likewise they are said to have aided Franz greatly in Mainz and allowed him to cross the Rhine in the Rheingau, and benefited financially in Mainz, etc.[2] Furthermore our chancellor, the knight Frowin von Hutten and our

* * * * *

1 Johann Hilchin or Hilchen von Lorch was in Albert's military service. Cf. his three-year contract of 1518 in Ingrossaturbuch 52, fol. 17, which shows his annual salary as thirty gulden.
2 I.e., when the loot was sold in Mainz.

marshal, Caspar Lerch,[3] aided and abetted Franz's actions considerably with their counsel, contrary to the imperial peace and the concord of the electors. Thus, dear sirs, you request and ask from our cathedral chapter and the city of Mainz, our Rheingau, our marshal Johann Hilchen and other connections of ours, to take immediate action concerning the damage and cost sustained and to reimburse and compensate you and keep an eye on things, etc.[4] If that should not come to pass, your dear Lordships would be obliged to bring action against the said parties for breach of peace, etc. and we were informed about the rest of the message.

This may be as you say, but the fact that our dear lord, the archbishop of Trier, was attacked with a military force by Franz was very much against our wishes and pleasure. We would have been willing to help Your Dear Lordships on request, as much as possible on such short notice, and to appear with cavalry and foot soldiers to assist you, as we indicated to Your Dear Lordships in more than one message and letter, as you will confirm.[5] The fact that some of our men, for example Johann Hilchen, was Your Dear Lordship's enemy and helped Franz and served him also in Mainz and put him across the river at the Rheingau, and that our chancellor and marshal aided and counselled Franz – all that was truly unknown to us, and if anyone crossed over at Mainz or the Rheingau, it happened against our strict

* * * * *

3 A letter incriminating the two men was found in the possession of Nickel von Minkwitz, a follower of Sickingen who was captured (see Planitz's report of 13 September 1522, #88). Frowin von Hutten (1472–1529), Albert's chancellor (*Hofmeister*, i.e., chief officer of the court), was from 1516 imperial councillor. As a result of his support for Franz von Sickingen's expedition, he was deprived of his estates in 1522. After helping to quell the peasant rebellions of 1525, however, he was reinstated. Being childless, he sold his estates to his cousins in 1528. Caspar Lerch of Dirmstein was Albert's marshal in 1522 (i.e., he supervised the day-to-day operation of the court and had administrative, judicial, and military power). Albert renewed his contract, which expired in 1522, for another three years at an annual pay of a hundred florins (see *Ingros-saturbuch* 53, fol. 140). Both Hutten and Lerch remained in Albert's service until their death.

4 Albert was eventually fined 25,000 gulden and had to take out a loan from the cathedral chapter, using his castle at Hoechst as collateral.

5 Albert had at first (August 1522) declined to send cavalry, claiming that he could not afford to do so because he was in danger himself. Later (September 1522) he offered to send foot soldiers, but the offer was declined by Richard Greiffenklau, as Sickingen had retreated and the troops were no longer needed. Cf. Planitz's report of 28 October 1522, #100.

order[6] and against our will and pleasure. But since our cathedral chapter, our city of Mainz, and our land of Rheingau, as well as our marshal stand accused of breaking the peace and compensation is demanded for the damage, etc., and I have pledged myself as elector to maintain peace in the land, I shall act on behalf of the city of Mainz and our Rheingau and our chancellor and marshal, in so far as they have broken the peace. I shall reimburse our friend the archbishop of Trier and guarantee it after (such is my request) the accused have defended themselves against the accusation of breaking the peace and a verdict has been passed by His Imperial Majesty's representatives and government or the privy court as constituted by his Majesty, that they disturbed the peace and broke it. This does not apply to Johann Hilchen, whose goods, according to the contents of the law concerning the imperial peace, we shall seize, as is our right according to the terms of the imperial peace, and I will likewise proceed against our associates mentioned, but not named, in Your Dear Lordships' letter, once Your Dear Lordships indicate who they are, even if we are not empowered by the letter of the law, but according to the spirit of the peace agreement. I am confident that you will be satisfied with the above response to Your Dear Lordships' writings and requests, and not take action against them and their retainers. If my dear lords consider it necessary and appropriate for the four of us to meet and discuss the matter further and act in the spirit of friendship, I shall not object, but agree to appear at a future meeting to be arranged with Your Dear Lordship. If, however, Your Dear Lordships do not desire such a meeting, which I do not expect in view of what is due and in the interest of the imperial peace, we shall wait until the next diet at Nürnberg[7] when His Majesty, the Roman King,[8] our most merciful Majesty's representative and regent and all unbiased princes and estates of the Holy Empire are gathered, and the Swabian league[9] with all its members has been invited according to the law. I am certain that Your Dear Lordships will not use force against us or our people, but act as we in kindness deserve, and I request a friendly

* * * * *

6 On 14 September 1522 Albert wrote to the authorities in the Rheingau, Mainz, Lahneck, and Gernsheim to see to it that no one intending to join Sickingen was ferried across the Rhine.
7 The second Diet of Nürnberg, which sat from November 1522 to February 1523.
8 Ferdinand, brother of Emperor Charles.
9 A peace-keeping alliance in southern Germany, founded in 1488. Its army razed twenty-five castles in response to the Knight's Revolt.

answer from Your Dear Lordships. Given at the Martinsburg in our city Mainz, Thursday after St Michael's, in the year 1522.

Albrecht, cardinal, etc. to Trier, Palatine, and Hesse.

Note: Whatever we should offer or do in addition or beyond what has been said concerning the imperial peace, I herewith offer and promise to fulfil in all points. Dated, as stated in the letter.

Letter 143: 4 November 1522, Mainz, Caspar Hedio to Capito

Quotation from a lost letter printed in *Briefe Oekolampads* 2:140, note 1a, #548

[*Summary*]: In less than three days Oecolampadius will meet with Hedio when he comes to visit his parents. From there, he will go either to Augsburg, if it is safe, or to Basel in order to publish the translation of Chrysostom's sermons.

Letter 144: 19 November [1522], Basel, Johannes Oecolampadius to Capito

Printed in *Briefe Oekolampads* 1:198–200, #135

[*Summary*]: Oecolampadius is writing from Andreas Cratander's house in Basel where he arrived two days earlier [see Ep. 143] and hopes that he will be able to stay there for a while. He was going to publish the sermons of Chrysostom, which he translated at the Ebernburg, but the printer wanted more material, namely, Chrysostom's commentaries on the letters to the Corinthians, of which a part has already been translated. Oecolampadius will translate the rest. The printers need the text, which Capito took to Strasbourg. Oecolampadius asks him to return it to Basel or to ask Friedrich Prechter to direct Nicolaus Gerbel or Ottmar Luscinius to do it. The manuscript he used at the Ebernburg has been translated in full. It is now at Caspar Hedio's [but cf. Ep. 147 below]; [the volume of] Gregory of Nazianzen is at Oecolampadius's parents. Oecolampadius would need the manuscript of Theophylactus. He sends his regards to Willibald Pirckheimer and other friends in Nürnberg.

Letter 145: 28 November 1522, Mainz, Caspar Hedio to Capito

The manuscript is in the Archives du Bas-Rhin in Strasbourg, Acquisitions 1940–4, 111J14/160

Greetings. The reverend Grosschlag[1] brought me your letter on the feast day of St Catharine.[2] I read it two or three times, and I think I understand your meaning. In many ways it would seem advisable to speak with you in person. I pray to Christ that this will be soon because there are many things that are troublesome and uncertain. I believe we would consult more effectively that way. I have not yet sent a copy of your letter to Strasbourg, partly because it will hardly be consistent with the former letters, of which I have twice now sent you a copy, most recently through Pfaffius, the procurator.[3] My reason for omitting your name from the letter was the fear expressed by Oecolampadius and Eberbach who did not want me to make you unpopular with the chapter, if the request is denied.[4] I had decided furthermore to come up after the feast of the Magi,[5] and I had prepared those former [letters?] in accordance with that plan, but that did not meet with their approval either. They thought it was more honourable if someone were sent to me. Oh, how often I wished you were present, my dear Capito! That is how clearly I recognize my lack of prudence, especially when I must deal with such giants, although, if they like me, I do not believe they will misinterpret what I have written. And whatever has been written, it is done, whether Christ withheld his counsel or directed us thus, for he knows what must be done for his glory and the glory of the gospel.

The business of inserting a clause (whether they wished to offer an unconditional contract) arose in this manner: On the Sunday before St Martin's

* * * * *

1 Balthasar Grosschlag von Dieburg (d. 1535), canon of the cathedral chapter from 1505.
2 25 November.
3 Millet suggests that this is Philipp von Helle, Albert's 'walpot' (architect) according to a contract of 1523 (*Ingrossaturbuch* 53, fol. 134). However, the reference must be to Beatus Felix Pfeffinger (d. 1554), who was named Capito's legal representative (procurator) in a document of 20 July 1521 (TB 1:175) and was a relative of Capito (cf. above, Ep. 50, note 7). Pfeffinger was a graduate of Heidelberg (Bachelor of laws, 1518) and a canon at St Thomas in Strasbourg. He turned Protestant and married in 1532.
4 These are the first cryptic references to an effort to recruit Hedio for the post of cathedral preacher at Strasbourg, a position for which Capito himself had hopes. Sigmund von Hohenlohe, the dean of the cathedral chapter, offered Hedio the position in a letter of 27 October 1522 (TB 1:254). After some hesitation, he accepted and took up the position in November 1523. His success embittered Capito, but the two men eventually reconciled. For Eberbach's and Oecolampadius's mediating efforts see below, Epp. 169–70, 173.
5 6 January 1523.

Day,[6] Hohenlohe,[7] the canon here, indicated that Petrus[8] would not easily yield without a pension, and they will perhaps agree on two appointments, so that compensation will be found for the successor from another source if they find a man who is popular and has their approval. Here no one so far knows whether this was put in writing, except Eberbach and his colleague, and it is not clear whether he said anything to the other gentlemen. About that, even if they know anything, they haven't divulged a word. Indeed I do not know whether or not it can be made public. You would think that zeal would generate friendly feelings for one's friends, but I fear that is not the case. Some people, if they knew, would say: why don't I leave when I am offered another post? For how many are there in Mainz who wished I had a position in another episcopal see! You would like me to stay in Mainz, as I do myself, even if the city recalls Chorazim and Bethsaida, and also: *even this little flock [will be given the Kingdom by the Father], to whom truth and simplicity is pleasing*, etc.[9]

I do not want to write more, for I certainly hope to receive your letter in which you will indicate what I should do and respond, either in writing or through some messenger you send to me. So far there are Gerbel,[10] or Oecolampadius, or Cap.[11] It would be a very good post for the provost of St Thomas, but I fear it cannot be obtained easily. I myself wish you could have it and be delivered from the business of the court. But the gentlemen will not likely tolerate two. But considering the spiritual wisdom with which they [provosts?] are endowed, the dignity of the provostship seems too great to be mixed up with the foolishness of the cross.[12] Seize an opportunity, my best teacher, to visit us, and then we could talk over many things at length, once you have decided to come down here. I cannot leave, first because it is

* * * * *

6 9 November 1522.
7 Ludwig von Hohenlohe (d. 1550) was a canon of the cathedral chapter at Mainz from 1516 on.
8 I.e., Petrus Wickram, the incumbent. Cf. above Ep. 72, headnote, and note 3.
9 Cf. Matt. 11:21, 27; Luke 12:32.
10 Nicolaus Gerbel (d. 1560) humanist, historian, jurist (doctorate in canon law from the University of Bologna, 1514), was the secretary of the cathedral chapter in Strasbourg and a close friend of Hedio. He worked for some time as a corrector of the Froben press in Basel, then for Schürer's press in Strasbourg. He edited a number of classical writers and in 1541 became professor of history at the Strasbourg academy. He was an early follower of Luther.
11 The significance of this list is unclear. 'Cap.' could be expanded to 'Capito' or 'Capitulum' (Chapter).
12 The reading is uncertain and the meaning therefore remains unclear. The sentence alludes to 1 Cor. 1:18.

Advent, and secondly because I daily expect a response. If there is anything to write, make sure that it is phrased as seems best. I shall most gladly do what you command. Wherever I am, I will have God as my protector.

I met the host of the Horse, gave him the letter, and after he read it, he replied that he had received no letters from anyone else, nor any money, otherwise he would gladly have done what I requested. I have received no clothes from Strasbourg, nor any books, and even if I receive any I am uncertain how to send them: by coach, perhaps, because the Main is not navigable.

Farewell, dearest benefactor. Mainz, 28 November 1522.

I have received Philip's commentaries.[13] May Christ be your reward. Your Caspar Hedio.

If I can achieve anything by travelling to Strasbourg after Christmas either for your sake or for any other reason, I would do it very gladly, just indicate how I should go about it.

Letter 146: 30 November 1522, Nürnberg, Capito to Hartmut von Kronberg

> Hartmut von Kronberg (1488–1549), a knight descended from the Wetterau family, was a relative and supporter of Franz von Sickingen and the author of several Reformation pamphlets. In the campaign against Sickingen (see above, Ep. 142, headnote), Kronberg's castle was destroyed (October 1522). Kronberg himself fled. For some years he resided in Basel and Strasbourg, then entered the service of Ulrich of Würtemberg. He repeatedly appealed to the imperial court and eventually was reinstated in his possessions in 1540. Luther wrote to him a letter of consolation similar to Capito's. Cf. WBr, 2:484–5, #466, March 1522.
>
> The manuscript of the letter, which is written in German, is in the Universitätsbibliothek, Basel, Ki.Ar. 25a, #144.

Salvation and grace in Christ Jesus, dear Junker and brother. Were I a little closer to you, I would make an attempt through personal conversation to ease the misfortune that has befallen you, that is, I would attempt together with you to find consolation in your constant faith. But I did not wish to write over such a long distance, which was risky, until I had a reliable courier, to avoid burdening you further and unnecessarily. For it is the custom of our enemy's servant to make a bold attempt to harm us. It furthermore

* * * * *

13 I.e., Melanchthon's *In epistolas Pauli ad Romanos et ad Corinthios* (Nürnberg, 1522).

seemed unnecessary to me to admonish him who seeks only God in times of tribulation, and whose soul will not accept any consolation or pleasure other than in the thought of God. I hope you are such a man, my dear Junker. This is how one comes to God and to salvation, this is how God usually visits his servants with great tribulation, so that the world judging by the flesh regards the friends of God as fools, evil doers, and rascals, so that hope in innocence remains immortal, etc.[1] If an unbeliever is struck by misfortune and loses his worldly honour, his goods and substance, then he has lost at the same time all consolation and everything he is, for he cannot place his hope in eternity, in God our Lord and in his strength, but only in his past worldliness. But the believer who is driven out and persecuted is strengthened and secure in himself. For he knows that he walks in the judgment of God and submits to God and suffers. The name of God and the thought of God is his only desire, and he knows how to glorify and bring honour to God through his obedient suffering and his ignominy. Sinners, moreover, are heavily burdened by the inescapable memory of their lost happiness, whereas the servants of God find relief in it, for they have no regard for the world and only heed the will of God, both in fortune and misfortune. Thus speaks the Lord: *Woe to you rich men, who have your consolation now*, etc. Luke 6:[24].

In sum, even the best men may be brought to despair by misfortune and out of despair give themselves up to pleasure and physical satisfaction, as the Jews did before the Babylonian captivity, for God sent them misfortune and tribulation, called them to penitence and sadness through the prophets, but they nevertheless went on seeking pleasure and entertainment, eating meat and drinking wine and said: *Let us eat and drink, tomorrow we shall die.* Isaiah 22:[13]. The children of God, however, sought God and his teaching in fear and sadness. We are like a pregnant woman in labour. We have conceived in the fear of the terrible face of God and now bring forth in some measure the Spirit of salvation through labour and fear and misery, etc.

We must see to it, dear Junker, that the world condemns us on account of the name Jesus and not for any other reason. For only our conscience and the truth matters, not the judgment of the world. No one wishes the world and its pomp to be victorious, for these are two things that we Christians despise. We must care for nothing but Christ. The prophets have always been persecuted, not as servants of God, but as offenders against the common weal, as slanderers of authority and the synagogues. You know also that the apostles and Christ himself were called seducers of the people, but

* * * * *

1 Cf. Job 4:7.

truly, the world has always persecuted God's name in this manner, although they pretended otherwise. We must ponder that and lift our eyes up to God, to the true *mountain of holiness*.[2] Then we shall be aided, for as long as we have not done justice, *no inhabitants have been brought into the world*. Isaiah 26.[3] Yet we hope that God will not take his word away from the world but that he will soon lift his hand and chasten all opposing powers on earth. In the meantime we must devoutly beg God from our heart that he may make us worthy of bringing his name to the peoples and keep us from backsliding through pusillanimity and lack of faith, for no one deserves heaven, who *looks back once he has laid his hand on the plough*.[4] We must hurry on to what has been set before us.[5] Please accept and understand what I write in my ignorance as written in the spirit of brotherly love, for I hope you will show us through your suffering and constancy the potent grace of God. Amen. From Nürnberg, on the last day of November, in the year 1522.

Letter 147: December 1522, [Mainz], Caspar Hedio to Capito

The manuscript is in the Archive Municipale of Strasbourg, IV 105b.

The great Chrysostom has been left behind at the Ebernburg.[1] Oecolampadius has written to Schweickard[2] about it, asking that he send it to the priest at Bingen,[3] and he in turn to me. When I have it, I shall send it to Strasbourg. If the Junker has been remiss,[4] I shall remind him by letter, if you wish. They have business at hand and therefore neglect books.

* * * * *

2 Zech. 8:3.
3 Cf. Isa. 26:18 (continuing the metaphor of the pregnant woman).
4 Luke 9:62.
5 Cf. Phil. 3:14.

1 This is presumably a manuscript belonging to the Dominicans in Basel, which Oecolampadius took with him to Sickingen's castle, the Ebernburg. He translated and published a number of homilies contained in the manuscript. See above, Ep. 109, and below, Ep. 148. In Ep. 144 above, Oecolampadius states that the manuscript is in Hedio's hands.
2 Schweickard von Sickingen (1500–ca. 1562), eldest son of Franz von Sickingen, from 1533 lord of Hoch-Koenigsburg. No such letter is extant.
3 Melchior Ambach (1490–1559) studied at Mainz; he was parish priest in Bingen from 1522 until 1524, when he was dismissed for his Lutheran leanings and moved to Frankfurt.
4 Or 'has left.' The meaning of Latin *cedere* is ambiguous.

Hartmut's whereabouts are unknown.[5] From a secret supporter I have heard that he is thought to be in Lorraine. I shall keep your letter[6] with me until I am certain where he is.

Letter 148: 4 December 1522, Basel, Johannes Oecolampadius to Capito

> Printed in E. Staehelin, 'Oecolampadiana,' *Basler Zeitschift für Geschichte und Altertumskunde* 65 (1965): 168–71

[*Summary*:] Oecolampadius is still perplexed about Erasmus and has received no counsel or support from him in his present difficulties [i.e., after fleeing the monastery]. He thanks Capito for his support. He was hoping for a decision at Nürnberg [i.e., at the Diet], but now there is the business of [the Sickingen Affair or the Turkish threat], and military questions take precedence over everything else. He has no desire to return either to Sickingen or to the monastery. He is staying with Cratander, who sends his regards. He has not yet succeeded in having his manuscript printed. If he had Chrysostom's commentary on the Epistle to the Corinthians, he would translate it, although Johannes Cono has already translated the greater part. He asks Capito to procure him a copy of the commentary. At present he is translating Chrysostom's commentary on Genesis. He wanted to dedicate his translation of Chrysostom's homilies to the pope, but the publication is being delayed, and he is considering dedicating it to another patron. He asks Capito for suggestions.

Letter 149: [1522], [Rome], Girolamo Aleandro to Capito

> Girolamo Aleandro (1480–1542) began his career in the church as secretary to Angelo Leoni, the papal legate in Venice. He entered the service of Cardinal Domenico Grimani in 1503. An accomplished scholar and linguist, he was involved in editorial work for the famous printer Aldo Manuzio of Venice. In 1508 he went to Paris, where he produced a series of Greek editions for the French printer Gilles de Gourmont. He became a successful lecturer at the Collège de la Marche. In 1513 he entered the service of the bishop of Paris, Étienne Poncher, a year later that of the bishop of Liège, and finally in 1517 that of Cardinal Giulio de' Medici. He began accumulating benefices and became librarian of the Vatican in 1519. In 1520 he was sent to Germany to implement the papal bull against Luther. Giulio de Medici, elevated to the papal throne as

* * * * *

5 I.e., Hartmut von Kronberg. See Ep. 146, headnote.
6 I.e., Ep. 146, addressed to Hartmut von Kronberg.

Clement VII (1524), made him archbishop of Brindisi the same year. He continued to go on diplomatic missions for Clement and his successor Paul III, and in
1538 was raised to the cardinalate.

The manuscript is in the Vatican Library, Rome, Cod. Vat. 8075, fol. 47. The
text is partly transcribed by W. Friedensburg in *ZKG* 16 (1896): 449. The lines
which Friedensburg could not decipher ('If you do ... for you') have been supplied by Kalkoff, *Capito*, 129, n1. On the history of Capito's ongoing litigation
for the provostship see also below, Epp. 161 and 163.

To show you that I am not a false friend and that the pope[1] is not so averse
to the humanities and humanists as some make him out to be, take note that
he has expedited the matter of your provostship free of charge. In return for
these favours, the pope asks nothing of you other than that you make as
great an effort as you can to serve the peace and tranquillity and order of the
Catholic Church (and indeed I beg and beseech you to do so). If you do it,
greater things are in store for you, both from the almighty God and from the
pope. If, however, you imitate Luther and yourself strive for revolution (but
I can never believe this of you), you can expect to turn the pontiff and
indeed the whole Catholic Church against you. This then is meant for you.

Farewell and be assured that I am wholly yours. Kiss the mostly holy
hands of your reverend and illustrious prince on my behalf and greet our
mutual friends.

Letter 150: 23 January 1523, Mainz, Caspar Hedio to Capito

The text of this letter was published by Herrmann, 220–1. There are a number
of errors in his transcription of the manuscript (Bayerische Staatsbibliothek,
Munich, clm 10.357, #26), which have been corrected as indicated in the footnotes to the electronic Latin text.

Hail in Christ. I have informed the landlord in writing that I am giving up
the house. I am not certain where I shall go in such sudden and instant des-
titution. If Scholl[1] reneges, things will be very bad, but I trust in the Lord,

* * * * *

1 Adrian VI.

1 Presumably Bernhard Scholl (d. 1548). He studied at Bologna (doctorate in
canon law 1510), was canon in the cathedral chapter of Worms and of St
Stephen, Victor, and Beatae Virginis in Mainz. In 1538 he was Albert's vicar-
general and from 1545 his protonotary. The nature of Hedio's business transaction with Scholl is not known.

and the world belongs to the Lord.[2] I am fond of studying that sacred language[3] and, *as through a lattice,*[4] I now see what it means to draw material from the sources. What you have noted concerning the difficult verbs of the second conjugation[5] has caught my attention, for there is a great difference between *schalach* and *schilach* and between *v'schalach* and *v'yischlach.*[6] Reading your note did indeed help me and made things clear. The rest, too, is sublime and arduous. I believe it will be worth my time to compare a great deal,[7] for I do not have the patience to tarry long over the rules, which are countless. Please let me know what you think about that. I would like a summary of what one needs to know about verbs. If you can conveniently do so, let me have a Bible similar to yours.

There is no end to the atrocious pamphlets in which my superiors and I are labelled poisonous heretics. A certain rogue, who could seem more changeable than Proteus himself,[8] is full of inconsistency: at one time Adrian VI is in agreement [with him], at another Martin Luther, etc.[9] Today we will be discussing in the chapter meeting whether we should respond from the pulpit for the sake of the people who might be offended by this imposture. I shall hear what the gentlemen decide, for some among them loathe the accusation of heresy. I know that it is my destiny to be slandered in God's name, and so my heart is not tormented. Indeed it brings me joy. I laugh and deride the weak counsel of those who thus want to alienate my hearers from me and in this manner find a way perhaps to drive me from their region. If they were wise, they would be quiet about a man who *breathes the spirit.*[10] This is not my teaching, but *the teaching of Christ who sent me.*[11]

Farewell. Mainz, 1523, 23 January.

Your Caspar Hedio.

* * * * *

2 Ps. 11:1 and 24:1. Hedio's Hebrew contains errors.
3 I.e., Hebrew.
4 Cicero *De Oratore* 1.35.162.
5 Cf. Capito's *Institutio* V4v 'verbum grave seu difficile.'
6 I.e., the Perfect, Imperfect, and forms with waw consecutive of the verb 'send.'
7 I.e., compare the Hebrew with a Latin translation?
8 Mythological figure who could change his shape at will; proverbial for evasiveness and inconsistency. Cf. Erasmus *Adagia* 2.2.74.
9 The meaning of 'subscribere' is ambiguous. The meaning could be 'at one time he signs himself Adrian ...'
10 Ps. 146:4.
11 John 7:16.

Letter 151: 7 February 1523, Nürnberg, Charles V to Capito

Printed in Ph. Mieg, 'Capiton le réformateur strasbourgeois. Quelques détails biographiques à propos de ses armoiries,' *Bulletin de l'histoire du Protestantisme français* 74 (1925): 179–83

[*Summary*]: This is an imperial brief giving armorial bearings to Capito, his brothers Johann, Heinrich and Symon, and their descendants.

Letter 152: 14 February [1523, Nürnberg], Capito to Francesco Chierigati

Printed in Kalkoff, *Capito*, 146

[*Summary*]: Capito thanks the papal legate Francesco Chierigati for his assistance [in obtaining the provostship of St Thomas in Strasbourg]. He will write to Joachim Vonstede, the archbishop's man of business in Rome. He asks that all correspondence be directed to him at Mainz, where he will be during the summer.

Letter 153: 14 February 1523, Nürnberg, Capito to Johann Bader

Printed in Kalkoff, *Capito*, 145–6

[*Summary*]: Capito writes from Nürnberg, where he is attending the Diet, to Johann Bader, the procurator of the bishop of Strasbourg at the Roman court, thanking him for his efforts of which Valentin Tetleben has informed him. He notes that there is a deficiency in one of the papers confirming him in the provostship and asks for a corrected document. He had not consulted a lawyer but left matters in the hands of his patrons Cardinals Schiner and Pucci. The papal chamberlain, Duke Johann Albert, will bring letters of reference from Archduke Ferdinand and Albert of Brandenburg, but there is no need to wait for their arrival. Time is of the essence. He is short of funds, but Joachim Vonstede, the archbishop's man of business, will supply the money necessary to complete the transaction.

Letter 153a: 17 February 1523, Anspach, Mariangelo Accursio to Capito

A reference to this letter, now lost, appeared in the catalogue of the Paris art dealer Benjamin Fillon, who offered it for sale in July 1878 (see BNF Richelieu Facs. 80 275, catalogue item #823). The letter was written from Anspach, Bavaria, and is described in the catalogue as '[une] belle lettre ou il lui donne des témoignages d'amitié et parle de son protecteur, l'empereur Charles-Quint.' Accursio (or Accursius, d. 1546), well known for his epigraphical and philological studies, was at the time tutor of Albert's relatives, Johann Albert and Gumpert of Hohenzollern. In 1522 he travelled with them in Germany and Poland; in 1523 he returned with them to Italy. Capito may have contacted him for help in securing the provostship at Strasbourg or asked him to carry letters to Rome (cf. above, Ep. 153).

Letter 154: 22 February 1523, Nürnberg, Capito to Heinrich Stromer

The manuscript of this letter is in the Stiftsbibliothek Zeitz, Katalog p. 29, fol. 59r. For the addressee, Heinrich Stromer, see above, Ep. 32, note 7.

Greeting. Please send the adjoined letter by way of a separate courier to the most reverend and illustrious cardinal[1] as soon as possible. There is much news, but you no doubt have heard it already. It is certain that Rhodes has been captured,[2] and the Venetians are using every effort in making preparations for a battle with the Turks. However, the princes prefer to believe what they wish to be the case, namely, that the Turks have waged war unsuccessfully. The knights and counts are forming a very close confederation.[3] Oh, what a tempest, what a flood of business is hanging over us! If Christ's teachings ever reigned, they reign here. Dominik[4] is our leading preacher of the Word. Farewell, most candid patron and friend. Nürnberg. Invocavit Sunday in the year 1523.

W. Fabritius Capito

* * * * *

1 Millet suggests that this is Albert of Brandenburg, who departed from Nürnberg on 16 February (RTA, 3:647), but it is not clear why Capito would send a letter to Albert via Stromer, who resided in Leipzig. Perhaps the 'cardinal' is Lorenzo Pucci, and the letter in question is the reference mentioned in Ep. 153.
2 The Turks attacked Rhodes in June 1522; it fell to them on 28 December under the leadership of the Sultan Suleiman I the Magnificent. Rumours of this reached Rome on 3 January 1523 and Antwerp on 15 February.
3 A reference to the support Luther enjoyed among the nobility? Cf. above, Ep. 104, section IX, 1: 'The knights ... now follow Luther ... as do the secular princes.'
4 Dominik Schleupner (d. 1547) studied at Cracow (BA 1500), Wittenberg, and Leipzig, and was a canon at the cathedral chapter of Wrocław from 1516 to 1522. During the winter of 1522–3 he moved to Nürnberg and was engaged in Lutheran preaching. On 23 February he was appointed preacher at St Sebald's, a position he maintained until the city council transferred him in 1533 to St Catherine's. Schleupner played a prominent role in the reorganization of state and church according to Lutheran principles in Nürnberg.

Letter 155: 17 February 1523, Mariangelo Accursio to Capito

This letter has been moved because it is out of sequence in Millet's list. It is now Ep. 153a.

Letter 156: 5 April [1523], Basel, Johannes Oecolampadius to Capito

Printed in *Briefe Oekolampads* 1:217–19, #150

[*Summary*]: Oecolampadius is pleased to hear that Capito is now in Strasbourg [he arrived there 14 March], but disappointed that he will remain there only for a short while because of plans to travel to Rome. Bernhard Adelmann has advised Oecolampadius to procure a papal dispensation for a release from his monastic vows. If Capito does travel to Rome, he hopes that he might assist him in obtaining such a dispensation. It was not safe for Oecolampadius to return to his father in Würtemberg. The theologians in Basel are plotting to prevent him from lecturing on Isaiah. They are intent on driving him out of the city. Oecolampadius asks Capito to mention a time and place for them to meet in order to discuss these and other matters.

Letter 157: 24 April 1523, Strasbourg, Capito to Michael Sander

Michael Sander (d. 1529) studied law in Bologna and served as a papal notary. He was secretary to Cardinal Matthäus Schiner and obtained a number of prebends, among them a canonry and deanship at St Thomas, Strasbourg, which he ceded to Nicolaus Wurmser in 1510 for a pension of seventy gulden. He obtained canonries at Young St Peter's in Strasbourg (1513) and in Constance (1523). His movements after Schiner's death in October 1522 and before he became master of ceremony for Cardinal Lorenzo Campeggi in 1524 are not well known. This letter furnishes evidence that he was for a time attached to the imperial court.

The manuscript, a draft in Capito's hand, is in the Strasbourg Archive Municipale, AST 40, #39.

To Michael Sander. 24 April 1523.

Greetings, reverend sir. I hear that you are at the imperial court. If it is in your interest and to your liking, I heartily congratulate you on this fortune. I have your success at heart, just as much as my own. But as for me, I want you to know, I am looking for peace and quiet, for I have overexerted myself and done a great deal and haven't accomplished anything yet. The worst evils are spreading everywhere throughout Germany. Therefore, as much as I am permitted, *I prefer to be at leisure*, as that man says,[1] *than to achieve nothing* in this way and running so many risks. But I am glad that a different approach has worked out well for you, for we believe that the good fortune of a friend is likewise ours. I commend to your trust Bernhard Wurmser,[2] a very brave knight, together with the rest of the delegates of the cities. For they have their job cut out for them, and once it is done, we shall either have hope of peace to keep the empire together or a most dangerous war and schism and private federations.

I, who worked so hard and made so many attempts, still don't have my *preces* yet. I beg of you to entreat the magnificent and illustrious lord chancellor[3] that he may keep me in mind. For I hear that the custodianship of St Thomas and positions in the chapter of Surbourg in the diocese of Strasbourg are vacant through the death of the persons who obtained these positions recently through *preces*. Since it is still unclear whether they have died, if you can obtain the position for a friend for free, use your role as a friend and see to it that my relative, Jacob Pfeffinger,[4] is nominated to the custodianship and my brother, Heinrich Capito,[5] to the chapter of Surbourg. Philip Nicola,[6] the secretary, will help you. Give my regards to him. My prince has obtained for me a benefice at the church of Halberstadt, but I will have no opportunity to take advantage of it. [Albert] knows that I do not want to spend my life there, and he would give it to me only on that account.

Furthermore, when I left Worms, since you were going to follow the imperial court, I gave you 22 gulden and entrusted to you the business of obtaining the *preces* on behalf of Master Johann Gebwiler[7] and the noble

* * * * *

1 Pliny the Younger *Epistulae* 1.9.8; cf. Cicero *Philippicae* 8.27.
2 Bernhard Wurmser (or Wormser, d. 1540), a member of the Strasbourg city council and representing the city at the second Diet of Nürnberg.
3 Mercurio Gattinara (1465–1530), president of Burgundy and councillor to the regent Margarete, from 1518 imperial chancellor.
4 Jacob Pfeffinger (1486–1593), related to Capito through Prechter (see Ep. 50, note 1). He did not succeed in obtaining the post at St Thomas. He left the Catholic Church and eventually became preacher in Worms (1556).
5 Cf. above, Ep. 151.
6 Philip Nicola (documented through his correspondence with Erasmus, 1522–30) held a minor post in the imperial chancery in Spain.
7 It is not clear to which of two Johann Gebwilers this refers. Johann Gebwiler (d. 1530) of Colmar studied at the University of Freiburg (BA 1470, MA 1476), and from 1507 taught theology in Basel, where he had also obtained a doctorate in theology. He was a staunch Catholic and had his salary suspended when Basel turned Protestant in 1529. He held benefices in Basel (canonry at St Peter's) and in Turckheim in Alsace. He is last documented as priest of Eichstetten, near

Lord von Falkenstein.[8] They now want their money back again. Please write to Friedrich Prechter,[9] the Strasbourg merchant, so that he may return that sum of money in your name, taking it out of the next payment of the pension for the deanship.[10] I shall remain here for a month or so and then, at the request of the prince, I shall return to the treadmill, the very turbulent life at our court. I will roll that stone[11] until I can conveniently leave, for I have been thinking of the peace and quiet I enjoyed before. Bernhard[12] will keep you up to date on our affairs. Farewell. Strasbourg. 24 April 1523.

Letter 158: 21 May 1523, Basel, Valentinus Curio to Capito

> For the writer, Valentinus Curio (Schaffner) of Haguenau, see above, Ep. 95, headnote. The manuscript of the letter is in the Universitätsbibliothek, Basel, Ki.Ar. 25a, #38.

Valentinus Curio to his patron W. Capito.

I resolved to visit you these days and talk to you in person about our common affairs, but lo and behold, I am told of the arrival in three days of Konrad Heresbach, the Maecenas of my office.[1] In the interest of my affairs, I have been eagerly expecting him for a long time now. I therefore hope and trust Your Excellency will consider me excused. Furthermore, since I recently wrote I would give you an account of the sum I have received in your name and which is now owing, let me tell you briefly what I have paid

* * * * *

___

Freiburg. Johann Sellatoris Gebwiler (d. 1545), also taught at the university and like his namesake had a canonry at St Peter's (appointed provost in 1533), but he favoured the Reformation.

8 Not identified. The Falkensteins were based in Solothurn, but sold their castle and lands to Basel in the fifteenth century. They played a prominent role in Basel and traditionally held canonries in the cathedral chapter there. There are also connections to Mainz. Albert had dealings with the brothers Philo and Wyrich of Falkenstein, who sold their estates to him in 1526 (see *Ingrossatur-bücher* 54, 2v–3v).

9 Friedrich Prechter, Capito's relative and man of business in Strasbourg. Cf. above Ep. 50, note 1.

10 Cf. headnote above.

11 Erasmus *Adagia* 2.4.40.

12 Wurmser. See note 2 above.

1 Konrad Heresbach, see above, Ep. 68, headnote.

out in turn: I have obtained 16 fl[orins], 2 s.[2] from the sale of the lexicon,[3] which is the third belonging to you, according to Cratander's calculations up to this point, including the interest on what is owed, but I do not want to burden you with that. Nor do I demand reimbursement for freight costs and expenses in Frankfurt, unless in your generosity you decree otherwise. In addition, I have two unsold copies of the lexicon, and Cratander[4] (as reported) has 20, of which a third is also owed to you. I do not know whether or not he has sold them. Conversely, here is what I have paid out on your behalf, kind sir: 50 gold florins to Johann Wiler,[5] 43 florins to Wattenschnee,[6] who constantly insisted that that sum was owed to him. In addition, according to our calculation before you left here, you owed money to Hartmann Hallwyl and Gertophius[7] for the binding of some books on your behalf as well as for books bought and other expenses: 2 florins and 19 s.; also for the Aldine books bought at Frankfurt in 1520, 13 florins and 3 s. The total sum is 118 florins and 13 s. Pay what you like for the books I gave you, I mean the volumes of the jurists, for which I am certain I paid no less than 50 florins, including the binding. But I don't say that in the expectation of receiving as much from you, my patron. Rather, I leave the amount to your judgment, although law studies are so unpopular now that over a period of six years I could barely do one printing of Bartolo[8] (and he was the only one). I will say nothing of the great many volumes that need to be sold, but

* * * * *

2 's,' further on in the letter abbreviated as 'tst,' stands for 'testes,' i.e., silver coins stamped with an image of the 'head' of the issuing prince. On sixteenth-century coinage and monetary values see the appendix to CWE 15 by J. Munro.

3 I.e., a Greek lexicon published in 1519 and jointly financed by Capito, Curio, and Cratander.

4 For Cratander see above, Ep. 109, headnote.

5 Johann Wiler (1491–1539), descendant of a Basel merchant family. His father and namesake was a partner in a jewellery business, but also sold books on behalf of the Basel printer Michael Wenssler. The younger Wiler took over the business after his father's death and served on the city council. In 1522 he became mentally ill and was eventually placed under guardianship.

6 Johann Schabler, called Wattenschnee (d. ca. 1540), matriculated at Basel in 1473. Since he served as a book agent in Lyon for publishers in Basel (Froben, Amerbach, Lachner) and Nürnberg (Koberger). He bought up Lachner's estate in 1522 and made other investments in the Basel book trade. His daughter, Anna, married Bruno Amerbach.

7 For Hartmann Halwyl see above Ep. 11, headnote; for Gertophius, Ep. 54, headnote.

8 The commentaries and questions of Bartolo da Sassoferrato (1313–57) had been standard textbooks for students of law. Cf. above, Ep. 79, note 15.

no more about that. My servants are putting pressure on me and telling me to produce the money. I believe it will easily equal the expenses of both, even if I do not need more. I will not press you for the fifty florins I lent you in Haguenau, but if it can be done conveniently and without loss to you, the payment would be a relief to me, for I am overwhelmed with debt. Farewell and I ask that you embrace Cratander and me as your friends, as usual. I shall see to it that you will not regret your patronage of me, and you will always have me under obligation. Again, farewell in haste. Basel, 21 May 1523.

Letter 159: 21 May 1523, Mainz, Caspar Hedio to Capito

> For Hedio see above Ep. 47, headnote.
>   The text of the manuscript in the Universitätsbibliothek, Basel (G2 I 37, fol. 22), has been published by Krafft, 52–3.

Greeting. The Lord's will is being done in Franz.[1] The state of affairs of the knights seems desperate to many now that their leader has been killed and so many of their fortresses have been deserted, though they were considered to be solid as a rock. Unlucky is he who depends on the flesh for his own strength.[2] The gospel should have other safeguards. It does not look as if the gospel teaching has been wiped out in its entirety, as the enemies of the cross of Christ are boasting, nor have the believers of the 'new' doctrine, as they call it, perished. Let me even respond to them with Tertullian: *We may not be equipped for war and we may be no match for their troops, yet we are willing to be butchered,*[3] if necessary, for the glory of Christ. Four days ago Carnatius[4] was released from prison where he had been detained for four weeks. As far as knowledge of Christ is concerned, he is more skilled than 600 anointed men and has been permanently blacklisted in his diocese, if I have rightly understood the strictest and most vigilant function of the right of the sword, which catches flies beyond the ken of eagles.[5] Those who *eat the flesh of my people and break their bones in pieces are*

* * * * *

1 Franz von Sickingen; for his unsuccessful campaign and death see above, Ep. 142, headnote.
2 Jer. 17:4.
3 Tertullian *Apologeticus adversus gentes pro christianis* 37.5.
4 Unidentified.
5 I.e., even more keen-sighted than the proverbially keen-sighted eagle (Erasmus *Adagia* 3.2.65).

going to burn in the cauldron, fate being unfailing.[6] They say that the bishop of Speyer[7] and Dieter von Dalberg[8] were chosen to settle the matter between the princes and Schweickard von Sickingen.[9] Franz Konrad,[10] the younger son, left with Balthasar[11] for some unknown place. A judgment has been handed down in the case of the Counts of Nassau and Hesse;[12] Hesse will cede nearly half of his realm.

Nesen[13] wrote these words today from Wittenberg: don't be worried about Capito. I have taken good caution with Luther so that he won't do anything that you were dreading, etc. The Swabian League is gathering an army in Dinckelsbühl.[14] Many of our men have left; they think that the League is going to lay waste also to the Frankonian fortresses. I feel sorry for Hartmut,[15] the poor fellow. He does not stand a chance of returning to Kronberg, unless there is some hope of doing so through the emperor, whom he may however have alienated with his writings, or through the count of Nassau.[16] The cantor of our church[17] still longs for your presence, which he foresees on account of a letter recently written to the reverend [bishop] of Strasbourg[18] and the chapter of St Thomas. He desires it for my sake, more-

* * * * *

6 Cf. Mic. 3:3.

7 Georg Count Palatine (1486–1529), bishop of Speyer from 1513 to 1529.

8 The barons von Dalberg held the hereditary office of majordomo at the cathedral of Worms. Dieter von Dalberg (d. 1530), son of Wolfgang von Dalberg and Gertraud von Greiffenklau, was the younger brother of the well-known humanist, Johann von Dalberg, bishop of Worms. He was married to Anna von Helmstatt and was related to Franz von Sickingen.

9 Cf. above, Ep. 147, note 2.

10 Franz Konrad (1511–72) was the third son of Franz von Sickingen.

11 Balthasar Schlör, notary of the bishop of Worms and in the service of Sickingen (see *Wormser Chronik mit Zusätzen F. Bertholds von Flersheim*, ed. W. Arnold [Amsterdam, 1969], 242).

12 An imperial commission had made a ruling concerning the Katzenelnbogen territory along the Rhine, over which the counts had been litigating. The contested territory went to Nassau. The ruling could not be enforced, however, and Philip of Hesse remained in de facto possession of the lands.

13 For Wilhelm Nesen see above, Ep. 76, headnote.

14 On the league see above, Ep. 142, note 9.

15 On Hartmut of Kronberg see above, Ep. 146, headnote.

16 In return for his services in the Katzenelnbogen affair? Sickingen and his followers had been active in efforts to obtain the Katzenelnbogen territory for Nassau. See above, note 12.

17 Christoph von Gabelentz. Cf. above, Ep. 100, note 14.

18 Wilhelm of Honstein, see below, Ep. 174, headnote.

over. Poor Hedio has once again taken a false step – I do not know what I did wrong and what will be the counsel of Doeg.[19] Do what the Lord commands and what seems appropriate for the benefit of the public; what concerns me is no great loss. Our Rode[20] will report the other news from Cologne and elsewhere. Eberbach,[21] who is more timid than a deer when it comes to writing letters to friends, greets you. Impudence is the least of my vices.

In haste. From Mainz. 21 May 1523.

Yours, Hedio.

Letter 160: 23 May [1523], Leipzig, Petrus Mosellanus to Capito

> For Mosellanus see above, Ep. 62, headnote. The manuscript of the letter is in the Universitätsbibliothek, Basel, Ki.Ar. 25a, #58.

Petrus Mosellanus to Capito, greetings. Since I had a convenient offer from a messenger who said he was travelling there,[1] and had decided to indicate to you by means of a letter that I will always remember you, I write this to you extemporaneously, with a hurried pen. There is nothing going on in Meissen at this time that would be worth reporting to you and worthy of your attention, unless it is your intent to spend good time badly. For you know: *Africa always brings forth a new monster.*[2] I therefore send you a sermon of Chrysostom, recently translated into Latin by me.[3] Our Hartmann[4] studies diligently. So far I can certainly be a proper witness to that. Farewell and write back. Leipzig, at the house of Stromer,[5] who sends you his regards and awaits your letter. On the day before Pentecost.

* * * * *

19 See 1 Sam. 22:6–20. The reference is to Doeg the Edomite who, on Saul's command, killed the priests of the Lord along with the men, women, children, and livestock of the town of Nob. The point of the reference is unclear.

20 Hinne Rode (d. ca. 1535), rector of the house and school of the Brethren of the Common Life in Utrecht. In 1522, he was dismissed on account of his Lutheran convictions and lived from there until 1526 in exile, mainly in southern Germany.

21 Johann Stumpf of Eberbach. See above, Ep. 140, note 14.

1 I.e., to Mainz.

2 A proverbial expression. Erasmus, *Adagia* 3.7.10.

3 I can find no reference to its publication.

4 Hartmann Hallwyl, see above, Ep. 11, headnote.

5 For Stromer see above, Ep. 32, note 7.

The provost of Halle[6] has left the monastery and went away taking with him certain provisions for the road.

Your Petrus Mosellanus

Letter 161: 18 June 1523, Strasbourg, Capito to Desiderius Erasmus

Printed in Allen 5:293–4, #1368 and CWE 10, Ep. 1368

[*Summary*]: Capito writes from Strasbourg, relating the continuing criticism he faces from both Lutherans and papists because he refuses to take sides. The Lutherans have published satirical dialogues and broadsheets against him. Pope Adrian VI is said to have deprived him of the provostship of St Thomas, but he can hardly believe that this is true. He asks Erasmus to put in a good word on his behalf. He has resigned his position at the court of Mainz and refuses to return, although the archbishop has written to him three times. He hears that Ulrich von Hutten has published his *Expostulatio*, in which he attacks Erasmus's moderation and accuses him of a lack of commitment.

Letter 162: 24 June 1523, Augsburg, Urbanus Rhegius to Capito

Urbanus Rhegius (1489–1541) studied at Freiburg, Ingolstadt (MA), and Basel (ThD). He was a good scholar of Latin and Greek. For a time he was in the service of Johannes Fabri (later bishop of Vienna) at Constance and was ordained priest in 1519. He took his clerical duties seriously. When he wrote this letter to Capito, he was serving as a parish priest in Hall (Tyrol). His congregation was receptive to evangelism, but the territory was ruled by Emperor Charles's brother Ferdinand, who was determined to suppress the Reformation. In 1523 Rhegius accepted a call from the reform-minded city council of Augsburg and served as a preacher in the city until 1530. At that time he moved to the court of Duke Ernst of Lüneburg and over the next ten years played a significant role in reforming northern Germany.

The manuscript of the letter is in the Universitätsbibliothek, Basel, Ki.Ar. 25a, #26.

Urbanus Rhegius to Wolfgang Fabritius Capito: may Christ favour you.

* * * * *

6 Nikolaus Demut was provost from 1519 to 1523. In April he left Halle for Torgau and married a former nun.

On the day which is sacred to John the Baptist, dearest teacher, my patron, Bernhard Adelmann,[1] showed me your letter. I was sorry when I read that your affairs are anything but tranquil on account of the Roman perfidy, but Rome is Rome. It hates virtues and heaps generous rewards on crimes. What camp follower ever left the curia without a present, as long as he has acquired the skill of a stable boy? But scholars are regarded of no account. But I know you have been given an ample measure of grace and will bear any adversity with fortitude. At the end of your letter you wanted to know where in the world Urbanus Rhegius dwells. Here is the whole story: on 22 April I went to Augsburg on a lark. There everyone favours my pursuits, except certain priests, or rather, stuffed bellies. I was quite unaware of the tricks which the bishop of Trent[2] had played on me at the court of Prince Ferdinand.[3] After some weeks I was about to return to Hall, when the council of Hall warned me in a letter not to return. Ferdinand, they said, was raging against the preachers of the gospel to such an extent that there was no safety for those who most deserved to live in safety. What was I to do? I immediately wrote an *apologia* in Latin, addressed to the prince, which the council tendered to him, but the prince has not yet replied. In the meantime I am staying with friends in Augsburg. Recently, on the request of the council, I have preached a few times. The people of Hall are trying everything to bring me back to the pulpit safe and sound. They strenuously oppose the bishop in the court of the duke. I myself would justify everything before the bishops,[4] but I am not admitted. Everyone sings the same old song: he is a Lutheran, Luther is a heretic. They admit no scriptural evidence. Do you see how powerful the *Lord of lies* is, upheld by alien forces?[5] I am content and prepared to accept any lot. I pray only that God give me understanding

* * * * *

1 Bernhard Adelmann von Adelmannsfelden (ca. 1459–1523), matriculated in 1472 at Heidelberg, in 1476 at Basel, and in 1482 at Ferrara. In 1486 he obtained a canonry at Eichstätt; in 1498 he became canon at the cathedral of Augsburg.

2 Bernard of Cles (1485–1539), bishop of Trent from 1514, studied at Verona and Bologna (doctorate in civil and canon law, 1511). He was an imperial councillor, and from 1522 in the service of Ferdinand, who made him his most trusted adviser and representative at successive Diets. In 1530 he was made cardinal. Rhegius's parish was in the Tridentine diocese.

3 Ferdinand I, brother of Emperor Charles V. Below, he is referred to as 'duke,' i.e., of Tyrol.

4 I.e., the bishop of Trent and Sebastian Sprenz, the bishop of Brixen, in whose see Hall was.

5 I.e., the pope. Urbanus is quoting Luther, who used the expression 'rex iste facierum' of Pope Leo X in *Ad librum ... Ambrosii Catharini ... responsio* (1521), WA 7, 742:30.

according to his word in this great confusion of all things. In this horrible tempest of evil, holy scripture is the only refuge and the true haven. This is my only strength: by frequently reading scripture I steel myself to bear all misfortunes. As for you, I beg you not to return to the court ever again, unless you want to put yourself into the most immediate danger. The court does not tolerate the truth, for flattery and slander rule in the courts. But I know your candid mind very well. You cannot bear deceit. You would not dissimulate continually, as is the habit of those who are brought up clothed in purple. My dearest Wolfgang, how happy I am to be born in this age. Times are dangerous, it is true, but the apostle has pointed his finger at it, so to speak;[6] and I take refuge in the ark of scripture lest this cataclysm of evils carries me away. May Christ give us fortitude and perseverance to the end. Amen. Farewell from Augsburg, on the very day of John the Baptist, in the year 1523.

Letter 163: 6 July 1523, Strasbourg, Capito to Urbanus Rhegius

> This is Capito's reply to the preceding letter. It is a rough draft in Capito's hand. The manuscript is in the Universitätsbibliothek, Basel, Ki.Ar. 25a, 37.

Greetings. Well, what great pleasure your letter gave me, dearest Urbanus! There was a rumour that Ferdinand had you killed or ignominiously expelled on account of the Word. They certainly stated that you had been taken. There were people who said you were no longer alive, for no living soul could find out where you had gone after you had been exiled. And therefore, being anxious about our friend, we are inclined to accept that rather sad report.[1] Just as we gladly believe what we wish to happen, we accept as fact reports of events we fear will happen, when we have good reasons for our conjecture. That is certainly the case in this century, which transmits to posterity many examples of tyranny. Your young prince whose mind is naturally inflamed does not need the bishop of Trent's encouragement.[2] He, together with the crowd of flatterers, will make the madman even more furious. Jesus will break his great power with our patient suffer-

* * * * *

6 Perhaps a reference to 2 Thess. 2.

1 This appears to be the meaning of the sentence, which is grammatically unsound.
2 Ferdinand was twenty years old at the time. See Rhegius's report in the preceding letter concerning his adviser, Bernard of Cles.

ing, for we have learned from the example of our forefathers to be victorious through suffering. What is this you are saying? You had in mind to defend your cause before bishops? As if such a defence could teach them about Christ, and as if, once taught, they would have qualms to suppress him with might and tyranny because they could not do it with tricks and malice![3] Here too we are called Lutherans by those most hateful men who know least how much Luther has benefited the world. The people know it very well, even women and children surpass our rabbis in Christian wisdom. They raise a tragic outcry: 'Alas the times, alas the morals! Was it necessary to profane the mysteries of scripture and bring them to the notice of the lowest rank of people?' As if Christ had been born only for the anointed, as if the people ought to have no business with faith, unless they claim perhaps that you can believe in things of which you are totally ignorant. My dear Urbanus, let us exercise ourselves and through diligent perusal of scripture strengthen our faith, if it appears that we must fight at close quarters.

Johannes Fabri[4] has been for some time the director of this rather unpleasant tragedy. He dragged many off to punishment. He made vigorous assertions, he wrote at length against Luther – if he acted sincerely, I wish him better judgment, if (as many think) he acted for profit and to boost his name, I shall pray that he changes his mind for the better. Yesterday I received a letter from him[5] in which he expostulates with me over my stubborn silence, using these words: 'Why have you not deigned to answer me?' [My reply:] 'I wanted to keep silent, in the belief, perhaps that neither I nor my thoughts were to your liking.' Another one wrote that I was safe if I did not hide my talent, that is, if I attempted boldly what is unjust and, I believe, cannot be done. You see it is now a crime to keep silent. What am I to do? I shall put my trust in Christ, who feeds the birds in the sky[6] and will care for me too, and I shall yield voluntarily[7] what they will take by force against my will to avenge my silence. I know that the tribe of priests have gathered witnesses from every quarter and accused me in Rome of the Lutheran heresy. I was secretly denounced, which is an easy method and open to the worst kind of

* * * * *

3 Yet a few months later, Capito himself addressed an *apologia* to his superior, the bishop of Strasbourg (see below, Ep. 174).
4 For Johannes Fabri, see above, Ep. 110a, headnote.
5 Not extant.
6 Cf. Matt. 6:26.
7 I.e., the provostship of St Thomas, which was once again under litigation. See AST 192, 12r (of 25 June 1523) for an appeal against Abel's renewed claims. Cf. also Epp. 161 and 164.

person and likewise the most wicked method of all, because once a hostile opinion is conceived and suspicion raised, they will overwhelm quiet innocence; and when the opportunity to respond is taken away their violence is less apparent, for the principal aim of the chaste is to expose the turpitude of the most corrupt whore. It is enough to utter a warning about what everyone knows. But do I turn tail so fast? Not at all. I shall play the brave man and with staunch heart confront them and make it difficult for my opponents. For some people kindle my hope in Adrian and say that he is a rather well-meaning man, of which he will give me evidence. If the evidence is good, I am saved, if it is bad, the case is the same: it will nevertheless be for the best.[8] Thus I find safety everywhere, indeed security, for I have no fear. Assist me with your pure prayers to obtain the hoped-for victory, for I have almost won *the first battle* (which they say) *is the worst*,[9] that is, the battle with my friends and relatives, with flesh and blood. One must pray for victory in him who comforts us, Christ Jesus. Amen. Strasbourg, 6 July, in the year 1523.

Letter 164: 6 July 1523, Strasbourg, Capito to Desiderius Erasmus

Printed in Allen 51:305–6, #1374 and CWE 10, Ep. 1374

There is a considerable overlap and the occasional verbal resemblance between Ep. 161 and Ep. 164 (see examples in summary). It is possible, therefore, that Capito dispatched only one of the two letters, likely the more elaborate Ep. 164. Although he explains that the delay in answering Erasmus's letter (now lost) was due to the lack of a courier, it is more likely that he held back because his own situation was volatile. Capito had relinquished his position in Mainz, but his provostship in Strasbourg was still the subject of litigation in Rome. Although he asks Erasmus to intercede on his behalf with the pope, he carefully omits any mention of the fact that he is about to take out citizenship – often a preliminary step to leaving the Catholic Church. See below, Ep. 167a, in which he defends his action.

[*Summary*]: Capito explains that due to the lack of a courier, his response to Erasmus's last letter is still in his possession. He has kept silent out of respect for Erasmus and in recognition of his own limited capacity [*reverentia tui ac meae imbecillitatis conscientia* in Ep. #161; *conscientia ... inscitiae meae atque tuae reverentiae* in Ep. 164]. He knew for some time that people ques-

* * * * *

8 The Latin text is ambiguous.
9 Terence *Phormio* 2.2.32.

tioned Erasmus's integrity, but did not wish to set himself up as Erasmus's adviser. A rumour was circulating in Nürnberg that Erasmus had attacked the importance of faith over works in a dialogue. Capito is defending Erasmus's reputation but fears that he will not be able to protect him against the accusation of hypocrisy. Yet he regrets Luther's virulence against Erasmus. Luther has also attacked Capito, which might in fact help his reputation in Rome. The provostship is once again under litigation, and he is burdened with debt. Nevertheless he has resigned his position in Mainz and will not return there, although the archbishop has asked him repeatedly to reconsider his decision. The Lutheran party has vilified Capito in print, accusing him of being a Judas, and mocking his silence.[1] Hutten's attack on Erasmus [*Expostulatio*] has been published. If Erasmus so desires, Capito will reply on his behalf.

Letter 165: 30 July 1523, Wittenberg, N to the Reader

This *apologia* is printed in WBr. 2:435–43 from a manuscript in the Universitäts-bibliothek, Basel, Ki.Ar. 23a. The identification of the hand as Capito's is doubtful.

Dated Wittenberg 1523, the *apologia* is an open letter to the reader (who is addressed in lines 1, 110, 160, and 174 of the printed version). The manuscript itself bears the address 'To Jakob Truchsess' (see above, Ep. 41, note 1) in a hand different from that of the writer. It is unclear whether Truchsess had any role in this affair beyond that of a letter carrier. In fact, nothing is known of Truchsess's whereabouts in 1523. In 1520, when he was still in Capito's employ, Egranus advised him to move to Wittenberg (see above, Ep. 47). Other members of the Truchsess family were resident in Basel.

The piece was composed in the wake of an unauthorized publication by the Strasbourg printer Hans Schott in January 1523, which contained Luther's *Iudicium de Erasmo*, Melanchthon's *Elogion de Erasmo*, both uncomplimentary to Erasmus, and a letter from Luther to Capito (Ep. 131 of 17 January 1521), which identified him as a crypto-Lutheran and criticized his underhanded methods. The *apologia*, which may have been ghostwritten by Capito, comments on this publication as well as on Hutten's *Expostulatio* which, like the *Iudicium* and the *Elogion*, was critical of Erasmus. In his last letter to Erasmus (above, Ep. 164)

* * * * *

1 This is a reference to the anonymous *Passio Doctoris Marthini Lutheri* in which Albert of Brandenburg is portrayed as Caiphas and 'Pedico,' likened to Judas, betrays Luther. 'Pedico' (foot) is a pun on Köpfel (head), Capito's name in the vernacular.

Capito had volunteered to compose a reply on his behalf. The present piece is, however, put into the mouth of a third person, who refers to himself as Schott's *affinis* (relative by marriage in classical Latin, but in the sixteenth century sometimes used indiscriminately for both blood relatives and in-laws) and ostensibly sent from Wittenberg. This person has not been identified so far. Millet suggests Felix Ulscenius, but there is no independent evidence to connect him with the piece. The question has been raised why the manuscript ended up in Basel. We can only speculate that it was submitted for approval to Erasmus, then resident in Basel, and that he decided against its publication. Perhaps he no longer wished to be associated with Capito and other Lutheran supporters mentioned in the *apologia*, or he preferred to write his own defence and to focus on Hutten's attack. Erasmus's *Spongia*, written in reply to Hutten's *Expostulatio*, was published barely two months after the date given in this *apologia*.

[*Summary*]: The writer regrets the unauthorized publication of Luther's and Melanchthon's *Iudicia* and Luther's letter to Capito. It gives the enemies of the Reformation cause to rejoice and an opportunity to point out that Erasmus, Luther, Melanchthon, and Capito disagree among themselves. The same effect has been produced by Hutten's *Expostulatio* against Erasmus. Capito had tried to persuade Luther to proceed with moderation and abstain from attacks on Albert of Brandenburg. His call for diplomacy aroused Luther's suspicion. Yet Capito incurred risks on behalf of the Reformation cause. The writer mentions other men at Albert's court who favoured the Reformation, among them Caspar Hedio, Johann Stumpf von Eberbach, and Johann Drach. Defending Albert, the writer notes that the actions taken against married priests in the see of Mainz had not been Albert's personal initiative. The letter continues with a defence of Erasmus against Hutten's aspersions and his accusations of hypocrisy. The writer wishes to counteract the impression created by the indiscreet publication of Schott and asks the reader not to pass unfair judgment on Erasmus, Luther, Melanchthon, and Capito.

Letter 166: 6 September 1523, Sélestat, Jacob Wimpheling to Capito

Printed in *Wimpfelingi Opera* 3:2, 871–2.

[*Summary*]: The Alsatian humanist Jacob Wimpheling (1450–1528) relates rumours that Capito is preaching against the veneration of saints and cautions him to show respect for the teachings of the church fathers and to honour the memory of his teachers at Freiburg. He fears that the teachings of Matthew Zell and Martin Bucer will cause a public uproar and recommends that they and Capito examine their conscience.

Letter 167: 16 September 1523, Strasbourg, Capito and Matthew Zell to the City Council of Strasbourg

Matthew Zell (1477–1548) studied at the University of Freiburg (BA 1503, MA 1504, BTh 1511) and was appointed cathedral preacher in Strasbourg in 1518. He was attracted by Luther's thought and began preaching in the evangelical style. Efforts by the bishop, Wilhelm Honstein, to have him dismissed failed because his sermons were popular and the members of the cathedral chapter were divided in their sympathies. He also enjoyed the support of the city council. Between 1521 and 1523, Zell was the principal spokesman for the evangelicals in Strasbourg. He was soon joined (and eventually eclipsed) by Capito and Bucer. In 1523 he married Katharina Schütz, who was also active in the Reformation movement.

   The manuscript, written in German, is in the Strasbourg city archive, AST 87 (50), #9. The draft is in Capito's hand and frequently uses the pronoun 'I,' which would suggest that the joint appeal was Capito's initiative.

Strict, most respected, careful, prudent, wise, most benevolent and ruling lords, we are duly at your service, etc. We have a reliable report that a priest said before several lords in the chancellery and then before the consistory that he would prove on the strength of scripture that we two are heretics and that I, the provost, am an evil man on account of my preaching. Since these statements came from a lowly person, we thought it of no importance and were quite convinced that it would have no effect and fall into oblivion by itself. In the meantime our benevolent lord's official[1] has given public notice to all who wished to enter into discussion with or make demands against that priest to appear before him within seven days and proceed according to the rule of the law under the threat of having silence imposed on them forever, etc. In addition, several troublemakers in barbershops and elsewhere said publicly and spread a rumour everywhere that that notice was for me, the provost, alone and that I should not respond to such a miserable village priest, who even today insistently offers to prove by means of scriptural evidence that I am a heretic and evil man. Yesterday, Tuesday

* * * * *

1 Jakob von Gottesheim, the bishop's vicar in spiritualibus and the official of the diocesan court in Strasbourg. See above, Ep. 15b, note 6.

morning at 6 o'clock, the knight Reimbold Spender and Martin Herlin,[2] senior *Stadtmann* and *Ammeister*, our two benevolent lords, indicated to me, as instructed by the honourable council, that the official of our noble lord of Strasbourg complained to you, our lords, on Monday that several people had appeared before him alleging that he was putting the priest in danger of life and limb. They said I would appear before him the next Saturday, at the fixed time, with a crowd of supporters and exert my influence, although he could hardly believe this of a doctor of holy scripture. For that reason no procurator or lawyer would give him written or spoken support. That is, an alarm was raised inadvertently, and a request was added that you, our lords, as the governing body should command me to abstain from such an unfair enterprise, etc. Thereupon you, my lords, ordered them to prevent me and make me abstain from such an enterprise and bring no more than three or four persons before the consistory, with a larger following, etc. To this, my lords, I reply briefly according to the truth, that I spoke to no man, nor had as yet decided to go before the official against such a person, who cannot (thank God) deprive me easily, with mere words, of the honour I possess. But when I reflected that the matter was becoming more serious and the priest more insistent in his desire to make me out a heretic and evildoer on the basis of scripture, I decided to take preventive action. After all, the report had been spread in the whole town, mockingly repeated, as I am told, by important persons in the consistory and would thus be regarded as the truth by many. Furthermore the day fixed in the notice is approaching, and once it has passed, it will be difficult for me to save my honour and the truth, after such grave suspicion has been cast upon me. It was suggested that I, the provost, assembled the people behind the government's back and wanted to cause an uprising to further a legal action, which I never wanted to carry on in that form. Thus I went on the same day at 9 o'clock together with Master Matthew [Zell], for he was likewise accused for the same reason, and appeared before you, our lords, and after defending myself against the suspicion raised by the official against me, we explained the origin of the matter, and as our lords are no doubt aware, asked you to name a time and meeting place and requested that some of you come to listen and bear witness. Likewise we offered to recant publicly and hold to the attested truth,

* * * * *

2 Spender, a descendant of one of the oldest patrician families in Strasbourg (d. 1534), and the furrier Herlin (1471–1547) were prominent members of the city council. The *Ammeister* (or burgomaster) was the figurehead of the city's goverment; the *Stadtmeister* was a member of the senate whose leadership was rotated every two months.

should [the priest] according to his claims prove our error on the basis of scripture, and if he was unable to offer proof (which no man can prove, in our opinion), there would be an end to the unrest, and the slander now broadcasted by many will be silenced and averted. We do not have in mind to make a counter claim against the priest, and so there is nothing in this matter that should be laid before the official and procurators and requires their judgment and execution. And since matters have come about in this way, we have desired and requested that the lords of the city also call the regular clergy and other preachers who every day whip up sentiment against us and abuse us, not without causing great ill will and resentment between the common people and the commendable clergy. Such a war of words usually has no other effect than to cause strife and unrest, since each man has his party and following. Yet we should make an effort to do away with all parties, sects, and factions, for we are the messengers of the gospel and of Christian love and concord.

We would also remind you that you, our benevolent lords, have the right and duty as governors to suppress in your city every faction and unrest and to aid and assist the peaceful word of God and promote it. We therefore ask furthermore that you agree that peace be made between us and all people, whether they are preachers or other learned and pious people, as long as they arm themselves with scripture and the spirit of God, from whom no one should depart, which we totally expect from them as faithful Christians. This is our request to you, our city councillors, which we herewith put in writing and want it understood with all goodwill that by the same measure we are humbly asking our lord of Strasbourg kindly to help us arrange such a meeting with your lords and that your Graces also deign to give instructions to several of your councillors [to attend]. Thus we ask your Honours once again most submissively to name a place for this fair and Christian undertaking and designate several of our lords to listen [to the debate]. Let the members of the orders and the preachers publicly state their opposition to our sermons and also cooperate with our noble lord of Strasbourg and our noble lords of the cathedral chapter by sending their own delegates, etc. and to promote the matter which will no doubt lead to peace, concord, revelation of the truth, and honour to God. Thus you, our lords, will please God and win glory before the world, which Your Lordships are doing and no doubt have the intention to do. We want to show ourselves worthy of this through our most obedient service to Your Lordships. Given at Strasbourg on Wednesday after the Exaltation of the Cross, in the year 1523.

We remain Your Lordships' obedient subjects, Doctor Wolfgang Fa[britius] Capito, provost of St Thomas, Master Matthew Zell of Kaisersberg, presently priest at St Lawrence cathedral at Strasbourg.

Letter 168: 20 September 1523, Sélestat, Jacob Wimpheling to Capito

Wimpheling copied this letter into his personal copy of Gerson's *Opera* (Basel, 1489), vol. 1, fol. 2, now in the Municipal library of Haguenau. The text has been printed in *Wimpfelingi Opera* 3:2, 873–4. The editors give the date of the letter as 'zwischen 6.IX. und 25.X. 1523.' Wimpheling does in fact provide a date, but the editors misread the words in question as 'verbi gracia Mathei auctoritate 23.' The correct reading is 'Vespera Matthaei anno 23,' i.e., 'On the eve of [the feast of] St. Matthew, in the year 23.'

[*Summary*]: Wimpheling complains that Capito replied harshly to his fatherly admonitions. He reminds Capito that he swore allegiance to the Catholic Church when he took office and asks him to admonish Bucer to moderate his language. At present he seems to emulate Luther and Hutten's strident tone. Wimpheling wants to see the church reformed, not destroyed through schism.

Letter 168a: Before 22 September 1523, [Strasbourg], Capito to [Johannes Fabri]

This letter appears in Millet's list as Ep. 178. It has been renumbered in view of the reference to it in Ep. 169, below, which provides a *terminus ante quem*.

The text of the letter, or pamphlet, is printed in O. Millet, 'Un pamphlet prolutherien inédit de W.F. Capiton,' *Revue d'histoire et philosophie religieuses* 63 (1983): 181–20. He identifies the unnamed addressee as Johannes Fabri (see above, Ep. 110a, headnote). Throughout the letter Capito emphatically supports Luther and his teaching, calling him 'the trumpet of the gospel' and 'a true preacher' (*est evangelica tuba Lutherus ... ecclesiastes est verus*, fol. 264, Millet, 190, 194). The letter is undated, but an approximate date is furnished by Johann Stumpf's letter, written 22 September 1523, in which he begs Capito not to publish what he has written. Stumpf is afraid that the pamphlet will reveal his indiscretion, i.e., that he shared with Capito a letter from Fabri to Schiesser. That letter is dated 3 June 1523. Thus, as Millet himself argues, Capito's pamphlet must have been composed after 3 June and before 22 September.

Capito's draft (Ki.Ar. 25a, #150 in the Universitätsbibliothek, Basel) is written in a careless hand, often barely legible, with many corrections, cancellations, and interlinear or marginal additions. The transcription is problematic, and scholars owe Millet a debt of gratitude for making the text available in print. I therefore offer the following corrections with due respect. My list contains only emendations affecting the meaning. Page and line numbers refer to Millet's printed text.

p. 185:   3 [Gr.] dielychthe >dielythe

            6 participabis > participares

            22 fidentiam>fidutiam.

p. 186:   6 id dicitis, fateor, quia > id vere dicitis, fateor, hereticus est, quia

            15 sensus > consensus

p. 187:   21 hospes > hospes tamquam

            28 id enim> ut id enim

p. 188:   11 tacuisse foret> tacuisse vitio foret

            27 consulere>consulere merito

p. 189:   3 solidissimum>stolidissimum

            27 repetita> ac repetitus

p. 190:   17 nititur>nitatur

            24 diuturnum>diutinum

p. 191:   6 nugarunt>nugatum

p. 192:   26 monachae>monachae nobiles

p. 193:   4 proficis industria>profers industriam

            23 verbo>verbo uno

p. 194:   9 Ciceronem usum >Ciceronem nullo usum

            32 lucem > Luther[i]

            33 tam>tenebras

p. 195:   1 praeibis>bibens

            25 ne>nae

            28 inferi>inferni

p. 196:   28 nexiit>nexuit

p. 197:   1 Fabrilia> fabrilia faber

            10 nescivit>nesciunt

            otiosis>otiosus

p. 198:   7 duos> duos, [Gr.] hoposos autos eig' exaiphnes polemikos
            kai meliphoron

            28 hoc est> hoc est praeterquam

p. 199:   1 perhibet>prohibet

            8 emeres>coemeres

            20 librarius>librariorum

            20 expingendis>expungendis

p. 200:   2 minis>minus

            9 humanissimus>humanissimus est

            [Gr.] epistemon>ho epistemon

            [Gr.] pamphilodorous > pamphilodorous [?] di' hon eunoustatos

            ... [illegible]

[*Summary*]: The manuscript consists of three sections, which Millet arranges as follows: [ff. 268r–269v] Capito presents an account of a dinner party given by Eberhard Schiesser (see below, Ep. 169, note 1). The conversation, which focuses on the Luther affair, is dominated by a cleric affecting to be a humanist. The guests deplore what they see as Luther's heretical views, his lack of refinement, and his aggressive criticism. One of them, who does not share the general opinion, responds with a tongue-in-cheek eulogy of the changes that have taken place in the church since the time of the apostles and of the wealth and power it has now acquired. The 'humanist,' oblivious to the irony of the eulogist, reacts enthusiastically. He volubly describes the worldliness and venality of the papal court and his own adventures in Rome. In a second section [fols. 262r–267v], the host raises the question why none of the learned theologians has written against Luther and rebutted his arguments if he is as ignorant as they say. The 'humanist' produces and reads from two anti-Lutheran letters, one from Johann Eck to Jacob Wimpheling, the other from Fabri to the host himself. Concluding his account of the dinner, Capito then addresses Fabri directly and critically reviews the arguments presented. In the third section [fols. 270r–71v] Capito discusses the Mass and the sacramentarian question and, more generally, the authority of biblical precepts versus human decrees and interpretations. He gleefully mentions that Fabri has been unable to find a publisher for his anti-Lutheran tract *Antilogiae* and concludes with an amusing sketch of their good-humoured host, Schiesser.

Letter 169: 22 September 1523, Mainz, Johann Stumpf von Eberbach to Capito

> For Eberbach see above, Ep. 92, note 6. The manuscript is in the Zentralbibliothek in Zurich (A63, fol. 14) and has been published by Herrmann, 232.

Eberbach to Capito, greetings. I beg and beseech you, dear Capito, take care to suppress the pamphlet in which mention is made of Schiesser and the letter from Fabri.[1] For the letter was copied in my house, whereas Schiesser sent it through a servant merely for me to read. Hence he can easily guess that I divulged the contents and this would give rise to serious enmities. Otherwise I would hardly be able to live among them. If the pamphlet appears, I will be in a very bad position. Therefore suppress it, not just for the glory of Christ but also for my safety.

* * * * *

1 I.e., Ep. 168a, above. As requested by Eberbach, it remained unpublished. Eberhard Schiesser (d. 1531) was a canon of the cathedral chapter in Mainz and dean at St Moritz's. For Fabri see above, Ep. 110a, headnote.

As for Hedio,[2] I have never thought differently and still know nothing other than that he was and is your best friend. I read the letter, which he wrote to Adelmann[3] recommending you and putting you ahead of himself. I would boldly swear an oath on Hedio's behalf, that he has never acted against you behind your back, at least not in our presence in Strasbourg, nor did we go there to negotiate about the terms. The first mention of it was made in the house of the lord dean of Strasbourg,[4] unless I am mistaken about everything. You see the will of the Lord, when things happen contrary to your plans. We shall oppose him in vain. Hedio is deeply upset that you are so disturbed, although he has high expectations of you, who knows how to repay everything *seventy times seven*.[5] It does not seem wise to traduce him everywhere among friends and make him unpopular as a result, for he will not fail to justify himself in turn. Thus, I fear, oil will be poured on the flames[6] and what comes will be worse than what preceded. I have better hopes of you all. If he erred, forgive him, for my sake at any rate. I would pray for that through Christ Jesus, who has not come to destroy but to save;[7] and it is obvious that hatred between you, if you continue thus, will be a bane. I know you will reflect on who is your inspiration.

The scribe of the chamber will render the money in four days, which I will then send on through a safe messenger. Farewell, Mainz, 22 September, in the year 1523. Yours, such as I am, Eberbach.

Letter 170: 29 September 1523, [Basel], Johannes Oecolampadius to Capito

Printed in *Briefe Oekolampads* 1:256–7, #176

[*Summary*]: Like Eberbach in the preceding letter, Oecolampadius tries to convince Capito to accept Hedio's appointment as cathedral preacher and show a more generous spirit towards his former protégé. He does not want their disagreement to spoil the friendship that ties him to both Capito and Hedio. Oecolampadius believes that God is punishing them for not being effective messengers of the gospel.

* * * * *

2 Hedio had been appointed cathedral preacher in Strasbourg, a position which Capito himself coveted. For Capito's reaction see also below, Epp. 170 and 173.
3 Cf. above, Ep. 162.
4 Sigmund of Hohenlohe; see below, Ep. 174, n 3.
5 Matt. 18:22.
6 A proverbial expression, cf. Erasmus *Adagia* 1.2.9.
7 Luke 9:56 (var.). The sentence, 'The son of Man has come not to destroy lives but to save them' has been removed from modern biblical texts.

Letter 171: [End of September 1523, Strasbourg], Anton Firn to Capito

Anton Firn of Haguenau (d. 1545) studied at Freiburg and was, from 1519 on, priest of St Stephen's in Strasbourg, and from 1520 parish priest of St Thomas. In June 1523 the dean of the chapter complained that he was preaching Lutheran doctrine. In November 1523 Firn took the provocative step of marrying his housekeeper. The bishop of Strasbourg ordered the chapter to dismiss Firn, but Capito did not enforce the directive and the parishioners baulked at Firn's replacement. They furthermore presented a petition to the city council, asking it to support Firn (see below, Epp. 176 and 177). In December the chapter yielded and allowed Firn to retain his post. In 1531 he became pastor of St Nicolaus.

The manuscript of the present letter is lost. The text comes from a transcript in TB 2:34.

To W. Capito, greetings. Please, give me instructions: in what manner would you like me to reply to the stupid question of the crazy old man and how ought I to react to what he writes about you? I never thought Wimpheling was stupid enough to think that it matters in what language the last supper is celebrated.[1] As if Christ had given instructions to do it in Latin or Greek. The important point is that it should be done in language which the people can understand.

I have a great and continuous pain in my chest, which makes me spit every moment. I have decided to eat no more food until that viscosity in my stomach or at the opening of the stomach subsides. I cannot sleep at night. The swelling of the legs has not yet gone away, my head is very feeble, perhaps as a result of this ongoing insomnia, and my whole body is weak. But may the Lord deal with his potter's clay[2] and his wretched creation as he pleases. If only he confers patience on me and strengthens my heart with the hope of future glory. Jacob Schütz asks for Latomus to come to him.[3] Please send your Reinbold[4] to him. He wishes to promote him to some parish. Farewell. A.F.

* * * * *

1 For Wimpheling's last letter to Capito, see above, Ep. 168.
2 Cf. Rom. 9:20–1.
3 Jacob Schütz studied at Heidelberg from 1507 to 1510 and was provost of St Martin's in Colmar. From 1534 to 1536 he was also a canon of St Thomas in Strasbourg. Latomus (Johann Steinlein, d. 1549) was a priest at the monastery of St John's in Strasbourg and held a number of posts in Strasbourg (at the cathedral 1523/4, at St Nicolaus's 1525–8, at St Aurelia's, 1531–49). From 1536 he was also a canon at St Thomas.
4 Johannes Remboldus? See above, Ep. 70, note 5.

Letter 172: [After 25 October 1523], Sélestat, Jacob Wimpheling to Capito

This letter, like Ep. 168, was copied by Wimpheling into his copy of Gerson (see Ep. 168, headnote) and has been printed in *Wimpfelingi Opera* 3-2, 874–5.

[*Summary*]: In a note preceding the letter, Wimpheling complains that Capito criticized him in a letter to Paul Phrygio, [parish priest in Sélestat]. He feels that he misrepresented his views. He was not implying that Capito was a liar or a hypocrite, but rather that he was arrogant, since 'on account of his knowledge of Greek and Hebrew he put himself ahead of St. Gregory.'

**Letter 173: 26 October 1523, [Strasbourg], Capito to
          Johannes Oecolampadius**

Printed in *Briefe Oekolampads* 1:260–3, #179

[*Summary*]: Capito is upset that Oecolampadius and others seem to favour Caspar Hedio over him. Though still bitter, Capito is willing to forgive Hedio. It will be difficult, however, to resume relations. He gave up his post as preacher in Mainz to Hedio, and in return has been ruined by his protégé. Hedio had been insincere, claiming at one point that he had informed him of his ambitions, at another that the post was offered him unexpectedly. He deserted the people of Mainz, who were thirsting for the gospel, and looked only after his own interests. He promised to preach inoffensively, and acted like a hypocrite. Meanwhile Capito himself is unpopular with the canons of St Thomas and the bishop of Strasbourg (see next letter). He continues to give vent to his unhappiness over what he sees as Hedio's betrayal. He will be reconciled only if Hedio preaches the gospel forcefully and sincerely. As it is, Hedio, like Erasmus, earns praise through flattery, whereas Oecolampadius and Capito are criticized because of their candour. Capito's affairs are in disarray.

Letter 174: 11 November 1523, Strasbourg, Capito to Christoph Ewiger

This is the preface to *An den hochwürdigen fürsten und herren Wilhelmen Bischof-fen zu Strassburg ... Entschuldigung* (An Apology ... addressed to the most reverend prince and lord William, Bishop of Strasbourg [Strasbourg: Köpfel, November 1523]). The text of the prefatory letter is on ff. AAi verso-AAii verso.

   The addressee is Christoph Ewi[n]ger or Ebinger (d. ca. 1548), a citizen of Basel, perhaps identical with the 'Christoph' mentioned in Ep. 47 of 1520. He married Kunigunde, widow of Arnold IV of Rotberg (see note below), in 1519. Ewinger is documented in a transaction of 13 December 1544 (Basel SA Fin. AA5, fol. 17v) when he invested four hundred pounds in a pension for life (*Leibrente*).

The *Entschuldigung* is addressed to Bishop Wilhelm von Honstein (ca. 1470– 1541, bishop from 1506). Honstein, who was the great-nephew of Berthold von Henneberg, archbishop of Mainz, studied at the universities of Erfurt, Padua, and Freiburg. He held benefices at Mainz, Cologne, and Strasbourg. In the *Entschuldigung* Capito justifies his recent conduct and in particular his taking out citizenship. As in Ep. 168a, Capito uses dialogue to camouflage his Lutheran sympathies, that is, he puts praise for Luther into the mouth of a third person. He carefully avoids tipping his hand by criticizing both Catholics and Lutherans. The Catholic clergy are mercenary and abuse their power, he says; the Lutheran preachers are disturbing the peace and inciting the people to riot. Although Capito claims that he is writing the *apologia* 'in the spirit of subjection' and 'as an obedient subject [of the bishop],' the *apologia* did little to allay suspicions that he was a crypto-Lutheran. After all, he himself acknowledged in the *apologia* that he had criticized the veneration of saints in his sermons, that he had used the phrase 'through faith we are saved,' and taught that the primacy of the pope had no basis in scripture. Yet he baulked at being labelled heterodox. His critics, Capito claimed, were misrepresenting him. He was willing to teach, for example, that works were essential for salvation, but he was unable to produce a biblical passage in support of such a claim, and he could not teach what he did not understand. His critics should instruct rather than denounce him. Throughout the *apologia*, Capito appeals for goodwill in settling the religious strife: 'If one were to interpret scripture in a spirit of peace and without contention, there would be an end to the factions among the people.'

Dr Hans-Günther Schmidt brought to my attention an autograph by the Erfurt Augustinian and Catholic apologist Arnold von Usingen (Universitäts- bibliothek, Würzburg, M.ch.o.34, fols. 41v–14r). On inspection, the pages in question turned out to be a partial translation of the *Entschuldigung* into Latin. Usingen, who was critical of Capito, may have planned a response.

To the noble Christoph Ewiger in Basel, my especially benevolent lord and friend: Peace and grace of our Lord God! Dear kind sir and friend, the fact that I have become a citizen of Strasbourg,[1] and that I have preached and

* * * * *

1 Capito took out citizenship on 9 July 1523 (cf. Ch. Wittmer, *Le Livre de bourgeoi- sie de la ville de Strasbourg 1440–1530* and AST 192, 1523, B1 12v).

asked for a public hearing against all who oppose the Word,[2] an opportunity to justify my words and listen in a friendly spirit to their objections in turn – all that has been counted against me and my actions are regarded as most shameful and interpreted as undertaken in defiance of the most reverend prince, Lord Wilhelm, bishop of Strasbourg, etc. my lord, of the common clergy, and especially of the chapter of St Thomas. That report was disseminated here and spread far and wide. It appeared to have some credibility and merit. As a result my good lords and friends living far and near became concerned on my behalf. Several of them have written to warn me and have offered their aid and assistance in the interest of justice and fairness. That is what, among other things, moved me to undertake a justification before my kind lord, addressing three specific points, and to issue it in print as a public statement of my just undertaking, of which I need not be ashamed, although here in Strasbourg, where my actions are well known, there is no great need for justification. Rather, people of both high and low standing know well that I never had any ill will against my lord and against my fellow members in the chapter and that I never had any problems with any priests in Strasbourg, whoever they may be. Even to the present day I have certainly, thank God, never been in disfavour with my benevolent lord and would not ever want to deserve it. Furthermore, I am too well known for anyone to believe that I am too quick in seeking revenge, and in any case I would never abuse the word of God for such an evil purpose, even if I had suffered injury. I know I have the same reputation in the praiseworthy city of Basel, where I likewise suffered criticism, but never sought revenge from the pulpit. And it may be that men of rank, such as the Christian prelate, my kind sir, Count Sigmund of Hohenlohe,[3] dean of the cathedral here in Strasbourg, and other creditable persons knew in advance my reasons for becoming a citizen and undertaking to preach. For the rest, there were many futile rumours circulating which are too insignificant to require much of an answer and which I have quite ignored. One was that I had attempted to force the priests to pay a significant amount into the poor box, each according to his income, as if I

* * * * *

2 See above, Ep. 167.
3 Sigmund von Hohenlohe (1495–1534), educated in France and Italy, became canon in the cathedral chapter at Strasbourg in 1506. From 1511 he was also canon of the cathedral chapter in Augsburg. He supported the Reformation and was one of those responsible for installing Hedio as cathedral preacher. He resigned his canonry for a pension and took out citizenship in 1527. A relative of the French royal dynasty, he entered French diplomatic service, for which he was placed under the imperial ban in 1529.

wanted alms to be given against a man's will and under duress rather than from the intention of the heart. Similarly it was said among you in Basel that by taking out citizenship I wanted to keep Abel from his right to the provost-ship.[4] I refer only briefly to this and other implausible talk. Time itself will sufficiently exonerate me. If I had wanted to injure Jacob Abel, I would have often had the opportunity at the Diet of Worms. As the noble and strong Jakob Truchsess von Rheinfelden[5] will remember, Abel was for a while in great disrepute with persons of rank because he once acquired a hundred benefices, of which he obtained twenty or thirty by supplication. He boasted that he was entitled to all the benefices, and even if there was no basis, he knew how to benefit from a lawsuit. Likewise, [it was known] that he sold the benefices he had hunted down and traded them for cash, etc. They also said that he by himself served as an example that any hope for law and order in Rome was utterly destroyed. At that time, dear Ewiger, best lord and friend, I could have had strong support, if that had been my intention. I will spare the reader who wants the facts, and will not reply at length to such tales. I beg, then, that you will read my apologia for the sake of our friend-ship and accept it as creditable and true. I also ask that you be kind enough to refer everyone to my apologia, when the occasion arises, notably the strict, severe, honourable, and wise councillors of the praiseworthy city of Basel and other honourable citizens, my dear and kind lords and old friends whose favour and goodwill I value and appreciate. For not everyone is inclined to read this stuff. I am at your service, etc. My best wishes and the grace of our Lord God to the virtuous lady, Kunigunde von Ropperg, your spouse,[6] to the noble and God-fearing lady Ursula Truchsess[7] and other good friends. I also would like you to know that I hope from many indica-tions the omnipotent God has given me, soon to be in good health again, etc. Given at Strasbourg on St Martin's Day, in the year 1523.

Letter 175: 12 November [1523], Strasbourg, Capito to Dietrich Spät

Dietrich Spät (Spett, Spat), documented in the records of the University of

* * * * *

4 For Capito's litigation with Abel see above, Epp. 50, 55, and 60, and for more recent developments, Epp. 161, 163, and 164.
5 See above, Ep. 41, note 1.
6 I.e., Kunigunde von Rotberg, whom Ewiger married in 1519. She was still alive in 1538, when the city of Basel granted her the right to a well (see *Urkundenbuch der Stadt Basel*, ed. R. Thommen [Basel, 1905], 10:231).
7 Perhaps Ursula, née Eptinger (d. 1538), who was married to Sebastian Truch-sess von Rheinfelden.

Tübingen in 1513 and Freiburg in 1521, was a jurist in the service of Cardinal
Leonardo Grosso della Rovere at Rome. In 1520, he acted on Capito's behalf
(see above, Ep. 50; cf. also Appendix, Document 1, for the cardinal's inter-
vention). Spät was dean of St Stephen's in Mainz from 1515 and provost of the
Collegiate church in Stuttgart from 1521. After mismanaging affairs there, he
resigned his provostship under duress in 1527 and entered the service of King
Ferdinand.

The manuscript of this letter, a rough draft in Capito's hand, is in the city
archive of Strasbourg, AST 40, #47.

Greetings. You are aware, my friend and true patron, what inconvenience
you have avoided by staying away from Germany during these fatal years. O
misfortune! What tragedies I have suffered here! The traits that should rightly
and justly commend a new man to both nobility and rulers have brought special unpopularity to the author in this evil time; and again what men of old
considered popular with the multitude has brought a veritable tempest and
blast of popular opinion on me.[1] I had earlier foreseen the conflagration that
now burns down the world. I have issued warnings in advance; I allied my
insignificant self with [Pope] Leo who was relying on certain moderate men.
When I was drawn into the court,[2] I begged and pleaded and did everything
to persuade those on whom the sum of things seemed to depend to remove
from our necks the peril threatening us.[3] I always preferred to see everything
done through their authority that would promote the glory of Christ and the
public welfare. What can I say? My labour was in vain. An inoffensive
bystander, I am publicly called into suspicion. People's minds are alienated
from me. The ears of the fortunate are so tender that they consider nothing
salutary unless it is corrupted with flattery.

The reverend cardinal of Sion[4] once told me always to maintain my simple candour and I could be sure that he would labour together with me to
counter the evil shortly with more suitable means, and without threats and
tyranny. For that prudent man saw that edicts exacerbated the situation,

* * * * *

1 The expression 'aura popularis' (popular breeze) was often used by Livy in the
   sense of fickle opinion, e.g., 3. *Ab urbe condita* 33.7, 22.26.4, etc; and Cicero *De
   haruspicum responsis* 43.
2 I.e., of Albert, whom he served from 1520 to July 1523.
3 This appears to be the meaning. The Latin sentence does not run.
4 Matthäus Schiner (d. 1522), diplomat in the service of Pope Julius II. After the
   disaster of Marignano (1515), he was *persona non grata* and lived at Zürich. He
   served the Hapsburgs and assisted the papal legate Aleandro in 1521. In 1522,
   after the death of Leo X, he returned to Rome, where he died of the plague.

that what is suppressed by force will rise up more forcefully, what is driven out by the sword, which some people boastfully threatened to do, would necessarily be strengthened forever. I still persist in that opinion, even now at this point in time. In their passion, pray, what can authority, what can the use of armed force effect? Therefore I kept silent, I kept my judgment to myself and shared it with no one among the people or among my less reliable friends. This cautious attitude has provoked the Lutheran camp to act harshly against me. How many pamphlets, I beg you, did they write cutting me to shreds, when I was innocent? Yet I never responded publicly, giving the appearance of a man who was most careless about his reputation. Again, how savagely did the leading powers tear me apart with openly voiced suspicions, expostulations, accusations, and injurious words spoken to my face, publicly, and in the most disrespectful fashion? I have suffered it all, trusting in the certain hope that there will come a time when those in authority will prefer solid councils to treacherous and flattering assent, and when the fickle people will pronounce a fairer verdict on a man who loves his country than it does now.

When I arrived [in Strasbourg] and matters were in astounding turmoil, I adopted a peaceful stand for the occasion. I praised both parties from the pulpit. I gravely admonished each party in turn, until the prudent would see a glimmer of peace and serenity. But the ignorant and obtuse monks, priests, and prelates were angry. How bitterly, how angrily, how bitingly they criticized what I had quietly said! On the other side, the Lutherans accused me far and wide of spelling the complete ruin of the gospel and did not even abstain from writing pamphlets. I send you one[5] that was given me the other day quite unexpectedly, which will give you a taste from which you can guess the rest of my fortune.

My affairs here were all uncertain and in doubt, elsewhere everything was certainly full of hostility. Whatever the fate that draws me unwillingly into the arena, most respected sir, I accept the condition under which I must exonerate myself in public as inevitable, but nevertheless forever foreign to my mind. And this happened at a time when I was gravely ill, tormented as much by physical as by emotional pain, for I did not leave the side of the stove for two months. I therefore make my excuses to the bishop.[6] For was there a more suitable person to whom I should render an account of my

* * * * *

5 Perhaps *Num recte dictum sit a concionatoribus Argentiniensibus* (Strasbourg, 1523), as suggested by Jean Roth (in *Investigationes historicae* [Strasbourg, 1986], 505–6) or the anonymous *Passio* (see above, Ep. 164).
6 Cf. above, Ep. 174, headnote.

faith and my actions? Whatever it amounts to, I shall publish it these days and bring it into the public realm if the printers who have had the manuscript in their hands for some time have not already done it. It has been done in response to the warnings of my friends everywhere and the criticism of my enemies on all sides, but certainly against my inclination. I cannot say whether it was done under happy auspices, but I am sure, unless I am completely mistaken, that it will do me no good, for it is easy for malicious people to harm the innocent. But truth, open and unstrained, does not flee the light. Thus, after these sufferings, I decided to give advance notice to you, kind sir, to the reverend lords Francesco Chierigati, Aleandro, Bombace, Joachim Vonstede, Bader,[7] and whatever other friends are in Rome, lest by defending me in vain, they share my danger, which I would certainly not want to happen, for I am the least ungrateful of all men and do not want to burden my benefactors, especially in a case against a scoundrel like Abel and when our effort expended over so many years has been useless.[8] Please ensure that my patrons, along with anyone else whom you know to be desirous of my safety, will read this. Aleandro understands me very well. What need is there for words? Farewell. Strasbourg, after St Martin's Day.

Letter 176: 14 November 1523, [Strasbourg], Martin Bucer to Capito

Printed in *Corr Bucer* 1:208–10, #52.

[*Summary*]: Bucer rejoices over the outcome of Firn's affair [see above, Ep. 171, headnote]. On the advice of Capito, Bucer will warn Martin [perhaps Enderlin, chaplain of the canon of the Rudolph Cathedral in Baden-Baden] not to waste his money and effort. He asked Firn to read the Bible in order to find consolation in the word of God rather than men. Firn ought to encourage his wife to dress more modestly. She continues to wear ostentatious and

* * * * *

7 For the papal legates Chierigati and Aleandro, both of whom had been involved in procuring for Capito the provostship of St Thomas, see above Epp. 149, headnote, and 152; for Paolo Bombace, secretary of Cardinal Pucci see above, Ep. 50, note 3; for the Dominican Johann Bader, procurator at the Roman court, see above, Ep. 153; the jurist Joachim Vonstede (see above Epp. 152, 153) was Tetleben's successor as the archbishop of Mainz's man of business in Rome.

8 I.e., his legal fight for the provostship of St Thomas, an office he retained, however, in spite of resistance in Rome and from those of his fellow canons who opposed the Reformation. For the history of the litigation and Capito's opponent Abel see above, Ep. 50.

indecent clothing despite repeated admonitions. Firn prefers that others instruct her. Either he does not dare to confront her or she refuses to comply with his wishes.

Letter 177: 12 December 1523, [Strasbourg], Parishioners of St Thomas to the city council of Strasbourg

The text of this petition on behalf of the parish priest Anton Firn (see above Ep. 171, headnote) was published under the title *Supplication des pfarrhers, unnd der pfarrkinder zu sant Thoman, eim ersamen Rath zu Strassburg* (Basel: Cratander, 1524). Millet included it in his list because Capito apparently helped with the composition of the parishioners' letter. The manuscript (Ki.Ar. 23a, #23, in the Universitätsbibliothek, Basel) has corrections in his hand. It bears marks showing that it was used as printer's copy and often differs from the printed version in spelling and, occasionally, word order. It is unclear on whose authority those changes were introduced.

Supplication of the common parishioners of St Thomas to the honourable council of the praiseworthy city of Strasbourg, in favour of holy matrimony and against the whoring priests. Presented and read to the council in session, with the delegates of the chapter of St Thomas in attendance.

Strict, worthy, provident, honourable, wise, gracious, and ruling lords. Master Anton,[1] appointed priest for the parishioners and residents of St Thomas, has been here in Strasbourg for one and a half years at St Stephen's and three and a half years at St Thomas's, living in disgrace and causing offence to many simple folk, for one is ever more inclined to follow evil. Now recently, however, reminded by the clear word of scripture of what offence, harm, and corruption of souls have resulted from his godless life, he has, after diligent counsel and consideration, put eternal before temporal concerns and entered holy matrimony in order to suit his works to his words. Thus he will no longer be a whorer while announcing God's truth, which says that adulterers and whorers will never possess the kingdom of God,[2] and he will also truly preach the gospel in his life, according to the honourable council's command. This heartens and edifies us not a little, just as before the contrast between his preaching and his life greatly hindered us. And we believe that through his respectable example as parish priest and superior, we might from now on more easily direct our lives towards

* * * * *

1 I.e., Anton Firn, see Ep. 171, headnote.
2 1 Cor. 6:9.

improvement. But the canons of St Thomas, who until now entrusted their parishes to public whorers (begging Your Graces' pardon for speaking thus, since we cannot very well call such obscenity other than what it is called in scripture) and who have never shown any displeasure at any vice, be it adultery, seduction of virgins, simony or anything else, now strongly complain of such Christian behaviour. And they no longer want to allow the priest in their company now that he intends to live in a Christian marriage like other good folk, him whom they previously requested and accepted for the priest's office when he was still a public transgressor of divine commands. And they adopted the doctrine *that comes from the devil*, as St Paul, 1 Tim. 4, calls it,[3] which forbids marriage, and have opposed God's command which maintains and directly commands marriage for everyone (other than those who are specifically exempted, such as men with a natural incapacity or with exceptional and rarely bestowed gifts of chastity), as we laymen now sufficiently understand and know ourselves. Therefore we have had no small concern and have most diligently begged the lords of the chapter of St Thomas to allow this man to remain as our priest. As is the custom of great lords, they have not considered us common persons worthy of their august answer. And that is where the matter rested for a while.

This Monday[4] they again acted in haste. Once again they dismissed the priest, removed the helper and sacristan from the house, ordered another one to preach, and without Firn's knowledge and in his absence had the priest's hat[5] carried out of the sacristy, and otherwise acted altogether as suits people who will not or can not bear piety, as being contrary to their own habits, and who not only tolerate whorers, but appoint and promote them, hold them in honour and dignity to the shame, disadvantage, and defiance of all Christian respectability. This, gracious and ruling lords, has moved a number of the parishioners, as many as could take counsel in a hurry yesterday in chance meetings, without being called together, so that they would not be suspected of insurrection behind your, our lords,' backs. For none of us desire to act so as to displease your Graces, nor would we want to rouse the suspicion of such evil thoughts against us. And thus we have, on account of the insufferable injustice of these dealings, found ourselves obliged to prevent, by suitable means within our capacity, our fellow citizen and brother, the priest of St Thomas, from being punished for keeping a divine command, whereas the canons' godless transgressions prevail.

* * * * *

3 1 Tim. 4:1.
4 7 December.
5 'kutzhut,' a hat worn by the confessor in the confessional.

Therefore grant us humbly to submit the present supplication to Your Graces, which we have undertaken so much more willingly since we know that its contents accord with divine will, Christian charity, and the worthy council's honour and welfare. For God has ever forbidden man to be unchaste and has given and instituted marriage as a remedy against it.[6] Charity also demands that we assist our brother, whom they undertake to punish for keeping the divine commands, while they themselves not only shamelessly transgress the divine command but are pleased when others also transgress it, who assist in and counsel it, and would even enforce it, if they were allowed to do so and if their sin were permitted.

Now it is the traditional freedom and custom of the gracious and honourable councillors of the praiseworthy city of Strasbourg to defend each one of their citizens against violence, to assist him and promote his rights. They are displeased and regard it unjust even when a man makes unjust payments behind the back of the worthy council, for if this were accepted, it would be injurious to the community and their descendants. It would be shameful for a ruling magistrate to tolerate that. How much more is it right and necessary for you, our lords, who diligently defend your burghers' fields and meadows, that you should defend and protect their souls and help avoid sins and provide that God's name be kept sacred among us, your subjects. For the promotion of which matter everyone should profess himself obliged who once in his baptism has promised and affirmed Christian obedience. This applies foremost to our superiors, from whose hands God will demand an account of our, the subjects,' blood.[7] We would rather not like to hear it truthfully said of Your Honours that you have tolerated public whorers in your city and moreover permitted them, the whorers, to persecute divinely instituted marriage in the face of such diligent requests and our calling on divine and human right, and want the parish priest to suffer bodily punishment, if this inquiry were to find him guilty of wrong doing. No one has yet appeared who has shown him that this was forbidden by God, despite many requests, as indeed no one can possibly show him as long as God lives, rules, and remains truthful. Yes, we, although simple laymen, are certain that God has commanded marriage and not forbidden it and has given nobody the power to forbid it. We've also had it reported to us that not only God the Lord and the holy apostles but also the four first councils, accepted by the popes, admitted such marriage and did not want to have it forbidden. In these councils there were many pious fathers, who showed in their

* * * * *

6 Cf. 1 Cor. 7:1, 9.
7 Cf. Gen. 5:7.

actions the influence of the spirit rather than the flesh and did so in a greater measure than their successors. Yet over time, as faith declined, decrees were issued against it (Dist. xxvii and lxxxi, and in the imperial laws *Autent. de Epis*),[8] to the effect that a priest who takes a wife is to be dismissed from his office, but he who has once committed whoring or has been found guilty of adultery is to be banished from his priestly office for life and to be banished generally and completely driven out of the Christian community. Now it is ever unjust that the lords of St Thomas want to use a few such new articles against the parish priest, applying that section which goes against God, and wishing to regard the other section, which cites the divine command against themselves, as powerless and ineffective. For these statutes do not accept a parish priest who is married as a legitimate priest, yet they let him remain a pious and good Christian, but his accusers, the public whorers, deprive him not only of the priestly office, but also cut him off from the community of the church and completely sever him from the spiritual body, like dead limbs. This article, which attacks the whoring priests, our accusers, so violently, is confirmed by God's spirit. You are not to share food with whorers, says scripture.[9] But sweet whoring has made them so purblind that they notice neither divine nor human laws that apply to themselves, although they want to be hailed as certified doctors, and keep a sharp lookout where they might find in their laws a clause denigrating hapless marriage, which is suitable only for us indifferent people and bungling riff-raff, as they call us, whereas for them, the soft-anointed and well-kept servants of God, nice, lovely whoring is proper. For as they enjoy and use all goods without toil and effort, so it is to be arranged that their belly-life and consequent pleasure is not to be spoiled by the burden of the married state. These are the terrible judgments of God, Gracious Honours, which they confound so wildly in scripture, which is clear as daylight, and want to persuade us Christians, contrary to Christ's word, that what the devil has introduced to destroy all natural and divine respectability is divine; yes, they are so blocked up that they won't understand their own law. Dealing with their prohibitions against marriage they have often given dispensations according to the common rule: where there is money there is cause for dispensation. But the prohibition against whoring has never lapsed, especially in written laws, yet they permit in actual life every shameful deed and vice or otherwise wink at

* * * * *

8 Prima pars dist. XXVII, cc. 1–9 and dist. LXXXI, c. XVI; Corpus iuris civilis (ed. P. Krueger [Berlin, 1880]) vol. 2, 37 in section I.3: 'De episcopis ... et de nuptiis clericorum vetitis seu permissis.'
9 Cf. Eph. 5:7.

them if the sinners pay. Furthermore, while the prohibition against marriage has repeatedly been lifted, they have never been allowed to declare in public writings that the injunction against the other unchaste acts has been lifted and is no longer in force. Instead everyone issues warnings against them in their spiritual laws. Old established practice that goes against scripture should be called a harmful error rather than a custom, which makes the transgression a graver rather than a lighter matter. And even if common abuse against the spirit of God were affirmed through papal and imperial law, it is nevertheless bad and to be shunned. For one should obey neither the pope nor the emperor when they command against God. Godlessness is so disgusting that it will only impose itself in the disguise of divine fear and obedience. If the accusers of the parish priest were to be judged according to the severity of papal laws, not only divine ones, and should they be told, like the Jews in the Temple at Jerusalem:[10] *Let him among you who is without sin pick up and cast the first stone* at the parish priest, they would not, like the Pharisees, decently leave one after the other, but would rush out the door in one heap; and the first out would be the leaders of this complaint, for whom lusty whoring is so pleasant, so habitual, so highly loved, and for whom hard respectability is so completely hateful and disgusting. These strict defenders of the faith, according to their claim, allow a trivial, soulless parish priest many benefices which he does not merit on account of his lack of skill, and in addition they allow him easy women, as opportunity permits, even virgins and wives, but as they say they cannot and will not tolerate a pious, God-fearing husband as their servant.

And perhaps they have good reason, lest in the presence of respectability their wickedness should become apparent and consequently more hated. For if the priests had wives and lived honestly, shame and vice would no longer be thought so honest. But now, as we can see, the vices have not only become a habit but an honour, and honour and respectability have become shameful among them. Otherwise we see no reason why they hire a whorer and shamefully dismiss a pious husband. That they refer to novelties unsupported by tradition and to the imperial mandate counts for nothing in divine matters. What prophet might not also have been reproached in this manner: 'You bring innovation, you speak and act against our custom; the council of the synagogues, the wisdom of the scholars, the spirituality of the Pharisees, the power of the king, etc.,' have condemned what you say? When pious King Josiah[11] issued the book of laws against long-standing idolatry and

* * * * *

10 John 8:7.
11 2 Kings 22–3.

established the true divine worship, he was also liable to punishment, for in the same action he renewed the old divine and fallen truth and abolished the specious inventions of the godless priests. And Christ himself punished, revealed, and unmasked proud hypocrisy, damned the men who relied on works for their salvation, re-established the justice of God his Father, which selfish hypocrisy had condemned and put down. We believe that if the priests of St Thomas had lived in the times of St Thomas and if Christ had shown his hands and sides, they would not have believed and would never have said, *you are my God and my Lord*,[12] but 'you introduce novel ideas, Christ! You say that what goes from the heart to the mouth defiles a man, such as adultery, whoring, etc.[13] This is a rebellious innovation and against our custom, which can make adultery and whoring sacred for us who wear God's vestments and which makes marriage, which does not suit us lusty priests, unclean and bad, etc.' That, Your Honours, is our opponents' pious protest against today's 'innovations,' which are truly a repetition and reestablishment of the old and divine. For what our parish priest has done is old, stemming from God, but has been darkened through human dross for many years, as in Josiah's times God's law had been quite lost. Our opponents use violence against God and holy scripture in order to introduce shameful vice everywhere, but they don't want to grant anyone to re-establish honour and fear of God against the devil and abusive practices. O the shabby priestly arrogance! Thus it is proper for everyone to bring about error, but him who takes truth to heart you frighten away from the spiritual life. For that is what you are now undertaking, as if we were still blinded by the old ignorance and could still be persuaded that white is black and black white.

Your Honours will also be told that the lords of St Thomas accuse us of being mutinous, claiming that they have cause to worry and are in danger because of us. Several of them are rumoured to tell such things, but we will not lay a complaint against them at this time. If, however, we were to hear something more certain or plausible, we would defend ourselves in such a manner that your Graces would be satisfied, and they would have to turn red with shame for their worthless and trumped-up accusation. The respectable citizenry at Strasbourg has traditionally (thank God) never thought of resisting the authorities. And especially nowadays, even if we were rebellious by nature, which is not the case, the gospel truth, which we hear daily, would make us better behaved and more submissive to all authority. We are mindful, moreover, of our oath of allegiance and our honour, and value

* * * * *

12 John 20:28.
13 Mark 7:15.

natural respect and fear of God. We are beholden and in debt firstly to God the Almighty and after that to Your Honours and your representatives, and this voluntarily and eagerly. We obediently bear civic burdens and common levies which our opponents desire to circumvent with much deceit and skill; they only want to benefit from you, our gracious lords: to be defended, protected, guarded, and luxuriously kept, but to help maintain the common city is quite beyond them and goes against their intent. Therefore we would more justly think them disobedient, burdensome, and rebellious, with their selfish freedoms, etc., owing to which we members of the community are burdened and the honourable council does not benefit. But, dear lords, among us citizens there must perhaps be brotherly love that reconciles all things,[14] and among priests priestly love must prevail, through which they seek to promote and raise only themselves to everyone else's detriment. In our community we find fault with this; if they attack us more clearly we shall offer a satisfactory defence at a hearing, showing that we are good citizens.

As for the imperial mandate and the mandate of the Holy Empire, they have miscalculated. They conform to the imperial laws and the current mandate, [they say], and expect the priest to do the same. Where have they ever acted according to the mandate with their parish priests? Where have they ordered them to preach the gospel alone, according to the exegesis of scripture accepted by the church? Where have they ever forbidden anyone to call their opponent a heretic, as several of their priests do so inappropriately, without any basis in scripture? And yet they strongly urge punishment for a Christian marriage. But these are the works of darkness, fit for the plaintiffs, to whom alone the light of truth is insufferably hateful. If one were to probe further into the ecclesiastic and imperial laws, the whorers would see a different punishment and find themselves banished from God and the church, and would forfeit not only their benefices and priestly freedoms, which they insist on and stand up for, but also the community of the church. But if one considers the new imperial mandate closely, one finds that it is not troublesome for Master Anton. It admits that according to ecclesiastic laws he has forfeited the freedoms, privileges, and benefices and that he should be punished according to the rules. Were one to take away his benefices and the fine spiritual freedoms, one would deprive him of a light-weight treasure; as for the rest, we are told, the established rules of the said ecclesiastic laws have no punishment against the divine marriage, etc. From which section of the mandate do they wish to conclude that they can take from the parish

* * * * *

14 Cf. Eph. 4:2–3.

priest the position for which they have contracted with him and are not obliged to keep their promise? We see no reason except that as a husband he is too respectable for them who are whoring priests and that he is therefore no longer suitable nor to be tolerated.

It would be fair to say, moreoever, that we are under the impression that His Imperial Majesty and the empire no longer think their mandate in force, for the main point is not being observed, which prescribes that within a year a Christian council is to be looked for, called, announced, and started, in order to prevent the torment of the poor consciences which afflicts the simple through the current schism. And afterwards the article on preaching and the marriage of priests is added as an appendix. Since now the main cause of the edict is gone, what is essentially attached to it is void, and we have also often experienced that public decrees have come to nothing. Even if the mandate were strongly and wholly against the parish priest, as it is not, it would nevertheless be incumbent on us Christians to interpret it equitably in its more lenient and better sense and on no account allow it to go against God. For we must expect better things of the Imperial Majesty and the imperial estates than that they would knowingly pass decrees against divine law, an interpretation that the priest's adversaries are not ashamed to give it. We don't at all believe that it was the intent of the Imperial Majesty to rule that one should allow, permit, promote, and provide for the priests' public adultery, the seduction of virgins, whoring, simony, avarice, together with other capital sins, and in turn to deprive a congregation of its pious parish priest for no other reason than that he has undertaken to live from now on without causing outrage and to give a good example to the people. By contrast, our opponents do not persecute vice, but respectability alone, which they dare to drive out since it is unfamiliar and strange for them. It is a serious matter with the heathens when vices become habit.[15] When vices are honoured and Christian virtue is persecuted by those who have from Christ an honest, comfortable, quiet, soft, lazy life, how, your Honours, is one to respect this? Is it not in the common interest to act against this without any concern or fear of disturbance? For truly, God is greater than the emperor, and this would amount to a violation of God's majesty, *who is jealous and punishes the children for the sin of the fathers to the third and fourth generation of those who hate him, and who is merciful a thousand times to those who love him and who keep his commandments.*[16] He alone is to be kept before one's eyes, to be looked at and

* * * * *

15 Cf. Seneca *Epistulae morales* 4.39: 'Quae fuerant vitia, mores sunt' (What was once vice, is now habit).
16 Exod. 20:5–6.

feared who has the power to destroy body and soul in hell, to whom we belong, him alone we justly consider, in all things that concern God. He will ever protect your city, you and us, Your Honours; where he does not stand guard and as a true guardian hold out his hand, there all watch, care and diligence are in vain.

Therefore, Gracious Honours, it is our submissive, humble request: look graciously on Master Anton and ourselves and to use in the present case the old traditional freedoms granted by kings and emperors to the praiseworthy city of Strasbourg, to help us, your citizens and subjects, to obtain justice in such a highly important matter, as you have never yet abandoned us in lesser ones, and may you weigh and consider that in your honourable wisdom, doubtless under the Almighty's guidance, you have orally, and subsequently in writing in a public mandate,[17] commanded and earnestly ordered the priest and his fellow priests, to preach only the gospel and divine doctrine, which he has obediently accepted. It was his understanding, moreover, that in giving such a Christian command, it was Your Graces' will, mind and definite opinion that he himself should also order his life according to the gospel message. As we cannot even today understand Your Graces' and the empire's law otherwise, for how else would it be of service to establish, through the power of the authorities, that all priests and preachers in your city should teach the clear word of God and persuade the people and at the same time not permit that a man accept the content of the spoken word and fulfil it in deed? Otherwise it would be with the divine law as with a game of Flüsslin,[18] in which you keep one card and let go of another, as the case may be. In the same way you look at the sins of the flesh in the most opportune and convenient manner, which, however, God has strictly forbidden. For he absolutely wants that we should not do what is good in our eyes but what his spirit demands from us through scripture, in which we must neither take away nor add a syllable.[19] Your Graces, this command pleasing to God has furthered and strengthened Master Anton not a little in taking up and accomplishing his Christian task, as his actions sufficiently show. You, our Gracious Honours, should take this fairly to heart and see to

* * * * *

17 On 1 December. Cf. T. Röhrich, *Geschichte der Reformation in Elsass* (Strasbourg, 1830–2), 1:455. The council decreed that preachers 'should preach nothing but the holy gospel' (nichts anders, dann das heylig Evangelium ... verkünden wöllt).
18 A card game in which the participants were allowed to discard or pick cards from a pack. See D. Parlett, *A History of Card Games* (Oxford, 1991), 101.
19 Rev. 22:18–9.

it, as far as you can, that an obedient citizen is not put at a disadvantage and come to harm when he has undertaken to confirm in his practices what Your Graces as his lords and superiors have commanded him to express in words. So that submissive diligence towards an honourable council, in divine things, will not be punished in a citizen, and proud defiance towards a praiseworthy city, in devilish things, will not be praised and elevated, etc. in proud, troublesome men, who are newcomers.[20] For truly, if in such an event we together with the parish priest are deserted, it might raise all sorts of thoughts in strangers. But if you help us to divine and human rights and don't drop the devil's bridle on his ears, it will serve your reputation in the eyes of many, for God's honour would be defended by it, as the honour of the community requires, whereas it is completely spoiled by our adversaries, as they prove by their action. And do not fear, strict, worthy, wise and gracious Honours, the imperial mandate, which first, as we heard, does not carry any verdict against the parish priest and should not be accepted if it goes against God. For no Christian power presumes to resist God. The mandate in question is in our view not highly regarded: its main point has already been abandoned, while other good mandates, against blasphemers, drinkers, deserters, and other trespasses are badly enforced even though they accord with divine law, and the present mandate, as the priests interpret it, is against divine scripture. What would, Your Honours, cause a praiseworthy empire to insist on this unchristian interpretation of a mandate, which is already obsolete, null and void with respect to its fair and honourable sections? One also knows what understanding our neighbours, other free and imperial cities, have of this mandate and how they daily decide in similar cases, and after all, they don't wish to be considered disobedient by the Imperial Majesty and the empire. We desire to fulfil the gracious will of all princes and lords, but first of all we desire the mercy of Jesus Christ. Otherwise it would become a heavy burden for the common man if the whorers, so well honoured, promenaded in front of them in the street, while the pious parish priest would be exiled by them for his Christian respectability, and we were robbed of him.

We therefore beg your gracious Honours in humble obedience for the sake of God, justice, and our diligent request, to help the parish priest of St Thomas, as our fellow citizen and dear brother, to obtain justice in this divine cause and not let him be exiled by force, but help that those of the chapter of St Thomas bring him before the Official or make other arrange-

* * * * *

20 I.e., the canons of St Thomas were not necessarily from Strasbourg and environs.

ments, as the occasion may be, and deal with him lawfully rather than by force, wilfully driving and chasing him out, while he is calling for justice and submits to be treated well or ill in accordance with the divine, papal, and imperial law, written rights and equitable traditions, as it suits the lords of St Thomas.

Your Graces should on no account allow it to be truthfully said that a burgher here at Strasbourg lacked help and assistance from the law. We wish to be eager in fulfilling our duty and offer our obedient humble services.

Given on Wednesday after the Conception of Mary, 1523.

Your Graces' humble citizens and parishioners of St Thomas.

Letter 178: Summer 1523, [Strasbourg], Capito to [Johannes Fabri?]

This letter now appears as Ep. 168a.

Appendix

The following two documents are notarized copies of records from the papal court which throw light on Capito's litigation for the provostship of St Thomas in Strasbourg (see above, Ep. 50, headnote) in 1520. The originals do not appear to be extant. The two documents (now in the Archive municipale, Strasbourg, AM IX 2, #4) were included in a dossier submitted to the city council of Strasbourg in 1534, when Capito's opponent, Jacob Abel, tried to enforce the papal judgment in his favour. Pope Adrian VI had awarded him the provostship of St Thomas in 1524 after Capito's apostasy from the Catholic Church. Abel had furthermore obtained a mandate from the imperial *Kammergericht*, summoning Capito and threatening him with fines. Capito turned to the city council for assistance. The council sided with Capito and defended his interests in representations before the *Kammergericht* and the League of Schmalkalden. The litigation before the *Kammergericht* continued until 1540. Nothing is known about the final judgment. It is possible that Abel had died in the meantime and the case was suspended. Capito, who retained the provostship de facto, died the following year. Cf. R. Schelp, ed., *Die Reformationsprozesse der Stadt Strassburg am Reichskammergericht zur Zeit des Schmalkaldischen Bundes (1524)/1531–1541/(1555)* (Kaiserslauten, 1965) 220–3.

Document 1:
Johannes Antonius de Trivultiis,[1] doctor of both laws, chaplain of our most holy lord, the Pope, prelate, domestic master of requests and auditor of the cases of the holy apostolic palace, specially appointed by our lord pope to the case and cases and parts described below. Greetings in the Lord to each and every lord abbot, prior, ...

* * * * *

1 Cf. Ep. 60, note 2.

Let it be known to you that our most holy father in Christ and lord, Leo X
by divine providence Pope, recently caused a certain note of commission or
of petition containing copies of two other commissions in its preamble to be
delivered to us by his secure messenger. We received the note with the reverence due to such things. And it stated:

[First Petition:]

Blessed Father, although the provostship, canonry, and prebend which the
late Jakob Rishoffer[2] held in his lifetime in the church of Saint Thomas,
Strasbourg, has pertained and pertains to your devout preacher, Wolfgang
Fabritius Capito, and although the right to them and in them belonged to
the preacher even while the aforesaid Jakob, now deceased, was still alive,
and thus no one is permitted to assert that the aforesaid provostship and
canonry and prebend belong to him, nevertheless, as it is rumoured, several
individuals in the city of Rome, and especially a certain Jakob Abel and
Sebastian Bender,[3] affirm that the aforesaid provostship, canonry, and
prebend belong more fully to them than to the preacher, although they
assert this improperly, and perhaps extorted certain general rulings in this
regard after the death of Jacob, now deceased, without summoning the said
preacher. Therefore, so that the improper ambition of those seeking these
rights might be restrained and so that the case regarding the ownership of
these benefices might be decided before a tribunal according to recognized
law, may Your Holiness deign to commit the case and cases which the same
preacher is initiating, desires to initiate or intends to initiate against the
aforesaid Jakob and Sebastian and any others ... to someone from among the
auditors of cases of your palace ...

[Reply:]

And other matters to the contrary notwithstanding, based on the mandate of
our lord pope, let Master Mercurius[4] hear the case and, the fact that there
was no proper legal access having been summarily established, let him cite
[the parties]. Let him restrain [them] under censure in accordance with the
edict, as it is sought, and let him decide on the aforesaid outcome. Let him
even excommunicate [them] with a summons.

* * * * *

2 I.e., Reichshofen, cf. Ep. 50, note 2.
3 On Abel and Bender, cf. Ep. 50, note 2.
4 Mercurio de Vipera was a papal auditor from 1505. In 1523, he was made
   Bishop of Bagnoregio. He died during the Sack of Rome in 1527. See H.
   Hoberg, 'Die Protokollbücher der Rotanotare von 1464 bis 1517,' in *Zeitschrift der Savigny-Stiftung für Rechtsgeschichte*, kanonische Abteilung 39 (1953):
   204.

Thus it pleases our lord, the pope, insofar as he does so in accordance with law and justice. Leonardus, Cardinal of Saint Peter ad vincula.[5]

[Second petition:]

Holy Father, it is asserted by some that, following the death of Jakob Rishoffer, the aforesaid Jakob Abel extorted a certain general ruling from the reverend father, lord Johannes Anthonius de Trivultiis, auditor of cases of the apostolic palace, against anyone collectively or individually asserting an interest [in the provostship] and that false ruling has passed into a formal judgment and executorial letters were decreed in this matter, which would apply if no one contradicted. And therefore they are in no way binding for the aforesaid preacher, since the same preacher, having been cited, was not present for the ruling and is a new litigant in the case. And in order that it might be determined by that same judge[6] whether the aforesaid asserted formal judgment should affect the preacher or not, or whether, since this was not taken into consideration, the said preacher might continue further, may Your Holiness deign to commit [the case] to the auditor, lord Mercurius, in accordance with the requests of the orator, Wolfgang, and may you deign to command that the same Mercurius [decide] to what extent the asserted judgment is binding and applies to the preacher and that Mercurius himself and not the aforesaid Johannes Anthonius proceed to the final execution, with the power to ... hear the case and cases and decide on whatever action appears appropriate to him ...

[Reply:]

By the command of our lord pope, let the same Mercurius proceed, as is sought, and let him judge. Thus it pleases the lord pope. Leonardus, Cardinal of St Peter ad vincula.

[Third Petition:]

Blessed Father, the said Wolfgang extorted the documents inserted above after the formal judgment and a decree of execution had been obtained. And it is not to be believed that it was Your Holiness' intention to withdraw through the documents inserted above the execution of the formal judgment obtained for the preacher Jacob. Therefore, the aforementioned Jakob Abel,

* * * * *

5 Leonardo Grosso della Rovere became bishop of Agen (a diocese in the Bordeaux region of France) in 1487. In 1504, he began serving in the papal chancery as master of requests. In December 1505, he was raised to the cardinalate. In 1511, he took over the role of penitentiary, which he held until his death on 17 September 1520. See T. Frenz, *Die Kanzlei der Päpste der Hochrenaissance (1471–1527)* (Tübingen: Max Niemeyer, 1986), 397.

6 I.e., Mercurius.

preacher, humbly requests that Your Holiness deign to commit [the case] to the aforenamed lord Johannes Anthonius Trivultius, auditor, before whom that very preacher Jakob obtained the formal judgment and executorial letters, and not to said lord Mercurius, and to command that he execute the sentence and order the aforesaid executorial letters to be executed and otherwise proceed in the business of execution on the assumption that the above-inserted documents were obtained without legitimate judgment and order of execution, and that the adversary is not the rightful owner ...

[Reply:]

Notwithstanding the September holidays recently mandated and any other impediments, two responses followed on this note of commission or supplication, of which the first was: In accordance with the mandate of our lord pope, let Master Johannes Anthonius hear [the case], let him cite [the parties to the suit], let him restrain [them] under censure and the aforementioned penalties. Let him proceed and execute [the decision] as it is sought, with the holidays and the other aforesaid impediments notwithstanding. The other said: Thus it pleases our lord pope. Johannes Casertanus.[7]

After the presentation of this note of commission or supplication to us and after its reception by us, as was mentioned earlier, we have decided in favour of the party of the venerable lord Jakob Abel, the principal actor in the aforementioned note of commission or supplication. Thus, in the usual fashion, we have deigned to inhibit [the parties] and to decree and concede to him [Abel] inhibitorial letters containing the appropriate threats of excommunication and censure. And we also deigned to execute other executorial letters on behalf of Jakob Abel in a certain case brought before us – first, a case between a certain Sebastian, cleric in the diocese of Strasbourg, who brought the action on one side, and on the other the late Jakob Fabri *alias* Rishoffer and, after the death of said Jacob Fabri, any and all individuals asserting an interest in the provostship of the church of St Thomas at Strasbourg, as well as the parish churches of Wergersheim zum Thunen, Ilkirchen, and Rumersheim, all located in the diocese of Strasbourg, and thereafter in a case between the said Jakob Abel and Sebastian Bender, who ceded his right to pursue a judgment. We have deigned to rule and execute judgment in and through all matters in accordance with the executorial let-

* * * * *

7 Giovanni Battista Bonciani (Johannes Casertanus) was a doctor of canon law and served as auditor and protonotary under Leo X. In 1514, he was named bishop of Caserta. In 1527, he was placed in charge of the datary, a position he held until his death in 1532/3. See A. Ferrajoli, *Il Ruolo della Corte di Leone X* (Rome, 1984), 547–50.

ters and the authority of a special commission given in the usual form and tenor ...[8]

Given and enacted at Rome in our place of residence in the year from the nativity of the Lord 1520, in the eighth indiction, on Tuesday, the 24th of September, in the eighth year of the pontificate of our most holy father and lord, Leo X, by divine providence, Pope.

Document 2:

In the name of the Lord: Amen. In the year 1520 from His nativity, the eighth indiction, on Wednesday, the fourteenth of November, the eighth year of the most holy pontificate of our father and lord in Christ, Leo X by divine providence Pope.

The venerable and circumspect men, dean Nicolaus Wurmser,[9] doctor of canon law, and the other chapter canons of the church of St Thomas in Strasbourg, gathered as a chapter in their chapter meeting room and in the presence of the worthy and distinguished Matthias Wildenroit,[10] provost of the church of St Stephen in Weissenburg and procurator of the venerable Jakob Abel, cleric at Strasbourg, in the presence of me, the public notary, and in the presence of the witnesses named below, have proposed and committed in writing, at the request of Matthias Wildenroit, the procurator, that they, based on the strength of the executorial letters presented to them by [Wildenroit] and executed on behalf of the aforementioned Jakob Abel, the principal, wish, as obedient children, in fear of threatened punishments and censures, to comply with, submit to, obey and give satisfaction to them. However, after the first stipulation had been fulfilled by the same Matthias, the abovementioned procurator, regarding the statutes and customs of the frequently mentioned church of St Thomas, the aforesaid Matthias Wildenroit, the procurator, promised by joining hands with me, the public notary, that he would pledge to observe on behalf of his principal the mandatory statutes and customs of the aforesaid church. After this promise was made and accepted, the statutes contained in the Book of Statutes pertaining to the promise of the provostship were first read for the information and on the urgent petition of the venerable Matthias Wildenroit, the procurator. Then the abovementioned venerable and circumspect men – the dean and the

* * * * *

8 Given the textual difficulties, the sentence is loosely translated.
9 For Nicolaus Wurmser see above, Ep. 57, headnote.
10 Matthias Wildenroit (Wildenraidt, also called Vassbender) matriculated at the University of Cologne in 1503 and graduated MD in 1504. He became parish priest at Dhünn (near Wermelskirchen) in 1522 and rector in Wermelskirchen, a position he resigned in 1524 for one at St Andreas in Cologne.

chapter – as obedient children who wish to comply with and obey the letters executorial under threat of punishment, and the dean and chapter informed him of the oath to be taken by the appointed provost and made him swear the oath. After putting his hand on the holy books of the gospel, he read and repeated in his capacity of procurator the words of the oath word for word as contained in the statute. Immediately and at once, after the oath had been made, the venerable men, lords Hieronymus Betschlin[11] and Martin of Baden,[12] canons in the chapter of the church of St Thomas, according to a special commission of the aforementioned venerable lords, the dean and chapter, led the aforementioned Matthias Wildenroit, the often-mentioned procurator and in his function as procurator into the choir of the said church during the singing of nones and finally they led him to the high altar to be installed in the usual seat of the provost in the choir of the same church. And finally, after he had been installed, they gave and assigned the real and actual possession to him in his capacity of procurator through the standard and customary words, in the name of the Father and the Son and the Holy Spirit. Concerning all these matters the venerable lord Matthias Wildenroit, the often-mentioned procurator, asked that one or more public instrument or instruments be made and prepared for himself and the said venerable lord Jacob Abel by me, the below-mentioned public notary.[13]

This was enacted in Strasbourg in the year, indiction, day, month, pontificate, and locations stated above with these honourable men present: Cristman Usinger[14] and Nicolas Beylfuss, vicars of the often mentioned church of St Thomas in Strasbourg, witnesses especially called and requested to attend on the aforesaid occasion.

* * * * *

11 Hieronymus Betschlin (Betschold) was made a canon in the chapter of St Thomas in Strasbourg in 1503. By 1515, he is mentioned as the cantor of the church. In addition to his position at St Thomas, Betschlin also held a prebend at Old St Peter's in Strasbourg and a chaplaincy at the altar of St Columba at the same church. He died on 22 September 1540.

12 Martin of Baden studied at the University of Basel, where he graduated in 1495. He became a canon of the chapter of St Thomas in 1500, advancing to the position of vice-dean in 1509, a position he held until Nicolaus Wurmser's flight in 1524. He died in 1532.

13 The document is signed by 'Johannes Buddel de Wynheim' on behalf of (the deceased) 'Ludovicus Rode.'

14 Christmannus Usinger was vicar of the altar of St Leonard at the church of St Thomas beginning in 1514. In 1524, he applied for an (absentee?) licence to study law at Heidelberg, but the matriculation records show no evidence that he ever completed his studies. And in 1525, he was registered as a citizen of Strasbourg. By 1530, he had become vicar of the church of Sts Michael and Peter.

TABLE OF CORRESPONDENTS

Index of Persons and Places

Lightning Source UK Ltd.
Milton Keynes UK
UKHW031056120220
358590UK00015B/267